Magic Maui
The Best of the Island

By M.J. Harden

With Jill Engledow

Aka Press
Maui, Hawai'i

Cover artist: Dick Nelson
Calligrapher: Patt Narrowe
Map maker: Beth Marcil
Layout: M.J. Harden

First Edition: September, 1987
Printed in the United States of America.

Published by: Aka Press
                  P.O. Box 1372
                  Maui, Hawai'i 96793

aka: 1. shadow; 2. reflection, image, likeness; faint glimmer preceding the rising of the moon...many words compounded with aka express clarity, brightness; 3. embryo at the moment of conception; 4. newly hatched fish in the stage in which its body is still transparent.

    Esoteric meaning: the ancient Hawaiians believed the aka cord to be the invisible thread that connects a person's three levels of consciousness—the unihipili (subconscious), the uhane (conscious mind) and the aumakua (superconscious).

May Aka Press and *Magic Maui* be a part of your connection to Maui.

Library of Congress Cataloging in Publication Data

Harden, M.J.
   Magic Maui The Best of the Island

   First Edition
   Bibliography: p. 355
   Includes Index.

Library of Congress Catalogue Number 87-71946
ISBN 0-944134-00-9

To Keopuolani
&
Ka'ahumanu

Maui's two
strong queens

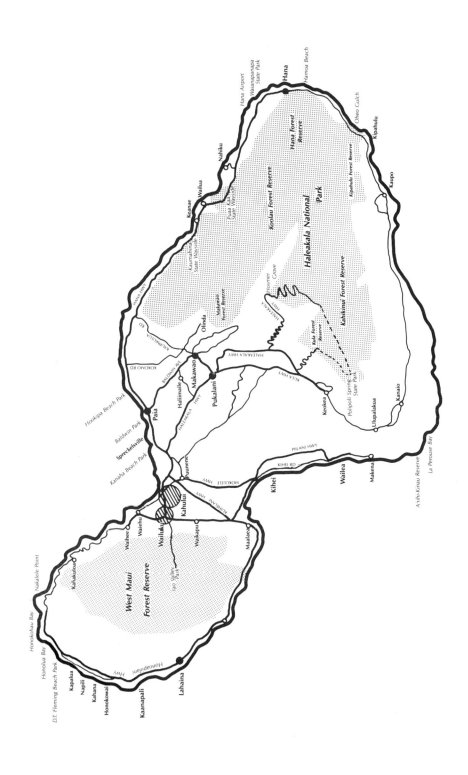

Contents

Acknowledgments

With joy and gratitude, Jill and I would like to acknowledge those who helped us put this all together. Multiple hosannas go to:

• Our "Maui Folk" who allowed us the privilege of writing their stories, thus adding warthm and spark to the book...Inez Ashdown, Coila Eade, Harry Hasegawa, Dana Naone Hall, Carol Kapu, Charley Keau, Jim Luckey, Hoku Holt-Padilla, Eddie Pu, Ken Schmitt.

• The artists (some of Maui's best and most famous) whose art perk up these pages...Cynthia Conrad, Curtis Wilson Cost, Eddie Flotte, Pamela Hayes, Ben Kikuyama, Piero Resta, David Ridgway, David Warren.

• Cover artist Dick Nelson for being such a fun guy, and for being sport enough to paint a pink waterfall.

• Map maker Beth Marcil and calligrapher Patt Narrowe for being such pros and for being wonderfully creative sisters.

• Tamara Horcajo and Hoku Holt-Padilla at the Maui Historical Society for letting us pick their brains and use their books and photos.

• Photographer Matthew Thayer for taking the authors' photos shown on the back cover.

• Steven Minkowski of Mink Productions for photographing the front cover painting.

• Our friends at *The Maui News* who lent their files and photos...Dave DeLeon, Kaui Goring, Lynne Horner, Wayne Tanaka, Jon Woodhouse, Ron Youngblood.

• Those who extended their support, their knowledge and their generosity...Ki'ope Raymond, Paul Fagan, Dorothy Pyle, Barbara Glassman, Charlene and Alan Walker, Lewis Eisenberg, Linda Rink, Mary Purdy, Kenji Kawaguchi, Susie Davis, Kathy Platt, Debbie Justice, Paul Winkler, Bill Geary, David Clark.

• My computer buddies who helped me learn Apple's amazing Macintosh...Steve Costa in Berkeley and Judy Plummer in Maui.

• Fellow writers Madge Walls and Kaui Goring for *not* writing this book.

• Jill Engledow...my personal thanks to my partner and my birth mate (born on the same day, a few years apart). As E.B. White wrote about Charlotte, the word-spinning spider of *Charlotte's Web*: "It is not often that someone comes along who is a true friend and a good writer."

mjh

Magic Maui
The Best of the Island

Maui

GOD AND ISLAND

Maui has always been a magical name. This is the only island named after a god. Maui was a god-man...half man, half god...a super being capable of powerful feats.

Like him, the island is half god, half man. Lahaina discos, Ka'anapali hotels, miles of roads, armadas of boats are man's inventions. Haleakala, Kipahulu, 'Iao Valley, Mt. Eke are the magic of God.

Maui-of-a-Thousand-Tricks

Maui the demigod has been known for centuries throughout Polynesia, with every island people adding to his legend. He is Maui-of-a-Thousand-Tricks, an endearing hero and trickster whose adventures helped create the world.

Though he is an obvious favorite, there is no worship of Maui. He may be a deified ancestor, a real person who lived in times of great upheaval, whose strength and creativity lived on in legends until he became like a god. He has a distinctive personality, and his name symbolizes adventure and change.

Fantasy beginning

According to legend, Maui and his brothers pulled the Hawaiian Islands up off the ocean floor. Maui invented a barbed fish hook, had a magical bird bait it, then had his brothers pull the fish line by paddling away in a canoe. He warned his brothers not to look back as the land rose from the sea. If they had done as they were told, the islands would have come all the way up and formed one great land mass. However, the brothers peeked back, thus only the tops—the Hawaiian Islands—emerged from the depths.

Geological beginning

Maui is a young island, its oldest part being less than two million years old. Its newest earth was heaved up 200 years ago on Haleakala.

The island was formed by two volcanoes. Lava from both spilled together and joined at the isthmus of Central Maui. The West Maui volcano is off the hotspot, so it is extinct. East Maui's volcano, Haleakala, is dormant—still on the hotspot, yet quiet for 200 years.

Only the tips of these mountains show, most of their bulk is under the sea. The volcanic chain of the Hawaiian Islands is the most massive mountain range on earth. The volcanoes themselves (from ocean floor to summits) are the largest structures on earth.

Island's birth

Maui the island had a rather laborious birth. Born eons ago, Maui started as lava spurting from a fissure in the ocean floor.

No one knows how long it took to build higher and higher until lava rose above the ocean. Underwater development of these huge volcanoes was long and complicated, and may never be scientifically determined.

The rocks on top of the ocean can, however, be dated. It is believed that Maui's two mountains are between one and two million years old...just babies in geological ages. Much developed during the Pliocene Age.

The West Maui Mountains are probably twice as old as Haleakala. They are almost half as tall as Haleakala—worn down with the erosion that accompanies age. The West Mauis are more jagged than East Maui; they are also covered with vegetation, while much of baby Haleakala is still bald-headed.

Birth of the demigod

Maui the god had a magical beginning, but the tale is told in many forms, depending on the island origin. The most common is the story of the mysterious malo, or loincloth.

Hina-i-ke-ahi, Maui's mother, went to the beach to gather seaweed. She found a man's malo on the beach, put it on, then fell asleep. When she awoke, she was pregnant with Maui, the youngest of her sons. Some say his father was a god.

Unfortunately, according to some versions of the story, Maui was born too early. His mother saw he would be unable to survive, and sadly she threw him into the sea. But the baby lived, adopted by the gods from whom he learned tricks and magic. As a boy, he returned to his human family, but he was no longer just a human. He had developed great mana (power) from being with the gods.

Maui improves the world

According to legend, the gods made the world, but left it half-finished. People lived without fire to cook their food. The sun raced quickly across the sky each day, leaving a chilled world. The sky was so low that people had to crawl like animals; they could not stand up straight.

Maui worked his magic and set the world straight. He stole fire (and nearly destroyed the world by setting it aflame), and he brought it home so his mother could cook.

Still, his mother's tapa cloth would not dry, so Maui set about slowing the sun. He made ropes from coconut husks and lassoed the sun's rays as it rose over Haleakala. Only when the sun promised to slow its daily journey would Maui set it free. Ever since, the sun has moved in a leisurely fashion across the heavens.

He lifted the sky from its low position by giving it a mighty heave from the top of Kau'iki Hill. He found the strength by drinking magic water from a woman's gourd. Some say the drink is a euphemism for sex.

Magic Maui

People of Polynesia have always been fascinated with Maui the demigod. Now people the world over are fascinated with his namesake island.

Maui improved the world with his magical tricks. Maui the island improves the world with its magical presence.

Nuts & Bolts

FAST FACTS

Motto	*Maui no ka oi.* Maui is the best.
Size	728 square miles 48 miles long 26 miles wide 120 miles of coastline Second largest of the Hawaiian Islands —Big Island is largest; O'ahu is third.
Height	From sea level to 10,023 feet
Highest Points	East Maui: Haleakala summit at 10,023 West Maui: Pu'u Kukui at 5,788 feet
Highest Waterfall	1,120-ft. Honokohau in West Maui Mt.
Longitude Latitude	156 degrees 21 degrees
Distance	Closest continental point is San Francisco —2,390 miles from Kahului Airport New York is 4,917 miles away
Population	More than 83,000
Time Difference	2 hours behind Pacific Standard time 3 hours behind during Daylight Savings Time...Hawai'i does not follow DST.

Rainfall	Pu'u Kukui in West Maui Mt. gets 420+" yearly...one of wettest spots on earth. Kihei & Lahaina—15" a year La Perouse area—less than 15"
Stream w/ most water per day	'Iao Stream—54.1 million gallons daily
Visitor Number	Average of 25,000 a day
Hotel Rooms	More than 5,900 on island...41.5% of these are luxury class. Maui has the highest concentration of luxury rooms in Hawai'i (O'ahu = 8.8% Kaua'i= 11.1%).
Condo Rooms	More than 7,100 rooms on island.
Latest Lava Flow	About 200 years ago in the La Perouse area
West Maui Mts.	An extinct volcano; twice as old as Haleakala, but half Haleakala's height.
Haleakala	A dormant volcano. Crater is 7.5 miles long, 2.5 miles wide, 21 miles around
Land use	Largest use of land is 188,000 acres used for cattle grazing. Second is sugar at 47,000 acres and pineapple at 9,500 acres. This includes all Maui County (Lana'i and Moloka'i).
Crops	sugar cane, pineapple, Maui onions, carnations, proteas
Wilderness	Over 75% of Maui is uninhabited.

Need Help?

Maui Visitors Bureau
P.O. Box 1738, Kahului, HI 96732 • 871-8691
Street address: 172 Alamaha, Kahului

This is not really a true visitor's bureau, but they are helpful. They are a membership organization, with various visitor industry companies as members. So they only have members' brochures.

They also have maps, information on all major hotels and some condos, information on some activities (like wedding services), plus camping, beaches and popular sites.

Their information is free unless you need to supply a large group, and then you might have to pay postage.

Information Booths

The small information booths seen all over the island are booking businesses. They have brochures and information for only those companies (boats, dive shops, bike companies, bus tours, etc.) that can give them a percentage of the booking.

They are helpful, but they are there to sell trips.

HawaiianWarrior Sign

Whenever you see this red, yellow and white marker sign on the road, know that a historical site or a tourist attraction is near. The sign is placed there by the Hawai'i Visitors Bureau. This marker is the official sign used throughout all the Hawaiian Islands.

PHONE NUMBERS

Police, ambulance, fire	911
Police non-emergency services	
Wailuku	244-6400
Lahaina	661-4441
Hana	248-8311
Medical	
Maui Memorial Hospital	244-9056
Hana Medical Center	248-8294
Poison Control Center (toll-free)	1-800-362-3585
Miscellaneous	
Maui Visitors Bureau	871-8691
Time of Day	242-0212
Recorded Weather Forecasts	
Island of Maui	877-5111
Marine	877-3477
Recreational Areas	877-5124
Coast Guard Rescue Center (toll-free)	1-800-331-6176
State Office of Consumer Protection	244-4387
County of Maui Complaints Office	244-7756
County of Maui Information Office	244-7866
Haleakala National Park Service	
General Information	572-7749
Weather Forecast	877-5124
Park Headquarters (open 7:30 to 4)	572-9306
'Ohe'o Rangers	248-8251
Social Services	
Maui Youth and Family Service	
Emergency shelter for youth	579-9591
Family Violence Hotline/ Shelter	579-9581
Child Protective Service	244-4330
(after hours, call police)	
State Commission on the Handicapped	244-4441
State Environmental Pollution Control	244-4228
Help Line (Suicide and Crisis Center)	244-7404
Sexual Assault Crisis Center	242-4357
Maui Humane Society	877-3680

Weather

Maui's weather forecasts are strikingly monotonous: mostly sunny, with a few windward and mauka showers, tradewinds 5 to 15 miles per hour.

Touristy areas like Kihei, Wailea, Lahaina and Ka'anapali are predictably pleasant. But there are several microclimates in Maui, and not all are sunny and hot.

The steep mountains of Hawai'i, rising up dramatically from the ocean, create an obstacle for weather. The result—wild variations of weather within a small area. Kihei and Lahaina may be roasting, while Haleakala is freezing, and Hana without sun for days.

Besides the obvious differences of the leeward and windward sides, there are tiny pockets of weather in different spots. Valleys, for instance, may have their own special combination of winds and rain.

Yet, for the most part, the weather is close to perfection. The tradewinds hold the weather stable and hot during the summer months. The wind pattern changes during the winter, with other winds joining the trades and bringing more of a flux (and more rain) in the weather.

The Tradewinds

These are part of a broad subtropical belt of easterly winds that circle the globe. They are called tradewinds because they powered the sails bringing the clipper ships of the early traders.

The stability of these winds keep Maui's weather even. The trades cool the island and bring much of the rain that keeps it green. The winds pick up moisture and form clouds around microscopic salt particles. When these clouds run into mountains, they are forced upward, so that large cumulous clouds build up over the mountains and the valley tops. One of Maui's high points, Pu'u Kukui in the West Maui Mountains, may receive more than 100 inches of rain a month during the winter rainy season.

On the windward northeastern side of the island, rain falls during most months of the year, thanks to the trades. Thus, the lush wetness of Ke'anae and Hana. On the leeward side, it's another matter—Kihei and Makena have desert climates.

Winter Storms
During winter months, as the earth tilts on its axis, Maui can have gale winds in the channels and brisk trades ashore. Some of the island's heaviest rains fall in the rainy season of October through April. Parts of the island may experience as much as 11 inches of rain in an hour.

Kona Storms
A major exception to the windward rain pattern of the island is the Kona storm. Kona weather comes in association with a low pressure front moving toward Hawai'i from the southwest. The wind pattern shifts; clouds gather in the south, and desert-like Kihei floods. These storms can be serious or just annoying. It may rain for days as the slow-moving low-pressure area lies over the islands.

Hurricanes
Only occasionally does Maui experience a severe tropical cyclone. The high winds and heavy rains of a hurricane are most likely to occur in August, but rarely reach the proportions of those that batter North America's southeast coast.

Waves
Waves result from far-off winds pushing on the ocean's surface, causing swells that break on Hawai'i's shores.

The islands create wind tunnels through which wind blows faster than on the surrounding open ocean. Thus, channels between islands are often filled with choppy waves. The strongest of all channel winds in Hawai'i are those southwest of Makena and Kaupo, which funnel between East Maui and the Big Island.

This wind and wave action make sailing in Hawai'i risky and challenging.

Tsunami
A tidal wave, more properly called a seismic wave or a tsunami, has nothing to do with tides. Tsunamis result from seismic action—an earthquake, landslide or volcanic eruption. Tsunamis that hit Hawai'i usually come from places like the Aleutian Islands or South America.

Such a wave travels up to 500 miles per hour in the open ocean with almost no trace on the surface of its presence. When it meets up with an island, however, the wave becomes steeper and taller as it drives up into the shallows around the island. By the time it hits land, its force is concentrated and damaging.

Due to the warning system installed after a big wave hit in 1946, there is now plenty of time to prepare for a tsunami generated outside Hawai'i. However, a locally-generated wave can be dangerous because it can appear with little warning.

The last tsunami hit Maui on November 29, 1975, striking both Kahului and Lahaina Harbors. No major damage happened, just some boats heaved on shore.

Sea Breezes

Sea breezes, bringing cold air inland off the ocean during the day, reverse the process at night, when cool air flows out to sea. When the trades meet a sea or land breeze, a cloud line forms. One exists on the slopes of Haleakala, where a sea breeze flowing around the western slope meets the tradewinds coming form the northeast.

Call for daily weather forecasts:

General weather	877-5111
Haleakala weather	572-7749
Recreational areas	877-5124
Marine weather	877-3477

Area	Mean Temperatures		Mean Monthly Rainfall	
	Summer	*Winter*	*Summer*	*Winter*
Kahului	78°	71°	.41"	4.21"
Lahaina	78°	72°	.19"	3.79"
Kula (3,000')	66°	61°	1.83"	6.25"
Haleakala (summit)	56°	50°	2.12"	10.18"

Airports

KAHULUI AIRPORT

This is Maui's main airport, serving domestic and inter-island carriers. It is currently in flux—it's being expanded to three times its present size. It will take several years, but when done there will be a new terminal and the runways will be strengthened.

No international flights arrive or depart from Kahului. Delta, United and American are the Mainland carriers that land here. Local Hawaiian airlines that use the airport are Aloha, Mid Pacific and Hawaiian Air.

United passengers arrive in a separate building located to the side of the main terminal. Several local commuter airlines arrive and depart from a small building about a half block from the terminal.

Need a lei?

There's a lei shop and a gift shop in the main terminal. There's snack food available, plus, there's a restaurant.

An information booth, run by the state, can offer some help to lost souls, but they can't book anything or help you find a hotel. Essentially, they give directions and hand out brochures.

Transportation

Check the Transportation Chapter for full details on bus schedules and car rentals.

Car rental stands are located to the side of the main terminal...a one minute walk. Bus information is in the same area.

The 4:15 afternoon shuttle bus is the last scheduled bus service of the day. Check with the tour bus companies to see if you can catch a ride after 4:15.

Only two hotels have regular airport pick-up service—Maui Palms and Maui Beach. Both are inexpensive hotels located in Kahului.

Airport fines

If driving, know that the fines for parking in the wrong zone are now $20. The security police will let you park in front of the terminal to unload your bags, but they'll tag you if you stay too long.

KAPALUA WEST MAUI AIRPORT

This is a small airport, opened in March, 1987, but it has the sophistication and feel of a large airport.

Only Hawaiian Air and Princeville Airways use the airport, and only for inter-island flights. From West Maui, Princeville flies to Honolulu, and Hawaiian flies to Kona and Honolulu. Those are their sole flights. Panorama Air Tours, a tourist company, also uses the facilities.

No jets are allowed, no helicopters and no private landings. Only day-time arrivals and departures; no night flights permitted. There were tussles with the neighbors about building the airport, and limiting the flights is an attempt to placate the residents.

There are no rental cars located at the airport. There are, however, several car agencies on West Maui. Most will pick you up at the airport.

There is no regular bus service at the airport. But, for guests at any Ka'anapali hotel or condo, there's a free shuttle that swings by every 35 minutes, from 9 to 5. It only goes to the Ka'anapali hotels or condo, no stops outside Ka'anapali.

For guests at any Aston resort (Mahana, Ka'anapali Shores, Paki Maui, Sands of Kahana, Maui Ka'anapali Villas and Napili Point) there's a special Aston shuttle bus. It's necessary to give advance notice of arrival or departure.

HANA AIRPORT

Only Princeville Airways flies into this tiny airport. They have four flights a day, flying to Kahului, Moloka'i and Honolulu.

Private planes and helicopters are also allowed to land here.

No rental car stands, no gift shops, no food available, no bus shuttles. This is a very simple little airport.

The only rental car service in Hana is National's—call Mary Purdy at 248-8237. She'll come pick you up.

If you're staying at the Hotel Hana Maui, you'll be picked up in style—in a 1938 Packard van. The hotel has two of these old classics, used mostly as their airport service. The Hana Maui does everything with class.

Transportation

Public transportation is not Maui's strong suit. A trip down the Honoapiilani Highway's gridlock of rental cars is proof of that. However, there are increasing attempts to provide bus and shuttle service.

BUSES

Buses at Kahului Airport

Grayline-Maui runs buses from the airport to Ka'anapali. The bus stop is across from the Hawaiian Air baggage claim, next to the Hertz Rent A Car booth. Departure times are 10:15, 11:45, 1:15, 2:45 and 4:15.

The bus stops in Lahaina and Ka'anapali at these spots: Lahaina Shores Hotel, Maui Islander Hotel, Lahaina Harbor, Royal Lahaina Hotel, Sheraton Maui Hotel, Ka'anapali Beach Hotel, Whalers Shopping Village, Maui Marriott Hotel, Hyatt Regency Hotel and Maui Eldorado Condo.

Return trips are by reservation only. Call 877-5507 for pick up at 8:30, 10, 11:30, 1, 2:30, 4 or 5:30. One adult fare is about a third the cost of a day's car rental; children are half fare.

Other airport buses, run by Robert's Hawai'i, Inc. and Trans Hawaiian Maui, are basically charter operations. Sometimes these charters have open seats...for a price you can ride along to whichever hotel the bus is going to. Ask at one of the bus offices, located with the rental car kiosks. If one company doesn't have an available seat, they can refer you to another company.

Hotel buses to airport

Maui Beach and Maui Palms Hotels in Kahului are the only hotels with regular guests pick-up and delivery. They are both inexpensive hotels situated on Kahului's bay...not terribly picturesque, but they are centrally located. Call them from their courtesy phone at the airport and a bellman will come for you.

Buses at Kapalua West Maui Airport

From 9 to 5, every 35 minutes, every day, Ka'anapali's free shuttle bus does airport runs, doing roundtrips to and from the airport and Ka'anapali condos/ hotels.

The Aston hotel shuttle will pick up Aston hotel guests, if guests give advance notice of arrival or departure.

Island-wide bus routes

Shoreline Transportation is Maui's only public transportation, serving all of West and Central Maui. They are still struggling to find the system that will allow them to survive.

Their fares are based on zones, with one-day or one-month passes available.

This schedule is their latest try. Call 661-3827 to check if it's still current and to see exactly where their stops are located.

Kapalua to Lahaina: daily from 7 a.m. to 10:45 p.m. departs every 30 minutes; stops in Ka'anapali and the Cannery.

Lahaina to Makena: leaves the Cannery at 8 a.m., 11 a.m. and 2 p.m.; stops at Ma'alaea Harbor, Sugar Beach Resort (Kihei) and Mana Kai Condo (Kihei). Turns around at the Maui Prince Hotel.

Makena to Lahaina: leaves the Maui Prince Hotel at 9 a.m., 10 p.m., noon, 1 p.m., 3 p.m. and 4 p.m.

Ka'anapali to Kahului: leaves Ka'anapali at 4:45 a.m., then approximately every two hours and 20 minutes until 8:55 p.m. It stops in Lahaina, Olowalu, Ma'alaea, the Kihei Junction, Waikapu, Wells Park in Wailuku, the War Memorial Complex in Wailuku, Ka'ahumanu Center and the Maui Mall.

Kahului to Ka'anapali: leaves Maui Mall at 4:45 a.m., also runs every two hours and 20 minutes until 10:05 p.m. Reverses the order of the stops listed above.

Ka'anapali-Lahaina bus shuttle

The Shuttle Bus runs daily from the Royal Lahaina Hotel in Ka'anapali to the Wharf Shopping Center in Lahaina. Runs at half-hour intervals from 8 a.m. to 10:25 p.m., stopping at all Ka'anapali hotels. There is a fee.

Ka'anapali bus shuttle to Tropical Plantation

Two trips leave daily from these stops: Sheraton Hotel, Ka'anapali Beach Hotel, Whalers Village Shopping Center, Maui Marriott Hotel, Hyatt Regency Hotel, Pu'ukoli'i Sugar Train Station (all in Ka'anapali), last stop is Lahaina Wharf. First pick-up (at the Sheraton) is 9:17, next trip starts at 11:15.

The bus goes to the Plantation, then goes to Ka'ahumanu Shopping Center. Return buses from the Plantation are at 12:30 and 2:30; returns from Ka'ahumanu are 12:45 and 2:45.

Ka'anapali shuttle

This open-air, free shuttle runs back and forth within the resort from 7 a.m. to 11 p.m., stopping at all hotels automatically, condos on request. It also goes to and from Banyan Square in Lahaina at 55-minute intervals.

Wailea shuttle

This free shuttle runs between the hotels, the shopping village and the golf and tennis clubs at 20-minute intervals.

Kapalua shuttle

This is an on-call service within the resort, serving both the hotel and the condo villas. Guests can call the hotel operator from wherever they are and go wherever they want to...within the resort.

Aston Hotels shuttle

Aston resorts are: Mahana, Ka'anapali Shores, Paki Maui, Sands of Kahana, Maui Ka'anapali Villas and Napili Point. Aston's shuttle bus runs hourly from 8 a.m. to 6 p.m., taking guests from these resorts to Whaler's Village in Ka'anapali and Longhi's restaurant in Lahaina. Only guests are allowed (you have to show a guest card to board). Napili Point condo is out of the way, so you must request pick-up in advance.

TAXIS

Maui has about 16 taxi companies, some offering tours and limo service. Only one company, Mita, is actually based at the airport, though all the rest go there for pick-ups and deliveries. Most companies are based in a specific area, and though they might drive all over the island, it's best to call the one closest to your area.

Most taxis are radio dispatched; you'll wait forever if you hope to flag one down on the street. This is not Manhattan.

Prices change, of course, but typical charges from the Kahului Airport are: to Wailea $21, to Ka'anapali $35, to Lahaina $28.

One of the companies, Classy Taxi, has an unusual service—for the same price as its standard station wagons, it can transport you in a 1928 Model A or a 1904 Oldsmobile. The Model A can do the speed limit, but the Olds is a little slow...35 mph is its max. Phone 661-2211 or 878-2211.

Hawai'i State Archives

HITCHHIKING

Hitching is illegal on Maui. The law came about when people grew alarmed by the influx of hippies in the the late Sixties, early Seventies, and the ruling still stands.

Yet hitching is done openly. There's just a different flair to it here. Extending the thumb is not done. Hitchers simply stand by the side of the road and stare at the passing cars. With no thumb out, the police can't cite you. Everyone knows you're hitchhiking...it's just a little game that's played to bend the rules, yet stay within them.

CAR RENTALS

Jeep, used clunker, Rolls Royce, Ferrari, Mustang convertible—they're all available for different prices. Most car rental agencies are near the airport. However, there are several agencies located elsewhere—in Kihei, Ka'anapali, Lahaina, even one in Hana.

Insurance

Venturesome drivers who go off the beaten path cannot expect insurance to cover them. The buck stops at the dirt. Once you leave pavement (even with four-wheel drive), the responsibility for repair or towing is yours. "It can add up to quite a bit of money, so people should take heed," one manager warns.

Uninsured, unpaved roads are past Makena, past 'Ohe'o, in Kaupo, up to Polipoli Forest, to Kahakuloa Village, plus numerous side roads that cross the island. Most drive guide maps indicate the areas not to go. In Kipahulu, Lindbergh's grave is a recommended turnaround point.

Four-wheel drive

A few companies have four-wheel-drive vehicles, but several remove the four-wheel-drive mechanism from their Jeeps and Suzukis, since the mechanism is easily damaged by incorrect shifting. The companies claim that people with four-wheel drives are tempted to go where they shouldn't, and when they get stuck, it can cost up to $1000 to pull the car from a ravine.

Only one company, Maui Rent-A-Jeep, allows drivers to go "anywhere on the island except the beach. Main thing, there's no abuse" (of the vehicle).

One veteran car rental manager suggests that people who want to see Kaupo or Kahakuloa should simply get a car that is high off the ground. Four-wheel drive is not necessary to go around the island.

RENTAL AGENCIES

AAA Scooter & Jeep Rental, Inc.
10-2 Halawai, Lahaina • *661-0606*
Vehicles: late model cars, 2-wheel Jeeps, Honda scooters, 3-wheelers.
Driver's age: 18.

Alamo Rent A Car
40 S. Hana Highway • *871-6235* • *877-3466* • *800-327-9633*
Vehicles: late models, 6-passenger vans, Suzuki 4-wheel drive. *Luxury:* Nissan Maxima. *Convertibles:* Dodge and Mustang. Driver's age: 21.

Andres Rent-A-Car, Inc.
Kahului Airport • 877-5378
Vehicles: new & used, 8-passenger station wagons. Driver's age: 21.

Arthur's Limosine Service
Lahaina • 661-LIMO • 800-345-4667
Vehicles: 2 limos (stretch and super-stretch); 7 or 12 passenger. Limos are chauffeured; drivers wear hats, gloves and tuxes.

Atlas U-Drive & Practical Car Rental
542 Keolani Place (P.O.Box 330069, Kahului HI 96733) • 877-7208 • 800-367-5238 (U.S.) • 800-433-5906
Vehicles: new cars, Jeeps. Driver's age: 21.

AVIS Rent A Car
Kahului Airport • 871-7575 (Kahului) • 661-4588 (Ka'anapali) • 800-331-1212
Vehicles: new models, 2-wheel Jeeps, 8-pax vans. *Luxury:* Cadillac Sedan DeVilles. *Convertibles:* Mustang. Drivers's age: 18.

Budget Rent A Car
W. Mokuea Place, Kahului • 871-8811 (Kahului) • 661-8721 (Ka'anapali) • 800-527-0700
Vehicles: new models, 4-wheel Wrangler Broncos, 8 to 15-pax vans. *Luxury:* Lincoln Town car, Oldsmobiles. *Convertibles*: Mustang, *Sports cars:* 200SX Datsuns, Firebirds, Camaros. Driver's age: 21.

Charton U-Drive
Dairy Road • 877-7836 • 661-3489
Vehicles: new. Driver's age: 21.

Convertibles Hawai'i
552 Keolani Place, Kahului • 877-6543
Vehicles: Used hardtop models. *Convertibles:* VW Rabbit and Mustang. Driver's age: 21.

Dollar Rent A Car
946 Mokuea Place, Kahului • 877-2731 (Kahului) • 667-5348 (Ka'anapali) • 800-342-7398
Vehicles: new models, 7 to 15-pax vans. *Luxury:* Cadillac Sedan DeVille, Ford Thunderbird, Chrysler Fifth Ave., Pontiac Fiero, Toyota MR2. *Convertibles:* Mustang and Chevy Cavalier. Driver's age: 18.

El Cheap-o Rent A Car
22 S. Hana Highway, Kahului • *877-5851*
Vehicles: used compact models. Driver's age: 21.

Hertz Rent A Car
Kahului Airport (P.O. Box 1519, Kahului HI 96732 • *877-5167* • *800-654-8200*
Vehicles: new models. *Luxury:* Lincoln Tour, Cadillac DeVille. *Convertibles:* Mustang & Sunbirds & Cavalier, 4-wheel drives. Driver's age: 21.

Kamaaina Rent-A-Car
Dairy Rd. & Haleakala Highway, Kahului HI 96732 • *877-5460*
Vehicles: late models. Driver's age: 25.

Kihei Holidaze Car Rentals
1979 S. Kihei Rd., Kihei • *879-1905*
Vehicles: late models. Driver's age: 25.

Kihei Rent-A-Car
22 Alahele Place, Kihei • *879-7257*
Vehicles: late model compacts, U-Haul trucks, big trucks. Driver's age: 21.

Klunker's Used Car Rentals
456 Dairy Road, Kahului • *877-3197*
Vehicles: late models. Driver's age: 21.

Maui Rent-A-Jeep
450 Dairy Road, Kahului (P.O. Box 89 Puunene, HI 96784) • *877-6626* • *871-2899* • *800-543-5357*
Vehicles: new & late models (some wrecks), 4-wheel Jeeps, Suzukis, Renegades. Driver's age: 21.

Maui Sights & Treasures
Sugar Beach Resort, Kihei • *879-6260* • *874-0663*
Vehicles: late models. Driver's age: 21. Serves mostly Sugar Beach.

Maui's Miser Rent A Car/ VIP
Dairy Road, Kahului • *871-2666*
Vehicles: late models. Driver's age: 25. Specializes in serving windsurfers.

National Car Rental

142 Mokuea Place, Kahului • *871-8851 (Kahului)* • *667-9737 (Ka'anapali)* •
248-8237 (Hana) • *800-227-7368*
Vehicles: new models, 4-wheel Suzukis, Samurai, Jeeps, 7-pax vans.
Luxury: Lincoln Tour Car. *Convertibles:* Pontiac, Chevy, Dodge.
Driver's age: 21.

Paradise Rent A Used Car

1939 S. Kihei Rd., Kihei • *879-8788* • *879-0031*
Vehicles: late model compacts, 4-wheel Suzukis. Driver's age: 25.

Rainbow Rent A Car

741 Wainee, Lahaina • *661-8734*
Vehicles: new & late models, 4-wheel Suzukis, 7-pax vans, pick-up
truck. *Convertibles:* Mustang, Suzuki. Driver's age: 21.

Sears Rent A Car

Halawai Dr., Napili • *661-3546 & W. Mokuea Pl., Kahului* • *877-7764*
Affiliated with Budget Car Rental—Sears credit card holders get a
discount rate on Budget's older cars.

Silver Cloud Excutive Limousine Service—Maui

P.O. Box 12152, Lahaina • *669-8580*
Vehicles: stretch and superstretch limos. Luxury 6-passenger vans
with TVs & VCRs. Rolls Royce, new & classic. *Convertible:* Ferrari.
Driver's age: 25.

Luxury Sports Car Rental

256 Paplaua, Lahaina • *661-5646 & 2387 S. Kihei Rd., Kihei* • *879-8977*
Vehicles: new models, 4-wheel Suzukis, Samurai, Wranglers, Rene-
gades. *Luxury:* Porsche, Masarati, Corvettes, Camaros. *Convertibles:*
Ferrari, 300 ZX Nissan. Driver's age: 25, but 21 for 4-wheel drives.

Sunshine of Hawai'i Rent-A-Car Systems

455 Dairy Road, Kahului Airport • *871-6222*
Vehicles: late model, 4-wheel Jeeps, 7-pax vans. *Convertibles:* Mustang.
Driver's age: 23.

Surf Rent-A-Car

711 L. Main, Wailuku • *244-5544*
Vehicles: late model. Driver's age: 25. Mostly rents to locals.

Thrifty Rent-A-Car
361 Hukiliki, Kahului • *871-7596 or Honoapiilani Highway, Ka'anapali* •
667-9541
Vehicles: new models, 2-wheel Jeeps, 8-pax vans. *Convertibles:* Chrysler. Driver's age: 21.

Trans-Maui-Rent-A-Car
Kahului Airport • *877-5222* • *877-2611* • *800-367-5228*
Vehicles: new & late models, 4-wheel Suzukis, 7-pax vans. *Convertibles:* VW Rabbit. Driver's age: 21. Get a 10% discount if you mention this guidebook.

Travelers USA Rent A Car
Kahului Airport (P.O. Box 1647 Kahului, HI 96733) • *877-7604*
Vehicles: new models, 4-wheel Suzukis. *Convertibles:* Mustang. Driver's age: 21.

United Car Rental Systems, Inc.
536 Keolani Pl., Kahului • *871-7328 or 888 Wainee, Lahaina* • *667-2688*
Vehicles: new & late models, 7 to 15-pax vans. Driver's age: 21.

VIP Car Rentals, Inc.
Dairy Rd. & Haleakala Highway • *877-2054*
Vehicles: new models. *Luxury:* Chrysler 5th Avenues. *Convertibles*: Chrysler La Baron. Driver's age: 25.

Word of Mouth Rent A Used Car
Dairy Road, Kahului • *877-2436*
Vehicles: late models. Driver's age: 25.

Annual Events

Can't drink another mai tai on the beach? Like to see how the locals live and celebrate instead? Stop playing tourist and get down with the folks...attend a local function, go to a fair, watch the paniolos at a rodeo. The real flavor of Maui is in its people. Ain't many local folks out there on those beaches at Ka'anapali. Won't find 'em on the golf course at Wailea either. Get thee to a local event.

Read *The Maui News* to find out what's happening. The following events are some of the biggies, but their dates often vary from year to year. The paper will print the correct times and places.

JANUARY

Chinese New Year: Based on the lunar calendar, this date falls somewhere between the Western calendar's Jan. 20th and Feb. 20th. On Maui, traditional dragon or lion dancers may show up anywhere. At Ming Yuen Chinese Restaurant in Kahului the Lion Dance happens on the front lawn after 200,000 firecrackers are fired off. Inside there's a feast of food...a giant party that lasts two or more nights.

FEBRUARY

Maui Marine Art Expo: An art exhibit of marine-related sculpture, painting, jewelry, pottery. Ceramic, gold, wooden and painted whales abound, with dolphins coming in for a close second. Located in the lobby of the Hotel Inter-Continental in Wailea. Runs for entire months of February and March.

MARCH

Carol Kai Bed Race: Celebrity singer Carol Kai sponsors this zany event—a bed race down Lahaina's Front Street. Businesses and clubs build vehicles that pass for beds, then their teams push the "beds" down

Front as fast as possible. Pledges collected go to Imua Rehab, an organization which aids handicapped children. Race happens in March or April.

Art Maui: Hundreds of local artists submit work to a jury, which then selects the top art for the show. Good opportunity to see Maui's best art. The show is hung in March or April.

Prince Kuhio Day: March 26 commemorates the last of the great ali'i. Prince Kuhio would have been king had the monarchy survived. Instead, he was Hawai'i's first delegate to Congress (under the territorial government). Usually some topnotch Hawaiian cultural events around this day.

Zoo Fest: Held the day before Easter (so could be in April) at the Maui County Zoo in Kahului. It's a mini fair with booths, cockroach races, entertainment, food, etc. Great for kids...they can see the zoo animals too. Proceeds benefit the Maui Philharmonic Society.

Spring Renewal: Usually attended by a couple hundred New Agers, old, young, families, singles...all are welcome. It's a week long spiritual camp held the week before Easter. No religion is stressed, but most participants are interested in Eastern religions plus a general huggy, feel-good brand of Christianity. What's offered?—lots of Sufi dancing and chanting, all types of meditaion, yoga classes, much socializing, very sincere folks and excellent vegetarian food. Price is kept quite inexpensive. Held in gorgeous Ke'anae at the YMCA camp. Accommodations are bunkbed dorms or bring your own tent. Check bulletin boards in health food stores for announcement of whom to contact.

Easter: Lahaina's banyan tree is the scene of an egg hunt held at 9 a.m. the Saturday before Easter. Sponsored by the West Maui Soroptimists. Check *The Maui News* on Good Friday for a listing of church services. Many churches have Hawaiian touches for their Easter celebration.

APRIL

David Malo Day: Held at Lahainaluna High School in Lahaina, the oldest school west of the Rockies. The day varies from year to year. David Malo was in the first class when the school opened in 1831. He later racked up an impressive list of achievements, becoming one of the first native Hawaiian ministers and the first superintendent of schools on island. He was also an authority on Hawaiian culture, writing the still-used book, *Hawaiian Antiquities*. During Malo Day there's food and entertainment offered at low prices on the historic campus.

MAY

May Day: May 1st is Lei Day in Hawai'i...an occasion for pageants at the elementary schools with traditional courts headed by queens and kings of Hawaiian heritage. Lei contests offer a look at the variety and beauty of lei making. One of the biggest is held at the Maui Inter-Continental Hotel.

Boy's Day: May 5th in Japan is Boy's Day. Local Japanese families follow the custom of flying colorful cloth carp over their homes, indicating the presence of sons. The carp symbolizes strength and other manly attributes.

Seabury Hall Crafts Fair: An all-day event (day before Mother's Day) exhibiting and selling the island's best crafts and art. Entertainment, pony rides, water slide for kids, an antique sale, and a chance to see Maui's exclusive, private Episcopal high school on Olinda Road.

Barrio Festival: Maui's Filipino community sets up a miniature Philippine village on the lawn in front of the War Memorial Complex in Wailuku for a weekend in May. There's a queen, plenty of Filipino food booths and games for kids.

Canoe Season: Starts in May. Each weekend for the next few months canoe clubs compete with each other along Maui's coasts. Their schedule is published in *The Maui News*. Special races: Ben Abiera Memorial Day relay along Kihei coast; Kamehameha Day regatta in Kahului Harbor in June; John M. Lake Maui championship regatta at Kahului in July.

Symphony of Chocolate: The best bakers on the island turn out fantastic concoctions for this YMCA-sponsored event held at the Maui Inter-Continental Hotel in Wailea. A chocoholic's paradise.

JUNE

Kamehameha Day: June 11—honors none other than the Great himself...King Kamehameha I, first to unite the combative islands of Hawai'i (in the late 1790s). Parade down Front Street in Lahaina, day-long entertainment, Hawaiian crafts fair at the Maui Marriott Hotel.

Upcountry Fair: A country fair held at the Eddie Tam Memorial Center in Makawao. Features flowers, produce, food, crafts, 4-H livestock, a petting zoo, a farrier making horseshoes...all country stuff.

O-Bon Festivals: These festivals honoring the ancestral dead take place throughout June, July and August at various Buddhist temples. Folk dances called Bon Odori are the center of the activities. Visitors are welcome to observe Bon dances; schedules and locations are listed in *The Maui News.*

Dance for Heart: A Heart Association fundraiser where aerobics buffs collect pledges, then dance for a day of fun and funds. Besides dancing, there are talks by experts on aerobic fitness and health.

JULY

Fourth of July: Maui goes all out...a parade in Kihei, fireworks in Ka'anapali and in Wailuku, a kalua pig cook-off at the Royal Lahaina Resort in Ka'anapali. Biggest event is the Makawao parade and rodeo. It's one of the largest rodeos in the state, with more than 300 cowboys/girls competing.

Kapalua Wine Symposium: Not a casual affair...several days of wine tasting and connoisseur nubbing costs about $250. Visiting vintners, lectures, wine trend talks, gourmet food and Kapalua's elegance are the draws.

Kapalua Music Festival: First-class classical music performances from selected artists across the country...elegant and high brow.

'Ulupalakua Invitational Rodeo: Paniolo from 'Ulupalakua, Kaupo and Hana meet each year for this local, down-home rodeo.

SEPTEMBER

Maui County Rodeo: The final rodeo of the year, held at the Oskie Rice Arena, about a mile up Olinda Road from Makawao.

Polo Season: This game has been popular here since Louis von Tempsky, a New Zealander who became manager of Haleakala Ranch, introduced it in the 1880s. Games begin Sundays at 1 p.m. from September through November. Held in a big field on Olinda Road, just past the Oskie Rice rodeo arena...watch for the "Maui Polo" sign.

Aloha Week: A week-long celebration of Hawai'i's heritage, held since 1946. There's a king and a queen and an elegant Monarchy Ball, plus several lu'au and talent shows held around the island.

OCTOBER

Maui County Fair: One of Maui's biggest events, held yearly since 1916. Typical county fair—carnival rides and games, food, agricultural products, livestock, homemade crafts, plus an extraordinary, large orchid exhibit...the flowers take up a whole building. Held at the fairgrounds on Puunene Avenue in Kahului.

Maui County Women's Conference: Workshops, speakers and classes in everything from politics to parenting. Good place for Maui women to meet and network. Visitors welcome. Men also welcome, but it's definitely not their day. Held at the Maui Community College Campus in Kahului.

Halloween: Lahaina's Front Street is the scene. Dress in whatever and parade yourself along with all the other weirdos. Goes on until the wee hours...just people prancing and watching. Good chance for visitors to join in with locals...who cares where you're from when you're in costume? Some of the costumes are quite wild, so have no hesitation about dressing up. There's also a children's parade on Front Street, but it's held before dark, and before the crazies are out in force.

NOVEMBER

Na Mele O Maui: Means "the songs of Maui"...it was started to ensure preservation of these mele (songs). Elementary schools island-wide compete in song contests held in Lahaina and Ka'anapali. Hawaiian craft displays, lu'au and concerts are also part of the week.

Maui Contractor's Auxiliary Annual Christmas Bazaar: The auxiliary is a group of building contractors' wives. They fill the War Memorial Gym in Wailuku with non-profit groups selling handicrafts. It's held on a Saturday in November between 10 a.m. and 2 p.m. Good place to buy Christmas presents.

Christmas Tree Festival: Exhibits of trees, wreaths, door hangings, ornaments made and displayed by the Maui Extension Homemakers Council. Held at Maui Community College. Some displays are sold at end of the two-day event.

DECEMBER

Ka'anapali Keiki Fishing Derby: Amfac sponsors this day of fishing for children, held at the water hazard on the Ka'anapali Golf Course. Tilapia fish reside there...not a great eating fish, but what the heck. Three different age groups, 5-8, 9 & 10 and 11 & 12 vie for prizes for the biggest fish. Kids should bring their own poles and worms. Amfac supplies free hamburgers and sodas. Can't fish all day; this is a golf course; just 9 to 11 a.m.

Messiah Sing Along: Anyone wishing to sing, comes to an afternoon rehearsal and potluck, then joins the famous choir at the Makawao Union Church. The audience is part of the concert. Watch newspaper for date or call the church. Christmas Eve service is a candle-lit choral event...very inspirational.

YMCA's Kids Overnighter on New Year's Eve: Go party with ease...leave the kids (aged 5 to 12) with the YMCA people. The kids have their own party, then bed down in sleeping bags. Call the Y for location.

THEATER GROUPS

Maui's theater is surprisingly good for such a small island. There are scores of talented folk living here and many consider acting more than a hobby. Don't expect avant garde, Off Broadway, however. Most shows are well-tested favorites.

The **Maui Community Theatre**, headquartered in the old 'Iao Theater in Wailuku, usually has a play in progress year round.

The kids' version, **The Maui Youth Theatre,** makes its home in the somewhat funky old community center in Pu'unene, a tiny sugar mill town. Their shows always change, of course, except they always have a dance show in July, called Pieces. At Christmas they have a big extravaganza, usually a major musical.

Baldwin High School, famous for its performing arts program, has a theater group of high school students, alumni and anyone else who's interested. They usually have a show happening, and it's often a cabaret type which includes audience participation. In January they present a scholarship show (either a Diamond Lil Revue or a USO show) to raise college funds for one of their deserving senior actors.

Safety

A New Yorker would laugh at these puny numbers; nonetheless, there is some trouble in paradise. The most recent available crime and accident records for Maui County (includes Lana'i and Moloka'i) are 1985. Crime statistics are:

Murder	1
Rape	28
Robbery	44
Assault	197
Burglary	1407
Larceny (over $200)	1420
Auto Theft	326
Prostitution	0

Traffic accident statistics:

Major accidents	1509
Traffic deaths	9

These statistics mean—lock your car and trunk; lock your hotel doors (particularly sliding glass doors). Don't put valuables in a locked car trunk (thieves know rental cars and can easily pop a trunk). Wear your seatbelt (it's law in Hawai'i). Don't camp alone. Don't walk the beach alone at night. Don't jog along desolate cane roads. Don't hitchhike. Don't tailgate. Don't pick your nose. Have a nice day...this is America.

Water & Sun

These are actually Maui's biggest threats. Both can do plenty of damage. The sun's rays are more direct and less filtered by the atmosphere this close to the equator. Sunburns happen even on overcast days.

For those who've already blown it and are burned, get an aloe vera plant or its packaged gel and put the soothing glop on the skin. It's magic stuff...used by native peoples for eons

The ocean is pretty, but powerful...
1. Before you enter, study the water—note location of rocks, breakers, currents and reefs.
2. Don't turn your back on the ocean.
3. Enter unfamiliar water feet first.
4. Breaker waves come in sets. Enter during calm periods between sets.
5. Never body surf a wave straight in; instead, ride at an angle to the shoreline.
6. Stay off reefs—you can damage them and they can damage you (coral cuts, sea urchin spines, eel bites).
7. Duck or dive *beneath* breaking waves before they reach you. Do not stand in their path or try to swim over them.
8. Never swim against a strong current. Let it carry you, if it's heading to shore. If not, swim across the current towards shore, not into the current.
9. Never swim alone at an unfamiliar beach.

(Special thanks to *The Maui News* for several of the tips.)

Local neurosurgeon Roger A. Slater says about two dozen visitors break their necks every year in water-related accidents.

The streams are sweet, but powerful...
1. In the rainy season, flash floods can happen in minutes. A gurgling stream can quickly become a raging torrent. Do not hike up streams when the water looks like it's high and getting higher.

2. Do not jump or dive into unfamiliar pools without checking the depth and the location of rocks. Legs and necks give before boulders do. Many paraplegics found this out the hard way.

Current beach etiquette...
Nudity, even on an isolated beach, is against the law. Yes, it's true the ancient Hawaiians swam and surfed naked, and it's a doggone shame about uptight Puritanical morals, BUT, nobody's listening. The police in the 1980s make arrests, particularly at Little Beach in Makena. Naked tourists are not excluded from police blotters.

This includes going topless, ladies. Makena is by no means the French Riviera...for which we can all be thankful.

Health Care

Sick on vacation? Not fair! But it happens only too often. Here's where to seek help and get health.

Emergencies

Call 911. State where you are and what the emergency is. There is no automatic tracer on the line to trace your call, so stay on until you've given directions. The dispatcher, headquartered at the Kahului police station, dispatches all emergency vehicles.

There are ambulance stations in Kihei, Wailuku, Makawao and Lahaina. Ambulances are state of the art and the paramedics are excellent, but there are not enough vehicles for the territory they cover. Thus, service is not always speedy. Best to start CPR or First Aid yourself.

Hana also has an ambulance, but it's not as fancy and up-to-date as those on the rest of the island. Hana's medical facility is quite good, though they do not treat serious cases there. If you have a heart attack or break your neck, they'll helicopter you to Wailuku.

Hospital

There is only one major hospital on Maui—Maui Memorial Hospital on Mahalani Street in Wailuku. This state-run facility has all the necessary modern equipment and is licensed for 150 beds.

Doctors

Maui has plenty of doctors—about 150 now have privileges at Maui Memorial Hospital. These physicians are listed in the Yellow Pages according to specialties, as are dentists, chiropractors, acupuncturists and other health care practitioners.

Listed in this chapter are the major clinics and health centers and those especially geared to care for visitors.

MAJOR MEDICAL CLINICS

Lahaina/Ka'anapali

Ben K. Azman, M.D. Inc., and Kathleen Welch, M.D.
Whalers Village, Ka'anapali • 667-9721 • 661-0475 • 667-9280
    Azman was the first doctor to move his office to Ka'anapali (in 1980), particularly to treat tourists. Welch is an expert on marine-related problems. They do house and hotel calls, and walk-in patients are accepted during office hours. Lab and X-ray equipment available. A dermatologist and a pediatrician are in the office some days. Open 8 a.m. to 10 p.m. daily.

Doctors on Call
Hyatt Regency Hotel • 667-7676
    Two doctors available for house or hotel calls 24 hours a day (for general medical practice) from Lahaina to Kapalua. Individuals or groups may retain a physician exclusively for themselves or for special functions by prior arrangement. Lab, X-ray and minor surgery facilities. Open 8 a.m. to 6 p.m. daily.

Kaiser Permanente Medical Care Program
910 Wainee, Lahaina • 661-0081
    Numerous doctors work regular 8 to 5 hours here (plus 8 to noon Sat.). And there's a physician's assistant available 24 hours a day. Doctors are on call evenings and weekends. Lab and X-ray available in the clinic.

Maui Medical Group, Lahaina Branch
130 Prison Street • 661-0051
    Four full-time doctors plus visits by specialists. Lab, X-ray, pharmacy. Open 8 to 5 Mon.-Fri. and 8 a.m. to noon Saturday. After hours, a physician's assistant takes minor emergencies until 9 p.m. Monday to Friday; noon to 3 p.m. Saturday, and 10 a.m. to 3 p.m. Sunday.

Kihei

Kihei Physicians
Kihei Professional Plaza, 1325 S. Kihei Rd. • 879-7781
    Seven doctors, including an orthopedic surgeon, pediatrician and an OB/GYN who is an infertility expert. Lab, X-ray, minor surgery in office (even some broken bones). Walk-ins are accepted without appointment. Hours: 8-8 M-F; 8-5 Saturday.

Kihei Pediatric Clinic
Kihei Professional Plaza, 1325 S. Kihei Rd. • 879-5288
This is the only clinic in Kihei with a pediatrician on duty six days a week; plus, he's always on call for emergencies. The clinic is run by Dr. Donald Roberts, a pediatric cardiologist who specializes in kids' respiratory and ear diseases. Open 8-5 M,W, Th, F; 8 to noon Th, Saturday.

Kihei Clinic & Wailea Medical Services
Island Surf Building, 1993 S. Kihei Rd. • 879-1440 • 879-7447
Two family practitioners who work often with tourists ...available for house or hotel calls 24 hours a day. Will accept walk-in patients during office hours. Open 8 a.m. to 5 p.m. Mon.-Fri. and 8 a.m. to noon Saturday.

Wailuku/ Kahului

Maui Clinic
53 Puunene Ave., Kahului • 877-6663
Fifteen physicians practice here. Their specialties include dentistry, opthalmology, pediatrics, psychiatry and general practice. The island's first neurologist and only neurosurgeon are here. Lab, X-ray, pharmacy, optical shop available. Open 8 a.m. to 5 p.m. Mon.-Fri. Closed Wednesday afternoons and Sundays. Saturday hours vary with the physician.

Maui Medical Group
2180 Main, Wailuku • 242-6464
Twenty doctors have offices here, including a cardiologist and an oncologist (cancer specialist). Lab, X-ray, pharmacy, physical therapy clinic are all on the property. Open 8 a.m. to 5 p.m. Mon.-Fri. and 8 a.m. to noon Saturday.

Upcountry

East Maui Clinic
Pukalani Square, 81 Makawao Ave. • 572-6114
An osteopath and a medical doctor offer family practice, sports medicine, allergy care, and more. Open 8 a.m. to 4 p.m. Mon.-Fri. and 9 a.m. to 1 p.m. Sat.; after hours in emergencies.

DENTAL CLINICS

Maui Dental Center
162 Alamaha, Kahului • 871-6283

Three dentists provide family dental care, cosmetic bonding and emergency service. They can do new dentures or denture repair in one day (about one visitor a week loses dentures in the ocean). Open 8 a.m. to 8 p.m. Mon.-Fri. and 9 a.m. to 4 p.m. Sat.; will come in Sundays for emergencies.

Tooth Tips:
.....Do not snorkel, SCUBA dive or body surf with dentures in, unless using a heavy-duty adhesive.
.....If a tooth is sensitive to pressure or to hot/ cold, do not get on an airplane. Pressure at high elevation can bring out a dormant abcess, and this will cause great pain...and there's nothing one can do about it on a plane. Have the tooth checked before traveling.
.....Teeth knocked out (common windsurfing accident) should be replaced in their sockets immediately and kept cold with ice. Then pronto to the dentist.

NURSING SERVICES

Akamai Nursing Service
878-6125

Nurses aides, licensed practical nurses and registered nurses available round the clock for full or part-time care in home, hospital or hotel.

Medical Personnel Pool
877-2676

This is part of a nation-wide company which is a subsidiary of H & R Block. Employees are insured and bonded. Registered nurses, licensed practical nurses, aides and chore workers are available for duty 24 hours a day. Aides are closely supervised. Travel escort and live-in services available.

Quality Time Professional Nursing Service
871-6244 or 879-4384

Companions, homemakers, aides, licensed practical nurses and registered nurses available for 24-hour care in home or hospital, or for travel assistance. Lower levels of care backed by RN supervision.

PHYSICAL THERAPY

Physical Therapy Care
358 Papa Place, Kahului • 871-7190

Three physical therapists and one myotherapist specialize in back injuries. Myotherapy is muscle re-education for soft-tissue injuries. Center offers regular physical therapy with heat, ice and electrical treatments, plus massage and assisted exercise. Facilities include a large gym area, treatment rooms, sauna and whirlpool. They offer exercise classes, nutritional classes and a wellness program. Their "Back School," which helps injured people learn to minimize pain and maximize function, is highly recommended by local rehab specialists.

Inter Isle Physical Therapy and Sports Medicine, Inc.
Puuone Towers Plaza, 1063 Lower Main, Suite C203, Wailuku
244-5541

This 3,000-square foot clinic holds a glittering array of advanced equipment—gym exercise machines for building strength, sophisticated testing gear, ice, heat, ultrasound and ultraviolet treatments, plus whirlpools. Two physical therapists specialize in post-orthopedic surgery care. Open 9:30 a.m. until finished M, W, F; 9:30 a.m. to 6:30 p.m. Tuesday, Thursday.

Valley Isle Sports/ Industrial Rehabilitation Center, Inc.
910 W. Honoapiilani Highway (West Maui Center) • 667-5384

This no-nonsense gym is tucked into 800 square feet in the West Maui Center. They specialize in rehab, with chiropractor Greg Song coming over from his Wailuku office twice a week. The 13 Nautilus machines are the only ones on this side of the island. Skilled trainers put people through the program. This is for serious work-outs...no shower rooms or lounge, just heavy metal. Open 7:30 a.m. to 7:30 p.m. Mon.-Sat. Anyone can use the gym, you don't have to be a chiropractic patient. But an appointment is recommended for use of the equipment to avoid overcrowding the gym.

ALTERNATIVE MEDICAL CLINICS

Healing Light Health Center
2119 D Vineyard, Wailuku • 242-9590

Christina Chang, who runs the clinic, practices an eclectic wholistic style of healing. Techniques include massage, herbs and supplements, acupuncture, diet and lifestyle counseling, and naturopathy. A naturopath and an osteopath also work out of the center. Much revolves around the use of an Interro medical computer developed by quantum physicists. By monitoring a patient's acupuncture points, the computer can evaluate all internal organs and functions, find an imbalance, and then prescribe a homeopathic remedy. Open 9 a.m to 5 p.m. Mon.-Fri. Students in massage apprenticeship programs give massages on Saturdays for reduced prices.

Maui Wholistic Clinic
2119 B Vineyard, Wailuku • 244-8144

Three naturopaths, two massage therapists, two colonic therapists and one acupuncturist offer natural approaches to healing. They use traditional diagnoses (blood tests and Pap smear), but alternative healing methods—herbs, diet, chiropractic, homeopathics and deep tissue work. They offer emotional counseling, and often work with chronic diseases. Open 9 a.m. to 6 p.m. Monday through Friday.

Center for Preventive Health Care and Research
90 Central Ave., Wailuku • 242-6668

Two naturopaths, a medical doctor, a psychiatrist, massage therapists, colonic therapists, an acupuncturist, a podiatrist and a Rolfer work here. Services include allergy testing and immune system evaluation, plus other diagnostic work involving a computer which analyzes blood, saliva or urine for unbalanced energy levels or other problems. Treatment all by natural methods. Open 9 a.m. to 5 p.m. Monday through Friday.

Grace Clinic
Baldwin Ave., Makawao (behind Whitey's Upholstery) • 572-6091

Run by acupuncturist Mallik Cotter, who studied and trained in both Maui and China. Two masseuses are also on staff. Open M,W noon to 7 p.m.; T, Th 8:30 a.m. to 6 p.m.

Lahaina Acupuncture and Massage Center
1287 Front, Lahaina • 667-6260

Four therapists (acupuncture and massage), a chiropractor (with X-ray facility) and a Rolfer work in this little building across from the Cannery. Their treatment and massage rooms open onto the ocean—relax and heal to the sound of waves. Open 9 a.m. to 5 p.m. Monday through Saturday.

Access &

The news is not great for travelers who have severe physical limitations. There is no van for rent with a wheelchair lift; many restaurants and other public places have steps rather than ramps or elevators; few hotels offer rooms specifically designed to accommodate a wheelchair.

Still, a holiday in Maui is possible. The State Commission on the Handicapped has two booklets that tell you how to do it—"Aloha Guide to Accessibility on Maui" (several years old, but much info still holds) and "Maui Travelers Guide" (more recently updated).

Commission on the Handicapped representative Linda Rink will send the guides for free. Rink is also very helpful with personal advice. Her address: c/o State Department of Health, 54 High Street, Wailuku, HI 96793. Phone is (808) 244-4441 (V/TDD - deaf).

Tips from Rink & the guidebooks

If traveling via electric wheelchair, only one inter-island airline, Aloha, can take a wet cell battery on most of its flights. On their 737s, they can stand the chair upright in the belly. Hawaiian Air can accept a wet cell battery only on their "dash" flight, which flies infrequently. All airlines can handle dry and gel cell batteries.

Notify the airlines at least one full day in advance, so they can make arrangements for your chair.

There are no battery rentals available on Maui, so you must bring your own.

Ground transportation

The only way to get an electric chair from the airport to a hotel is to rent the Maui Economic Opportunity van, which has an electric lift. This van is used mostly by residents, but can be hired by visitors (with advance notice). Call well in advance and speak to Agnes Groff or Norita DeLima at (808) 877-7651.

Both Avis and Hertz rent cars with hand controls installed. To reserve one, call the toll free number in your local telephone directory.

Bring along your handicapped-parking permit. If you don't have it, you can get one from the drivers license section at the War Memorial Complex in Wailuku (corner of Kanaloa and Ka'ahumanu Avenues)...best to have a statement from your physician stating that you are a qualified permit holder in your home state.

There are no sightseeing tours designed for disabled people, and the regular tour vans do not have wheelchair space.

Equipment

Medical equipment, including manual wheelchairs which tuck into a car trunk, plus walkers, oxygen, lifts, overbed tables and other supplies can be rented from Crafts Drugs (877-0111), GASPRO (877-0056), Hawaiian Rentals (877-7684) or Maui Rents (877-5827). All are located in Kahului.

Sightseeing

The Travelers Guide lists parks and sites that accommodate disabled people. All the most frequently-visited places are wheelchair accessible.

Hotels

Hotels that have accessible entry and exit, plus specially-designed or adapted rooms with at least 29" entry into bathrooms and grab bars are:
—Kapalua Bay Hotel (two rooms)
—Maui Marriott (six rooms...MEO says most of their van customers stay here)
—Royal Lahaina Resort (four rooms; grab bars in shower only)
—Stouffer Wailea Beach Resort (two rooms)
—Hotel Inter-Continental Maui (All rooms have grab bars in showers; two have grab bars by toilet; two more are in the works.)

Other hotels may be sufficient for those with less severe limitations. Tell the hotel exactly what you need when you call or write for reservations.

Bedding Down

BED & BREAKFAST

Bed & Breakfast Maui Style

If a homeowner rents a room solely for the income, that's the wrong motivation, according to the owners of B & B Maui Style. Jeanne Rominger and Margaret DelCastillo will not book with a money-minded owner.

"Our people like to have guests in their homes," says Rominger. "It's an aloha gesture...the aloha spirit." They practice what they preach—both Rominger and DelCastillo have B & B rooms in their Kihei homes.

They have about 25 host homes with prices from budget to moderate. They range from a rustic Makena house with a floor futon in a small room to a Lahaina studio with a kitchen and a hot tub to a luxurious, isolated home on the slopes of Haleakala in Olinda.

P.O. Box 886, Kihei, HI 96753 • (808) 879-7865 • 879-2352

Bed & Breakfast Hawai'i

This is a professionally-run outfit that books B & Bs on all the islands. Owners Al Davis and Evie Warner started in 1979 with their own home in Kaua'i. Then there were few, if any, B & Bs available. B & B Hawai'i changed that—they now have more than 35 host homes on Maui alone.

Write them and they will send out three pages of sample listings, or send $10 (plus $1 postage) to receive their book of B & Bs on all the islands. Only the B & Bs that list with them are in the book.

Prices are budget to moderate. All homes are inspected for location and cleanliness. Home owners are expected to serve breakfast and interact with guests.

P.O. Box 449, Kapaa, HI 96746 • (808) 822-7771
(808) 572-7692 • Maui rep Natalie Powell

HOSTEL

There is only one hostel on the entire island. It's perched on a beautiful, isolated peninsula that is, unfortunately, a 32-mile, 2-hour drive from the airport. Catch 22 for budget travelers: the only way to get there is by car; there is no bus. Hitchhiking is an alternative.

Once there, you'll find a simple wooden building with metal bunks, men and women together dorm style. Bathhouse is separate with hot showers. Kitchen is also separate and is huge. Other buildings on the property are used for retreats and outings, so you may share space with local groups. The camp is beautiful...set in a rugged area overlooking the crashing sea. It is the cheapest place to stay on the island. The hostel is run by the YMCA which also owns the property.

Come equipped with your own bedrolls and food. There are no groceries for miles. Check-in is 4-6 p.m. Maximum stay is 3 nights.

P.O. Box 820, Wailuku, HI 96793

244-3253 • 242-9007.

Hawai'i State Archives

PRICES: HOTELS & CONDOS

All Maui's hotels and all its best condos, from budget to stratosphere, are listed in this book in the areas where they are located. The Hyatt Regency Hotel, for instance, is in the Ka'anapali Chapter.

No prices are given because prices change constantly. Instead, they've been divided into ranges—for hotels there are budget, mid-range and expensive.

Budget in 1987 means anything under $75 a night for a couple (remember, Maui is expensive). If it's low-end of budget, it'll be marked "very budget." Mid-range means a room between $75 and $199. Expensive is anything $200 and above...and there are plenty of them on Maui.

Since there are so many condos, they are divided into five categories—budget, moderate, high, expensive and stratosphere. Prices break down as follows:

Price Range	1-Bedroom Unit	2-Bedroom Units
Budget	$40-55	$56-75
Moderate	$56-75	$76-95
High	$76-100	$96-125
Expensive	$101-139	$126-249
Stratosphere	$140 & up	$250 & up

Camping

HALEAKALA NATIONAL PARK

This is the only national park on the island. It includes Haleakala Crater plus the 'Ohe'o Gulch area in Kipahulu. Tent camping is allowed in four areas: Hosmer Grove, 'Ohe'o Gulch and near Holua and Paliku Cabins.

Hosmer Grove : At 7,000-foot elevation, this place is cold at night. It's a pretty, wooded area with a marked nature trail through the trees. Six campsites with room for 25, groups limited to 15. No permits needed—first come, first serve.
Facilities: pit toilets, drinking water, tables, fireplaces, cooking shelter with grills. Max. stay = 3 nights

'Ohe'o Gulch (Seven Sacred Pools): Pristine, gorgeous area to camp—on a grassy field right on cliffs above the crashing surf. Nearly 50 acres are designated for camping, but only 15 acres are usable; the rest are too overgrown. No permit needed; no limit to the number of campers.
Facilities: toilets, tables & grills; no water, so bring your own.
Max. stay = 3 nights a month
248-8251: phone for the 'Ohe'o rangers

There are three cabins within the crater itself. Two of these, **Holua Cabin** and **Paliku Cabin**, have grassy areas near them where tent camping is permitted. Limited to 25 per campground; groups limited to 15. Permits are required. They are issued at Park Headquarters (as you drive into the park) on a first-come basis on the day you intend to camp. Reservations are not possible; bookings are given only on the day of camping. Headquarter's hours are 7:30 a.m. to 4 p.m. daily.
Maximum stay = 2 nights per campground; 3 nights max per month
Facilities: toilets & drinking water.

Haleakala Cabins

The three cabins in the crater are often difficult to reserve. A written request is required 3 months in advance. Give a first and alternate choice of days and a first and alternate cabin. "The key to getting a cabin," a ranger says, "is flexibility." Each party is given one cabin; limit of 12 per party. Cabins have bunks, water, firewood, stove, kitchen utensils, but no bedding.

Holua Cabin is 3.9 miles from head of Halemau'u Trail;
...7.4 miles from head of Sliding Sands Trail.
Kapalaoa Cabin is 5.8 miles from head of Sliding Sands Trail.
Paliku Cabin is 9.8 miles from head of Sliding Sands.

Address: P.O. Box 369, Makawao, HI 96768
Phone : 572-9306 or 572-7749
Office hours : 7:30 a.m. to 4 p.m.

STATE PARKS

Three state parks allow camping; only two of them have cabins. No fee for camping, but the cabins have a minimal charge. Maximum stay for both cabins and camping is five nights. After five nights, you cannot camp in the same campground for the next 30 days. Then you're free to camp there again. There are a limited number of campers allowed in each campground.

These three state parks are well tended, and the campgrounds are in beautiful areas. Facilities and cabins are fairly rustic, but they fit the surroundings. No one will be disappointed.

Reservations are a must; you may apply up to a year in advance for either cabins or campsites. Permits are required for both. To apply for permits by mail, write: P.O. Box 1049, Wailuku, HI 96793.

To apply in person, or to pick up permits or bedding, visit the state parks' office—Department of Land and Natural Resources, 54 High Street, Wailuku, on the ground floor of the state office building.

Phone: (808) 244-4354
Office hours: 8 a.m. to 4:15 p.m.

Waianapanapa State Park

Three miles before Hana is a turnoff to gorgeous Waianapanapa. Here there are 12 basic wooden cabins that sleep up to six people. The cabins are quite large. All have electricity, a bathroom with hot shower, a big kitchen, two bedrooms, a living room area and a lanai. Linens and towels are provided. You are expected to sweep your cabin upon leaving.

The very budget price and the dramatic setting make the cabins popular with both locals and tourists. Reservations are a must; they are often booked months in advance. There is an office in the park where you show your permit and pick up your key.

Tent camping is available for 60 people in an area separate from the cabins. Permit required; pick it up at the state office building in Wailuku. No fee. Campground facilities: cold showers, flush toilets, drinking water, tables & grills.

Polipoli Spring State Recreation Area

A magical, misty, foggy forest...something never expected on a tropical island. Serene and quiet, Polipoli is 6,200 feet up in the Kula Forest Reserve (on the west slope of Haleakala). Four-wheel drive is often needed to reach the park...the dirt road is bumpy and rutted.

Nights are cold; winter nights are often freezing.

A campground with room for 20 is located next to the parking lot. Facilities: toilets, picnic tables and potable water.

One cabin, usually booked far in advance, has space for 10. Facilities: bunks, toilet, cold shower, stove, drinking water, kitchenware. Sheets, blankets, pillows, dish towel (but no bath towels) can be picked up at the state office building in Wailuku. Pick up the cabin key (at the state office) the day you'll occupy it.

Early Haleakala campers share morning brew.

(Hawai'i State Archives)

Kaumahina State Wayside
A forested rest stop area on the way to Hana (Highway 360)...about 28 miles from Kahului Airport, a two-hour drive. This is a rain forest area with great views of the coastline. Room for 30 campers. No cabins. Permit required—state office building in Wailuku.

Facilities: toilets, showers, tables and grills.

MAUI COUNTY PARKS

Only two county parks allow camping. Neither site is sensational. Both have been the scene of local violence and rapes.

Maximum stay is 3 nights per campsite; fee is $3 a night. A tent is required. So are permits. Write the Department of Parks and Recreation, County of Maui, Wailuku, HI 96793, or visit War Memorial Gym near Baldwin High School in Wailuku. Phone: 244-9018. Hours: 8-4.

Baldwin Park near Pa'ia is right on Highway 36 (Hana Highway)...nothing scenic about it. The small campground looks like a fenced-in cage of tents. The ocean is a block away.

Facilities: 2 portable toilets near the campsite, more toilet, showers, picnic tables are close by in Baldwin Beach Park.

Rainbow Park is on Baldwin Avenue between Pa'ia and Makawao (Road 390 near mile marker #3). The park was landscaped in the 1920s and many types of trees were planted—monkeypod, koa, banyan, Norfolk Island Pine, coconut, shower trees, etc. There is also a sweet little Japanese teahouse and garden. The park is pretty and secluded, and, unfortunately, often dangerous.

Facilities: toilets, showers.

Reality Talking...
A county administrator (who prefers to be unnamed) admits these two piddly campsites have "deplorable conditions." Local people never use them, yet locals camp out a lot. It's a Hawaiian tradition that you camp wherever you want. Whole families park themselves for a week on a favorite beach. It's illegal, but the police rarely bother you.

Renting camping gear
There's only one place on island—Silversword Stoves on Baldwin Avenue in Makawao. This used to be a sporting goods store, but now they focus more on stoves. Still, they rent tents, sleeping bags and mats. They also carry some dried food. Phone 572-4569 to see what's in stock and to check rental rates.

East Maui

East Maui is Haleakala. The great and mysterious crater area is generally called Haleakala; but, in fact, the whole of East Maui is one volcano—Haleakala.

This volcano reached the surface around one million years ago. It last popped a vent or two just 200 years ago...the lava produced being the youngest earth on Maui. The paths of these latest flows are easy to see in the La Perouse area.

Haleakala is now considered dormant, still on a hotspot, but not actively producing lava...not now, anyway. Scientists make no predictions. More volcanic activity is possible.

East Maui's highest point is at the summit—10,023 feet. Here at the crater area much of the earth is barren, too porous and too young yet to support much plant life. The slopes of the mountain have diverse botanical zones—from the desert-like Kaupo, La Perouse and Kihei to the lush jungle areas near Hana and Kipahulu.

Meanings of Place Names

La Perouse	18th century French explorer
Makena	"many gathered"
Wailea	"water of Lea" (goddess of canoe makers)
Kihei	"cape" or "cloak"
Pa'ia	"noisy"
Makawao	"forest beginning"
Haleakala	"house of the sun"
Kipahulu	"fetch (from) exhausted gardens"
Kaupo	"landing (of canoes) at night"
Hana	"work" or "to make"...no one knows if either definition applies to town

La Perouse

La Perouse is primitive. The earth lives isolated, all by itself, way out here. Nobody and nothing can exist on its piles of rocks.

La Perouse is the scene of Maui's last lava flow. Sometime around 1790 Haleakala popped off two vents and liquid lava ran all the way to the ocean. The a'a lava cooled into its characteristic chunks, and remains unchanged today. Nothing but rocks and chunks and boulders.

The landscape is bizarre. Only the moon is this surreal. Hardly a drop of green in acres of brown. Rugged, dusty, desolate, austere.

Jean-Francois de Galaup, Compte de La Perouse, the first European to set foot on Maui, did so at La Perouse (then called Keone'o'io) on May 30, 1786. In his journal he called it *"a dismal coast, where torrents of lava had formerly flowed..."*

The French explorer spent only a day on Maui, visiting, as he described: *"four small villages of about 10 or 12 houses each, built and covered with straw in the same manner as those of our poorest peasants."*

Still these villages exist, though they are empty of inhabitants. They are relics amidst the lava. In fact, they are lava themselves—the lava foundations and walls and heiau of days gone by.

Their ruins haunt La Perouse. They give the area a presence like no other place on the island. It is ancient Maui...as close as we can get.

The Road

Past the Maui Prince Hotel the paved road ends and a dirt and gravel road begins. The farther you drive, the worse it gets. It is possible to drive to Maonakala Village, and it is possible to go on to the La Perouse area. But beyond that it's tough. Jeeps and trucks are recommended. Foot travel is better.

The rugged Jeep road ends at the Hanamanioa Lighthouse. Beyond that it's a fisherman's foot path leading into desolate rockiness.

Legend

A jealous and angry Pele, fire goddess extraordinaire, created the last lava flow on Maui. It is named Paea Flow after a young man whom Pele coveted. Pele transformed herself into a beautiful woman to seduce Paea, but he was already in love with Kalua, and he was not a man to be tempted.

A local priest recognized Pele and warned Paea that he was dealing with a powerful goddess. Paea took Kalua and ran down Haleakala to escape. But, too late—Pele caught on and sent lava cascading after them. If she could not have him, no woman would.

HISTORIC SITES

This region and farther east (from Makena to Kaupo) is littered with ancient villages. No ruins are marked, and most have not been excavated. None of the thatched roof charm remains. It's strictly foundations left. They begin to look like just so many piles of rocks after a while. It is best to leave them untouched since they have yet to be excavated properly.

The King's Highway

There are two versions of who built this old road. Whichever is right, the fact is that this is an amazing feat of engineering—a road built from lava rocks that originally encircled the entire island. Much of it is gone now, but in La Perouse the road is in good condition.

In the State Register of Historic Places the road is called Hoapili Trail. This is the missionary version. In 1851, minister Henry Cheever rode a mule along 20 miles of the road, and he wrote that it was constructed in the early 1800s during the governorship of Hoapili, a high ranking chief. Cheever said the trail was built by a labor force of "convicts of adultery." He called it a trail "which Sin has wrought."

Most do not take kindly to such an unromantic idea. Locals call it the King's Highway or Pi'ilani Trail. It is generally believed that King Pi'ilani and his son Kiha-a-Pi'ilani built the road in the 1500s. To do so, stones were supposedly passed along a line of men, then set in place...a rather torturous task.

The road was often wide enough for eight people to walk abreast. Much of it had lava curbs along each side. This wide construction is particularly evident in La Perouse.

The truth might be that Pi'ilani started the road, his son Kiha-a-Pi'ilani finished it, and Hoapili improved it. Possibly the road the missionaries saw being "built" was actually just being rebuilt in places.

Do not drive a vehicle along the old highway. Go on foot.

Makena

Makena is an island favorite...one of the last pristine, isolated areas with great beaches. Some people think of Makena solely as a beach. For many years that's all there was. Then a few houses started creeping in. Now there's a hotel. Soon there will be more. Golf courses, tennis courts, parking lots—the wave of change has begun. Makena was slated for resort development in the early Seventies. In the Eighties the building began.

Less than 15 inches of rain falls a year, so sunshine can be expected daily.

HISTORY

Makena was never a bustling area, but villages and communities did exist from ancient times until the 1920s. In the 1800s the Makena Landing saw plenty of action. Then Makena was an active port, shipping cattle and sugar from this side of the island.

By the 1920s, Kahului became the central, most modern port, so there was little need for small landing areas. The inter-island ferries stopped calling at Makena Landing. Population dwindled as Makena residents lost their quickest source of contact with the rest of Maui.

Beach Hippies

Makena was left to the kiawe trees until the late Sixties when mainland hippies decided Makena's beaches were home sweet home. A hundred at a time could be found camping out on the golden sand. The draw was nature and seclusion. They would bother no one way out there, and no one would bother them. Or so they thought...local newspaper headlines indicate that not all was peace and love.
—"Maui Councilman Wants Them Quarantined" • 4-18-70
—"Easter Love-in a Desecration of Hawaiiana" • 4-5-70
—"Mayor to Crack Down on Transient Squatters" • 4-15-70
—'Pitiful Half-Nudes, Serious Trippers" • 8-16-7

By 1972 the hippies were evicted from Makena. They went else-where—to small farms and wild areas all over the isle. Makena is still a favorite beach, still popular with the New Agers who flock to Maui.

BEACHES & PARKS

Po'olenalena Beach

Part of this beach is sometimes called Paipu Beach or Chang's Beach (after a local family that has long lived there), another part is often called Blue Tile Roof Beach (after the roof of a house on the beach). Officially, it's Po'olenalena, meaning "yellow head," referring to a large rock on the golf course that has yellow streaks in it. Locals love Po'olenalena's beauty and seclusion.

Good swimming; bottom generally sandy.

No facilities.

Naupaka Beach

This is the beach in front of the Maui Prince Hotel. Obviously popular with hotel guests.

Great swimming; sandy bottom.

Facilities: showers, toilets, parking.

Oneuli Beach

After the pavement ends and the dirt road begins (past the Maui Prince Hotel), look for the first makai turnoff. You need a Jeep to get down the turnoff, it's so rutted. The beach is Oneuli, also known as Black Sand Beach (Oneuli means "dark sands").

Not a popular beach, some days you can have it all to yourself. A reef is at water's edge, so swimming is difficult.

No facilities.

Pu'u Ola'i Beach (Little Beach)

Named after Pu'u Ola'i cinder cone which separates Big and Little Beaches (both beaches were named by the Seventies' hippies, and the names stuck).

Little Beach can only be reached by walking through Big Beach over to the cinder cone, then climbing up the cone part way. A path across the base of the cone leads to secluded Little Beach...in its own cove. Its seclusion makes it Maui's most popular nude beach, but authorities are now making arrests.

Swimming and snorkeling good.

No facilities.

Oneloa Beach (Big Beach)

Popular place, wonderful beach. Oneloa means "long sand;" it is 3,000 feet long and 100 feet wide. This is the last large beach area on Maui that is undeveloped. Residents are holding their breath and are ready to fight for this one.

After the paved road turns to dirt, the second, third, fourth and fifth turn-offs along it all lead to the beach. Parking is amidst the kiawe trees. It's dusty and littered with garbage, but the beach is great.

Good swimming, good snorkeling, good body surfing. Waves, especially in afternoons, can sometimes be rough.

No facilities. Everything is primitive and natural.

'Ahihi-Kina'u Natural Reserve

Here Hawaiian nature is left alone to flourish as it would without human interference. This is a marine and land reserve that includes Cape Kina'u and parts of 'Ahihi and La Perouse Bays. No hunting, fishing, picking, shelling, etc. are allowed.

Snorkeling is excellent; swimming is fine, but there are many rocks and entering the ocean is often difficult.

No facilities.

SIGHTS

Keawala'i Congregational Church

Means "calm harbor." It was built in the 1860s from white coral and lava rock. The timbers used were cured for two weeks by soaking in the ocean. Sunday 9 a.m. service includes a few prayers in Hawaiian.

Pu'u Ola'i

One of the last cinder cones to erupt on the island. Sometimes called "Earthquake Hill," sometimes called "Red Hill" (the cinder is red). It rises 360 feet from the ocean's edge. An ocean cave beneath the cone is said to be a sacred dwelling place for guardian sharks, often thought to be ancestral dieties.

Maonakala Village

On the 'Ahihi Bay side of Cape Kina'u, is a small hamlet where all the sites have been excavated and explained by archaeologists. This is the village of Maonakala, now a state reserve. Few people visit it, yet it's the most accessible example of a fishing village on the island.

Directions: Look for the first 'Ahihi Kina'u sign on the right side of the road. Five houses past it (including a deserted home), take the first right into a small parking area. This is just beyond a home surrounded by a low lava rock wall. There is no sign posted.

Diagram of MaonakalaVillage

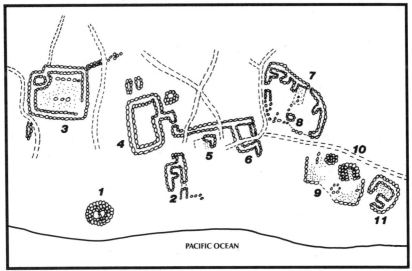

Redrawn from "Endangered Hawaiian Archaeological Sites Within MauiCounty: A Bishop Museum Report to the County of Maui" by K.P. Emory and R.J. Hommon, Dept. of Anthropology Rep. 72-2. Copyright 1972 byBishop Museum. Used by permission.

1: Well—two pits encircled with rocks (now full of garbage)
2: Canoe house—could once hold both hulls of a 45' double canoe
3: Choice house lot. Small waterworn pebbles within most
    structures are 'ili 'ili—used to make the floor less rough.
4: Two-house yard divided by loose wall of small stones
5: Corner of house floor
6: House yard with a solidly pebbled floor
7: Area for several houses, but only one is clearly defined.
8: Imu—cooking pit
9: Large house-yard complex
10: Ko'a—a fisherman's shrine. Coral placed with the rocks
    indicates the sacred nature of the structure.
11: Vague house site built directly on a recent lava flow.

NOTE—Please heed the words of the Bishop Museum:
"Every year the unwritten history of Hawaii is being lost as hundreds of archaeological sites are utterly and irrevocably destroyed. Most of this destruction is the direct result of large scale economic development and the activities of collector-vandals."

HOTELS

Maui Prince

The Prince is the first structure in a 1,000-acre planned resort that will include golf courses, possibly another hotel and 6,000 housing units. The large Japanese corporation Seibu bought the thousand acres for $12 million from 'Ulupalakua Ranch. Locals weren't too crazy about commercialism creeping into pristine Makena, but there's little they can do—it's all slated to be developed.

The hotel is a 6-story, "V" shaped, stark white building. All 300 rooms have an ocean view. There are three restaurants plus 24-hour room service...a necessity way out here in the boondocks.

Expensive.

5400 Makena Alanui, Kihei, HI 96753 • 874-1111 • 800-321-MAUI.

CONDOS

Stratosphere: On Beach

The **Makena Surf** is the most expensive condo on this side of the island. And worth the money. The Surf is exclusive. It's tucked far away from any hustle bustle...the condo farthest from Kihei. The white tile entryway in all 86 units leads to very large living and dining rooms. They face a wall of glass—huge windows that look straight into the ocean...no buildings, no civilization in sight. Furnishings are elegant, rooms are spacious. The Surf is luxury and seclusion with an exquisite natural setting. Both 2 & 3-BR units available.

96 Makena Road, Kihei, HI 96753 • 879-1331.

RESTAURANTS

$$ Mid-Range

Hakone: They try to be as authenticly Japanese as possible. Everything is imported from Japan from the chefs to the rice. The restaurant's interior, both tables and sushi bar, are artistically simple, typically Japanese. Service is geisha gracious. The a la carte menu is moderate (under $18); but kaiseki "traditional" dinners are expensive—$30 to $40. Open 6-10 nightly. *Maui Prince Hotel. 874-1111.*

$$$ Expensive

Prince Court: The only expensive island eatery that specializes in the trendy American cuisine, often called California or nouvelle cuisine... buckwheat blinis with caviar, Kansas steak, free range chicken, Maine lobster. Creative menu, elegantly beautiful restaurant. Wear your dress-up clothes. Open 6-9 nightly. *Maui Prince Hotel. 874-1111.*

Wailea

Wailea is manicured. Nothing out of order here, everything is perfectly groomed. The grass grows barely an inch before the ubiquitous blades swoop over it. Even the banyan trees get their hanging roots trimmed...no shagginess allowed. Wailea looks expensive, and it is.

It was all planned for perfection. The Hawaiian conglomerate Alexander & Baldwin, Inc. had 1,500 acres they thought would be great as a resort and residential area. They began in 1971 with an 18-hole golf course. Since then they've added another golf course, plus 14 tennis courts, a shopping center, two hotels, and hundreds of homes and condos. Only 700 of the acres are developed thus far. Eventually, there will be four or five hotels, about 5,000 condos and 1,000 homes.

Wailea is three times as large as Waikiki and twice the size of Ka'anapali, yet it seems small and compact, possibly because it is so well organized.

HISTORY

Once upon a time there were ancient villages along Wailea's coast, but bulldozers rarely value old rocks. The golf course designer kept a heiau and a few walls as part of his two courses, but golfers are the only ones to see those. There are village remains in some of the kiawe forests surrounding the golf courses, but this is private land, not open to the public.

BEACHES & PARKS

Wailea has one and a half miles of coastline laced with five crescent-shaped beaches...each more perfect than the next (what else in Wailea?). They are not as crowded as one might think, and the resorts keep them very clean. No trash, as you find in other areas.

Keawakapu Beach

In 1957 the fish and game people decided to build an artificial reef to increase the fish population just off Keawakapu. They dumped 150 old cars in 80 feet of water about 400 yards off shore. You never see the cars, and you rarely see many fish.

Great little beach, about a half mile long...fairly quiet. Good swimming, sandy bottom. No protective coral reef, so the waves can sometimes get high.

No facilities.

Mokapu Beach

Before WW II, Mokapu (meaning "sacred island") was a small offshore rock island favored by sea birds. "Sacred" means nothing to the armed forces, though—they blew the rock apart during war time drills. So much for the island...but the beach is still great. You share it with the Stouffer Hotel crowd. Look for the concrete bunker on rocks between this beach and Ulua—remnants of WW II.

Great swimming, good snorkeling.

Facilities: showers, toilets, parking.

Ulua Beach

A long strip of a beach fronted by Elua condos and the Inter-Continental Hotel. Has bigger surf than the other Wailea beaches, so it's good for bodysurfing. Also great for swimming.

Often a great area for snorkeling.

Facilities: showers, toilets, parking.

Wailea Beach

No condo or hotel fronts this beach, so it has a more public feel to it. You don't have to walk through a hotel or search for a beach access road...the clearly marked road ends in a large parking area. There's lots of white sand, and it's rarely crowded.

Great swimming; good snorkeling around the rocky point where Wailea Point Condos are located.

Facilities: showers, toilets, grassy area for picnics, parking.

Polo Beach

To get to this beach you have to walk along a path beside the Polo Beach Condo. It's not easily seen, so the beach is often deserted.

Swimming is fine. The bottom is sandy, but there are many large rocks.

Facilities: showers, toilets, parking.

HOTELS

Stouffer Wailea Beach Resort

Stouffer Resort, built in 1978, receives AAA's Five Diamond Award year after year. That's because this is a true luxury hotel.

Part of the 15-acre grounds resembles a rain forest garden (albeit a very groomed one). Fountains, waterfalls, wandering streams, 400 coconut palms and oodles of green exotica make this one spectacular front yard. It takes 60,000 to 100,000 gallons of water a day to keep this once desert terrain brimming with chlorophyl. This little oasis is right on a perfect sandy beach.

Guests in the 347 rooms receive complimentary coffee and newspapers every morning. Rooms are elegant and beautifully designed. Celebrities like the privacy of the Mokapu Beach Club, a separate beachfront building with 26 units where guests are coddled at a higher room rate.

Special kama'aina rates are available. Expensive.

3550 Wailea Alanui Drive, Kihei, HI 96753 • 879-4900 or 800-468-3571.

Maui Inter-Continental

Running neck and neck with Stouffer's, but twice as large (and less expensive) is the 600-room Maui IC (opened in '76). Six low-rise buildings plus a 7-story tower are spread over 18 acres.

It's gracious and spacious, but it is not dull. The IC has one of the most extensive guest programs imagineable—quilt making, juggling, hula lessons, aquacize, scuba, snorkeling, lei stringing, etc. ...and all free. Three pools, a whirlpool, morning aerobics and plenty of jogging on the beautiful grounds for the health conscious.

It must be a friendly place—25% of the original employees still work here...surely a record in transient Hawai'i.

Mid-range to expensive.

P.O. Box 779, Kihei, HI 96753 • 879-1922 or 800-367-2960.

CONDOS

All three Wailea villages—Ekahi ("one"), Elua ("two"), Ekolu ("three")—have gorgeous grounds, beautiful views and similar units. Prices for all three are in the expensive range.

Elua's 152 units are the most expensive of the three and they are considered to have the nicest interiors. Frankly, it's hard to tell. They all seem interchangeable. All are beautiful. Elua's 24 acres face the ocean, and the property fronts a perfect sandy beach. Elua has a variety of 1, 2 & 3-BR units.

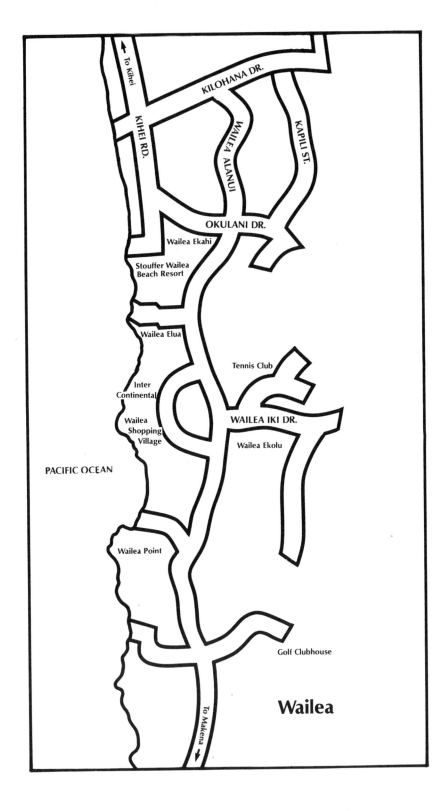

Ekahi is a gorgeous village of 294 units on 34 acres. All units are sold as garden views; but, in fact, about 50% have ocean views too, so that's a pleasant surprise. Part of Ekahi's property is on a sandy beach. Ekahi has studios and 1 & 2-BR condos.

Golfers like the **Ekolu Village** because its 18 acres sit right in the middle of Wailea Golf Course. All 148 units have views of both the greens and the ocean. It is about a half mile from the beach, and thus is the least expensive of the three. 1 & 2-BR units available.

Same address and phone for all three: *3750 Wailea Alanui, Kihei 96753 • 879-1595 or (800) 367-5246.*

RESTAURANTS

$ Budget

Maui Onion: Stouffer's coffee shop—situated outside by the pool in the hotel's garden-like atmosphere. Great setting, great little place. Famous for onion rings (made from sweet Maui onions, of course). The menu is small, mostly salads and sandwiches, and food is good. Hours: 8:15 a.m. to 6 p.m. daily. *879-4900.*

Set Point Cafe: Cute little airy place, never crowded. It's tucked above the tennis courts at the Wailea Tennis Club, high on a hill with long views of the ocean and West Maui. It has a lovely wooden interior with open windows all around...easy to watch the tennis players. Breakfast and lunch only: 7-10 a.m. and 11-3 p.m. Cocktails from 3-7 p.m. *879-3244.*

$$ Mid-Range

Wailea Steak House : A classy steak house set high on a hill with a view that stretches across a golf course pond to the ocean. The building is a low-rise beauty with an open patio area—great for romantic sunsets. The menu is classic steakhouse fare of various meats, fish and fowl. Food and service has always rated an excellent reputation. Hours: 5:30-10 nightly. *100 Wailea Iki Drive   879-2875.*

Hibachi: A traditional Japanese restaurant situated across the courtyard from the Wailea Steak House. Two individual tatami rooms are great for small groups. Sunset views are wonderful. Hours: 5:30-10 nightly. *100 Wailea Iki Drive • 879-7211.*

Palm Court: You get your money's worth here...it's a huge buffet that changes every night. This is the only restaurant on Maui that has a different country's cuisine each night. There's French night, English night, Oriental, Italian, Hawaiian, American, and a general seafood night. If the buffet's not right, there's an a la carte menu as an alternative. Breakfast and lunch are not such elaborate affairs. Hours: 6-11 a.m.; 11-2 p.m.; 6-10 p.m. daily. *Stouffer Resort • 878-4900.*

$$$ *Expensive*

La Perouse: This is the Inter-Continental's fancy, expensive restaurant. It has a dark, woody elegance. The menu is French, but has exotic twists...callaloo soup, for example, a creamy mix of crabmeat, coconut milk and taro leaves. Or try breadfruit vichyssoise—rarely found on Parisian tables. Service is impeccable. Suit and tie type dress is preferred, but nothing is rigid. Hours: 6:30-10:30 nightly. *879-1922.*

Raffles: The kudos keep stacking up here year after year—AAA's Five Diamond Award, Travel/Holiday magazine's highest award, to name just two. Stouffer Resort can always be trusted to do things right. Named after the famous Singapore Raffles' Hotel, the restaurant maintains that same old-world ambiance and elegance. Food is continental with a Hawaiian touch. The Sunday champagne brunch is the fanciest and most expensive on the island (served 9 a.m. to 2 p.m.). Dinner served nightly 6:30-11. *879-4900.*

SHOPPING

The Wailea Shopping Village is the only place to go. There is no other shopping area in Wailea. This modern mall has about 20 shops, two restaurants, a bank and several offices—all geared to tourists. The best of the bunch are: **Chapman's**—one of the few men's clothing shops on the island, has casual, conservative wear. For women, try **Alexia**, cotton and raw silk clothes from Greece. The simple elegant designs can be hip or chic; most is dressy, though there is some beachwear. **Michele's** has fancy, expensive, unique clothes...lots of pizzazz, sequins and spangles. **Superwhale** has kids' clothing and toys...many of the clothes are made in Maui, and most have a Hawaiian flair.

For Your Eyes Only—a national chain that sells sunglasses of all styles and all costs. **Isle Style**—an artsy-craftsy gift shop that features Maui artists. The **Elephant Walk**, another gift shop, has classy gift items—baskets, jewelry, glassware, pottery, a few paintings. For beautiful seashells, **Sea & Shell Island Gifts.** They also also have fine shell jewelry and other gift items. **Maui's Best** specializes in Maui-made gift items. They also have a line of Maui-made candies (macadamia nut brittle, chocolate covered Kona coffee beans, etc.).

Kihei

Sand and sun are synonymous with Kihei. This is the "desert" area of Maui. Less than six inches (30 cm.) of rain falls per year. Perfect for sun seekers. Hot in the winter, hotter in the summer.

There's not much of a town to Kihei, just one long strip of a road that passes beach after beach. Yet rarely are the beaches seen—concrete slab buildings jut from the sand, obscuring the view.

Forty-five years ago beach front property went for two cents a square foot. A mere $300 would buy a half acre. Then the land was just kiawe (mesquite) trees and sand. No one considered it glamorous.

"When I was growing up here, we thought the beach was crowded if two tourists walked past." So says a 30-year old who doesn't much like the Kihei of today.

Development started innocently enough. In the 1960s and 1970s Maui was economically depressed. The population was dwindling as people left to seek their fortunes. Tourism seemed the only answer. Beaches were marketable, and Kihei has nearly six miles of golden sand.

Now it is condo country. More than 50 condos line both sides of Kihei Road. The town often gets rapped on the knuckles for its adolescent growth spurt. Never again, islanders say, will developers be allowed to run amuck.

Still, this is not Waikiki. Many of the condos are small low-rise places with little pretention. This is one of the few areas on Maui that offers numerous budget and moderate accommodations (many listed in the next pages).

HISTORY

Hawaiian villages once dotted the beaches along the present Kihei Road. The original Kihei itself was a single village located near the Kihei Pier. The next villages were Kalepolepo and Kama'ole (now names for beaches).

During World War II the Navy took over several Kihei, Wailea and Ma'alaea beaches to use as training ground. Hundreds of men were taught reconnaissance and demolition. Their concrete bunkers still dot some of the beaches.

Until the condo craze of the Seventies, Kihei was a sparsely inhabited, quiet area. Land was not worth much money. The beaches were beautiful, but it was hard to grow any produce...too little rainfall. The sun and sand that once kept Kihei's population down now draw the crowds.

SIGHTS

Kihei Wharf

This small landing area was built in 1890 to get freight and produce in and out for the farms and sugar plantations. Was also used by inter-island boats until 1915, then the area sanded in so much that boats could not reach the pier. Once a 200-foot wooden wharf, it burned in 1959, leaving only a few pilings and a small stone section. Located across from Suda's Store, north end of Kihei.

Vancouver Memorial

A homemade-looking monument erected by the original owner of the Maui Lu Hotel in memory of Captain George Vancouver, a British explorer who visited Hawai'i five times between 1778 and 1794.

Vancouver was good friends with Kamehameha I. He brought the king cows—the first such critters introduced to Hawai'i.

Trinity Church-by-the-Sea, a.k.a. David Malo Memorial Church

Built in 1853 by the Kalepolepo congregation of Hawaiian scholar David Malo, one of the first ordained native ministers. Malo spent his last years as pastor in this once remote village (now part of Kihei).

Malo died the year it was built. His congregation dispersed and never again met there. The church stood empty in a kiawe forest for over a century. It was in ruins, with nothing left but the stone foundation and a few crumbling walls, when the Episcopalians took it over in 1976.

The "church" is peaceful and isolated, located down a dirt road. A 9 a.m. Sunday service is held within the ruins—a ceiling of sky, walls of trees—gloriously natural.

Location: First road south of Koa Resort on South Kihei Road. Look for the Hawaiian historical marker sign (red-cloaked Hawaiian warrior), then turn down the dirt road, following it to the end until it dead-ends into the church.

Maui Folk...
Hawaiian Scholar and Minister

David Malo was an extraordinary Hawaiian pulled by two opposing forces. He was a historian who wrote of the ancient Hawaiian ways he lived as a youth. He was also one of the first native ordained missionary ministers. He taught his countrymen about the religion of the white men...the people whom he knew were overpowering his own.

Malo was in the first class of men when Lahainaluna School opened in 1831. It was the first school west of the Rockies, and Malo proved to be one of its best students. He was in his late thirties, a driven man intent on learning as much as he could.

Besides being a dedicated minister, he was a scholar whose book, *Hawaiian Antiquities*, is a treasured litany of Hawaiian culture.

He must have been a busy man—he was Hawai'i's first school superintendent and he served in the legislature in the early 1840s.

He was never able to learn English, but he read and wrote in Hawaiian, and supposedly owned every book printed in his language. Missionary doctor Dwight Baldwin said he had "perhaps the strongest mind of any man in the nation."

Malo was born on the Big Island in the late 1790s—a time when foreigners were just beginning to sail into the islands. He was raised in the household of Kuakini, brother of Queen Ka'ahumanu (favorite wife of Kamehameha I).

He left the Big Island in his twenties to live in Lahaina. After meeting Rev. William Richards, his life changed completely. He became a devoted Christian and a lifelong friend of the Richards family.

The missionaries he considered upstanding, but the foreign invasion he feared. *"If a big wave comes in,"* he wrote, *"large and unfamiliar fishes will come from the dark ocean, and when they see the small fishes of the shallows they will eat them up....white men's ships have arrived with clever men from the big countries. They know our people are few in number and our country is small, they will devour us."*

Prophetic words.

BEACHES & PARKS

Kihei beaches are generally windy in the afternoons, so swimming and sunning are best in the a.m. None are outstanding for snorkeling, but all are excellent for swimming.

Mai Poina 'Ole Ia'u Park

Means "forget me not." Locally called Memorial Park, it is dedicated in memory of the war dead. Good swimming, okay snorkeling. Popular with windsurfers in afternoons.

Facilities: pavilion, toilets, showers, grassy park area, picnic tables, parking.

Kalepolepo Beach

Once the site of a large Hawaiian village. Deserted by the late 1800s, all that remains are the stone walls of an old fish pond used by Kamehameha I. The pond was built before his time, but he had it rebuilt. It supposedly took 10,000 men to do it.

The large shallow pond makes a good pool for children. Waves break against the walls, leaving the pond water smooth. Good swimming. Quiet beach. Great for small kids.

Facilities: shower, toilet, small grassy park with picnic tables.

Waipuilani Park

Narrow, small beach off a large grassy park. Very quiet, almost deserted. Good swimming; no snorkeling.

Facilities: toilets, picnic tables, parking, tennis courts.

Kalama Beach Park

A 36-acre, well-used local park. Has two pavilions, showers, toilets, telephones, soccer field, baseball field, basketball courts, four tennis courts, volleyball court, picnic tables, grills and parking.

The park is bordered on the ocean side by a rock retaining wall. There is no beach. Swimming is uncommon...better areas are a blink away down the road.

Charley Young Beach

Actually not a separate beach—it's the north end of Kama'ole I Beach. This little section is known locally as Charley Young Beach. Named for the Young family who have lived near here for 30 years. Charley was a local newspaper man and civic leader.

Popular swimming beach with locals. Beach is sheltered from wind by rocks. Sometimes good snorkeling.

Kama'ole I, II, III Beach Parks

Kama'ole means "childless" for some obscure reason. These three popular "local" beaches follow each other down the coast. Each one is excellent for swimming, though each has a deep drop off. They all have grassy areas that are popular when the wind starts up and blows sand around on the beach.

All have toilets, showers, parking, picnic tables and grills.

Lifeguards—very rare on Maui beaches—guard these three.

Kihei Boat Ramp

Located across from the Maui Hill Condo. Just a boat ramp, no slips. No overnighting.

HOTELS

Surf & Sand

Rooms are basic here—small and a bit dull, but they are clean. Twenty of the 100 rooms include a bit of a kitchen—toaster oven, hot plate, small frig. Phones and TVs in rooms, air conditioning and maid service. No pool, but there's a whirlpool. The hotel's ambiance is reminiscent of a Fifties' motel. Walls are thin, so expect some noise. Hard to complain at such a price. Plus, it's right on a sandy beach...surf and sand, that's the promise.

Budget to mid-range.

2980 S. Kihei Rd., Kihei, HI 96753 • 879-7744.

Maui Lu

This is a Kihei institution. It once stood alone on the beach—the first hotel on this part of the island. Built by a Canadian man, the current rustic lobby used to be his summer home.

The hotel still has an older, gracious feel about it. Numerous wooden buildings and cottages dot 30 acres. Neither grounds nor buildings are spectacular, the whole place is low-key and moderate.

Fifty of the 170 rooms are on the beach in their own separate, secluded area. The rest are across Kihei Road on the main hotel acreage. Here there's a Maui-shaped swimming pool and two tennis courts.

Also on the main acreage are 16 large, 1-BR cottages, each with a screened-in lanai. They have no air conditioning, but the hotel rooms do. The oceanfront rooms and the cottages are $10 to $20 more than the regular garden view rooms.

Budget to mid-range.

575 South Kihei Road, Kihei, HI 96753 • 879-5881 or (800) 367-5244; Canada-collect: (808) 879-5808

CONDOS

Budget Condos: On Beach

Waipuilani was one of the first condos built along this strip of serenity. Now it is crowded in by high-rises, but it still retains its little low-rise integrity. Not to say that the building is any beauty—it has 42 units in a 3-story concrete block structure. The rooms are modern with fully equipped kitchen facilities, both 1 & 2-BR units available. The stunner about Waipuilani is the grounds...all lawn and palm trees, very gracious with a definite tropical feel. The greenery gradually recedes into a sandy beach. Four public tennis courts are a stone's throw away. Stay two months and you get a 20% discount. *1002 S. Kihei Rd., Kihei, HI 96753 • 879-1458.*

Another "oldie" is the **Kihei Kai**, built in 1970. This 24-unit (all 1-BR), 2-story condo has a very homey, quiet feel about it. Its wooden, brown-shingled exterior gives the place a certain charm. The manager says guests have known each other for years since they all keep returning, so the atmosphere is friendly and intimate. There's just a dinky lawn area fronting the condo, but it bleeds into Kihei's 6-mile white sand beach mentioned above. Tropical views galore. *61 N. Kihei Rd., Kihei, HI 96753 • 879-2357.*

Budget Condos: Off Beach

The **Nona Lani** ("heavenly Nona") cottages are infused with the personalities of owners Dave and Nona Kong. More than 30 years they've lived on the property, raising seven children who now have eleven kids of their own. Dave Kong, once a County Council member, remembers the days when there were no strangers in Kihei. He runs his cottages with that same family spirit. They're rustic wooden cabins, all one bedroom, though they can sleep four. Kitchens are fully equipped. Furnishings are fine; the whole place is full of charm. Guests are welcome to pick from the variety of fruit trees in the yard. Daughter Jean says the cottages are the closest thing to the dream of a little grass hut in paradise. *P.O.Box 655, Kihei, HI 96753 • 879-2497.*

Built in 1958, the **Lihi Kai** is the oldest condo in Kihei. Perhaps that's why it has such character. All units are one bedroom. Eight are in two apartment buildings and nine are separate "cottages." These are more like concrete block bunkers than cottages, but they are homey and their price is low-end of budget. The summer rates are a steal. "It ain't that this place is so great, it's just that it's so cheap," laughs Jeanette DiMeo, the vivacious and talkative owner. "I tell it like it is. Eccentric is a very good word for it. We're not fancy, but we're clean and

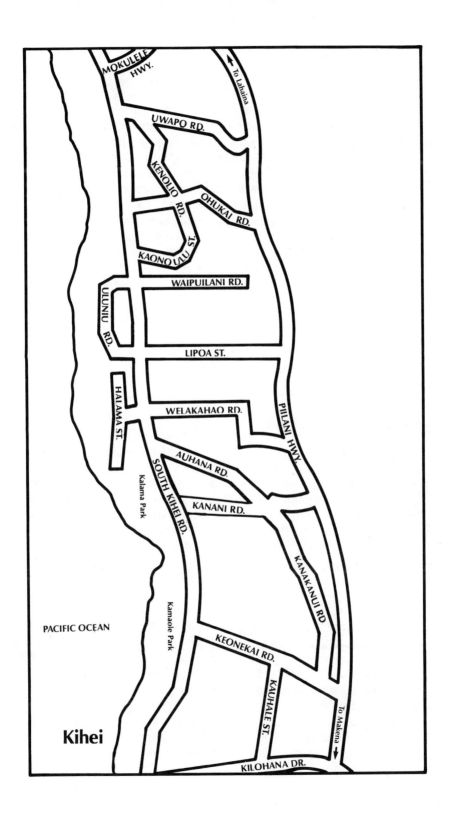

comfortable. We're always busy. The same people keep coming back. It's like family. I look forward to them coming. We have millionaires stay here who could buy the place with their spare change." Jeanette's of the opinion that tourists should spend their money seeing the island and having fun. "I couldn't sleep if I charged the amount most condos get," she says. *2121 Ili'ili Rd., Kihei, HI 96753 • 879-2335.*

The **Kihei Kai Nani** is a deal for the price. Covering five and a half acres, this group of 13 low-rise buildings has the appearance of a residential apartment complex. The lawn area is very pretty, and supposedly has one of each of Hawai'i's most typical plants. Inside, the apartment units are all one bedroom, all with good-sized rooms and nice furnishings. *2495 N. Kihei Rd., Kihei, HI 96753 • 879-9088*

"Nothing posh here," one tenant said while showing his room at the **Wailana Sands**. But he returns every year because the price is low budget rate. The units are small and basic, the furniture a bit eclectic, still everything is comfortable. The lawn area around the small swimming pool is very pleasant and includes a putting green. The 11-unit building is on a quiet side street with a sandy beach just a block away. The building has studios, 1 BRs & 2 BRs. *25 Wailana Pl., Kihei Rd., Kihei, HI 96753 • 879-2026.*

Moderate Condos: On Beach

What a surprise **Kapulanikai** is. Just off the main Kihei Road, down a short dirt street, through a patch of kiawe trees... voila—there it is at the end of a deadend street...refreshingly low-key, a true sleepy secret. No noise except the sounds of birds and ocean waves. There are 12 one-bedroom units in this simple wooden building. The apartments are fine, but they are not the main draw. The quiet, gracious setting is. The condo faces a sandy beach, and between the beach and the building is a half-acre lawn dominated by three magnificent banyan trees. A hammock strung from one of them adds a lovely, lazy touch. *73 Kapu Place, Kihei Rd., Kihei, HI 96753 • 879-1607.*

Also on a quiet back street is the **Kihei Beachfront Resort**. This is a nice looking building with eight units, all of them two bedroom, all with very modern, well-designed interiors. There is a small lawn area around a pool, but the big plus, of course, is the sandy beach. *P.O. Box 1746, Kihei, HI 96753 • 879-6343 or (800) 628-4776.*

The **Kihei Sands** almost fits the budget rate (in fact, its 2-BRs do). It's small and pleasant—30 one and two-bedroom apartments in two stucco buildings. The two bedrooms are townhouse style with one bedroom in a loft area. The manager calls it "homey," and says that a "congenial atmosphere" dominates, the place being small enough for everyone to know each other. *115 N. Kihei Rd., Kihei, HI 96753 • 879-2624.*

Another good buy is the **Waiohuli Beach Hale** condo. Here there are four low-rise, two-story buildings with 52 units (1 & 2 BRs). The buildings are spread out over a quiet lawn area that includes two small fountains, a putting green and a pool. There are also shuffleboards and barbecues. Altogether the place gives the impression of a well-done, comfortable motel. The beach in front can't be beat. *49 Lipoa St., Kihei, HI 96753 • 879-5396.*

Moderate Condos: Off Beach

A full-time resident here calls the **Koa Resort** Kihei's best kept secret. It is. Hard to imagine the moderate price because everything seems luxury range. Interiors of the 54 units are beautiful and airy with lovely furnishings and great kitchens. Units have 1, 2 or 3 bedrooms. The exterior, both buildings and grounds, are equally well done. Five two-story wooden buildings are spread out over 5.6 acres. Much of the acreage is manicured lawn area. The 120-foot long pool has a bridge spanning it and has the only diving board in Kihei. Other extras include a whirlpool, two tennis courts, an 18-hole putting green, shuffleboard and a picnic table/cabana area. *811 S. Kihei Rd., Kihei, HI 96753 • 879-1161.*

At the **Hale Kamaole** eight white stucco buildings are set in a U-shape around a well landscaped lawn area that includes two pools and one tennis court. It looks like an apartment complex, and has a gracious, spacious feel to it. The 1 & 2-BR units are fine—very modern—but the beautiful lawn is the draw here, plus the ocean view and the proximity to a great beach. *2737 S. Kihei Rd., Kihei, HI 96753 • 879-2698.*

Windsurfers often stay at the **Kihei Holiday** because the beach across the road has good waves. After a day in the surf, the whirlpool on property can help soothe the muscles. There's also a pool, with a small lawn area around it. Each of the 48 units is a 2-BR townhouse, very pleasant and surprisingly reasonable, almost budget. *483 S. Kihei Rd., Kihei, HI 96753 • 879-9228.*

Though the **Kihei Resort** has 64 units and five buildings, it somehow has a small, homey size to it. The yard is what does it; it seems more like a courtyard than a lawn. A lovely clump of palm trees separates the buildings and adds privacy—you're not staring into each others' windows. The 1 & 2-BR units are modern and well equipped. The two-bedrooms have a loft for the second bedroom. *P.O. Box 1471, Kihei, HI 96753 • 879-5504 or (800) 367-5634.*

Staying at the **Na Hale Kai** is like having your own home across from the beach. In fact, each of the six units is a separate 3-BR, 2-BA wooden house, and each has its own yard. If three to six people share a house, the price per person would be budget category. These are commonly rented for a month or two at a time. *317 S. Kihei Rd., Kihei, HI 96753 • 879-1079.*

High Condos: On Beach

All the extras come with the **Luana Kai**—hot tub, two tennis courts, a putting green, two saunas, shuffleboard, barbeques. The property is quite large, certainly spacious enough for 113 units (1, 2 & 3 BR) The lawn area is huge and beautifully groomed. The units are well furnished and large with loft areas in the 2 and 3-BR condos. *940 S. Kihei Rd., Kihei, HI 96753 • 879-1268.*

Health fanatics should stay at the **Maui Sunset**. It is the only Kihei condo that has a health spa (gym and weights). Other benefits are a large pool, a sauna, a whirlpool, four shuffleboards, two tennis courts, an 18-hole putting green, a volleyball court, croquet and barbeques. The complex is big—225 units (1,2 & 3 BR) in two 5-story concrete-block buildings. *1032 S. Kihei Rd., Kihei, HI 96753 • 879-0220 or 879-0674.*

High Condos: Off Beach

Tennis players and swimmers like the **Maui Vista**. It has six tennis courts and three swimming pools. The place is much like a modern apartment complex with three separate 4-story buildings housing 280 units (1 & 2 BRs). Kama'ole I, a popular beach, is right across the street. *2191 S. Kihei Rd., Kihei, HI 96753 • 879-7966 or (800) 367-8047 ex. 330.*

Expensive Condos: On Beach

Ma'alaea Surf Resort is a classy place both inside and out. The 1 & 2-BR units have large rooms with high ceilings and lots of windows (particularly the corner units). Many of the two bedrooms are townhouses with an upstairs loft. The 60 units are spread out amidst eight charming wooden buildings. Every unit has a view of the sandy beach in front. Two pools and two tennis courts complete the complex. *12 S. Kihei Rd., Kihei, HI 96753 • 879-1267.*

Expensive Condos: Off Beach

Maui Hill has the most beautifully-done interiors in Kihei. The 1, 2 & 3-BR units are large and elegantly decorated with expensive rattan furniture. Ground floor apartments have sunken living rooms. All kitchens have koa wood cabinets and microwave ovens. The exterior is just as striking—70 Mediterranean style buildings (containing 140 units) staggered up a hillside overlooking the ocean. Much of the twelve and a half acres is flowering, manicured grounds. Everything in the complex is beautiful and spacious. Worth the expensive bill. *2881 S. Kihei Rd., Kihei, HI 96753 • 879-7751.*

Kamaole Sands has the distinction of having the most rooms (440) in a Kihei condo. It is a huge complex of 10 buildings bowed in a U shape around a gorgeous lawn area. The grounds are manicured to perfection, and include a small waterfall, a rock garden and several fountains and ponds. The 1, 2 & 3 BRs all have similar furnishings, all modern and lovely. A Colony Resorts' management team runs the place efficiently like a hotel. There's even a front desk office area staffed by very helpful "concierges." *2695 S. Kihei Rd., Kihei, HI 96753 • 879-0666.*

RESTAURANTS

$ Budget

Polli's Mexican Restaurant: A spacious restaurant with a big lanai right over the beach. Very popular with locals because the food is good and the margaritas are decent. Part of the menu is vegetarian. Hours: 11:30 a.m. to 10 p.m. except Sundays when it's 10:30 (brunch) to 10 p.m. Local entertainment offered Wed.-Sat. 8-11 p.m., plus Sunday afternoon jazz 2-5. *Kealia Beach Center • 879-5275.*

La Familia: A popular Mexican restaurant, located in the Kai Nani Shopping Center, this place is especially popular at Happy Hour...a local cruise spot for singles. Good, cheery drinking atmosphere on their open deck. Hours: noon to midnight every day. *879-8824.*

The Sand Witch: Small place at the Sugar Beach Condo with tables and take-out service. Nice koa wood bar attracts the thirsty. Food is burritos, sandwiches, burgers, salads, hot dogs—simple, quick fare. Hours: 10 a.m. to 11 p.m. daily except Sundays (12-11). *879-3262.*

Munchies: Tucked away in back of the Kai Nani Village, this is a healthy, cheap place for breakfast and lunch. The owners had a Munchies in Key West, but left when the Keys got too crazy, so now Maui is the place. They have great coffee drinks, milkshakes and smoothies, plus healthy sandwiches, salads and omelettes. Hours: 7:30 to 4 daily. *879-9330.*

Painting by Beth Marcil

Paradise Fruit Stand: This is the Kihei hangout for everyone—from hippie haoles to traveling tourists. Want to meet someone? Need to tack a notice on a bulletin board? Want to socialize? Paradise is the place. Both a grocery store and a deli, it's one of the rare places in Kihei open 24 hours (though the deli does close for three hours from 2-5 a.m.). The food is excellent and much is health conscious—huge sandwiches, tofu burgers, salads, fruit smoothies and shakes, sugarless frozen yogurt. Not all is health food, though, the counter is loaded with killer brownies, macadamia nut cookies and cinnamon rolls (baked in the kitchen...the best rolls ever). It's an alternative food store where the products are fresh and local. The people who work here are friendly and helpful. They'll box and certify local fruit to send to the Mainland. It's a true Maui place...not to be missed. *1913 S. Kihei Road (next to McDonald's)* • *879-1723.*

$$ Mid-Range

Island Fish House: Has always had a great reputation for quality. They buy their fish whole from fishermen, then filet it in their own kitchen. Steaks are also good here. Very popular place, reservations are important. For those who find the prices a bit steep, during low season (summer and fall) there's an early bird special from 5-6 p.m. for the $12. Hours: 5-10 nightly. *1945 S. Kihei Rd.* • *879-7771.*

Kihei Prime Rib House: There are more seafood selections than prime rib, plus steak, chicken and a salad bar...a varied menu, all very good. The interior is very woody with wood sculptures by local artist Bruce Turnbull. It's located upstairs above La Familia in the Kai Nani Village Shopping Center. Hours: 5-10 nightly. Early bird special during low season from 5-6:30. *879-1954.*

Idini's: The only fine dining place right on the ocean in Kihei. Bob Idini had such success with his Kahului deli that he decided to go upscale with this restaurant. He tries to keep dinner prices just below the expensive range, but still have elaborate French entrees. Lunch is a soup, salad, sandwich affair, much like the original Idini's, just fancier. The sushi/seafood bar seats only four, but you can order from your table. Hours: 11-2:30 p.m.; 6-10 p.m. daily. Seafood bar open from noon till closing. Sunday brunch from 10-2:30. *760 S. Kihei Road • 879-1356.*

SHOPPING

Kealia Shopping Center (north Kihei Road)

One of the only shopping areas located right on the ocean. **Natalia** is certainly the only island beauty salon where your hair is cut while you watch the waves. You can also get your legs waxed, your nails done and your skin vacuumed...all to the pounding surf. It's a stylish, chic salon.

Azeka's Place (middle Kihei Road)

Azeka's was one of the original stores in Kihei. Bill Azeka started here in the early 1950s with one small grocery. Not many customers back then, just a few local fishermen. Azeka's modern grocery is now famous for its Korean Kalbi (marinated) ribs.

The only bookstore in town is **Silversword.** It's small, but great for Hawaiian books, kid's books and cards. Also has several stands of popular paperbacks.

The largest selection of gold charms on the island is at **Alchemist's Garden,** a jewelry and gift store. The best and biggest choice of earrings in Kihei is at **Rainbow Connection,** a clever little gift shop.

WOW says it all. Find your itsy-bitsy, teeny-weeny polka dot bikini here...snazzy, glitzy suits. You can mix and match bottoms and tops. Size 14 bottom, size 8 top?—no problem.

Cover the suit with a cotton T-shirt from **Crazy Shirts**...some of the best T-shirts on island. This now popular chain of stores began in the Sixties in Waikiki when the now very rich owner was selling hand painted shirts for $5. The T-shirt craze caught on, as did his business.

Rainbow Shopping Mall   (middle Kihei Road)

The smell alone will pull you in—**Maui Fudge Kitchen**— cookies and fudge made daily on the premises. A few doors down is **Le Grand Ice Cream**...they also make their own ice cream (32 flavors) and cones daily. You can watch them make the waffle cones in front.

If you still can fit your regular size, go to **Four Winds,** a locally-owned clothing store, both men and women. No aloha clothes; this is up-to-date, chic casual wear, mostly 100% cotton.

Nishiki's Farmers' Market

Ever buy your produce from a politician? You can on Maui. Wayne Nishiki, a County Council member and a true character, makes his living selling produce from Maui's farmers, both vegetables and fruit. His sales technique is very low-key—he sets up his crates in Suda's parking lot (61 S. Kihei Rd.) and rings up purchases on a makeshift counter. His prices are good, and so is his produce. Hours: Tues. & Fri. 2:30-5:30 p.m. North end of Kihei in Suda's Store parking lot.

Yee's Orchard

If you notice a humble looking wooden fruit stand along Kihei Road, you've found a very local, down-home business. The small sign says "Yee's Orchard." For more than 50 years, the Yee family has owned 20 acres not far from Azeka's Shopping Center. They don't live there, but they still farm the land. Dr. Wilbert Yee "is very interested in his orchard," says wife Virginia, "He's nurtured it all these years."

It's mainly a mango orchard, but they also raise and sell grapefruit, tangerines, pomelo, guava, sour sop, papaya, pineapple, banana, tomato, onions and sugar cane. You can also buy live chickens, peacocks, fighting chickens and squabs. The stand is open for business Wednesdays and Sundays, 9 a.m. to 4 p.m.

Pa'ia

Nothing seems to change the integrity of this little town. It remains its sweet little self through various waves—first the plantation workers, then the hippies, now the windsurfers. Somehow it manages to be both quaint and hip. It's a great little town..one of the best on the island.

HISTORY

Ancient villages were probably here, but there are few traces left. Pa'ia's environs have been plowed and planted with sugar cane for more than a century. The first cane was planted in the 1870s, then a mill was built (on the site of the current mill). Plantation camps grew around the mill, most of them populated by a single ethnic group.

Workers had free housing—simple wooden structures with outhouses. Several old houses still stand in an area called Skill Village (previously a placea where the skilled workers lived).

Lower Pa'ia was a line-up of shops..much as it is today. Capitalistic-minded immigrants opened stores and restaurants. Sing Kee Shoemaker, Toyama's Piggery, Hew Fat Restaurant...the names tell the story eloquently. *

Eventually, Pa'ia had the biggest population on the island—8,000 in 1940. Nearly 1,300 students attended Pa'ia School, then the largest school on Maui.

During WW II Pa'ia boomed. A nearby Marine camp brought thousands of GIs in and out of town.

Ghost Town

After the war, Alexander & Baldwin began to fold the camps. The company encouraged workers to buy their own places in the new "Dream City" of Kahului. The workers were eager to own, and Pa'ia fast became a near ghost town.

A small wave of hippies came through in the 1960s and '70s. Many just drifted in and hung out, but others stayed and opened small businesses. The once ethnic shops now had Woodstock names...Bounty Music, Touchstone Gallery, Sundance Incense and Trading Co., Good Stuff, Pa'ia General Store.

Today it's boards and sails and casual clothes. Pa'ia is back on its feet as the windsurfing capital of the world.

Many hats this town has had. All seem to fit.

BEACHES & PARKS

H.A. Baldwin Park

This is a well-used local park just off the Hana Highway between Kahului and Pa'ia. A blue sign along the highway announces the park.

The beach is often crowded, more with locals than tourists. The waves are reputed to be good for body surfing.

Harry A. Baldwin was the son of sugar king H.P. Baldwin. Harry was a politician, a ranch owner and the manager of Maui Agricultural Company. The park is a memorial to his achievements.

Facilities: pavilion, picnic tables, BBQ, toilets, shower, baseball and soccer fields, swing set, plenty of parking, camping area.

Lower Pa'ia Park

The park is a small fenced-in grass field right next to the Maui Crafts Guild building. In front is a simple little beach a bit littered with rubbish. Not terribly scenic, but not bad for swimming.

No facilities.

Ku'au Bay

Outside town on the road to Hana is a large house with a blue tile roof; turn left here and you're in Ku'au. It's a sandy cove, very pretty, but the ocean bottom is rocky.

No facilities.

Father Jules Papa Beach

Father Jules Papa was a priest from Belgium who ministered to Catholics in Ku'au and Pa'ia in the early 1900s.

The beach named after him is in the beautiful cove behind Mama's Fish House. Parking is available right by the restaurant. The beach is small and pretty, but swimming is not good—it's too rocky. There are small tidal pools, however, so it's safe for kids.

No facilities.

Painting of Pa'ia Town by Eddie Flotte

Hamakua Poko Papa Beach

Just before Holomua Road is a dirt parking ledge above the ocean. The beach is just below; it's a nice sandy spot, but swimming is not great (bottom is rocky.) The parking area is a good place to catch views of the Ho'okipa windsurfers.

No facilities.

Ho'okipa Beach Park

This is the most famous windsurfing beach on earth. Ho'okipa means "hospitality," and most days the beach lives up to its name, playing host to guest surfers from all over the world. They come here as if going to Mecca. The waves and wind combine for perfect windsurfing conditions in this cove. Waves can be as high as 10-15 feet. When the wind is down, the board surfers come out in force; when the wind is up, colorful sails dot the ocean.

The beach and the ocean are usually crowded with expert surfers. This is not the place to learn to surf or sail...the pros do not appreciate floundering beginners; plus, the waves are too intense for learners. Swimming is not suggested, the waves are too strong.

There's a paved sightseeing point right above the beach...great for spectator sports.

Facilities: toilets, showers, pavilions, picnic tables, BBQ, paved parking.

HOTELS

Nalu Kai Lodge

Find it behind Larry's Restaurant on the Hana Highway that cuts through Pa'ia. This is the only lodging in town.

It's so basic the manager was hard put to even discuss it. She hardly knew what to say. Cheap, though, so no complaints. The eight rooms are plain little boxes. Most have twin beds; one room has a double. All have bathrooms; none have kitchen facilities. Short walk to the beach.

Very budget.

Box 188, Pa'ia, HI 96779 • 579-9035.

RESTAURANTS

$ Budget

Picnics: Great place; favorite windsurfer spot. Perfect for tourists heading out to Hana. Essentially a sandwich joint, but breakfast, salads and pastries are also good. They have pack lunches for Hana trips. Hours: 7:30 a.m. to 3:30 p.m. *30 Baldwin Avenue • 579-8021.*

Charley's: Named after the owner's dog, Charley P. Woofer. This is a very Pa'ia place—woody, somewhat funky interior. Good, honest food, and lots of it. Breakfast is especially good. Lunch is mostly sandwiches, burgers and pizza. Dinner is Italian—pizza, calzone, lasagne, chicken cacciatore, shrimp scampi.

The bar in back is a local favorite...sometimes rowdy, never dull. Willie Nelson (who owns a home in Spreckelsville) drops by occasionally to drink with the regulars. Restaurant hours: 7 a.m. to 2 p.m. & 4-11 p.m. Bar hours: 6 p.m. to 2 a.m. *142 Hana Highway • 579-9453.*

$$ Mid-Range

Dillon's: A low-key, tropical looking place; bamboo and wood interior with local art on the walls. You can get a snack or a full meal any time of day...a sandwich or a steak for dinner. The menu is large; the food is typical American fare. Juicy hamburgers are a house specialty. Hours: 7 a.m. to 9 p.m. daily. *89 Hana Highway • 579-9113.*

$$$ Expensive

Mama's Fish House: Has a reputation as the best seafood restaurant on Maui. When it opened in 1973 it was the only fresh seafood restaurant; now it has many competitors. Meat and chicken are also available. It's a lovely place with beautifully-landscaped grounds sitting right on the ocean. Kama'ainas get a 20% discount. Hours: 11 a.m. to 2 p.m.; 5-10 p.m. Happy hour & pupus 2:30-4:30 p.m. *Location: 1.5 miles from Pa'ia up the Hana Highway on makai side of road • 579-9672.*

SHOPPING

Pa'ia is tiny, so there are only two small streets with shops. Yet some of the most innovative stores, especially women's apparel, are found here. Most places are open 9 a.m. to 6 p.m. Some are open Sundays, but many are not.

The first building in town as you enter from Kahului is a green two-story home that houses the **Maui Crafts Guild** (43 Hana Highway). Here are the best crafts made on the island, done by artists who run the store. Raku vases, pottery, woodwork, jewelry, hand-dyed silk blouses and scarves...many imaginative creations.

Of the many clothing stores, **J.T. Swan** (27 Baldwin Ave.) is the most unusual. This is the outlet for Juliette Van Dyke's handmade, handpainted designs. Her clothes are in good stores all over the island, but they're often twice as much as they are here. Van Dyke has been designing, sewing and painting for years on Maui. Her work is unusual and creative.

Rona Gale's Boutique (120 Hana Highway) has beautiful hand-made, handpainted clothing made by local designer Rona Gale. She also carries beaded, sequined dresses from India and Bali.

Summer House (120 Hana Highway) has hip, young clothing for women, most of it with a certain razz-ma-tazz style. **The Clothes Addict** (12 Baldwin Ave.) is a small shop of women's clothes, some of them unusual, one-of-kind items. **Jaggers** (100 Hana Highway) has both men's and women's casual clothes. They also carry a good selection of T-shirts.

If Bay Area tourists miss the Body Shop (started in Berkeley), go to **Anuenue** (means rainbow) at 120 Hana Highway. They sell bath and body potions and lotions, some bought from the Body Shop. This small shop has soaps, shampoos, perfumes, incense, makeup, etc.

Bears Forever (76 Hana Highway) is for kids. It's a small place, but a fun place. Toys, stuffed animals, handmade quilts, books...a cuddly little shop.

The little wood sculptures and knickknacks in **Maui Exotic Woods** store (83 Hana Highway) are fine little pieces, but they do not tell the whole story. Their workshop in Haiku is a huge space piled high with beautiful wood slabs—koa, mango, monkey pod, African ear pod. Anyone looking for custom-made furniture or for a slab for a desk top, should inquire at the Pa'ia shop, then take a trip to Haiku.

Painting by Eddie Flotte

Makawao

Makawao is Maui's cowboy town. Paniolos, they call them here. Paniolos are rarely seen in town; they work the surrounding ranches. They all come out for the annual 4th of July rodeo—three days of cowboy contests—Hawai'i's largest rodeo.

It's a small town...just a strip of shops along three blocks of Baldwin Avenue...Dodge Street, Maui style. Wooden boardwalks and 50-year old wooden stores keep the Western flavor. No building is allowed over two stories high. Residents don't want the town "developed;" they like the country atmosphere.

HISTORY

Portuguese immigrants were the first to farm and settle the area. They moved Upcountry after finishing their sugar plantation contracts.

It remained rural until WW II when thousands of troops were stationed nearby. Businesses opened with a flurry, only to close after the war, and the town went back to sleep.

Two of these local mom & pop businesses still anchor both ends of town. Komodo's general store opened in the 1930s and Kitada's Kau Kau Korner started serving inexpensive local meals in 1947. They are simple, old style places...Makawao as it once was.

Tourism and an increase in residents keep the town alive today. Still, it is country quiet—an honest little town with plenty of character.

Paniolos

This is not a Hawaiian word. Paniolo is a bastardized- Hawaiianized version of Espanol. The first cowboys in Hawai'i were imported Spanish-Mexican vaqueros from California...hence the name. They were brought in to teach the natives how to handle their proliferating wild cows.

Hawaiians had never seen a cow until British explorer George Vancouver brought a few to Kamehameha I in 1793 on the Big Island.

Vancouver insisted on a 10-year killing tabu; he wanted the animals to have a chance to multiply...which they did with fervor. By the time the vaqueros were called in, thousands of cattle were roaming about, trampling fields and causing havoc. The Hawaiians knew nothing about cowpunching.

The first horses were brought to the islands in 1803. These mustangs were also allowed to roam wild. Before they could tackle the cattle, the vaqueros first had to tame the horses.

Today there are two major cattle ranches on Maui—Haleakala Ranch and 'Ulupalakua Ranch, both located upcountry on the slopes of Haleakala.

On the Big Island, Parker Ranch is the largest privately-owned ranch in the United States. It was started on two acres in 1809; it now spreads over 200,000-plus acres.

Drawing of Baldwin Avenue by Pam Hayes

RESTAURANTS

$ Budget

Kitada's Kau Kau Korner: The oldest restaurant in town. It's a small joint, and is a favorite with locals. Food is basic, nothing fancy...beef hekka, pork tofu, saimin, sandwiches for less than $2, hamburgers. Good place to sit and watch the "real" people. The Kitadas themselves are as real as you can get...long time Makawao folks. Hours: 6 a.m. to 1:30 p.m. Closed Sunday. *572-7241.*

Zambala's: An upstairs coffee shop with a small balcony overlooking Baldwin Avenue. Tiny place with good coffee drinks, plus sandwiches, bagels, breakfast (any time), pastries. Hours: 8-5:30; Sun. 8-2. *3660 Baldwin • 572-6401.*

Polli's: Good Mexican restaurant with a cosy interior. Run by the same people who own Polli's in Kihei. (And there is a real Polli.) Favorite Up-country spot. Food is good, margaritas are great. Local entertainment plays at 9 p.m. Wed.-Sat. Hours: 11:30 a.m. to 10 p.m. *1202 Makawao Ave. • 572-7808.*

Casanova Italian Deli: A big, bright, very Italian deli. Good food, great space. The deli is owned by six Europeans (five are Italian) who moved to Maui in 1986 looking for the tropical lifestyle. They had the place running within three months of being here. Hours: 8 a.m. to 7:30 p.m. weekdays; 8:30-7:30 weekends. *1188 Makawao (next door to Partners) • 572-0220.*

Partners: A spacious cowboy place that serves simple food—sand-wiches, pizza, salads, chicken, steak, ribs. Hours: 5-10. Dancing after 10 Th-Sat. Teen disco Wednesday night. *1188 Makawao Ave. • 572-6611.*

$$ Mid-Range

Makawao Steak House: Famous for serving good fish and meat; been around a long time. It's a nice woody looking place that insists it's the "only restaurant on Maui that serves real prime rib" (served Fridays and Saturdays). They make other claims on the menu...real butter, fresh fish, real scallops, fresh fettucine (not packaged)...all these pro-clamations are not necessary, the food should speak for itself. Hours: 5-9:30 p.m. *3612 Baldwin Ave. 572-8711.*

SHOPPING

There are no hotels or condos near Makawao. Besides country beauty, the only draw for tourists is shopping. All the stores are originals. No chain stores,, no big businesses. The shops are run, sometimes on a shoestring, by locals who care about their products.

Most stores are open 9 a.m. to 6 p.m. Monday through Saturday. Nothing much happening on Sundays in Makawao.

Starting at the top of the Baldwin Avenue and heading down, the first store of interest is located in a converted gas station, address 3682. The smell of potpourri hits you at the front door of the **Country Cupboard**. It's that kind of store—cute and sweet. There's sexy lingerie and cutesie kids' stuff and women's apparel...all crowded into this tiny place.

Komoda's Store and Bakery (3674) is a general/grocery store where goods range from eggs to coveralls. They are famous for their cream puffs, selling several hundred a day. Much of the pastry is the gooey, white flour variety. Hours: 6:30 a.m. to 6 p.m.; Sunday 7 to noon.

Collections, across the street at 3677, is a favored store with many Maui women. The clothing is casual and hip; accessories are great.

Upcountry/Down Under (3647) sells New Zealand products— sheep and lambs' wool items (furry stuffed animals, car seat covers, sweaters, etc.).

Silversword Stoves (3640) is the biggest stove store in Hawai'i. Yes, stoves—it's cold Upcountry in the winter. Owner Gary Moore stocks 30 lines of stoves and has about 20 of them on display in his shop. This used to be a sports and western store, and Moore still rents and sells camping equipment...the only place on island that rents tents and sleeping bags. Moore also carries knives (the largest selection in Hawai'i, he says), telescopes and binoculars. He's a friendly guy and knows Makawao well; his store has been here since 1973.

There's a rainbow of colors and objects in **Goodies** (3637). Essentially a women's clothing store (unusual clothes), the shop also carries toys, wind chimes, jewelry. It's jam-packed, full of goodies.

Bamboo Forest and **Tutu's Palaka** (3625) are two small souvenir stores run by two local women. Both sell Polynesian items. One of the women, Jo-Anne Kahanamoku Sterling, has sailed Polynesia in an old-style Polynesian canoe, and knows the islands well.

Mountain Fresh Market is a large health food store with a bulletin board out front...always a good place for buy/sell/rent notes, plus dance/seminar/workshop/concert notices. Hours 9 a.m. to 7 p.m. Monday to Saturday; 9-6 Sunday.

Upcountry

Upcountry Maui is the midsection of Haleakala—the area that's roughly 3,000 to 4,000 feet elevation on the side of the mountain. It's cool up here; the weather is generally temperate, and it's often downright cold.

The scenery is woodsy and green, reminiscent of northern California. Much of Upcountry is farm land. The Kula district is particularly fertile—protea flowers, carnations, onions, potatoes, cabbages—all kinds of produce thrives here.

Upcountry is also ranch land, with 'Ulupalakua Ranch stretching across more than 25,000 acres.

HISTORY

There are a number of heiau and ancient sites in Kula. Archaeologist Winslow Walker visited and listed many of them in the 1930s. Their existence indicates that early peoples lived, not only in seaside fishing villages, but also at this high elevation, half-way up Haleakala.

The large village of Kahikinui ("great Tahiti") is farther east in the desolate ranch country between the ranch and Kaupo. Here a sizeable ancient society once lived in a large terraced village. The ruins still exist, but they are not accessible to the public.

Ranch History

Much of Upcountry's modern history is tied to the 'Ulupalakua Ranch. In the 1840s, Kamehameha III agreed to lease a couple thousand Upcountry acres if the renters would build a sugar mill where he and his chiefs could grind sugar from the cane they grew. The mill was built, but the owners soon turned the land over to someone else, who decided to grow both cane and potatoes. The new owner then went bankrupt and someone else took charge.

Painting by Curtis Wilson Cost

By 1856 Captain James Makee bought the property for a song. Under him, the ranch began to thrive.

Makee was captain of a whaling ship. One fateful night, a man who was denied shore leave slashed Makee in the face with a knife. Makee was treated for the wounds in Honolulu, and he subsequently decided to stay. A few years later, Maui beckoned, and Makee once again changed careers.

His wife had a love of roses, so they planted many varieties and named the property Rose Ranch. Makee was also a tree lover. It's believed he planted more than 150,000 trees; many of the eucalyptus, Cook pines and Norfolk pines still stand.

After Makee's death, the ranch went through several hands. Then in 1963, C. Pardee Erdman became the seventh owner of the ranch now known as 'Ulupalakua ("the place where breadfruit ripens").

SIGHTS

Pukalani

Means "hole in the clouds," supposedly because this area always has a bit of sun shining through the clouds. The town is mostly a bedroom community. Not much action—few restaurants, few shops, little for tourists to see or do.

Church of the Holy Ghost

Located on Lower Kula Road just off Alanui Place, beyond the small town of Waiakoa. The church was built in the 1890s for the Portuguese community. Its odd octagonal shape and tall belfry make it visible from afar. It looks like a pink and white wedding cake. Some say it's supposed to replicate Portuguese Queen Isabella's crown. Nobody knows for sure.

Tedeschi Winery

The only vineyards and winery in Hawai'i. Emil Tedeschi, a vintner from California's Napa Valley, teamed with 'Ulupalakua ranch owner C. Pardee Erdman in 1974. They planted Carnelian grapevines on the ranch, and thus far have produced a rose, a beaujolais, a champagne and a wine made from pineapples. They have a delightful tasting room in the old ranch jail. The whole area is very picturesque— the sugar mill ruins are across the street, and several lovely ranch homes and buildings are next door. The tasting room is six miles from Keokea down a rough, bumpy road...the same road that continues on to Kaupo. Hours: 9-5 weekdays; 10-5 weekends.

Keokea

Once a large Chinese farming community with two groceries, two meat markets, two opium dens, three gambling joints and the Tong fraternal social club. Many Chinese settled in Kula after their sugar contracts were up. They were farmers, and Kula was one of the few places where affordable land was available.

Sun Yat-sen, the man who led the overthrow of China's Manchu Dynasty, was in touch with Keokea's Chinese community during all the years he plotted the revolution. His brother lived in Keokea, so Sun

Yat-sen sent him his wife, mother and two children. They lived there in seclusion for at least 10 years. Sun Yat-sen had a price on his head, so, to ensure their safety, much about the family's whereabouts was kept secret. It is known that Sun Yat-sen himself visited Keokea many times. By 1911, he won the revolution and thus became the first president of the Chinese Republic.

Now all that's left of Keokea are the small Ching and Fong Stores and their gas pumps. There's also a community park.

Keokea's Fong Store in the 1940s.
(Maui Historical Society)

HOTELS

Both of Kula's two hotels are isolated and quiet even though they're on the main Haleakala Highway. Both have a woodsy lodge appeal.

Kula Lodge

This is a charmer—only five units in two wooden cabins, a small rustic country place built in the Forties. Three of the units have fireplaces and four have lofts furnished with two single beds (there's also either a queen or a double downstairs). No TVs or phones...the idea is to escape.

Much of the three acres is left untouched with minimal landscaping. Right outside the lodge's dining room window is an immediate view of forested hills; farther down you can see the ocean. The dining room and bar are large and lovely.

Also on the property are a gift shop, a protea co-op (they'll pack flowers for you to send home) and a gallery devoted to Curtis Wilson Cost, a well-known Maui artist who paints the Kula area.

Budget.

RR1, Box 475, Kula, HI 96790 • 878-1535.

Silversword Inn

Six redwood cabins sit perched on Haleakala's slope with a view that stretches to the ocean. Rustic it is, but it is also run down. It's a deal for the price, but a little work would add charm.

The cabins are large one-room affairs, a bit worn looking, but functional. They have bare rooms with Goodwill type furniture. No TV, no phone; shower, but no tub. Best part are the large lanais with great views.

There's a nice large dining room and lounge in a separate building. You check in here any time between 7 a.m. and midnight.

Budget.

RR1, Box 469, Kula, HI 96790 • 878-1232.

RESTAURANTS

$ Budget

Pukalani Terrace Country Clubhouse: One of the few Maui restaurants where you can get Hawaiian food daily. Sample kalua pig, laulau, Pulehu ribs, squid, tripe and lomi salmon...all at decent prices. American food is also available, but Hawaiian is the draw. The salad bar has homemade Portuguese bean soup, a local favorite. Hours: 10-2 & 5-9. *360 Pukalani. (Turn on Pukalani Road toward the shopping center and keep following it until you reach the golf course.) 572-1325.*

$$ Mid-Range

Kula Lodge: A small woodsy kind of place with windows all around to catch the wonderful view of the lower elevations. Great stop for breakfast after a sunrise visit to the Crater. Dinner is a continental, steak and fish menu, but is only served Friday, Saturday, Sunday. Hours: 7 a.m. to 3 p.m. daily; dinner only Fri., Sat., Sun.—5:30 to 9 p.m. *878-1535.*

Haleakala

Haleakala is one of the wonders of the world. At 10,023 feet high, with a "crater" area 7.5 miles long, 2.5 miles wide and 21 miles around, there is nothing like it on the planet. Many think of Haleakala as just the stark summit area, but it is, in fact, the entire East Maui Mountain.

Genesis

In the beginning was a hotspot, situated beneath the Pacific Plate. From this spot Haleakala built itself during three periods of volcanic activity—named Honomanu, Kula and Hana periods.

Starting during the Ice Ages, a million-some years ago, **Honomanu** flows lasted for thousands of years, slowly building East Maui's foundation as a huge shield volcano. The mountain grew to 8,500 feet. It spread out, building the isthmus of Central Maui (Kahului and Wailuku). Haleakala joined hands with its older sister, the West Maui Mountain volcano. Maui's shape was formed; the two other volcanic periods would ice the cake.

Kula activity built the mountain 900 feet higher than it is today. Most of the lava now seen at the summit is from Kula flows. These were the most explosive and dramatic eruptions on Haleakala. After them came long periods of inactivity. The crater area began to form.

Rain created streams and waterfalls, and their force carved out the mountain top. Four great valleys—Ke'anae, Kipahulu, Kaupo, Waiho'i—were formed by this erosion. The heads of Ke'anae and Kaupo Valleys nearly fused together at the summit, creating a deep depression on top.

Lava during the **Hana** period filled in this depression and leveled the crater floor we now walk on. All the magnificent, colorful cinder cones seen along Sliding Sands trail and farther east popped up during the Hana period. The largest, Pu'u o Maui, is 1,000 feet high.

Old lithograph of crater courtesy of Lahaina Printsellers

Enormous amounts of lava flowed through Haleakala's two huge gaps—Kaupo and Ko'olau. Lava flowing through Ko'olau spilled into Ke'anae Valley, spreading out at the bottom to form the Ke'anae Peninsula. A peninsula also formed at the bottom of Kaupo Gap.

Hana activity ended 800 to 1,000 years ago. Since that time, the most recent eruption occurred around 1790. This happened far from the summit, on Haleakala's slope above La Perouse Bay. Two vents went off, sending lava to the ocean, and forming Cape Kinau Peninsula.

The volcano has been quiet ever since. Not extinct, it is still partly over the hotspot on the ocean floor. But it is dormant, slowing moving off.

When is a crater not a crater?

Answer: when it is an erosional depression. You do not peer into a true volcanic caldera when you look down into Haleakala. What you see 3,000 feet down on the floor is the work of erosion.

A volcanic crater is created when the mountain sinks in or when its top explodes off. Haleakala did neither. Haleakala is a volcano, but there is no "crater." Nonetheless, the depression area 3,000 feet below the summit is commonly called a crater.

History of people activity

To the ancients, Haleakala was a sacred place. They did not live here—too cold and no food. But they did use it for spiritual ceremonies, and they did cross it on foot. It's the shortest route across East Maui. Remains of the ancient Pi'ilani Highway still exist within the crater.

Several heiau (temples) were built, including a very sacred one at Mt. Haleakala, an 8,201-ft. peak along the south rim (near the Kaupo Gap). Some believe kahunas were initiated at this powerful heiau. Stone sleeping shelters and other platforms are still present along the rim near the heiau. (It takes a keen eye to recognize the heiau ruins and the sleeping shelters amidst the other rocks.)

In 1920, archaeologist Kenneth Emory of Bishop Museum surveyed the crater and found 58 stone terraces and platforms, 9 stone shelters, part of the Pi'ilani Trail and hundreds of ahu (cairns that marked trails). Many now are gone, blown under the shifting cinders.

The first white men who climbed Haleakala to view the summit were three missionaries—Lorrin Andrews, Jonathan Green and William Richards. Of their experience at the summit, they wrote: "...*we beheld the seat of Pele's dreadful reign. We stood on the edge of a tremendous crater, down which, a single misstep would have precipitated us 1,000 or 1,200 feet. This was once filled with liquid fire, and in it, we counted 16 extinguished craters.*"

The first to explore it officially was a 1841 U.S. Exploring Expedition. They were a bit more accurate in their description: *"The crater of Haleakala, if so it may be called, is a deep gorge, open at the north and east, forming a kind of elbow..."* (the crater is actually an elbow shape, so they were very observant).

Soon Haleakala saw its first tourists, and as its fame grew, many climbed the mountain to take a peek. In 1894 a grass-hut shelter for visitors was built at Kalahaku Lookout.

In 1916 Haleakala became part of Hawai'i National Park—lumped together with Kilauea and Mauna Loa craters on the Big Island. In 1961 Haleakala was made a separate national park. The road up to the crater was built in the 1930s, finally paved in 1935. The summit visitor center went up in 1936, and the three crater cabins were built the following year. Until then, people camped and slept in lava tubes and caves.

Hikes

Hiking Haleakala is obviously the best way to experience the volcano. There are 36 miles of trails, plus numerous caves, lava tubes and ancient sites to explore. After a hike through Haleakala, you may want to spell it Hallelujah.

You can cross the crater on a 12-mile hike in a day, or you can go down Sliding Sands Trail and out Kaupo Gap in two days, or you can mosey down for an hour or so just to experience ultimate stillness.

Main Trails

Halemau'u Trail: This rocky trail was built in 1937 by the National Park Service. Halemau'u means "grass house," named after a thatched roof shelter that used to be near the trailhead. The trailhead is near 8,000 feet elevation, and is a mile from the rim (the walk to the rim is along a gentle grassy slope). From the rim it's a switchback trail 1.9 miles down to the crater floor at 6,640 feet. Trail is rocky. Scenery is rough a'a lava with some greenery, plus views of Ko'olau Gap.

Sliding Sands: As the name indicates, this is a sandy, cinder trail, easy going down, tough going up. It starts near the summit at 9,780 feet, and descends 4 miles to the crater floor. Scenery is desert-like, colorful and dotted with cinder cones.

Kaupo Gap: Usually traveled to exit the crater. Begins near Paliku cabin at 6,400 feet and descends down the gap through private ranch-land, eventually to Highway 31 by Kaupo Village. The trip can easily take eight hours. It is all down hill, but not to be taken lightly—people occasionally pop off toenails and ruin their knees.

Hosmer Grove: This is a forested area reached .7 miles after entering the park, just before Park Headquarters. Named after the first territorial forester, Ralph Hosmer, who planted temperate-zone trees at this altitude in the early 1900s. The nature trail here is an hour walk through both native and exotic trees and shrubs. A brochure available at the trailhead maps and describes the trail well.

Guided Walks & Talks

Park service rangers give two talks daily—a Haleakala geology lecture at 12:30 in the House of the Sun Visitor Center, and a silversword and Haleakala natural history lecture at 11 a.m. at the Red Hill Summit. There is also a self-run 5-minute slide show at the Visitor Center explaining Haleakala's basic story. The slides and talks are available year round.

Summer Programs (June through August)

—Ranger-guided walk partly down Sliding Sands trail for 1.5 hours roundtrip. Starts at Visitor Center at 9 a.m. daily.

—Star trekking at 8 p.m. Fridays at Hosmer Grove. A ranger talks about myths and the night sky.

—Waikamoi birding walk: a 2-hour hike in the Waikamoi Forest Reserve to spot and discuss native Hawaiian birds and plants. Meet at Hosmer Grove Saturdays at 9 a.m.

Hiking Mileage

2.9 - Halemau'u trailhead to crater floor
3.9 - Halemau'u trailhead to Holua Cabin
2.5 - Sliding Sands trailhead to first cinder cone (Kalua o Ka Oo)
7.4 - Sliding Sands trailhead to Holua Cabin
5.8 - Sliding Sands trailhead to Kapalaoa Cabin
9.8 - Sliding Sands trailhead to Paliku Cabin
3.7 - Kapalaoa Cabin to Paliku cabin
9.0 - Paliku Cabin down Kaupo Gap to Highway 31

Camping and Cabins

There are two grassy campgrounds within the crater, one near Holua Cabin, the other near Paliku Cabin. Camping is limited to 25 per campground, and permits are required. They are issued at Park Headquarters on a first-come basis on the day you intend to camp. Reservations are not possible; bookings are given only on the day of camping. Headquarter's hours are 7:30 a.m. to 4 p.m. daily. Maximum stay is 2 nights per campground; 3 nights maximum per month. Both campgrounds have toilets and drinking water.

Camping is also available at Hosmer Grove, located outside the crater in a wooded area. Here there are 6 campsites with room for 25. No permits are needed; it's first come, first serve. Facilities include pit toilets, drinking water, tables, fireplaces, cooking shelter with grills. Maximum stay is 3 nights.

The three cabins in the crater are often difficult to reserve. A written request is required 3 months in advance. Give a first and alternate choice of days and a first and alternate cabin. "The key to getting a cabin," a ranger says, "is flexibility." Each party is given one cabin; limit of 12 per party. Cabins have bunks, water, firewood, stove, kitchen utensils, but no bedding. Holua Cabin is the closest to the trailheads, Kapalaoa the second closest, Paliku the farthest. All can be reached within a day's hike.

Clothes Alert: Wear clothing in layers. The crater is cold. It does warm up, often to shorts and T-shirt weather, in the day; but sun-up and sun-down are *cold*. Do not go camping without a warm bag. Rain gear is often needed. Gloves, down vests, coats, woolen scarves...all appreciated in the winter.

Safety Alert: From the Park Service brochure...*"Haleakala is a fragile, yet harsh environment. High, thin air may cause problems for those with heart conditions, emphysema, or high blood pressure. Only those in excellent physical condition should attempt to enter the crater. It may be sunny and warm one minute, yet cold and rainy the next."*

Silversword

The most famous native endemic plant is the Haleakala silversword, a silvery mint-green sphere that looks delicate, yet is able to live in a rugged environment. It thrives at high elevations, between 6,000 and 12,000 feet. It plants itself in loose cinders, gets very little rain and endures diverse temperatures of hot and cold.

The plant's body has adapted to handle Haleakala's extremes. Sunlight and ultraviolet rays are more intense at high altitudes, so its silvery color reflects the sun's brightness. Silver hairs cover the leaves and also reflect the sun. The thin leaves curl inward like a rosette, protecting the growing tip deep within their middle. This inward curl produces a natural bowl which catches and holds water. The leaves are filled with a gel that also stores water.

The silversword takes from 7 to 30 years to mature, finally shooting up a 3 to 9-foot stalk which bears hundreds of flowering heads. The stalk terminates the growing tip, and once the seeds ripen, the plant dies. Flowering season in Haleakala is May to October.

Silverswords are of the *Compositae* family. Its family members include daisies, dandelions, artichokes and sunflowers. There are other types of silverswords in Hawai'i—on the Big Island volcanoes and on Mt. Eke and Pu'u Kukui in the West Maui Mountains—but all are different, peculiar to their areas.

The first visitors to Haleakala in the 19th century reported an abundance of silverswords in the crater. Within a short time, vandalism from these tourists and grazing from goats put the plant near extinction. With park service efforts, the silversword is now making a comeback.

Science City

Maui, the demi-god, lassoed the sun from the summit at Haleakala. As the legend goes, Maui's mother wanted more day time to dry her tapa cloth. So Maui lassoed the sun and demanded that it slow its pace across the sky.

Modern Mauians still lasso celestial bodies, but they now do so with lasers. From the summit of Haleakala they track satellites and bounce lasers off the moon, and heavens knows what else. Maui the god didn't tell the secrets of his strength, and the scientists don't tell their secrets either.

Science City is an 18-acre, off-limits area just outside the park's boundaries. The white dome-shaped observatories are as obvious as giant mushrooms sitting on the landscape. Most of the observatories are run by the University of Hawai'i's Astronomy Institute and the U.S. Air Force.

Kipahulu & 'Ohe'o

This area is far from Park Headquarters. Though Kipahulu and 'Ohe'o are part of Haleakala National Park, they are 180 degrees different than the crater. Thus, they are generally considered separate. No way can both the crater and 'Ohe'o be visited in one day.

Kipahulu Valley starts at the top of Haleakala and cuts down the mountain to the sea. The Nature Conservancy purchased Kipahulu Valley from various land owners in the late Sixties and early Seventies. They did so because the valley is a unique habitat for Hawaiian native plants and bird life. It is fragile territory that the Conservancy wants to preserve, thus it is rarely visited by the human species. The public is not allowed access. A foreign seed brought in on someone's shoe could disrupt the natural Hawaiian order of Kipahulu within years.

'Ohe'o Gulch is at the base of this giant valley. The valley cannot be hiked, and 'Ohe'o can be reached only at the base of Haleakala on the Hana side. Check the Kipahulu chapter for more.

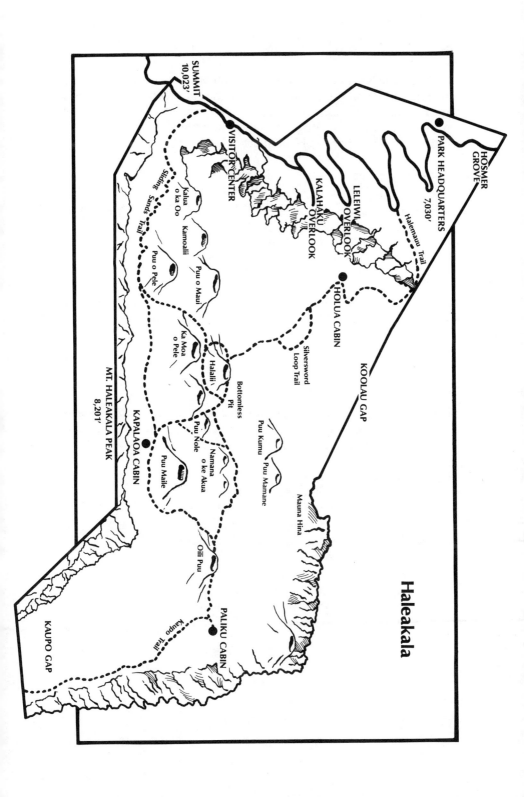

Haleakala

SUMMIT 10,023'

PARK HEADQUARTERS 7,030'

HOSMER GROVE

VISITOR CENTER

KALAHAKU OVERLOOK

LELEIWI OVERLOOK

Halemauu Trail

Sliding Sands Trail

Kalua o ka Oo

Kamoalii

Puu o Pele

Puu o Maui

Ka Moa o Pele

Halalii

Bottomless Pit

HOLUA CABIN

Silversword Loop Trail

KOOLAU GAP

Puu Kumu

Puu Mamane

MT. HALEAKALA PEAK 8,201'

KAPALAOA CABIN

Puu Nole

Namana o ke Akua

Puu Maile

Mauna Hina

Oili Puu

Kaupo Trail

PALIKU CABIN

KAUPO GAP

Fast Facts

Haleakala National Park is 43 square miles. It includes the "crater," plus Kipahulu Valley and 'Ohe'o Gulch. The park is open 24 hours, but Park Headquarters near the crater is open 7:30 a.m. to 4 p.m. daily. During the summer, the Visitor Center near the summit is open sunrise to 4:30 p.m. The phone at Headquarters is 572-9306.

Park entrance fees: $ 3 per car
                                    $10 annual pass
                                    free - under 12 and over 62 years

Elevation: Park Headquarters...7,030 feet
             Visitor Center...9,745 feet
             Summit (Red Hill)..10,023 feet

Average elevation of crater floor...6,700 feet
Descent from summit to crater floor.....................................3,000 feet

Dimensions of crater: 7.5 miles long
                            2.5 miles wide
                            21   miles around

Distances: Kahului Airport to Park Headquarters...........27.0 miles
             Lahaina to Park Headquarters.........................52.4 miles
             Visitor Center to Park Headquarters................9.6 miles

Hiking Distances:
     2.9 - Halemau'u trailhead to crater floor
     3.9 - Halemau' trailhead to Holua Cabin
     2.5 - Sliding Sands trailhead to first cinder cone (Kalua o Ka Oo)
     7.4 - Sliding Sands trailhead to Holua Cabin
     5.8 - Sliding Sands trailhead to Kapalaoa Cabin
     9.8 - Sliding Sands trailhead to Paliku Cabin
     3.7 - Kapalaoa Cabin to Paliku Cabin
     9.0 - Paliku Cabin down Kaupo Gap to Highway 31

Hana Road

The famous road to Hana...52 miles with 56 bridges amd more than 600 curves. What a reputation it has—great beauty, but treacherous driving. A local T-shirt proclaims: "I survived the Hana Highway."

So is it really dangerous? No. Absolutely no. It once was, but now it is a smooth two-lane blacktop; it is not a bumpy road. Some hairpin turns are a bit harrowing; some sections are not wide enough for two cars; the bridges fit only one vehicle. Those are the problems, the rest is magic.

The road bends around the edge of East Maui, the wet, windward side where the prevailing northeasterly tradewinds run into the mountain of Haleakala. Water spills from the clouds to create dozens of streams. It is these streams which carve out the valleys the 56 bridges cross.

Do not be scared out of going. You will never see another such highway. Dense jungle vegetation almost swallows the road. Ferns drip down from the banks. Trees line the roadside. Waterfalls cascade into pools. Tropical flowers fill the air with fragance.

It is the exotic Hawai'i of your dreams. It is nature at its best.

Note: All the streams have names; most are painted in black letters on the bridges that span them. The bridges, built between 1910 and 1912, are early examples of arch-stressed concrete work, now successfully carrying many times the load for which they were designed.

Note: Summer and fall are dry seasons, so the waterfalls may not be running, thus the roadside pools may be stagnant. Still, you may swim in them.

Note: Makai means sea side of the road; mauka means toward the mountain. These are used instead of left or right.

Note: Tourists generally travel slowly; Hana residents do not. They've seen the scenery; they just want to get where they're going. Pull over and let faster-moving cars and trucks by.

Pa'ia
Last chance for gas.
Last chance for a full meal (though there are roadside snack stands along the way).
Last chance for groceries.
(Read Pa'ia chapter for info on town.)

Ho'okipa: *2 miles from Pa'ia's MM 7 (mile marker 7)*
Best windsurfing beach on Maui; possibly best in world. Expert sailors practice here. Colorful sails dot the ocean when the winds & waves are right. A lookout turn-off allows for spectators.

Maliko Gulch: *first bridge after Ho'okipa, just past MM 10*
Beautiful, secluded bay, mostly used by fishermen. Has a small boat ramp. Beach area is all rocks; swimming is not great. The gulch starts from the bay and goes deep into the mountain, a steep and dramatic place. Some people live back here, but they do so because they don't want to be bothered.

Haiku: *begins around MM 11.*
This is a lush, green, rainy district popular with artists. It is the beginning of "country" on Maui. Many residences are way off the beaten track.

MM 16
Just past this mile marker, the famous road with its twisty turns really begins. From now on the road is narrow, kept so by common agreement, both because it would be exorbitantly expensive to widen, and because it serves as a sort of moat, keeping Hana isolated from the rest of the world.
After MM 16, the mile markers start over again with 0. No logical reason...this is, dontcha know, Maui.

Twin Falls: *first bridge (Ho'olawa) after MM 2*
Park by the bridge and walk up along the right side of the stream. The first pool has twin waterfalls, but the second pool (1/4 mile up) is larger and has a taller falls.
These pools are great swimming/picnicing areas for families. The land is private property, so be considerate.

Huelo: *makai, by school bus shelter & phone booth*
The dirt road down into this district leads past two old churches, Door of Faith and Kaulanapueo.

Huelo is a rainy, fertile area. Thousands of Hawaiians lived here once upon a time. It is now sparsely populated.

Kailua: *1/2 mile past MM 5*

Many residents in this small community work for East Maui Irrigation Company, the arm of Alexander & Baldwin that regulates the vast aqueduct system for the cane fields. E.M.I.'s base yard is located in Kailua. From here, workers maintain the tunnels and ditches that divert mountain stream water to lowland fields. It was an extraordinary engineering feat when built in the 1870s, and it still functions perfectly well for the 1980s.

Eucalytus Groves: *MM 6 & 7*

Towering rainbow and robusta eucalytus are predominant here, the trees lining the road majestically. Eucalyptus are originally from Australia and Malaysia. More than 50 eucalyptus species were introduced to Hawai'i during the past century.

Waikamoi Ridge: *no sign, just a dirt pull-off*
metal turnstile at head of trail

This short trail along Waikamoi Ridge quickly leads into a silent world of trees, through forests of native and introduced species. "Quiet, Trees at Work," proclaims a sign along the path. Name placards mark several of the species. The walk is a delight, and it's short and easy...can be done in a half hour.

On the road again...

There are three pool/waterfall areas within two miles of each other. Each is part of a different stream. If you miss one, just catch the next one. They are the following:

Waikamoi Stream: *first white painted bridge after the ridge*

Small pool and waterfall—picturesque and good for a quick dip. Metal pipe sticking out of the rock wall just beyond the bridge has spring water constantly running from it...wonderful drinking water.

Puohokamoa Stream: *next bridge, MM 11*

Bigger pool and falls than Waikamoi. More space for parking cars. This is the only one of these three waterfall/pool areas that has picnic tables, so people often stop here.

For the adventurous: walk up to the left of the first pool where there's a larger falls and pool. Or, hike down the stream (makai of the road) to the edge of the world.

Hawai'i State Archives

Haipuaena Stream: *next bridge*

Walk up along left side of stream (behind white cross painted on rock) to pond and falls. Can't see falls from road.

Kaumahina State Wayside Park: *.2 mile past MM 12; sign*

Flush toilets, picnic area, beautiful coastal overlook to Ke'anae Peninsula. Camping allowed with permit.

Lots of lonely, wild cats hang out here. Cat lovers should definitely feed them.

Honomanu Valley: *view from MM 13*

Huge valley carved into Haleakala's side during its first long period of dormancy. Within the canyon is some of the oldest rock seen on Haleakala (not covered by subsequent flows). At the head of the canyon are 3,000-foot cliffs and a 1,000-foot waterfall—almost impossible to reach. Hikers would have to be hardcore adventurers to even try it. Definite Indiana Jones stuff.

The dirt road to the left after MM 14 leads to Honomanu Bay. The bay is beautiful, but it's not a good beach; dangerous for swimming, but often great for board surfing.

YMCA Camp/Hostel: *just beyond MM 16, makai side*

Gorgeous area for the YMCA; spectacular views that overlook the Ke'anae Peninsula. Large groups can book the whole camp (several lodging buildings plus a kitchen structure). Hostelers can book a bed. Maximum stay is 3 nights. (More in Hostel chapter.) Call 242-9007 or 244-3253.

The buildings were once part of the old Ke'anae prison. In the 1920s, prisoners helped plant and maintain the arboretum down the road.

Ke'anae Arboretum: *makai side, .2 mile from YMCA*

Here there are lovely walks through both native and introduced trees and plants. The Pi'ina'au Stream meanders through, and has a decent swimming pond.

A large area is devoted to taro, showing many varieties growing in water-logged sections. At the far end of the taro is an unmarked one-mile trail that ends in a native forest. The hike is a bit tough, is usually muddy, and can take a couple of hours. It is easy to lose the trail, so be prepared for an adventure.

Ke'anae Peninsula & Village: *next makai turn from arboretum; sign*

Lava formed this peninsula when it burst through the Ko'olau Gap in Haleakala and flowed to the sea, spreading out like a fan to become Ke'anae.

Since ancient times it was inhabited, and still the village is much like old Hawai'i. Taro patches, a few houses and an 1856 missionary (Congregational) church are the whole town. Some Hawaiian families have lived here for generations.

The road off the highway and down into the peninsula is rough, and it deadends at the sea. But it's a beautiful, picturesque side trip.

Had enough?

If you drive as far as Ke'anae, and you find this is not your schtick, you might as well turn around and head back. The scenery is much the same from here to Hana, and Hana itself is just a simple little town. If you're missing the beach and don't really care about ferns and falls, then head back...you've had a taste of Hana Road.

Palauhulu Bridge: *second bridge past Ke'anae turn-off*
Favored swimming hole of Ke'anae kids.

Ke'anae Overlook: *just past MM 17*
Good view of the peninsula. Good photo angle.

Waianu/Half Way to Hana Fruit Stand

This is the pioneer fruit stand, the first one established along Hana Road. Roadside fare includes ice cream, banana bread, shave ice, sandwiches, hot dogs, fruit, smoothies, soda, etc.

Uncle Harry's

This food and souvenir stand is run by Harry Mitchell and his family. Harry, born in Ke'anae in 1919, is actively involved in issues involving Hawaiian rights and land use.

His son Kimo was lost at sea in the 1970s when he and singer George Helm paddled surfboards to Kaho'olawe to protest the Navy's bombing of that island. Harry himself made the trip several years later, successfully hiding out on the island against Navy wishes.

Now the Mitchell family, including Harry's son "Uncle Harry, Jr.," are building a mini museum by their fruit stand with displays of Hawaiian artifacts. They've also built a hale pili, (grass house made of rare pili grass) to show how their ancestors lived.

Joanne Mitchell is the kupuna director of Maui's Hawaiian culture teachers, so she knows her stuff. "I'm always thinking in terms of how to educate," she says. The family built the hale pili, she adds, "To teach people that Hawaiians had grass houses and not grass shacks."

The Mitchell philosophy, Joanne says, is to take "the Hawaiian concepts of aloha (love), ohana (family) and lokahi (harmony that exists with man, nature and God) and show how we as a Hawaiian family are perpetuating that. We have something special to offer visitors, because we're a Hawaiian family operating our business on our property. Where else can visitors go and get that kind of flavor?

"We want people to feel the warmth of the genuine aloha that we have here, to share and learn with us as we share with you what we have."

The Mitchells find they sometimes have to correct "the wildest stories" visitors have been told by tour drivers, who in some cases, "just got off the plane themselves."

The Mitchells plan to start selling Hawaiian foods—"the kind we eat," Joanne says. "Hawaiian food the way we prepare it, not the kind you get at a hotel lu'au" (she thinks hotel poi is "yucky").

"Once in a while tourists ask for poi," Harry Jr. says. "So I run in the house, get 'em. They say it tastes good, because ours is homemade, rich, heavy poi, kind of white, not real pink. They taste and they like it."

Harry Jr. makes killer banana bread with whole wheat flour, which allows wife Joanne to say, "I perpetuate an ancient Hawaiian custom—men did all the cooking!"

Wailua: *immediate makai turn from Harry's stand*

A one-road village straight out of old Hawai'i. Taro patches dominate, but a little shrine has the most fascinating story.

Our Lady of Fatima Shrine was the original St. Gabriel's Catholic Church (new one is next to it) built in 1860 out of coral. As the tale goes, church members had to dive 6 to 10 feet deep off shore, pry coral loose and bring it up in buckets—a laborious task. They prayed for help and a freak storm hit. After several days of raging waters, the storm passed, leaving chunks of coral on the shore. The amazed Catholics carried in enough coral to construct the entire building.

Supposedly, the Protestants knew the coral was meant for the Catholics, so they didn't touch it until the Catholics had enough. Then the Protestants went to the seashore to collect the remnants, only to watch as a great wave came in and washed to sea all traces of coral.

Believe it or not.

Wailua Lookout: *.8 mile from Uncle Harry's, almost to MM 16*

From the parking area there's a good view of the giant Wailua Canyon that cuts down the north side of Haleakala.

Walk up the concrete steps under an archway of tangled hau bush; looking out in the other direction at the top, there's a grand view of Wailua village.

Waikane Falls: *.6 mile from Wailua lookout*

This is the most spectacular falls on the road before Hana. The E.M.I. is not allowed to divert its water as long as people raise taro down below in the Wailua Valley.

Pua'a Ka'a State Wayside Park: *past MM 22*

This is a picnic park built along a stream and pools...a sweet, idyllic little place with two small waterfalls. Perfect for families. Last restroom till Hana.

Nahiku: *first turn makai past MM 25*

This road heads down 1,000-foot elevation for three miles to the small village of Nahiku...interesting little community, part hippie, part Hawaiian. Now there are less than 100 people, but in ancient times there were many hundreds.

Nahiku was a plantation town in the first decade of the 1900s. Rubber, though, not sugar. More than 25,000 rubber trees were planted. They grew rapidly and their rubber was good quality, but labor and production were too costly, so the first rubber plantations in America met a quick finale.

This is a lush, tropical area where house plants grow into trees. Above Nahiku on the other side of the highway (in Kuhiwa Valley) is one of the wettest spots on Maui; some say it is the rainiest area on the island (though this is hard to measure precisely).

Danny's Country Kitchen: *big sign*

Funky little "cafe" popular with locals and tourists both. You can take your food and go, or eat in booths under the trees. The food is basic hot dog, chili and saimin fare. Open 10 a.m. to 5 p.m. Closed Sunday. Telephone booth on property.

Last place to eat before Hana.

Hana Gardenland: *mauka; sign*

This was Maui's first certified nursery. Certified means that plants and flowers are washed and groomed so they're bug free. Thus, they can be shipped or taken back to the Mainland.

It's a pretty nursery landscaped with a koi pond. Tiny plants, flowers and souvenirs are sold here.

Their hours are a good indication of life in Hana. The sign says:

> Weekdays 9-4 (about)
> Sundays 11-3 (maybe)
> Someday maybe we go fish too!

Pi'ilanihale Heiau: *just past MM 31, turn makai on Ulaino Rd.*

This is a massive and amazing structure—the largest heiau (temple) in the Hawaiian Islands. Pi'ilanihale means house of Pi'ilani, and it is assumed the heiau was built in the 1500s by the Pi'ilani family. Pi'ilani, one of the great kings of Maui, was the first to unify the districts of Maui under one reign.

The heiau's enormous size indicates that it could have been a war heiau. It is believed to have been the scene of human sacrifices.

The heiau is on land owned by the Pacific Tropical Botanical Garden. They are planning escorted tours, but as yet do not offer it as a tourist attraction. You cannot see it from the road; you do need to be escorted in.

Wai'anapanapa State Park: *sign*

Beautiful coastal park for picnicing, hiking and swimming. Camping is allowed under the trees, and large cabins are available (both require permits from the Department of Land and Natural Resources in Wailuku...see camping chapter).

For hikers there are ancient burial sites and heiau to find. For swimmers there's a black sand beach plus several water-filled caves.

One of these caves has a dry chamber, reached only by swimming underwater through the first chamber. Legend has it that a Hawaiian princess hid with her maid in the dry chamber to escape her jealous husband. He found her, however, and killed both women. Since then, the water often appears red in this cave. Some say it's due to the murders; others say it happens when there's an abundance of tiny red shrimp.

Helani Gardens: *sign*

This is the granddaddy of all the island nurseries. Helani means "a heaven," and it's definitely a slice.

For a slight fee you can drive through more than 65 acres of wondrous foliage and flowers. The place is so extensive they give you a map at the gate so you won't get lost.

Hana native Howard Cooper owns the garden and has his own private treehouse in it. Howard is a local character, and his philosophy, a blend of individualism and and rugged conservatism, pops up on signs all over the garden. He espouses tried-and-true sayings like: "We cannot direct the wind, but we can adjust our sails."

Howard doesn't know how many varieties of plants he grows, but it's several thousand. He claims to know the Latin name for most of them, and can recall which of his international network of friends sent him the original seed or cutting.

Tourists cannot buy plants or flowers certified to send to the Mainland. Retail plant sales are not Cooper's business; he sells seeds, cuttings and air layers wholesale to Mainland florists.

Open 10 a.m. to 4 p.m. daily.

Hana town

Hana is a mere blink from Helani. It is a sweet little town where there's little to do. That's its allure.

Do remember, the road to Hana is a goal unto itself. You do not drive the road with Hana town as Mecca. You drive the road to see the scenery along its 52 miles.

Hana

So big deal, you say after you make your first trip to Hana. This is it?—two stores, a fancy hotel, a few houses, a bank and a post office? Why do they wax so poetic about it? What is the Heavenly Hana mystique? Beauty, islolation, serenity, a feel of old Hawai'i—all of these make this a small town not easily forgotten. Hana is a place to relax and enjoy Hawai'i as it once was.

Forget the scenery, what's for lunch?
If you stay in Hana, know this about it:
—There are only two stores with groceries, and their selections are limited.
—The only restaurants are those of the Hotel Hana Maui (and they can be expensive); there is a snack bar on Hana Bay.
—Gas is expensive at the town's two stations.
—There is no launderette in town; closest one is in Pa'ia.
—Bank is open 3-4:30 p.m. M-Th; 3-6 Fri. Deposits are not recorded until they reach the bookkeeping center in central Maui, and that takes a few days by mail.
—Post office is open Monday through Friday 8:30 a.m. to 4:30 p.m. Mail is dispatched once daily at 9 a.m. Monday through Saturday.
—Hana Medical Center is open 8 a.m. to 5 p.m. Monday through Friday. An on-duty nurse answers at all other times. 248-8294.
—There is an ambulance here, but people in serious trouble are flown to Wailuku by helicopter.

Transportation
You need a car in Hana, there is no bus or taxi. If you fly in to Hana's airport, there is only one car rental agency. It's **National Car Rental**, run by Mary Purdy. She has no booth at the airport; you have to call her office at 248-8237. She stays open for all the flights (usually 7 a.m. to 7 p.m.). You can book through Purdy or through any National Car office.

HISTORY

Hana was popular in ancient times. Thousands of people lived here and along the neighboring coasts. It was isolated from the rest of Maui, so it long had its own chiefs.

The village was located in a strategic military position—angled close to the Big Island. Both Maui and Big Island warring parties would sail back and forth attacking each other.

There are many heiau along the Hana coast. These were not just places of worship; they were often built for particular battles. The presence of this many heiau indicates the warlike nature of the times.

Fortress & Lookout

Ka'uiki Head, the red cinder hill on the south side of Hana Bay, was a natural fortress and lookout point for the town. Kalaniopu'u, king of the Big Island, conquered and held the hill for several years in the mid 1700s. Then Kahekili, king of Maui, defeated Kalaniopu'u in Kaupo. Kahekili retook Ka'uiki Head by shutting off the water supply to the warriors positioned on top. Thus the Big Islanders were effectively pushed back home until Kamehameha came into his prime and put an end to fighting by conquering and unifying all the islands.

A sweeter time...

The story of modern Hana is tame in comparison. Sugar cane was introduced in the mid 1800s and did well until the end of World War II when the last plantation folded. With it went most of the jobs. The population dwindled from several thousand to several hundred as people went elsewhere for work.

Enter Paul I. Fagan, San Francisco entrepreneur extraordinaire. Fagan and wife Helene bought up much of the available land and started a cattle ranch in 1946.

A social man, Fagan would invite his millionaire Mainland friends over, but then had no place for them to stay. So he built a hotel. Money was apparently no issue with Fagan. The next year he opened the hotel to the public—the first Hawaiian hotel opened outside Waikiki.

Fagan's ranch and hotel have kept the town folk employed since the late 1940s. It's been a company town, and it still is.

When Texans bought the ranch and hotel in 1984, Hana folk worried about their future. But no need. Caroline Hunt Schoellkopf and her Rosewood Corporation value the town's unique, homey atmosphere. Their $25 million renovations were needed; the hotel was getting a bit ragged. Now it is elegant, but it still has the special feel of 'ohana (family).

Maui Folk...

"I've been blessed."

Carol Kapu grew up in Honolulu's Waikiki area when Waikiki was charming. "That was in the Forties," she says. "Waikiki was so gracious and now it's so awful.

"Look what's happening to Lahaina—it used to be quaint, but it's tacky now along Front Street."

Because of this, she fears for her beloved adopted Hana. "It makes me ill to think of it becoming commercial. I am very possessive of this area, and I don't want to see it spoiled.

"Hana is special because of its people and because of its serene beauty and noncommercialism.

Carol says she "speaks as an outsider who can appreciate the area." She doesn't have a narrow, provincial view of Hana. She lived on the Mainland for 17 years and loved it...Minnesota, Wyoming, Iowa and Washington State.

A Woman of Many Hats

It is rare for a small community to have its own museum. Hana does...thanks to Coila Eade. Coila raised funds ($60,000 for starters) for Hale Waiwai ("House of Treasures"). She donated 139 stone artifacts. She designed the museum's interior. She was the building contractor, and she handcarved the koa wood front doors herself.

She is supposed to be "retired." She and her husband Les (now deceased) came to Hana for one day in 1956. "We fell in love with it," she says. "We went back to Pasadena, sold our business and we've been here ever since. It's been a very busy retirement.

"When I first came here, I got about 20 books from the library on Hawaiian history. Everything just fascinated me—everything to do with Hawai'i's past. I think of these natives before the white man came and how they lived. They had no metal to make things with; they had to use stone tools. They were really artists."

Coila too is now an artist. "Hana influenced us both artistically. I don't know how to explain it. My husband started painting and I started carving."

She carved the kapa design in the museum doors for a month in the evenings. By day she'd be at the museum working with the builders.

Coila was awarded a 1986 Preservation Certificate by the Historic Hawai'i Foundation for her museum

"I've been blessed," she says, "I've always been able to adapt."

Still, during all her Mainland years, she kept the hope of coming home. And she did. First to Kaua'i, then in 1978 to Hana.

She worked eight years as Social Director for the Hotel Hana Maui. Now she runs a Halau, training Hana children in the art of hula.

"I'd like to leave a legacy," she says, "that the children learn our culture. I teach them their language and culture (through the hula), so they'll have a love for the 'aina (land) and for their heritage. It's a wonderful heritage; they have a lot to be proud of.

"When I was growing up, our culture was dying out. When the Hawaiian people were spoken of, it was derogatory—Hawaiians were lazy or no good.

"I knew I was okay and my family was fine, but, being a young-ster, I thought the Hawaiians in general were not too swift.

"It was through the hula and the chants that I learned this was not so. There was much beauty in their thinking and in their love of the land. They described it through the chants. They were an intelligent people and they were very industrious."

Hana's Hawaiian people affect Carol deeply. "I tear up when I think about them," she says, explaining the tears in her eyes. "I treasure them. They have so much aloha.

"That's why the hotel guests come back year after year. The people and the beauty. That's Hana."

work...an award she calls "an unex-pected honor."

Her next project is to build an ancient Hawaiian living compound on property next door to the mu-seum. It was rumored the land was slated for condo units...which horri-fied Coila. She and her fellow mu-seum directors quickly raised the funds and bought the property.

"It's so important to preserve this," she says. "We're going to build two Hawaiian grass houses, a canoe shed, two small taro patches, and we're going to plant Hawaiian me-dicinal and food plants. I'm so ex-cited about it. We'll use no nails; all the joints will be wrapped. We want to fix it up as much as possible as the olden days."

SIGHTS

Ka'uiki Head

This is a cinder cone turned red due to the oxidation of the iron in its lava. The hill is a natural fortress; on top an army would be isolated and protected. Thus it was the scene of many battles.

Captain Cook anchored right off this hill. He never touched foot on Maui, but a young Kamehameha was in the party of Hawaiians who canoed out to meet him. Cook apparently recognized the potential in Kamehameha. Ka'ahumanu, Kamehameha's favorite wife, was born in a cave at the base of this hill.

'Alau Island

A four-acre lava island near the coast by Koki Beach Park. Fusae Nakamura, owner of Aloha Cottages, says that years ago when they were fishing, her father and brother planted two coconuts on the once-barren island.

Lyon's Hill

This is the high hill on pastureland overlooking the hotel (once owned by the Lyon's family). It's obvious to all because of the huge black cross that tops it. This lava rock cross was erected in memory of Paul Fagan, original owner of the ranch and hotel. You can walk to the top (it's a very aerobic 15-minute climb), or you can drive up if you get the gate key from the hotel.

Hale Waiwai (House of Treasures)

Hana's museum was opened in 1983 by a volunteer group of Hana residents (see Coila Eade's story). It is a small, charming museum full of Hawaiiana. Entry is free, but a donation is appreciated. Open 10 a.m. to 4 p.m. daily.

Next door stands the old police station and courthouse (the judge used to visit twice a month). Neither are used anymore. Get the key from the museum staffer and visit the dark, ramshackle little jail behind the courthouse.

Wananalua Church

Located at the corner of Hauoli Road and Hana Highway. The first structure, built in 1838 near Hana Bay, was made of grass. Construction on the present lava rock building was begun in 1842 and lasted for 20 years. There's a Hawaiian language Bible on a table near the altar, open for anyone to leaf through. The cemetery by the side of the church has many old Hawaiian graves.

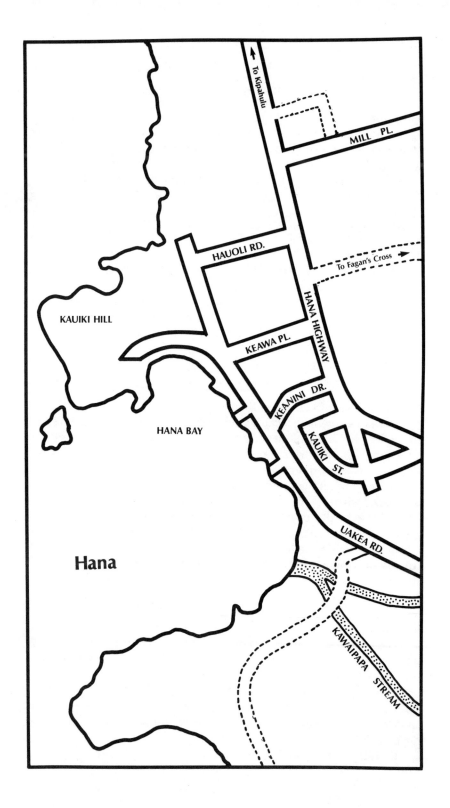

BEACHES & PARKS

Waikoloa

Located on the side of Hana Bay opposite Ka'uiki Head. Two streams meet here and flow into the ocean. To reach it, take Waikoloa Road (garbage dump road) off the highway and follow it to the area closest to the Bay. This is a state park, but it's undeveloped.

Swimming is poor. Both bottom and beach are rocky. It is, however, a good surfing area.

No facilities.

Hana Beach Park

On Hana Bay, this park is a favorite with Hana residents. It's a safe swimming area with a sandy beach. The old wharf at the far end of the harbor is now used only for small boats. Pu'u Ki'i is the small island with the lighthouse on it; there are stairs to the lighthouse, but the island is not for public use.

Snorkelers should stay between the lighthouse and the pier. Beyond the lighthouse, the strong current goes out to sea.

Facilities: picnic tables, pavilion, toilets, showers, boat ramp.

Red Sand Beach (Kaihalulu Beach)

This is a gorgeous volcanic cinder beach. The sand is red and so are the cliffs of Ka'uiki Hill that cradle this secluded cove. For years it was considered Hana's private nudist beach. Now, as more tourists discover it, it is less private.

Swimming and snorkeling are good near the beach. Outside the lava rock "barrier," the currents are strong.

Getting to the beach can be dangerous for the unsure of foot. Anyone afraid of heights should not attempt to go. Start from the community center at the end of Hauoli Road, then walk along the outside of Ka'uiki Hill following the well-worn path. Do not go up towards the Japanese cemetery (unless you want to see the graves).

No facilities.

Koki Beach Park

The park is a narrow strip of grass and ironwood trees. There's a small sandy beach, plus a larger rocky beach. High surf and heavy currents sometimes make swimming dangerous.

The park is located down Haneoo Road, a loop road a mile from Hasegawa's Store. Farther along the loop (but before Hamoa Beach) are some obvious ancient fish ponds—little pools where the chiefs raised fish to eat.

Facilities: picnic tables, BBQ grills.

Hamoa Beach

Located on the other end of Haneoo Road, this is a beautiful, white sand beach, favored by Hana residents. Swimming can be dangerous due to the often high surf, but there is usually a lifeguard on duty, and people are always swimming. Not particularly good for snorkelers or surfers.

Hotel Hana Maui guests use this beach, and most of the facilities were built by the hotel for them. Nonguests are welcome to use a toilet and shower provided for all. Beach chairs and umbrellas are strictly for guests, though.

HOTELS

Hotel Hana Maui

There is no other hotel like this on Maui. It is, in fact, unique in all the islands. Low-key and unpretentious, still it attracts the rich and international set. Kennedys honeymoon here and no one blinks. It is a world class hotel without the pomp.

For 40 years it has been run by the same Hana families. The cooks, the maids, the various staff are all related—cousins, parents, siblings— they've seen three generations of guests since the hotel's opening in 1946.

The buildings and furnishings started showing their age by the Seventies, and occupancy began falling, sometimes to 50%. Not so anymore.

In 1984 the Rosewood Corporation bought the hotel and the 4,500-acre ranch. This company is owned by millionairess Caroline Hunt Schoellkopf, who also owns three exclusive Texas hotels, plus L.A.'s Hotel Bel Air. She is the daughter of legendary oil tycoon H.L. Hunt, so she just happened to have the $20 million needed to buy the property.

Rosewood pumped nearly $25 million into renovations and they did an exquisite job. The 105 rooms, suites and cottages seem all beige and bamboo, very airy and light—something straight out of a decorator's magazine. All the perks are there—thick bathrobes, bathroom scales, coffee beans plus grinder and coffee pot, Hawaiian quilts on the king-sized beds, orchid plants in huge baskets.

It is expensive, but the price includes three meals a day—a necessity in Hana where there are few restaurants and inadequate food stores.

Expensive.

Hotel Hana Maui, Hana, HI 96713 • 248-8211 • 800) 421-0000 • (800) 252-0211 (in California)

Heavenly Hana Inn

You enter the property through a wooden Japanese gate guarded by two stone lions. A rock path leads to a house converted into an Oriental inn. There are too many knickknacks and clutter to call it a serene, simple ryokan. Still, it is peaceful and rustic...a quiet place in a quiet countryside.

There are only four units, each with two bedrooms. They're decorated with Japanese shoji screens, bamboo towel racks, Asian art, and some antique furniture. All four have small kitchen areas.

It's an eccentric looking, eclectic place with a lot of character. Price is very reasonable. It's two miles from town, so if that's too remote, the Inn has two separate cottages in town—a one-bedroom on a rocky beach and a family cottage near Hasegawa General Store that sleeps up to eight.

Budget.

P.O. Box 146, Hana, HI 96713 • 248-8442.

Joe's Place

This is an odd little place, but clean and cheap. The downstairs is all one flat—3 bedrooms, a living room, a large kitchen and a bath. It's decorated in funk—lime green carpet, plastic roses in an Aunt Jemima jar, dusty crocheted doll, etc. If you can live with the carpet, the price is definitely right.

Upstairs is split into five rooms. Only one has its own bathroom. The others share a bath. Three are very dinky with two twin beds; the fourth is slightly larger with a double and a single bed.

Owner Joe Akana lives right next door. If you want better units, he also rents two of the Hana Kai Resort condos at a moderate price. They're right across the street from Joe's Place.

Budget.

P.O. Box 536, Hana, HI 96713 • 248-7742.

CONDOS

Moderate Condos: On Bay

Though it's nearly 20 years old, the **Hana Kai Resort** looks quite modern. The 19 units are reasonably priced considering the location—on a rocky beach right on the bay. Both the 1-BR units and the studios are large and well done. The manicured grounds are beautiful. The most unusual feature is the spring fed pool...a small swimming pool built with lava rock.

P.O. Box 38, Hana, HI 96713 • 248-8426.

RENTAL HOMES AND COTTAGES

Aloha Cottages

This is a very homey place, aptly named Aloha. Owners Zenzo and Fusae Nakamura feed you papayas, bananas, avocados and lychees from their trees. Fusae washes your laundry and hangs it on her line. "If guests do their own, they waste a lot of time," she explains. "I want them to go out and enjoy themselves."

Fusae was born in Hana and is now "retired" from working in the school system as an aid. Zenzo was raised in Japan, but came to Hana in '49. He's been the local barber for more than 30 years. They live on the property. It's right in town with a close view of Hana Bay.

They keep their wooden cottages clean and simple. Each has a full electric kitchen. Furnishings are basic, but adequate. Three of the units have two bedrooms (and sleep six), and one is a studio.

Budget.

P.O. Box 205, Hana, HI 96713 • 248-8420.

Home O Hana

Just across the street from Aloha Cottages and a blink from Hana Bay is a 2-BR cottage and a 1-BR apartment run by John and Thelma Akana, Hana residents all their lives.

The Akanas live on the property and keep it neat as a pin. Neither apartment nor cottage are fancy, but both are very comfortable. If they're full, Thelma's sister next door has a 1-BR apartment that might be available.

Budget.

P.O. Box 477, Hana, HI 96713 • 248-7716.

Hana Kauhi

Coleen Church's parents run the eight Nona Lani cottages in Kihei, so when Coleen moved to Hana in the mid Seventies, she thought she could do the same—but on a smaller scale.

She and her family live on 5 acres on the airport road just .4 miles from the airport. They rent out a beautifully-done, wooden duplex cottage that's situated in a private area 200 feet from the Church's home.

The downstairs unit is a one bedroom with a double bed. Upstairs is a studio with two twin beds. Both have full kitchens and baths. The cottage is brand new and squeaky clean, obviously built with care.

Minimum stay of 3 nights in the 1 BR; no minimum for the studio.

Budget.

Box 296, Hana, HI 96713 • 248-7029.

Hana Bay Vacation Rentals

"We have quite a variety—we like to accommodate all pocket-books," says Suzanne Collins of her rental agency. She and husband Stan are the rental agents for nine homes and cottages in the Hana area.

Cheapest is a 1-BR wooden cabin with loft; most expensive is a 2-BR, 2-BA modern pole home with washer/dryer, dishwasher, stereo, color TV and a whirlpool spa on the encircling deck.

On request, the Collins send out a list describing their homes with a map showing where they are. All but one are right in Hana Town.

They claim to be booked all the time, but occasionally do have openings for overnighters.

Budget to mid-range.

P.O. Box 318, Hana, HI 96713 • 248-7727.

Hana Houses

Bobbie Sanders handles the rentals for three 1-BR homes in and near Hana. All three are in lovely spots and have at least an acre of land. One is right in Hana overlooking Hana Bay, another is near Waianapanapa State Park, another is just past Hamoa Beach on the highway outside town. All three have modern conveniences.

Mid-range.

P.O. Box 248, Hana, HI 96713 • 248-8976.

B & B

Kaia Ranch

There's no electricity here, just kerosene lamps. It's a country place with oodles of dogs and cats and horses roaming about. It's on 27 acres of land three miles from Hana town, one mile from the airport.

The house has a barebones, unfinished look about it. Floors are linoleum and the roof is tin. The guest room is huge and comfortable; it has one double and two twin beds, plus a large sitting area. The one bathroom is shared with the hosts.

Owner JoLoyce Kaia is a generous, accommodating woman willing to share her stories of Maui life. She and her husband and six of their eight kids lived on the land for two years in large tents while building their house. By the time the house was done, the kids were gone, so now they have room and time for guests.

Of her unique place, JoLoyce says, "It takes a special type of person to stay here—someone who enjoys farm life." (She "farms" flowers.)

Prefers a minimum of 2 nights. Budget.

P.O. Box 404, Hana, HI 96713 • 248-7725.

RESTAURANTS

The restaurant scene is quite sparse in Hana. You can either eat at the hotel or eat at the hotel. THE hotel meaning, of course, Hotel Hana Maui. The ranch restaurant is also run by the hotel people.

Restaurants don't do well in Hana because the locals eat at home, and restaurants need more than tourists to keep them going year round. The following three are the only three, but they are here to stay.

$ Budget

Tutu's: Located right on Hana Bay in the green civic center building.
This is an over-the-counter concession; seating at picnic tables in front. Food is basic—sandwiches, plate lunches, ice cream, snacks. Cherie Hanchett opened Tutu's in 1971 because Hana folk needed somewhere to eat. She just serves breakfast and lunch. No dinner, she says, because "this is Hana, ya? I tried dinner, but it didn't work. Nothing much happening at night in Hana." Hours: 9-4 daily. *248-8224.*

$$ Mid-Range

Hana Ranch Restaurant: You can buy over the counter from a chicken, beef, hamburger, hot dog type of menu, then eat outside on picnic tables. Or, you can eat inside the cheery restaurant. Lunch inside is a buffet or salad bar; dinner is a steak-chicken-fish a la carte menu. Breakfast is not served inside. Breakfast at the take-out counter daily, 6:30 to 10. Lunch from the take-out counter, daily 11-4; buffet lunch in the restaurant 11-3 daily. Dinner served only Fri. & Sat. nights, 6-10; last seating at 8:30. *Located up the hill by the post office • 248-8255.*

$$$ Expensive

Hotel Hana Maui Restaurant: Most diners at this beautiful restaurant are hotel guests, and their meals are included in their hotel bill. Nonguests are welcome, they just have to pay dearly for a meal...but the food is excellent, as is the service.

The hotel has arranged different dining experiences so their guests won't get bored with the same food. Tuesday nights they have a steak cook-out on Leho'ula Beach, Friday it's a lu'au on Hamoa Beach, and Wednesday and Sunday they offer an amazing buffet with local hula performers as entertainment. Reservations are a must for dinners. Breakfast and lunch can handle drop-ins. Hours: breakfast 7:30 to 10; lunch 11:30 to 2; dinner 6:30 to 8:30. *Located in the hotel • 248-8211.*

SHOPPING

If you're looking for souvenirs, this is not the town to buy them. If you're looking for clothes, this is not the town to buy them. There is no shopping district in Hana. Even grocery shopping is bleak here. There are two grocery stores—the Hana Ranch Store and Hasegawa's.

Hana Ranch Store is run by the same people who own the hotel and ranch. The store has more meat and produce than Hasegawa's, but it's not a very big grocery. Hours: 7 a.m. to 6:30 p.m. daily.

Hasegawa's is a very famous store; it even has a song written about it. It is a crazy, funky, everything sells and anything goes kind of place. In the front part you can buy groceries, bluejeans, whiskey, rifles, you name it; the back storehouse area is more utilitarian—barbed wire, chain saws, nails, horse shoes, etc. Harry Hasegawa sells it all under one roof because Hana folk need all this stuff. There's no other place to go for it. Located at the far end of town on the Hana Highway. Hours: 7:30 a.m. to 5:50 p.m.; Sundays 9 a.m. to 3:30 p.m., but Harry cautions that "we're not real prompt."

Maui Folk...
The Man, Not the Store

There is a real Hasegawa behind the famous store. In fact, Harry Hasegawa is the third generation of Hasegawas to live in Hana and run the town's most extensive, but eccentric store.

Harry's grandfather and his brother opened shop in 1910 after their sugar plantation contracts ran out.

"The idea then," says Harry, "was to come to Hawai`i, make your money and go back to Japan." But the brothers stayed on for a while. They saw an economic need and were smart enough to jump on it.

"There were a lot of Japanese in Hana then, and all the stores were run by the sugar plantations, and they didn't service the needs of the Oriental groups," Harry says. "They thought they could do well filling that need."

Grandfather and brother eventually did return home, leaving the store to Harry's father. They sent him a picture bride from Japan (Harry's mother). "They're still together," Harry laughs, when asked how things worked out. "They had four sons."

All the boys worked in the store growing up, but, Harry says, "The pace was nothing like what we have now. The volume was entirely different. Everything was strictly on a charge basis in those days. Everybody got paid once a month and that's when you got your money."

Being the oldest, Harry was expected to take over the store, and he did so with no hesitation. "It usually follows that the oldest does what the father wants," he says of the Japanese way.

He does not, however, expect his own son to necessarily follow suit. "We're working on him. But if he became a successful businessman somewhere else, we wouldn't ask him to come back."

For Harry though, the question was moot. He studied to be a CPA at the University of Colorado, worked in L.A. for a year, then did his time in the Army. "I saw enough to see that this was not too bad a life. In fact, it's a nice life," he says simply.

He went to college in Colorado because it was in the middle of the U.S. He figured he could

easily travel around and see the rest of the states.

"I had no idea what distance was. I have yet to go east of Colorado," Harry admits with a laugh. "It sounds funny, but I didn't know you could drive a car for days. The island was all I knew. The longest ride for me was three hours to Kahului."

Those were in the days when you'd meet 5 or 6 cars along the highway to Kahului. Now, there are hundreds of cars a day.

Even though Hasegawa's would get more business, Harry does not encourage increased traffic. "I wouldn't fix the road to get more tourists," he says. "You want San Francisco or Honolulu here? I'd rather go to those places. I don't want Hana to become them. We've got to stay the way we are to succeed.

"I'd say we're 10 to 30 years behind compared to the rest of the island. I like the slower pace better."

He does, however, hope some day to move his jammed and cluttered store to a larger, more modern building that he's planning down the street.

"We've been talking about it for 20 years. We need wider aisles; we need a more comfortable place to shop. We've got the property, but..." This is Hana; things take their own sweet time.

Besides, as Harry says, "We've got to keep the character of the store, and I don't want any heart attacks."

Kipahulu & Kaupo

The 10 miles between Hana and 'Ohe'o Gulch is perhaps the most beautiful drive in Maui, full of wondrously lush and spectacular scenery. The road itself is narrower and more twisty than the Hana road, so it is not for the faint hearted.

Tourists usually drive beyond Hana for two reasons—'Ohe'o Gulch and Lindberg's grave. But there are many other surprises along the way. In fact, it is fascinating to drive clear around East Maui on the Kaupo side (but only if your car can take it).

Kipahulu (where 'Ohe'o Gulch is located) is very rainy and fertile. Kaupo and beyond gets drier and drier until it is quite like a desert. Drastic changes of scenery happen within a few miles.

The Road

The road from Hana to Kipahulu is bad, but at least there is some semblance of asphalt on it. Just past Lindberg's grave in Kipahulu , pavement stops and gravel/dirt begins. For the next seven long miles into Kaupo and beyond, the road is unpaved.

Kaupo scenery is stark and rugged. Most of it is cattle country. Past the Kaupo Store the road remains unpaved and cranky for three miles. Even though it's paved from there on, until Keokea it's narrow, bumpy and full of potholes. Insurance companies do not want their rental cars out here, so they won't insure you if you get in a bind.

Sometimes you don't have the choice anyway. The road is often washed out and no one can even get to Kaupo, let alone get beyond it.

If your vehicle is up to it, the drive is worth it. It is desolate ranch country, but it has its own magnificent beauty.

HISTORY

Both Kipahulu and Kaupo districts were populated in ancient times. Fishing villages and heiau sites are scattered throughout the area. None are marked, and most take some hunting to find.

In a barren area past Kaupo are traces of a very large village called Kahikinui (meaning "great Tahiti"). It is now in ruins, of course, but the numerous house sites indicate its size. The village remains cannot be seen from the road, and they are difficult to find. Plus, they are on private ranchland, and trespassers are not appreciated.

Several old churches along the Kipahulu-Kaupo road (many of them now abandoned) prove that the missionaries were after souls even way out here.

In the typical Maui scenario, missionary times were followed by sugar blues...from fighting Cain to raising cane. All that's left of the Kipahulu Sugar Mill is a smokestack and a few concrete remains. No longer is there a large population. Kaupo, in fact, has less than 100 residents.

SIGHTS

Helio's Cross

Located on a high promontory in the Wailua district, this large white cross marks the grave of Helio Koa'eloa, who was born in this valley. As a young man he heard of the Catholic religion and it seized his imagination. Catholic priests were not yet allowed on Maui, so he paddled a canoe to Honolulu to learn the faith. He spent the rest of his life back on Maui converting thousands of Hawaiians. When he died in 1848 his body was brought back to the valley of his birth.

'Ohe'o Gulch

Often called Seven Sacred Pools, an incorrect appellation given it years ago to promote tourism. No one knows whodunnit or why "seven" and "sacred" were pulled out of the hat. Call it 'Ohe'o, that's the true name (pronounced o hay o).

There are, in fact, more than 20 pools along the first mile of 'Ohe'o Stream from the ocean up. It is a gorgeous area of ocean cliffs, pools, waterfalls, pasture land and bamboo forests. Great for hikers.

The pools and streams are fun to swim in, but heed the words of the National Park Service:

> "'Ohe'o Stream has been known to rise 4 feet in 10 minutes. If you see the water level rising, get out fast! Never swim during high water.
>
> "An invisible layer of extremely slippery microorganisms coat rocks in and near Hawaiian streams. Be extra careful around wet rocks.
>
> "Hidden rocks, ledges, shifting boulders, gravel bands and turbid water make diving dangerous."

'Ohe'o is part of Kipahulu Valley, the second of the three large valleys on this side of Haleakala. Kipahulu Valley became part of Haleakala National Park in 1969, thus ensuring its conservation. Part of the upper valley (difficult to reach and closed to the public) is home to many rare native birds and plants.

Lindbergh's Grave

Though most residents wish people would not bother his simple grave, many tourists are keen on seeing the final resting spot of famous aviator Charles Lindbergh—first man to fly solo across the Atlantic.

Lindbergh spent his last years living on five acres in Kipahulu with his wife Anne. He thought the area was one of the most beautiful places on earth. When East Coast doctors diagnosed his final illness as cancer, he told them he'd rather live one day in Maui than a month in New York. He then flew home to die (in August of 1974).

The famous man's simple funeral was attended by 15 people. His grave is in the cemetery of Ho'omau Congregational Church, built in 1857. In typical Hawaiian style, his grave is covered with small, smooth lava stones. On his marker are these words from Psalm 139: *If I take the wings of the morning, and dwell in the uttermost parts of the sea.*

The church is one mile from 'Ohe'o on the makai side. It is not marked and not clearly seen from the road.

Souvenir hunters are reminded to leave everything in place.

Kaupo Gap

The largest of the three valleys on this side of Haleakala. It is possible to walk from the crater down the Gap to Kaupo or vice versa (walk up). It is an unrelentlessly steep, tough hike. Occasionally knees go out and toenails pop off. It is a glorious hike, but be in shape for it. Linda Domen at the Kaupo Store tells of many a hiker who crawls in on his/her knees.

SHOPPING

Yes, it's true, there is a store way out here in no man's land. And a long-lived, famous one at that. The **Kaupo Store** has a small amount of merchandise, but a big history.

The current structure was built in 1925 by Nicholas Yee Soon. His uncle built the original store in 1886. This was a hard-working Chinese family—they had other stores in Kipahulu, Nahiku, Ke'anae and Honolulu.

Nick Soon was an interesting and clever character. He studied via mail and learned to build his own windmill, his own clocks, radios, telephones, even Model T Fords. He ordered car parts from the

Mainland, then assembled them himself. He could not even drive until he built his first Model T. Soon continued to run the store until 1975, then died the next year.

Linda Domen and her family now own the historic store. She tries to keep the traditional hours of 10:30 a.m. to 4:30 p.m., but when the road's washed out and few cars pass by, she reduces her hours...sometimes to just an hour a day.

What next?

There is no other store or food stand from here until Keokea—27.5 miles away. Sounds like a short distance, but on the Kaupo Road it's a good hour. Keokea only has two small groceries; the closest restaurants are in Pukalani, 38.5 miles from Kaupo.

Maui Folk...
Smiling Eddie

Park ranger Eddie Pu has seen a lot of people come through 'Ohe'o since he started as a ranger in 1972. Once a few hundred came a month. Now that many and more come every day.

Does he mind? "Not really," he says with his characteristic smile. "They make my day. The more people the better for me. I love them all. People are people. They'll keep coming, so all we can do is accept them.

"I guess there are too many," he will admit when pressed, "but there's nothing you can do about it. How can you stop people from coming?"

Pu (pronounced "pooh"), who was born in Hana, feels a responsibility to welcome visitors with Hawaiian aloha. "That's my purpose for being here," he says simply. "This is my roots. I ran around here as a kid, not knowing how valuable the park would be today."

He sees the national park system as land preservation for tomorrow's children. And he has one wish for the tourists of today—"I hope that all visitors take something back with them," he says. "Love of the land."

He thinks 'Ohe'o and the Kipahulu Valley easily give this gift, if people tune in to it, as Eddie himself has done over the years.

"For me," he says, "it's a spiritual thing. There's lots of good energy here. Sometimes we lose feelings or faith in ourselves because we haven't done what we're supposed to do. But if one walks into the valley, the valley cleanses. It gives me a better energy for the day.

"I sense that the land provides energy. Every morning when I get up, I look out towards the east and say, 'Thank you, Lord, for this beautiful morning. Thank you for giving us this sun.' That's where my energy comes from—the sun, the land.

"When I come to the park, I think, `Aina (land) accept me for this morning. I'm coming through. And I may not be humble today, but let me receive your energy into my body so I can share with all who come into the Park.'

"When I first came here as a ranger," he continues, "I couldn't blend in with the environment. But after a year or two went by, it became so simple. I understood.

"The land gives me all the energy. Twelve hours of talking...doesn't matter."

Eddie seems always to have a smile on his happy face. As he explains it: "People ask why am I always smiling? I don't know that I am. Smile...it gives me...hard to explain. When the wind blows, the leaves are waving—they're smiling. When you throw a rock into a pool and the ripples go out—the water is smiling. That's the energy. That's what I call my energy."

Eddie thinks the highlight of 'Ohe'o is the four-mile Waimoku Falls hike—across a cow pasture, over a stream bed, through a bamboo forest, finally dead-ending at Waimoku Falls. It's unique, but it's more than many people want to undertake. Most visitors hang out at the lower pools. Thus, so does Eddie Pu.

He was hired as the water safety officer, and has saved 5 people from drowning in the ocean below the pools. Before coming to 'Ohe'o, Eddie was a lifeguard for 21 years at Hamoa Beach, and there he saved countless people.

For his courage at 'Ohe'o, Eddie was given a Valor Award in Washington, D.C. The trip, he says, "was the thrill of my life. I never thought I would see Washington, D.C. I had studied about this place in high school. I will never forget it." For once Eddie Pu could be the tourist.

His award and his ranger work at 'Ohe'o—he ties it up eloquently with this parting statement: "I'm just a simple Hawaiian. I like to do for the people."

Central Maui

This is the isthmus between two great volcanoes. East and West Maui join here...a bridge across the water. Lava from both volcanoes spilled down until the two mountains laced together.

It has not always been so. Many times during the past million years the sea has risen above the isthmus, flooding it and leaving the two volcanoes as separate islands.

The rock-hard sand dunes present on the isthmus had their start during the Ice Ages. The then lower seas exposed large amounts of sand, which blew with the tradewinds into dunes. It is on these dunes that rest two of the greatest heiau in Maui. From their high perch, these ancient temples oversee the whole of Wailuku and Kahului...the past keeping tabs on the present.

Meanings of Place Names

Kahului	"the winning"
Wailuku	"waters of destruction"
Ma'alaea	"where the ma'a wind begins"

Kahului

There's nothing old Hawaiian about Kahului. This is modern Maui. Much of the town is devoted to tract homes, shopping centers and office space...it's a very utilitarian place. Maui's workers live here. The town was built for them in the 1950s.

HISTORY

Kamehameha I landed his war canoes in Kahului's harbor when he came to battle for Maui in 1790. He chased Maui's warriors up 'Iao Stream and brutally defeated them.

In later years the harbor became Maui's chief port since it's the only deep water harbor in the island.

The small town that grew up around the harbor was infected with bubonic plague in 1900. The town was purposely burned to the ground to destroy the rats that carry the disease.

"Dream City"

The major town that Kahului is today was created in a planned development scheme by brothers Frank and Harry Baldwin. Alexander & Baldwin, Ltd., owned the land, so the brothers decided to build a "Dream City" affordable to plantation workers.

A & B wanted out of its "landlord" role of providing free plantation camp housing, and workers were eager to own their own homes.

In 1949, when construction on Kahului began, there were 66 plantation camps (with about 4,000 basic wooden homes) located near A & B's mills. These camps dwindled as Kahului sold.

Building started in 1949 with the first house and lot selling by the following year. Within the next 13 years all the houses sold quickly. Prices ranged between $6,600 and $9,200.

Kahului became the first successful new town development in Hawai'i. "Dream City" might not look like a dream to outsiders, but affordable housing is definitely a dream for Maui residents.

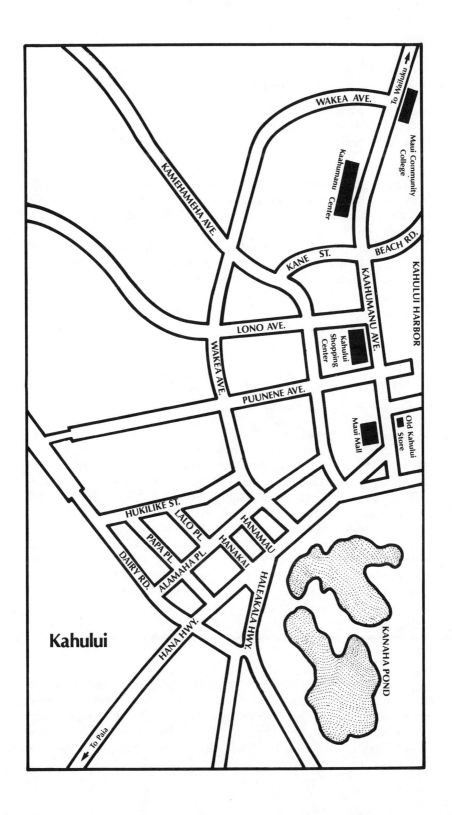

Kahului

WAKEA AVE.

To Wailuku

Maui Community College

Kaahumanu Center

KAMEHAMEHA AVE.

KANE ST.

BEACH RD.

KAHULUI HARBOR

KAAHUMANU AVE.

LONO AVE.

WAKEA AVE.

Kahului Shopping Center

PUUNENE AVE.

Maui Mall

Old Kahului Store

HUKILIKE ST.

LALO PL.

PAPA PL.

HANAMAU

HANAKAI

ALAMAHA PL.

DAIRY RD.

HALEAKALA HWY.

HANA HWY.

To Paia

KANAHA POND

BEACHES & PARKS

Kahului Harbor

Don't bother, don't even consider it, forget it. Murky and polluted. Why swim here?—view and water are much nicer down the road.

Kanaha Pond

Located at the junction of Haleakala and Hana Highways (36 & 396), this wildlife refuge was once a royal fish pond, supposedly built by King Kiha-a-pi'ilani in the early 1700s, and used later by Kamehameha I.

In ancient times it was kapu to catch ocean fish for 3 to 5 months of the year while fish were breeding, but there was no kapu on pond fish. Kings and chiefs would fatten their favorite breeds of fish in the pond.

Most Hawaiian fishponds had brackish water, but Kanaha is fed by fresh water springs. Thus, it attracts waterfowl, some who migrate from as far as Russia and Alaska.

Since 1952 the pond has been a waterfowl refuge, harboring a large number of Hawaiian stilt and Hawaiian coot. Herons, ducks, cattle egret, plovers, and many others paddle around the pond.

Its ancient importance has been formally recognized; it is now a National Natural Historic Landmark.

Kanaha Beach Park

This is a long strip of golden beach fronted by a nice grassy park. There are three cul-de-sac turnoffs to the park, each one leading to the same beach. On windy days the beach can be crowded with windsurfers, but on still days it's quite empty. Swimming is safe because the bottom is shallow and sandy, but the water is often murky. It's a great jogging/walking beach; it stretches unbroken for a good mile or two and runs right into Spreckelsville Beach (where you can continue your exercise).

To get there, take Keolani Place (the airport road) to the airport. Turn left at a green sign that says "Car rental return turn left." There is also a small blue Kanaha Park sign at the intersection. The airport being so close, there is a constant rumble of jets in the background.

Facilities: toilets, showers, picnic tables, BBQ grills, paved parking.

Spreckelsville Beach

Claus Spreckels planted sugar here in 1878 and soon became a millionaire sugar magnate. There's no plantation in Spreckelsville now, but there is money. It's a pricey, exclusive place to own property. Willie Nelson has a home here. Expensive beachfront homes and the Maui Country Club line the beach. Still, there is public access—best found by turning off the Hana Highway on Spreckelsville Beach Road or Nonohe Place (look for the two stone pillars).

The beach is not as good as Kanaha down the road. The sand at Spreckelsville is eroding and it is a bit rocky.

No facilities.

Hoaloha Park

Across from the Kahului Shopping Center is this run-down looking park. It's essentially just a big lawn area fronted by the ocean. The park is mainly used by local people.

Facilities: two portable toilets, concrete picnic tables.

HOTELS

A four-block strip along Kahului's main drag (Ka'ahumanu) is motel row. Here are the town's only tourist accommodations. All are clean, honest places with budget to moderate rooms.

They line up right next to each other along the busiest street in Kahului, but are set far enough back from the road so they're quiet. The best shopping centers on Maui are directly across the street.

Behind the hotels is Kahului Harbor. Each hotel has a little beach on the harbor. Not a good idea to swim (though some do)—the bay is murky. Views tend to be of cargo ships rather than sunsets.

Maui Palms

This is the oldest hotel in Kahului, built in 1953. There's a large, rather plain lawn area behind the hotel, plus, there's a pool.

The 11 low-rise concrete block buildings still have a Fifties' motel-like style—not fancy, just functional. The 103 rooms are large and clean...a good buy for the money.

Budget.

150 Ka'ahumanu Avenue, Kahului, HI 96732 • 877-0071.

Maui Beach

This is the fanciest and most expensive of the four hotels on the strip. It's right next door to its sister hotel, the Maui Palms. Both are managed by Hawaiian Pacific Resorts. Maui Beach is newer and costlier. Still, it's reasonable...has both budget and mid-range rooms, depending on the view.

Its 154 rooms are in one U-shaped, two-story building that faces Kahului Bay. The hotel has a small swimming pool on its second floor.

Budget to mid-range.

170 Ka'ahumanu Avenue, Kahului 96732 • 877-0051.

Hukilau

This hotel and its neighbor, Maui Seaside, are operated by the same management (Sand and Seaside Hotels—an island chain). They share the same office phone, registration desk, pool and restaurant.

The Hukilau is older, less attractive and less expensive than the Seaside. The Hukilau's 81 rooms are in two long low-rise buildings that face each other across a simple yard and pool. Rooms are clean, freshly painted with tiled baths (tub and shower). Motel like, but adequate.

Budget.

100 Ka'ahumanu Avenue, Kahului, HI 96732 • 877-3311 • (800) 367-7000.

Seaside

You have to cut through the Hukilau to get to the Seaside—a three-story white building next door. It looks like an apartment building, and, in fact, it once was.

The 110 rooms here are bigger and nicer than the Hukilau's, thus they cost about $10 more. They have two double beds and a small refrigerator. Baths have both tub and shower.

Budget.

100 Ka'ahumanu Ave., Kahului, HI 96732 • 877-3311 • (800) 367-7000.

RESTAURANTS

$ Budget

Ichiban's: Very inexpensive, simple place with basic Japanese food—teriyaki, donburi, noodle dishes, sashimi. Hours: 7 a.m. to 2 p.m.; dinner 5-9. *Kahului Shopping Center • 871-6977.*

Ming Yuen: A favorite for its service and its cooking—both Cantonese and Szechuan. So predictably good and popular it's a Kahului institution. Food is excellent. Take-out is available—just call ahead. Hours: 11:30 a.m. to 9 p.m. M-Sat.; 5-9 p.m. Sun. *162 Alamaha St. • 871-7787.*

Idini's: It's a deli, a cafe, a wine shop and a bar all in one. There's even entertainment some nights. Very popular and crowded at lunch; it's a place to see and be seen. Pastries are great; salad bar is good. Soups and sandwiches are always tops. Breakfasts are capuccino and croissant affairs. Hours: M,T,W, Sat. 7 a.m. to 9 p.m.; Th & F 7 a.m. to 10 p.m.; Sun. 8 a.m. to 5 p.m. *Ka'ahumanu Center • 877-3978.*

Aloha Restaurant: Known for its Hawaiian food. It's a family-run eatery that has been around since the 1940s. Here you can try kalua pig, poi, lomi salmon, lau lau, loko—all Hawaiian dishes. They also have

American food for queasy stomachs. Sunday brunch is a Hawaiian buffet for under $10—served all day and night from 11 a.m. till 9 p.m. Hours: 11 a.m. to 9:30 p.m. daily. *127 Pu'unene Avenue • 877-6318.*

Coconuts: Kahului had no health food restaurant until Coconuts opened in 1986. The food is excellent, cooked with care, and it's very cheap. The menu is salads, sandwiches, fresh juice, smoothies, gourmet coffee, plus breakfast. It's not a sit-down restaurant; you order food over a counter and sit at tables in the mall's courtyard. Hours: 7 a.m. to 5:30 p.m. except Sunday. *Kahului Shopping Center • 871-4512.*

Lopaka's: The restaurant has a fresh pine wood interior with a high ceiling...very clean and Swiss looking. Food is plain American fare—roast beef, fish and fries, deep fried shrimp, ribs, fish, steak. Their hamburger was rated one of the "best" on the island by a local magazine. Lunch is popular with Kahului workers. Hours: 11 a.m. to 10 p.m. M-F; closed weekends. *161 Alamaha St. • 871-1135.*

Sir Wilfred's: Started with the idea of a tobacco shop and an espresso coffee bar, but now it's much more. Salads, sandwiches, quiche, breakfast served at any hour—the food is good and the ambiance is chic (for Maui). Attracts a local stylishly-hip crowd, plus anyone else who likes good coffee. They sell the beans too, more than 30 types. Hours: M-Th 9 a.m. to 6:30 p.m.; Fri. 9 a.m. to 9 p.m.; Sat. 9 a.m. to 5:30 p.m.; Sun. 10 a.m. to 4:30 p.m. *Maui Mall • 877-3711.*

Artful Dodger's Feed 'N Read: A coffee shop and book store. Food is light fare, mostly sandwiches and pastries. It's a great place to sit for hours reading or talking. The crowd here is different than at Wilfred's; Dodger's group is a more beatnik, literary type. Hours: M-F 7:30-7:30; Sat. 9:30 a.m. to 7:30; Sun. 10-6. *55 Ka'ahumanu Avenue • 871-2677.*

Safeway: The ubiquitous grocery store has a deli and it's open 24 hours ...very rare on Maui. Deli food—sandwiches, cheeses, salads, enchiladas, fish dishes, and much more. *170 Kamehameha Ave. • 877-3377.*

$$ Mid-Range

The Chart House: They have a great reputation, plus they have a wonderful, spacious, airy building on the less than wonderful Kahului Bay. But you go for food, not the view. The salad bar is beautiful; the simple fish, steak, crab, lobster food is always plentiful and excellent. The mud pie is beyond words (and they even give you their recipe). Hours: 5:30-10 p.m. daily. *500 N. Pu'unene Avenue • 877-2476.*

Island Fish House: Consistently good; known for its fresh fish. Menu also includes steak and chicken dishes. Nicely done interior. There's always a classic old car parked out front. Hours: lunch M-F 11 to 2; dinner M-Sat. 5:30 to 9. *33 Lono Avenue • 871-7555.*

SHOPPING

Kahului Shopping Center (Ka'ahumanu & Lono Avenues)

This was the first mall on Maui. When it was built in 1951, it was the center of town. It was part of the planned community of "Dream City," a place for the sugar workers to shop. The mall is a bit old and creaky now, but still functioning with some odd and uniquely Maui stores. It is also a gathering place for local men to sit and talk or gamble. If the shopping doesn't intrigue you, go for the local experience of the mall and these men.

Peggy and Johnny's clothing store and Toda's Drugs are relics from the Fifties. Both opened when the mall was built, and they've lasted through time. **Peggy and Johnny's** has very functional, workers' clothes—apparel that doesn't change with fashion. Hours: M,T,W,Th,Sat. 9-5; Fri. 9-6; Sun. 10-2.

Toda's Drugs has the feel of an old-fashioned American drug store complete with fountain where they serve up basic, inexpensive food from the old green formica counter. Hours: 8-5:30 weekdays; 8-5 Sat.; 8-12 Sun.

Other old timers in the mall are the two groceries—**Noda** and **Ah Fook**. Both are very local stores, so they lean heavily towards local food (that includes Chinese, Japanese, Filipino, Korean, Hawaiian, fresh fish, local produce). Noda's hours are: M,T,W,Th,Sat. 6-6; Fri. 6-8; Sun. 6-12. Ah Fook's hours are: M-F 8-8; Sat. 8-7; Sun. 8-4.

Most of the stores here are quite small and specialized. **Golden Palette**, for instance, is a tiny art supply shop, one of the few places on island that sells art supplies. Hours: 9-5 M-F; 9-4 Sat.

The **Island Biker** is one of two bicycle shops on Maui. They sell Univega, Specialized and MT Racing brands. They also have numerous kids' bikes and scooters, plus the Da Hon folding bike. They take used bikes as trade-ins and sell them, and they do repairs.

Anyone looking for used furniture, dishes or appliances should check out **Big G's** large and cluttered joint. This is the biggest and best used store on Maui. Hours: M-F 9-4:30; Sat. 9-3.

Maui Mall (Ka'ahumanu & Puunene Avenues)

Built in 1970, this mall is anchored by three large stores—**Long's Drugs, Star Market** (grocery) and **Woolworths.** Most stores in the complex stick to these hours: M-Th 9-6; Fri. 9-9; Sat. 9-5:30; Sun. 10-4.

However, the big three (Long's, Star and Woolworth) generally open earlier and close later.

The **Hobby Habit** is the only hobby store on island. **Waldenbooks** is one of three Waldens on Maui. Good selection of Hawai'i and Maui books.

Rainbow Beauty Supply has girlie things galore—curlers, hair dyes, rinses, brushes, shampoos, make-up and nail polish.

WOW is a mix and match swimsuit store. Size 10 bottom and size 6 top? They can suit you up, and their styles are the latest and snazziest. Go right next door to get a mu'u mu'u to cover your suit. **Island Mu'u Mu'u Works** is a large shop with the biggest selection and lowest prices of long dresses on Maui. They also have men's aloha shirts, plus T-shirts depicting Hawai'i's endangered birds.

Amazon women will be glad to know about **Judge's Place**, a stylish clothing store that specializes in large sizes (12-52). **Baby's Choice** has the opposite—tiny sizes from zero to size 6. The clothes are darling, and very few are Hawaiian designs...nice for locals who might prefer a sailor suit to a tropical dress.

The Old Kahului Store (across street from Maui Mall)

The structure was built in 1916, but it's now renovated and houses the most unique shops in Kahului.

The **Artful Dodger**'s motto is "Feed 'N Read." It's a coffee shop and book store, mostly used books. It's a wonderful, spacious place, popular with Maui's literary, hip folks. Easy place to pick up a chess partner, perfect spot to read the Sunday paper. Local entertainment often plays, and there's always a changing display of local art hanging. Tuesday evenings anyone can join in—it's open mike night. Hours are: M-F 7:30 to 7:30; Sat. 9:30 to 7:30; Sun.10-6. Hours aren't strict, though. Many nights run later when there's a poetry reading or a band playing.

Tiger Lily is the best, classiest women's clothing store on this side of the island. Working women with style shop here. The clothes are not Maui at all, they're more San Francisco. Hours: 10-6; closed Sunday.

Bamboo Breeze is an old lace, Japanese kimono, Hawaiian shirt, chunky costume jewelry kind of place. Eclectic, but beautifully done. They also make cotton-filled futons and pillows to order. Hours: weekdays 10-6; Sat. 10-5; closed Sunday.

Most Maui surfing shops are devoted to windsurfing. **Lightning Bolt** is one of the few that specializes in board surfing. All their boards are handmade, most done in O'ahu, some in California. They also carry sportswear (men and women's) for all ocean-oriented sports. Hours: 10 to 5:30 M-Th, 10 to 6 Fri., 10 to 5 Sat., 11 to 3 Sunday.

Ka'ahumanu Center   (Ka'ahumanu & Wakea Ave.)

This is Maui's largest, most modern mall. In fact, it's the largest shopping center in Hawai'i outside Honolulu. There's one of everything here—Computerland, Waldenbooks, Phone Mart, Dairy Queen, Baskin Robbins, Zales Jewelry, Merle Norman Cosmetics, Hopaco Stationery, Crafts Drugs, Ben Franklin, to name a few. It's anchored by Sears on one end, Liberty House on the other. Hours are: M,T,W 9-5:30; Th & F 9-9; Sat. 9-5:30; Sun. 10-3.

Shirokiya is one of the three department stores here. This is a branch of the large Tokyo store which is Japan's oldest department store (opened in 1662 as a notions shop). All merchandise is from Japan—jewelry, TVs, clothes, luggage, vacuum cleaners, toys, dishes, even food.

Honsport has equipment for nearly every sport, including weight machines for muscle builders. They also carry sports clothes and shoes.

Only items made in Maui are sold at **Maui's Best.** This cute little shop does not focus on arts and crafts; instead, it carries gift items like kid's clothing, handpainted T-shirts, coffee, candies, jewelry, books, quilted pillows, etc.

Nani Pacifica is a tiny store filled to overflowing with trendy knickknacks and gift items. They have a constant display of Christmas decorations, and they're the only place on island that sells miniature doll house items.

111 Hana Highway

The Cycle and Sport Shop sells and repairs bicycles. The brands they stock include Nishiki, Montana, KHS and Cyclepro. Hours: 9 to 5:30 except Sunday.

If you need to rent equipment, **Canyon Rent to Own** is the place. You can simply rent or rent-to-buy any number of items—TVs, VCRs, stereo, refrigerators, washer-dryers, microwave ovens. Hours: 10-7; closed Sunday.

Across the highway and down a bit (at 230 Hana Highway) is **Nevada Bob's**, a tennis and golf store with the largest selection of equipment on the island.

Maui Swap Meet

This is the biggest flea market on Maui. Held every Saturday from 8 a.m. to 1 p.m. at the County Fairgrounds at Pu'unene Avenue near Wakea Avenue. Typical flea market—everything sold from vegetables to old junk.

Wailuku

At a major corner in downtown Wailuku (Market & Vineyard) is a ramshackle, abandoned building. It belongs in a western ghost town, not in the Maui of Wailea and Ka'anapali. But this is precisely the charm of Wailuku. It is old Hawai'i....sometimes funky, always local, never touristy.

Wailuku is the county seat. Yet even government buildings cannot make this a high-powered town. Wailuku is sleepy and casual, old-fashioned and gracious. The back streets with their simple wooden houses seem straight from the plantation era.

Wailuku feels like a Hawaiian town. It looks like one too. Much of the old town area (on High Street around the 1907 Court House) is on the Register of Historic Places. Market Street is being preserved with its old wooden facades intact.

Why is it named "waters of destruction?" Wailuku sits at the base of the West Maui Mountains. The mountains attract clouds, and rain is frequent in the peaks. 'Iao Stream, which runs through Wailuku, often flooded...thus, "waters of destruction." Now, however, lower 'Iao Stream is usually dry. Most of its water is diverted to aqueducts that irrigate cane fields. As added protection, concrete walls were built along part of the stream to contain flood waters.

HISTORY

Two massive heiau stand on sand dunes overlooking modern Wailuku. These temple/fortresses are reminders of what once was. From this perch high on the dunes, Maui kings and their warriors could see in every direction.

No one knows how old the heiau are or how long people lived here. But it is assumed that ancient villages flanked the sand dunes.

It is known that Kahekili, the great Maui king of the 1700s, occasionally lived at the Wailuku heiau. Keopuolani, a tabu chiefess of high rank, was born here. Kamehameha I, who became her husband, used the heiau in 1790 to call on his war god after conquering Maui.

Wailuku Town c. 1890

Maui Historical Society

Missionaries & Money

Modern Wailuku began with the coming of the first missionaries to the area in the 1820s. Much of the old religion died or went underground. The heiau were deserted and destroyed. Attention now focused on the mission. People began to settle near the church and the town of Wailuku began to grow.

The most prominent of the Wailuku missionaries were Edward and Caroline Bailey. They came to run the first Hawaiian girls' school on the island. Reason for educating girls?—so they'd be proper young ladies, suitable for the lads they'd been educating across the island at Lahainaluna School since 1831. The girls' school lasted from 1833 to 1849, then funding ran out and the school shut down.

Edward Bailey quit mission work and turned to business and building. He designed and built a church. He supervised road and bridge building. He settled land claims for the government. He taught music, and he painted landscapes of Maui. His paintings hang on the walls of his former home (now a museum).

By the 1860s sugar was the focus in the central plains. The Wailuku Sugar Company was founded, and Edward Bailey, jack of all trades, became its first manager. Bailey designed a water-run mill to grind sugar and wheat. With Bailey's mill, the company was able to manufacture the first sugar in Wailuku.

For the next century, the whole center of the island was planted with sugar cane. A two-mile railroad took sugar from the mill to Kahului's port.

Eventually, however, sugar was not a viable crop. The mill closed in 1979. Now the main employer in town is the government. Wailuku is the civic center, the county seat of Maui. Tourism is not big here, so without the government offices, Wailuku might well be a ghost town.

SIGHTS

Pihana & Halekii Heiau

A bit hard to find, but worth the search. Both heiau sit on a high sand dune with a spectacular view of Wailuku. These two Hawaiian temples are some of the most important Hawaiian sites on Maui. Their age is unknown, but they could be ancient structures. Both are massive temples, built from smooth, water-worn rocks probably collected from 'Iao Stream.

The heiau closest to the parking lot is Halekii. It measures 300 by 150 feet, and was partially reconstructed in 1958. Hale means house, ki'i means image. There probably were one or more chiefs' houses within the temple, and carved images (ki'i) of gods undoubtedly guarded the heiau.

Some believe there were several houses at the base of Halekii with more house sites located between the two heiau. Chiefs and kings certainly did live here. It's possible that the entire dune was reserved for ali'i. The ruling chiefs could isolate themselves here during times of crisis.

Pihana-a-ka-lani is the full name of Pihana heiau; it means "gathering place of the kings." It is 300 by 120 feet, slightly smaller than Halekii. People lived here, but they also died here. It was a sacrificial temple. Pihana is just beyond Halekii, higher up on the dune. It's difficult to see much of it. It is not reconstructed and it's covered with sand and foliage.

Both heiau are on the National Register of Historic Places, and the site is a State Park.

Directions: Take Waiehu Beach Road over a bridge that crosses a dried-up stream bed, turn left at Kuhio Place, then left at Hea Place where a sign points the way up to the park.

Ka'ahumanu Church

This gracious, white stone church with its old-fashioned spire is a Wailuku landmark. Completed in 1876, it is the fourth church built on the site. Queen Ka'ahumanu, Kamehameha's powerful wife, visited the first church (a thatched shed) in 1832 and asked that the finished church be named for her. The land around the church once belonged to King Kahekili, Maui's brave warrior king of the 1700s. His personal heiau supposedly stood where the church now stands.

Honoli'i Park

Right on the corner at Main and High Streets, this tiny park was once the property of King Kahekili. His house was across the street where the police motorpool is now located.

Bailey House a.k.a Hale Ho'ike'ike

Hale Ho'ike'ike means "house of display," and it is—it's a museum housed in an old missionary home once inhabited by the Bailey family. Construction began on the house in 1833 and continued until 1850 when the third floor was added.

This was the residence of Edward and Caroline Bailey, missionaries who came to run the Wailuku Female Seminary. The school was open from 1833 to 1849; then money became tight and the girls' school was the first to lose funding.

It was unusual to educate girls at the time, anyway. A major reason for doing so was to make them suitable companions for the boys at Lahainaluna School. They learned "employments suited to their sex" (manners, sewing, weaving, cooking, religion, etc.).

The school dining room is still intact; it stands next to the house. The school building no longer exists; it was made of adobe and was not strong enough to last.

The Baileys and their five sons lived here until 1885 when they left for California. The place now houses a museum run by the Maui Historical Society. The first floor has a display of Hawaiian artifacts; the second floor shows how furnished rooms looked in the 1850s.

Museum open 10 a.m. to 4:30. Donation requested.

Tong Society

The Chee King Tong Society was a Chinese fraternity that immigrant sugar workers transplanted to Maui. It was a political organization in China, but in Maui it was a social group. The "clubhouse" building is a wooden Victorian at 2151 Vineyard (quite similar to the Tong building in Lahaina). It now looks like a haunted house—boarded up and dilapidated. No one has yet restored it.

'Iao Theater

Built in 1927, this charming old classic is the oldest theater in Maui. Back then, the 750 seats went for 25 cents for general admission and 50 cents for reserved. Films, bingo games, high school graduations, political rallies, singing contests...the theater has housed them all over the years.

There was once serious talk of gutting the old building and putting offices and shops in it. Then the Maui Community Theatre started using it as their headquarters, and such talk ended. The MCT usually has a play in progress. The accoustics are good, so the stage is still set for plays, performances and occasional lectures.

Painting by Cynthia Conrad

Maui Tropical Plantation

Claims to be Maui's number one tourist attraction...proof that agriculture does not have to be a dull game. It's located outside Wailuku near the small town of Waikapu on Highway 30. The plantation shows visitors how pineapple, sugar cane, macadamia nuts, guavas, bananas, etc. are grown. A 30-minute tram ride tours through the various fields with a guide giving details of all the crops.

There's also a restaurant, a plant nursery and a large souvenir store. It's all geared for tourists...bit of a tourist trap, but very well done.

Barbeques with an entertaining Western show are staged every Monday and Wednesday at 5:30 p.m. Square dancing held a half hour earlier. Reservations required for the dinner and show (244-7643). The Plantation is open daily from 9 to 5.

OLD CIVIC BUILDINGS

Courthouse
Hawai'i became a U.S. Territory in 1898. The islands of Maui, Lana'i and Moloka'i were lopped together into one county six years later. The courthouse was built in 1907 to handle county business. It was wired for electricity when built, but the lights didn't come on for five years (when electricity became available). Many immigrants made a pilgrimage to the Courthouse to become U.S. citizens. The building now stands empty.

Old Police Station
Near the Courthouse on the corner of High & Kaohu (opposite the library), this was built in 1924 as the county building. At that time Wailuku was booming—it had 5 hotels, 132 new businesses, 9 churches and 4 movie theaters. Later the building housed the police station, but now it's empty, waiting for county offices to fill it up.

Public Library
Built in 1929, the library has a large collection of Hawaiian books, and a very helpful staff of librarians.

Territorial Building
Across from the Courthouse, this was built in 1930 to handle increasing government business. It now houses the state agriculture department.

BEACHES & PARKS

Waiehu Beach Park
Just outside Wailuku on Waiehu Beach Road is the small local community of Waiehu. To find the beach/park area, turn right on Lower Waiehu Beach Road (just past the Church of Christ church).

This is a small, rocky, narrow strip of beach, often quite deserted. The park area and the pavilion are run down; they don't look well tended. It's not a great beach or park.

Facilities: pavilion, toilets, showers, picnic tables, BBQ.

Waihe'e Beach Park
On down the same road is the local community of Waihe'e. To find the beach, follow the signs to the Waiehu Golf Course. The beach is right next to the golf course.

This is a grassy park fronted by a nicer beach than in Waiehu (are all these Wai words making you crazy?). It is a narrow, long strip of a beach, often deserted, with great views...not a building in sight.

Swimming is okay, but the bottom is rocky.

Facilities: toilets, showers, picnic tables, paved parking, grassy park area.

HOTELS

The only hotels in Wailuku town are all budget range. Each of the three hotels oozes character, and their proprietors are all characters themselves...friendly, a bit eccentric, and definitely individuals.

Wailuku Grand

Only a small sign by Hazel's Cafe indicates that there's a hotel behind and above the cafe. You have to go down an alleyway, into a funky little yard and then up an unmarked staircase to find the "lobby."

Very casual. Owner Gene Bagley keeps it that low-key because, "a sign would attract more people," he says. "I don't need to advertise. I can't handle people walking in off the street—I don't have any place to put them. I turn away about 30 people a week who write for reservations."

They write because the place is cheap. Once they get here they find out it's funky, but fun. Just your basic clean room, 23 of them. Five shared baths. About 70% of the guests are local residents who live in the hotel a few months, then move on.

The Grand has been around a long time. Bagley says 75 years. He bought it in '84 in a foreclosure. Then it was a $5-a-night flophouse. And, he says, "Even at $5 it was only a third full...that's how bad it was."

Bagley has had no vacancies in over a year. He's slowly renovating the rooms and the building. He'll cutesie it up and make the place proud.

For reservations write months in advance.

Very budget.

2080 Vineyard, Wailuku, HI 96793 • 242-8191.

Molina Hotel

Forget reservations here—they're never taken. Just call when you're in town and take a chance. First take a look at the place and see what you think. It's behind Molina's Bar, a local hang-out that can be loud.

Some think the bar makes the place dangerous. Owner Manuel Molina poo-poos such a notion. "I've never had trouble. We may be noisy, but fights are rare. I have women living here (in the hotel) alone and I tell 'em it's safe depending on them. "

Molina has been in the bar business since 1943. He came to Maui from Spain at age one in 1911. Since then he's picked pineapples in the fields, opened a federal credit union, been a County Council member and run the bar and hotel. A character, and a busy one.

He built the hotel in the early Sixties for construction workers who just needed a place to rest their heads. It's still best for single men with no illusions of grandeur.

The rooms are very tiny...14 one-bedrooms with a single bed, all with baths. No cooking allowed; no space for a pot anyway. There are two larger rooms with room for a double bed, but those are often taken by long-term residents.

Very budget.

197 Market, Wailuku, HI 96793 • 244-7981 • 244-4100.

Happy Valley Inn

If you're a serious windsurfing tourist, you should stay at Happy Valley. Period. This place is it...the hangout, the only place to park your board and lay your head.

The owners bought a very rundown tenement house/hotel in '84 and decided to renovate it as the premier windsurfing hotel in Maui. Why? Because, as one of the innkeepers says, "They're a great group of people. A high percentage are professional people. They're active all day, and they want a clean room to come home to. They don't need extra amenities like swimming pools and golf courses."

The Inn is never advertised, there's not even a sign on the building. Bookings are strictly word of mouth, and the place is always full. The first year open, people came from 36 different countries. It's not unusual to have visitors from 10 to 12 countries every night.

The guests are known as the HVI group...kind of a quick family situation. They meet easily, then eat, surf and play together.

The rooms are clean, bright and airy. The four baths are shared. Boards and sails rest in their own locked shed.

Very budget.

310 N. Market Street, Wailuku, HI 96793 • 244-4786.

RESTAURANTS

Being such a local town, Wailuku has lots of inexpensive local joints, most of them loaded with character. The food is generally basic, nothing fancy or gourmet.

$ Budget

Archie's: Famous for its noodles—many varieties of udon and somen. Has other typical Japanese favorites like sashimi, tempura, teriyaki, etc.

Also has American staples—steak, omelette, pork, chicken, hamburgers. The menu is written both in English and in Japanese characters. Hours: Mon.-Sat. 10:30-2; 5-8:30. *1440 Lower Main* • *244-9401*

Chums: Opened in the spring of '86 and was popular with locals from the start. The large interior is sleek and modern, but the food is down-home and old-fashioned. Plate lunches (piece of meat or fish, over-cooked vegetables and a scoop of rice and macaroni) are popular. Hours: 5:30 a.m. to 11 p.m., Fri. & Sat. till midnight. *1900 Main* • *244-1000.*

Down to Earth: Both a health food store and a deli...not exactly a deli, but not exactly a restaurant. Whatever it is, it's great food—all vegetarian fare. There's a daily special and a daily soup, plus an unchanging menu of brown rice and tofu type standbys. All food is packaged for take-out, but you can eat at tables under a covered area in the back...not particularly charming, but it is a good meeting place. Hours: M-F 7-7; Sat. 7-6; Sun. 10-5. *1910 Vineyard* • *242-6821.*

Fujiya's: Very plain Japanese place with good, cheap food. Unbelievable amounts of sushi for budget prices. A dinner under $10 can include tempura, yakitori, fried salmon, miso soup...the works. Hours: 11-2 for lunch; 5-9 week nights, 5-11 Fri. & Sat. *133 Market* • *244-0206.*

Hazel's: With a name like this, you know it's an unpretentious place. Hazel Yasutomi is the owner and cook. She serves up "real" American food, no "cuisine" here—just cook-it-up-and-serve-it food. Spam & eggs, hamburgers, pork chops, mahi mahi (breaded & fried, not grilled on mesquite). Nothing over $6. A local scene. Hours: 6 a.m. to 9 p.m. daily. *2080 Vineyard* • *244-7278.*

Moon Hoe Seafood Restaurant: Finally, a Chinese restaurant that leaves out the MSG when you ask it to do so! Food is delicious here. Inexpensive, but still cooked perfectly. Large menu—way over 100 choices, both Cantonese and Szechuan. Fresh fish comes from local fishermen. Take-out orders available. Hours: 11-2; 5-9:30; Sunday no lunch. *752 Lower Main* • *242-7778.*

Osaka House: A large Japanese restaurant with a sushi bar. The menu has pictures of all the selections...good idea for those who don't know what sukiyaki and tempura are. Hours: 5-10. Sushi bar open till 11 p.m.. Closed Sunday. *Located on the bottom floor of an apartment/office building at 1063 Lower Main* • *244-3414.*

Sam Sato's: Very basic, very small place with booths and formica tables. You order your food and you get it in minutes. Food is very simple—chow fun, chop steak, saimin, tuna sandwich, hamburger, etc. Wailuku to the max. Local, local, local. Famous for their manju, a Chinese dessert of sweet beans packaged in rice flour. Hours: 8 a.m. to 4 p.m.; closed Thur. & Sun. *318 N. Market • 244-7124.*

Siam Thai: Possibly the best food in town. Very tasty Thai cuisine. Favored place with residents who appreciate food cooked with care. Many vegetarian choices of the 70-some selections on the menu. How a place this good can have budget prices is a mystery. Hours: Mon.-Fri. 11-3 ; 5-10 daily. *123 N. Market • 244-3817.*

Tasty Crust: Has the ambiance of a truck stop, but that's its charm...kind of a real-life diner. It's a favorite with locals...been around nearly 30 years. Food is truck stop fare—simple, basic and local. Breakfast is served at any hour. Their pancakes are renowned. Hours: Sun.-Thur. 5:30 a.m. to 11 p.m.; 5:30 a.m. to midnight Fri. & Sat. *1770 Mill • 244-0845.*

Tokyo Tei: Been around a long time and has a faithful clientele. Food is simple, good Japanese cooking, very inexpensive. It's a small place with 14 tables. It's located on the first floor of an ugly office/apartment building in an area where tourists rarely show up. Hours: 11-1:30 (lunch); 5-8:30 (dinner). Closed Sun. for lunch, open for dinner. *1063 Lower Main • 242-9630.*

Yori's: Across the street from Sato's and just as local, but Yori's has a more varied menu. It also has a bar. Mostly it has Yori himself—a friendly guy who takes everybody's picture, then hangs the photos (thousands of them) on his walls. Go in one year, come back the next and he'll still remember where your picture is. The place is a riot of faces. It's a great little joint. Go for booze or food, or just go for local color. Hours: Tues.-Fri. 1-10:30; Sat. & Sun. 11-10:30. *309 N. Market • 244-3121.*

$$ Mid-Range

Pino's: An authentic Italian place owned by an Italian who grows herbs in his own back yard. Pino Manzo and his family run Pino's like a comfortable neighborhood cafe. Lunch is very popular with Wailuku business people. Hours: 11 a.m. to 9 p.m. weekdays; 5-9 p.m. Sat.; closed Sunday. *2065 Main Street • 242-9650.*

Wailuku Grill: The most high style, uptown, "chi-chi" restaurant in central Maui. It's very slick and modern. Unfortunately, the nouvelle cuisine did not catch on for dinner, so the Grill is open just for lunch . Food and service are excellent. It's a fun place, not at all snobbish, though the clientelle is usually a hip crowd. Sit by the open windows and watch the action at Wailuku's main intersection. Hours: 7:30-3 weekdays, 8-2 weekends. *2010 Main • 244-7505.*

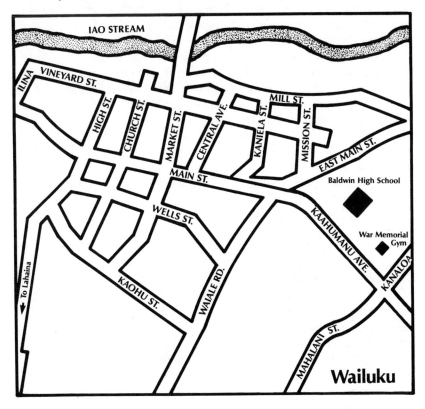

SHOPPING

Market Street

Market Street lives up to its name. It's Wailuku's main shopping street. It's also the focal point for merchants who are trying to revitalize "Old Wailuku Town." The shops are all small and unique, and not at all touristy. The buildings that house the shops are a mishmash—false front Western style, Fifties vintage and broken down, crumbling edifices.

Market Street has three shops that sell eelskin products. The best is **Golden Eel Import Co.** (11 Market), a large store with oodles of eel at decent prices. Many varieties of purses, wallets and briefcases, plus boots, shoes, belts, even earrings. Hours: 9-5 Mon.-Sat.

Maui Sporting Goods (92 Market) is an old-fashioned, small-town type of sports store with something for everyone—snorkeling, basketball, baseball, camping, fishing, hunting, weights, volleyball. They carry both equipment and clothing. Hours: Mon.-Fri. 8:30-5; 8:30-6 Sat.

For a completely different antique store go to **Things from the Past** at 160-A N. Market. Knickknacks, bric-a-brac, framed pictures, Buddhist thankas (artwork), hanging lamps, glassware, "silkie" Hawaiian shirts, costume jewelry, a few furniture pieces...this is a fun place crammed with everything imagineable. A collector's toyhouse. They both sell and rent. If you need a picture for your wall, they have a storeroom full that you may rent or buy. You can't miss the place...a 6-foot brown Santa Claus statue stands directly in front in a permanent waving pose. Hours: 10-6 Mon.-Sat.

Right next door (158 Market) is **Traders of the Lost Art**...clever name for a unique shop. The tiny store is crammed full of artifacts from New Guinea. Anyone who loves primitive art should stop here. But first call the owner, Tye Hartall—he's a wild, busy man on the go, so he's often not in the shop. An appointment may be necessary to catch him. Hartall lived in New Guinea, teaching English. He fell in love with the art and collects it himself along the Sepik River villages. Phone: 242-7753.

Off Market...around town

Crystals, magic wands, metaphysical books, visionary cards, beaded jewelry...**Miracles Unlimited** (82 Central Ave.) is a place of fantasies. It is unofficial headquarters for the New Agers who trek through Maui. Stop in at Miracles to find out the current workshops, lectures, dances, gurus in town, happenings in general. Hours: 10-5:30 M to F; 10-4 Saturday.

The **Herb Shop** (58 Central Ave.) is just that—a tiny store full of tinctures and teas and herbs and vitamins. All kinds of natural cures and holistic advice is handed out over the counter. Owner Ken Redstone has studied natural healing and herbs since the early Seventies. He also is a licensed acupuncturist. Hours: M-F 10-5:30; Sat.10-3.

Need a box? The **Maui Box Shop** will have it (either corrugated or gift box). Owners Sharon and Michael Higa are so nice they'll probably pack your box for you. They've got bubble wrap and wrapping paper and ribbons. They also have a great selection of balloons, party items, toys and novelties. Cute little store in an out-of-the-way location—1870 Mill Street. Hours: 8-5:30 M-F; 9-4:30 Saturday.

Kalima O Maui is not really a store, but it often has a selection of crafts, including Christmas ornaments. They also have a wonderful plant nursery. The crafts are made and the plants are tended by handicapped people. Kalima O Maui is a sheltered work place that offers jobs for the handicapped. Their workers also do ironing for a reasonable price.

Their workspace and nursery is located in the **Cameron Center** at 95 Mahalani Street. This is a unique center for human resource agencies. More than 20 service agencies have office space and share meeting rooms there.

Groceries

Takamiya Market is a Maui institution, been around since 1946. It's a small, very local store with the best selection of local food on the island. There's a deli case full of prepared food—just the place to get lau lau, poke, poi, ogo, lipoa, sushi, limu kohu. You can also get more recognizable items like fried fish, turkey tails, beef broccoli, fried gizzards, sweet and sour pork, and fried squid. Owner Jimmy Takamiya is a big-hearted man, called "the little giant of Happy Valley." It's located in the Happy Valley section of Wailuku, a very earthy, sometimes funky, always local area. 359 N. Market. Hours: 6 a.m. to 6:30 p.m.

You can't beat **Ooka's** prices. This is a large grocery store started in 1930 by a Japanese contract laborer. If you're tired of shopping in sterile, modern groceries, Ooka's is a downhome, earthy store favored by locals. Besides food, they have a good selection of locally-grown flowers—sold at bargain prices. Hours: M, T, W, Sat. 7:30 a.m. to 8 p.m.: Thur. & Fri. 7:30 to 9; Sun. 7:30 to 6.

Ma‘alaea

Ma‘alaea is a boat harbor. It is also a little community of ten large condos, a few beachfront homes and two restaurants. Ma‘alaea is tucked away...no shopping, no traffic, no noise. Nothing elegant, but the views are great—Haleakala in the foreground, the West Maui Mountains in the background.

The tradewinds blow constantly. For some it's too windy; for most the winds are a breezy blessing against the heat. "Without the winds," says one resident, "we'd be just like Kihei. Hot."

HISTORY

There were villages in and around Ma‘alaea, but most traces are gone. An important village near McGregor Point was destroyed by the contractor who built Ma‘alaea Harbor's breakwater. He used boulders from the village to build the breakwater, thus demolishing the site.

It was a fishing village of 45 house sites plus a well-preserved heiau, a fishing ko‘a (shrine) and several petroglyphs. Bishop Museum archaeologists considered it one of the best such villages on Maui, and they planned to excavate and study it in the future. However, there was no future.

The two rocks mentioned below were the only artifacts saved from destruction.

SIGHTS

Two boulders

Behind Buzz's Restaurant are two large rocks from the village mentioned above. A small brown sign announces "Sacred Ancient Hawaiian Stones," but other than that, there's no hoopla. The rocks lie forgotten in tall grass right behind a metal gas tank.

One boulder is an adz grinding stone, the other is a *pohaku piko*, a stone where villagers hid the umbilical cords of newborns.

BEACHES & PARKS

Kealia Pond
A salt-water marsh set aside as a nesting and breeding refuge for birds, most notably the indigenous Hawaiian stilts, black-crowned night herons and Hawaiian coots.

Ma'alaea Beach
A long, long strip of white sand that curves around Ma'alaea and joins up with the Kihei beaches...very popular with joggers and walkers. Usually windy in the afternoon.

Good swimming, but the sandy bottom drops off quickly, so can be dangerous for children. Decent surfing in some areas.

Facilities: showers & portable toilet in a grassy area by the last condo (Makani A Kai) on Hau'oli Road.

Ma'alaea Harbor
Many tourist charter boats, both fishing and sightseeing boats, are docked here. There's also a Coast Guard station in the harbor. Large parking area, plus toilet facilities.

McGregor Point
Right beyond Ma'alaea, on the highway heading to Lahaina, is a small white lighthouse on the makai side of the highway.

In the late 1800s a Scottish sea captain by the name of McGregor made a safe overnight landing here during a treacherous storm. Thus he discovered one of the few parts of Ma'alaea not buffeted by the Ma'a'a winds.

Soon after, a wharf was built there for inter-island ferries. It was destroyed in a 1906 tidal wave, rebuilt, then destroyed again.

The area around the lighthouse is rarely visited. It's not that interesting, but you can hike a short distance down and sit on rocks at the ocean's edge.

A plaque near the lighthouse commemorates the 1881 arrival of a Norwegian ship that brought in the only mass immigration of Scandanavian immigrant field workers. About 600 Norwegians, Swedes and Danes dropped anchor here.

CONDOS

Considering the beauty and serenity of Ma'alaea Bay, the condos here are disappointing esthetically. There are 10 condo complexes along Hau'oli Road, all lined up side by side like monolith concrete slabs. All are modern units equipped with everything you need, and all but one are moderately priced. All are a few feet from the ocean, but only three are on a sandy beach (the rest are rocky). Two of these are detailed below.

Budget Condos: On Beach

Rental agent Jeanne McJannet, whose husband Jim is the manager of the **Hono Kai Resort**, is very enthusiastic about her property. "It has a certain charm about it...good vibes...seriously, I can't explain it," she says. "Once we get people here, they all want to come back." That includes the McJannets. They kept returning themselves until Jim retired as an L.A. fireman, and then they stayed for good. They host a nightly sunset cocktail party to mingle the guests. The Hono Kai has 45 units, both 1 & 2-BR, in four long buildings. *R.R.1 Box 389, Ma'alaea Village, Wailuku, HI 96793 • 244-7012 • (800) 367-6084.*

Moderate Condos: On Beach

The **Makani A Kai** is Ma'alaea's smallest condo and its most unique one. It has only 24 units (1 & 2-BR) and they're spread out in four nicely-designed buildings. The units are large and modern. The two bedrooms have one bedroom in a loft and one downstairs. The grounds are much prettier than most in Ma'alaea. Jeanne McJannet calls this condo the "Cadillac" and its neighbor the Hono Kai the "Chevrolet." Both are charming. *R.R.1 Box 389, Ma'alaea Village, Wailuku, HI 96793 • 244-5627.*

RESTAURANT

Mid-Range

Waterfront: Sits right on the harbor, so one would expect the seafood to be good...it is. The interior is plush and dark with leather banquette booths. The open-air verandah gives a different ambiance. Whatever mood fits your day—airy or intimate. Hours: 11-3 p.m. & 5:30-10 p.m. *Located on ground floor of Milowai Condominium. 244-9028.*

West Maui

This is the old, jagged, wrinkled side of Maui, born somewhere between one and two milion years ago. The volcano was once higher (about 7,000 feet), but the top collapsed and formed a wide caldera. That, plus erosion, has carved it down, its highest point now being the 5,788-ft. Pu'u Kukui. Eons ago, at its mightest height, the West Maui volcano reached more than 20,000 feet from its base on the ocean floor.

What is left of the volcano crater is deep within the peaks at the head of 'Iao Valley. From this amphitheater-like crater radiate out several magnificent valleys...'Iao, Kahakuloa, Ukumehame, Olowalu and Honokohau.

The West Maui Mountains have dramatic peaks and ridges that jut upwards...many impossible to climb. Much is inaccessible land with its head in the clouds.

Meanings of Place Names

'Iao	"cloud supreme"
Olowalu	"many hills"
Lahaina	"merciless sun"
Ka'anapali	"rolling cliffs"
Honokowai	"bay drawing water"
Kahana	"cutting"
Napili	"the joinings" or "pili grass"
Kapalua	"arms embracing the sea"
Kahakuloa	"the tall or faraway master"

ʻIao

ʻIao is the most magnificent of several great valleys that carve into the center of the West Maui Mountains. This is a very special valley...a sacred place since ancient times. Still the deepest parts of it, beyond the park area, remain untouched and aloof from humanity.

In ʻIao there is an eerie sense of history, of ghosts still drifting within the confines of the valley's massive vertical cliffs. Hundreds of warriors died here in one of Maui's bloodiest battles. Numerous aliʻi were buried high in the canyons in caves secret to all, their spirits still guarding the sacred valley.

This is the oldest part of Maui. More than two million years ago the West Maui Mountains were born as lava pumped from a hotspot in the sea. As the magma cooled, it formed a crater, which is still the head of ʻIao Valley.

The mountains have shifted off the hotspot and West Maui is an extinct volcano. But ʻIao Stream is still much alive, daily cutting the valley deeper as water flows from the crater heights to the sea.

HISTORY

Hikers can find a few ancient structures and heiau in ʻIao Valley, but there were no large villages deep within the canyon. It was easier living on the plains of Wailuku. Ancient peoples did use the valley, however, and they planted taro along the banks of the stream.

The valley was a sacred burial place, reputed to be the preferred spot for ancient kings and chiefs. Bones of the aliʻi were hidden secretively in caves. So secret, that years later modern king David Kalakaua searched to find the ʻIao graves and could not.

Why hide the bones?—because bones were thought to hold the mana, the energy, of the person. Aliʻi bones held a high, powerful mana, thus they were often hidden so no one could disturb them or misuse the power still within them.

Drawing by Ben Kikuyama

The stream runs red...

Kamehameha left plenty of bones in 'Iao, though none of them his own. In 1790 he waged a dreadful battle here, beating Maui's warriors, and thus winning the island.

Kahekili was the king of Maui at the time, but he was on O'ahu, so his son Kalanikupule fought the battle. From the plains of Wailuku, Kamehameha and his Big Island warriors drove Maui's men up 'Iao Stream into the valley.

The match was grossly uneven. Kamehameha was assisted by two Englishmen manning cannons. Kalanikupule and his chiefs escaped through 'Iao, out a pass in Olowalu Valley. The warriors defending them were murdered en masse, their corpses supposedly damming 'Iao Stream until the water ran red with their blood.

SIGHTS

Kepaniwai Park

Kepaniwai means "damming of the waters," commemorating Kamehameha's terrible battle near here. The park is now a heritage park with small buildings depicting the various ethnic groups that are Hawai'i's people. There is a Hawaiian thatched roof dwelling, a missionary style New England cottage, a simple wooden Japanese home with a tiny garden, a Portuguese home complete with outdoor oven, a small Chinese building and a Filipino grass and bamboo structure.

The park is popular with locals. It has several covered picnic pavilions plus a kids' swimming pool (pool open 9-12 a.m. and 1-4:30 p.m. daily). Toilets and showers also available.

The park is marked by a large blue sign. Hard to miss.

'Iao Park

This is the end of the road. Here there's a small botanical garden along the confluence of the 'Iao and the Kinihapai Streams. Kinihapai is the one that heads up towards the 'Iao Needle. Once joined, the streams become the single 'Iao Stream that flows to the ocean through Wailuku town.

Many people visit the park to see the famous 'Iao Needle which rises 2250 feet straight up. The Needle is merely a sturdy piece of rock that resisted erosion. There is no magic to it—the magic is beyond, deep into the valley itself.

RESTAURANTS

$$ Mid-Range

Mark Edison's: Beautiful, romantic spot to dine, surrounded by giant cliffs. Chicken, steak, fish kind of menu, all very good. The salad bar is a standout—probably the most extensive on the island, includes everything from raw fish to hearts of palm. Service is friendly and excellent. Hours: 10 a.m. to 3 p.m. and 5-10 p.m. daily. *Located right beyond Kepaniwai Park • 242-5555.*

Maui Folk...
Maui's Archaeologist

Maui's one and only local archaeologist was not the least bit interested in old rocks and ancient ruins when he was first introduced to the subject. That was in 1971 when Kenneth Emory, the dean of Polynesian archaeologists, was on the island, studying Maui's sites. Emory took a liking to Charley Keau and decided to take him under his wing. At the time, Keau thought differently.

"I told him I didn't want to do it," Charley says today. "I thought it was a waste of time...that it should be left alone. Whatever the ali`i and the kupunas had left should not be disturbed.

Emory emphatic

"He told me I *was* going to do it. He said, `Charley, if you don't take care of these things, who's going to protect them? What's going to happen to them?'

"My first answer was—to hell with them. I said I'm a hupo, which means I'm stupid. I don't know anything.

"But Dr. Emory saw that I did know much, and there was something in me that he wanted to promote. I told him I never graduated from high school, and I never knew about archaeology. He said he'd teach me."

The mayor asked Charley to work with Emory and his crew cleaning up Wailuku's two great heiau, Pihana and Halekii. Charley was born at the foot of the sand dune where Pihana stands, so he was joining up on his own territory. Before he knew it, he was hooked, and he wasn't as hupo as he thought.

"Somebody told me the heiau stones came from Ma`alaea, and that burned me up. They came from the mouth of `Iao Stream...I was born and raised right there. I knew I had to get these things straightened out."

He began reading as much as he could find. A knowledgeable friend gave him Elspeth Sterling's archaeological manuscripts.

"The more I read, the more I became interested because that's what my mother was telling us. And we never listened to her. The old folks, they don't know nothing, you know. Then this lady (Sterling) was writing the same things! I felt shamed. Here was Dr. Emory trying to teach me, and I had said to hell with it.

"I kept reading—Kamakau, Fornander, Malo—these were stories the old folks were talking about. I don't

think they ever read Kamakau and Fornander. You go to their houses and there's no library, no books; but they tell me the same things that are in the books. That really made me feel so good inside. Hey, this is what my mother said!

"From that time on, I had to do the job."

Maonakala Village

After the heiau work, Emory took Charley to the small village of Maonakala past Makena. They worked there together for two or three weeks, then, for the next six months, the crew went all over the island.

"I became more involved because I thought I could do something for my people. I could do something for the children. I have a lot of aloha for that," Charley says.

"I saw all the artifacts *in situ* on the ground. I started to learn about the scientists' way of understanding the stones. I didn't know the scientific words, but I caught on fast. Even when I was working construction jobs, I'd go back to archaeology and work with the Bishop Museum."

Caretaker in 'Iao Valley

Charley is still involved today. He has a full-time job as caretaker of Kepaniwai Park in 'Iao Valley, but in his spare time, he's back at his old hobby.

Charley is not rigid about keeping all things Hawaiian as is. He is not against development and progress. He thinks land should be used.

"The old folks told me as a young kid that every land is valuable whether it's dry, rocky, no good—that land is a valuable land.

"Who ever thought Wailea, Kihei, Makena would be developed as it is today?...because there is no water. You cannot plant fields. But the land was still valuable. Along come the guys with brains. They put in a water line, the land becomes valuable. Who would think?

"But the old folks always say every land, every stone is valuable because somehow it produces life. Put the land into use—let it feed us. Aloha 'aina means that."

This does not mean Charley wants development to go unheeded. He has seen too many sites bulldozed. "It's sad," he says, "I know about it, but I can't do a damned thing about it."

Lahaina and Ka'anapali are nearly bare of ancient sites. Management at one Ka'anapali hotel once had plans to reconstruct a Hawaiian village. "I burst out laughing," Charley says. "They had it all there—the villages, the taro patches, but they destroyed them. Now they want to build a new one? Kinda stupid."

Charley's dream

His dream is to "preserve all the stones, all the historic sites." But reality is that very little money is allocated for archaeological work. "It's a shame," Charley says. "We know so much about the island. We have so much history to share with visitors, so much beautiful things in this 'aina. But the state and county and federal governments don't protect the sites. 'No more money' are the famous three words we hear time and time again. But if we don't protect them, we'll lose the sites to development. We'll lose the future of our Hawaiian culture."

Olowalu

You wonder why you suddenly have to slow to 30 mph on the highway to and from Lahaina. Then you see it—a blink of a town. Olowalu...a tiny, odd combo of a simple general store and an expensive French restaurant. That's it, plus a few houses you can't see from the road.

Olowalu is not just a tiny town; it is a V-shaped valley that cuts into the West Maui Mountains. The town sits on the alluvial fan that spreads out from the valley.

HISTORY

Villages have existed here for eons. Not much is known about them except for one village that earned a spot in history the hard way.

In 1790, an American ship captain took revenge on the village when he lost a small craft and the sailor in it. Seems the thieves were from Olowalu...presumably reason enough to wreak havoc on all its people.

When he learned the boat was in pieces and the man dead, the captain planted his ship in front of the village. He encouraged the residents to paddle up in canoes to trade. When in close range, he fired his cannons, killing more than 100 and wounding many others.

A get-away trail...
An ancient trail once led from 'Iao Valley through Olowalu Valley...probably the only way to get through the near-impassable West Maui Mountains. This was the trail that Maui chief Kahekili's son, Kalanikupule, took when he escaped from Kamehameha during the bloody battle of Kepaniwai.

It is probably the same trail that Keopuolani's guardians used to spirit her out of Wailuku and over the mountains to keep her from Kamehameha (during the same battle). She was the highest ali'i on Maui, so they hid her in Moloka'i...to no avail. When he won Maui, Kamehameha went after her and married her, thus ensuring that his children would be of high rank.

A few hardy missionaries wrote in their journals of passing through the mountains on this trail. It is no longer accessible, however. Rock slides have made the going tough. Some hardcore hikers have been known to make it through, but others have nearly lost it trying.

SIGHTS

Old Road

Look mauka as you drive between Ma'alaea and Olowalu and you'll catch glimpses of the road that once was. The current highway and tunnel were built in the early Fifties; the 315-foot tunnel was the first such tunnel built in Hawai'i. The early road was narrow and twisty.

Olowalu Church

Built in 1859, all that's left are the coral block walls. The ceiling is an open sky. The church is in ruins. It is located on property occupied by Teen Challenge, a Christian drug rehab organization.

BEACHES & PARKS

Papalaua State Wayside Park

This rather stark-looking park is a kiawe jungle with picnic tables. The beach is secluded; bottom is rocky, but swimming is good.

Facilities: toilets, picnic tables, grills.

Ukumehame Beach Park

You'll know it by a rickety wooden fence, many ironwood trees and a big orange dumpster...no sign. And little sign of life—not a popular spot. It is located between Ma'alaea and Olowalu. No facilities.

Olowalu Beach

Mile marker 14 is the clue. Pull off and park anywhere near it...the beach goes on for quite a distance. Famous for snorkeling, one of the best spots on Maui. No facilities.

RESTAURANT

$$$ Expensive

Chez Paul: What is such a restaurant doing in the middle of nowhere? It is one of island's best—the menu changes nightly according to what food is fresh that day. Belgian owner/chef Lucien Charbonnier has the place styled after a simple French cafe. Only open for dinner; seating at 6:30 & 8:30 every night. *661-3843.*

Lahaina

Lahaina is a rarity—a cute little town that has somehow remained cute. True, there is much commercialism, yet tourism has not turned it into Waikiki. Front Street, bordering the ocean, still has early 1900 structures. Some are a bit rickety, but that's the charm.

The old is intact because Maui was smart enough to designate much of Lahaina as National Historic Landmark property. There are strict rules about what can be torn down and what can be put up. Any new building must look as if it came from a time before 1920.

Most of the genuinely old buildings in town are either from the missionary times of the 1830s or from around 1920. A 1917 fire burned up one end of town, and many of the late 1800 structures were destroyed. Several of those built immediately after the fire are still standing.

Many think Lahaina is supposed to look like a whaling town. It does not. It was a much cruder, simpler town in the whaling days. Much is made of those rowdy times, but they lasted only 50 years. There have been many other faces of Lahaina. The town has the most varied history of any place on Maui.

HISTORY

The ali'i, the Hawaiian ruling class, favored Lahaina since the 1600s. They liked it for the same reasons we like it today—it has little rainfall with lots of sun (plus, it's a good surfing area). It also had abundant water. In earlier days there were several mountain streams running down to the sea; these streams have since been harnessed by the sugar industry, and the streambeds are no more.

Lahaina was often considered the islands' capital town. In truth, the "capital" was wherever the king was...and royalty moved around the islands as they pleased. Kamehameha I did build his Brick Palace in Lahaina and lived in the village quite a bit. His two sons also spent much time there. In the 1840s, however, Kamehameha III officially and permanently moved the capital to Honolulu.

Saints & Sinners

The year after Kamehameha died, 1820, whalers began stopping in Hawai'i. They had hunted whales to scarcity in the Atlantic. Thus they turned west to hunt the sperm whales of Japan and Alaska. Hawai'i was a strategic middle ground.

Here they weren't after the humpback—R & R, rest and recuperation, is what they needed. Captains restocked provisions, while their men sought grog and women.

Some 549 ships stopped in Hawai'i in 1859. During the heyday of 1840 to 1860, 40 to 400-some ships a year, each carrying 25 to 30 men, would visit Lahaina's port. The town boomed commerically. In 1825 there were 23 grog shops within a mile strip. "No god west of the Horn" was the whalers' motto.

All seemed carefree and easy except for one major factor—the missionaries arrived in Lahaina in 1823. These were people as sturdy as the whalers, and the two groups were often at odds with each other.

The missionaries had the upper hand—the Hawaiian chiefs were on their side. In 1825 Chief Hoapili (later governor of Maui) banned the sale of alcohol and forbade women being on the ships. A sundown curfew was enforced—all sailors had to be on their ships by sunset or they'd be thrown in the clink.

None of this was taken graciously. Several times hundreds of rowdy sailors rioted through town. They once fired four cannon balls from a ship towards the missionary house. Twice angry sailor mobs threatened the lives of missionary William Richards and his wife. The couple was stoic and not easily intimidated, plus the Hawaiians protected them.

The missionaries were favored by the Hawaiians. Both Queens Ka'ahumanu and Keopuolani (wives of Kamehameha I) accepted the faith. So did numerous other ali'i...and with them came the commoners. The Christian god replaced the old gods in an easy sweep.

Baldwin

Rev. Dwight Baldwin, who took over for Rev. Richards in 1838, had a kinder attitude towards seamen. He journeyed with them for 161 days during his voyage from New England to Hawai'i, and he admired their courage and stamina.

He wrote in his journal: *"Did the church exhibit half the enterprise of the whalemen, this world would soon be another sort of picture from what it is now...This ship is to be cut off from the world and almost independent of it for three years; in the meantime, they are engaged in a most hazardous work..."*

Hawai'i State Archives

Back to Sleep

By 1871 the whaling era was over. Petroleum oil was discovered in Pennsylvania, and it replaced whale oil in lamps.

The supply of whaling ships was depleted during the Civil War when they were used for war purposes. Those left whaling could dump their cargoes of blubber, oil and bone in San Francisco—the new transcontinental railroad transported it quicker than a trip around the Horn. There was no need to stop in Hawai'i; provisions were restocked in San Francisco.

Lahaina's economy fell. With jobs gone, much of the population left. The town grew quiet and stayed that way for a century.

Lahaina would now become a company town...immigrants and Hawaiians all worked for the sugar and pineapple plantations. Ambitous children would move away. There was nothing for them to do on sleepy Maui...until the hotels in Ka'anapali brought in a new era.

Tourism brought prosperity. But like the whalers, tourists brought change. The Sheraton opened in 1963. Year after year, chunks of beaches fell to giant concrete monoliths. From Lahaina to Kapalua there is nary a view devoid of buildings.

SIGHTS

Very few pre-European sites and remains are left near Lahaina town. Most remaining history is of the missionary and whaler era. It's this 19th century architecture, combined with early 20th century Front Street shops, that make Lahaina unique.

Banyan Tree

Planted by the sheriff of Maui in 1873 when the tree was only 8 feet tall. Over 100 years old, it is now the largest banyan in Hawai'i. The banyan is from India, and is considered sacred by the Hindus.

Every evening at sunset, mynah birds (also from India) perch in the tree, singing and screeching. It is a nightly symphony of riotous dimensions.

Court House

Originally built in 1859; rebuilt in 1925. It's a deserted looking building now, though an art gallery and the district court have offices there.

Fort

Not the real thing...these two corners look like ruins, but they're not. The fort was torn down in 1854; it was never in ruins. The two corners in front of the Old Courthouse were put up in 1964. The stones are blocks of coral—built authentically as it was in 1832 when Governor Hoapili erected it as a defense against unruly sailors. Its canons were never fired, never needed.

Four Cannons

These guns point over the seawall, ready to protect Kamehameha I who dredged them up from a sunken ship to guard his Brick Palace. They were never used.

Brick Palace

The first western structure built in Hawai'i. All that's left is a cleared space in front of the Pioneer Inn with several odd rectangular holes sectioned off. The holes used to have plexiglass covering them with evidence of the old bricks underneath. Vandals destroyed the exhibit.

Not much to view, but it is interesting to see where Kamehameha I chose to live. He had the two-story brick house built, then only stayed there one year, 1802. Favorite wife Ka'ahumanu refused to live in it, so it became a storehouse. It stood for 70 years, then fell to ruins. The mud bricks simply were not strong enough.

Hauola Stone

This rock at the edge of the seawall resembles a low reclining chair. It was thought to be a healing rock. The sick would sit in it with their legs dangling in the sea and let the waves wash over them, and hopefully be cured.

Pioneer Inn

Built in 1901, oldest hotel on Maui. It stands on land where Kamehameha I once had a taro patch. It is said he tilled it himself to show commoners the dignity of work.

The hotel capitalizes on the whaling era (whaling paraphernalia decorates the lobby); but, in fact, the hotel never had a whaler customer—whale ships were years gone when it was built.

Pioneer Inn's House Rules: 1901

You must pay you rent in advance.
You must not let you room go one day back.
Women is not allow in you room.
If you burn you bed you going out.
You are not allow to gambel in you room.
You are not allow to give you bed to you freand.
If you freand stay overnight you must see the manager.
You must leave you room at 11 am so the women can clean you room.
Only on Sunday you can sleep all day.
You are not allow in the down stears in the seating room or in the dining room or in the kitchen when you are drunk.
You are not allow to drink on the front porch.
You must use a shirt when you come to the seating room.
If you cant keep this rules please dont take the room.

Brig Carthaginian

The only authentically-restored square-rigged brig in the world. It is a replica of the type of ship that brought the missionaries around the Horn from New England. The first missionaries came on the Brig Thaddeus in 1819.

The Carthaginian is a German-made schooner built in 1920. It was a cement carrier in the Baltic Sea before being rebuilt in Maui in the 1970s. It took lots of research and plenty of work to make it authentic.

Go inside—the interior is charming, plus there are continuous whale documentaries shown. One shows close-ups of the birth of a whale (not a humpback, though).

Open daily 9 to 4:30; small admission fee.

Lahaina Harbor Lighthouse

This is the site of the oldest lighthouse in the Pacific. The original, fueled by whale oil, was built by King Kamehameha III in 1840.

The present lighthouse was built in 1927. It is a small, white structure overlooking Lahaina Harbor. It is not the lighthouse that contained the lens on display in the Spring House (next listing).

Spring House

This small lava rock structure was supposedly built by the mission-aries over a source of fresh water, used by the community and the whalers alike. Now the structure houses a dazzling, giant Fresnel lighthouse lens, once considered the brightest light in the Pacific. The lens nearly takes up the entire building, though there is a maritime exhibit squeezed in with it.

Hard to explain how beautiful and incredible this lens is. It weighs 3.4 tons, and is an engineering marvel of handcut, ground optic glass. It could change 1000 watts of light into 680,000 candlepower...visible for 25 miles at sea.

It was originally in the lighthouse at Kalaupapa, the famous leper colony in Moloka'i. It is on loan to Lahaina until Kalaupapa can house and show it properly.

The lens was replaced in Kalaupapa's lighthouse in 1986 with a modern lens, but not because it wasn't strong enough. In fact, the new lens is not as bright as the old. Problem with the Fresnel sytem—it has 200 pounds of toxic mercury within the lens. The Environmental Protection Agency feared the mercury might leak, so they replaced the lens.

Now the Fresnel lens stands as a piece of art in a tiny Lahaina building. The Spring House is located in The Wharf Shopping Center at 658 Front Street (next to Island Sandals). Open 10 a.m. to 6 p.m.

Hale Pa'ahao, Old Prison

Built with planks in 1852 by prisoners themselves. The coral block wall around the wooden building was built two years later from coral hauled over from the fort that was torn down that year.

The prison was needed to hold rowdy sailors, most commonly imprisoned for breaking curfew. Sailors were to be on their ships and out of town by sundown...if not, they went to the clink.

The old prison burned down in 1958, but was rebuilt the next year.

Waine'e/Waiola Protestant Church

First stone church on Maui, erected in 1832. It was built by the Hawaiian people and paid for by the chiefs. It was two stories high and could accommodate 3000. Governor Hoapili first named it Ebenezer, but it was later called Waine'e after the district it is in.

James Michener referred to the church in his book *Hawai'i* as the church that couldn't stand. Twice it burned down and twice it was destroyed by winds.

The current structure was put up in 1953 and renamed Waiola Church.

Waine'e/Waiola Cemetery

Dates from 1823 when Queen Keopuolani died and was buried here. She was considered sacred, the highest ranking ali'i in Hawai'i, more noble than her husband Kamehameha I. Said to be the first Christian convert, her support gave the missionaries tremendous credibility.

Other ali'i buried with her include her second husband, Governor Hoapili; Hoapili's first wife Queen Kalakua (once one of Kamehameha's wives); Keopuolani's daughter Nahi'ena'ena; King Kaumuali'i, king of Kaui, the only king not conquered in battle by Kamehameha; plus many other chiefs.

Missionary families are also here. Rev. William Richards' tomb (1847) proclaims: *"Mark the perfect man and behold the upright; for the end of that man is peace."*

Maria Lanakila Catholic Church

Built in 1928 as a duplicate of the previous 1858 structure. The same ceiling was used in both.

Catholic priests did not reside in Lahaina until 1846, but when they came, there were already 4000-some converts waiting to be baptized...the work of visiting priests and resident catechists.

Seamen's Cemetery

Next door to the Catholic church, but not a part of it. This is full of whalers and ordinary folk..a funky little graveyard with old and interesting headstones.

Melville's ship visited Lahaina. One of his shipmates died of a "disreputable disease" (as they called it) and is buried in this cemetery. Melville's cousin is also buried here.

U. S. Seamen's Hospital

Built in the 1830s as a party hideaway home for Kamehameha III. Early in his reign, as a youth, Kamehameha III liked to drink and gamble with the whalers. He also liked to rendevous with his beloved sister whom he would have married had the missionaries not disapproved.

To avoid detection, the king put a Chinese store on the ground floor and had his parties upstairs. As he matured, the king began to live more in Honolulu, so he leased his party house to the U.S. Government. It was used as a hospital for seamen from 1844 to 1862.

Whaling life was tough, and Lahaina saw many of its casualties. As one missionary wrote: *"In a few weeks they will be thronging in, a forlorn crew, with all shapes of scurvy, rheumatism, dysentery and consumption."*

In the 1970s, vibration from nearby condo construction crumbled the structure's walls. It was rebuilt in 1982.

During reconstruction a skeleton was found in the northeast corner of the building. The old custom was to bury a body under important buildings so the spirit would guard the place forever. The skeleton was given a new blessing and reburied in the same spot...still a constant guard.

Lahainaluna Seminary

First school west of the Rockies, it was built by Protestant missionaries in 1831. The first students were 25 men, all in their twenties and thirties, including Hawaiian scholar and minister, David Malo.

It is no longer a seminary; it became a public school in 1923, called Lahainaluna High School, and it is now coed. It has the only public boarding school program in the State, though most of its students are not boarders.

Hale Pa'i Printing Museum

The first newspaper printed west of the Rockies was printed here by Lahainaluna students. The first issue of the four-page Ka Lama Hawai'i (The Hawaiian Torch) was printed February 14, 1834 in Hawaiian. The hand press pumped out religious books, paper money, the Hawaiian constitution, and many other documents until it shut down in 1846.

The building is a delight—a New England coral and lava structure, considered one of the most significant remaining missionary buildings. It is located on the campus of Lahainaluna High School

Open 10-4 daily except Sunday.

Lahaina Whaling Museum

One wall of Crazy Shirts store at 865 Front Street is devoted to whaling artifacts—scrimshaw, harpoons, cannon, pikes, gaffs, etc. It's a mini museum put up by the store's owner, Rick Ralston, a T-shirt millionaire with a penchant for whaling memorabilia.

Mala Wharf

Called a "monument to error" in the Maui newspaper. This deep-water wharf was built for $220,000 in 1922 to handle increasing inter-island traffic, but its engineers failed to notice strong currents and high swells in the area. Only two passenger ships ever docked here. Other ships tried, but got banged up so much by surf, the wharf was declared unsafe, used thereafter only by small craft. Now the wharf is condemned.

Sugar Cane Train
A replica of the train that used to chug through Lahaina and Ka'anapali transporting cane to the mills. It's a 12-mile, one-hour round trip, not terribly exciting, but kids like it. There are three boarding stations along the route, each with plenty of parking. Call 661-0089 for departure times.

Wo Hing Society
A pretty little Victorian house that served as a club house and temple for a Chinese fraternal society commonly known as Chee Kung Tong. The 1912 building has Chinese artifacts downstairs and a Taoist temple room upstairs.

A cookhouse next door shows films of Hawai'i taken by Thomas Edison in 1898 and 1906.

Baldwin House
Fascinating house full of antiques and missionary memorabilia...home to Dwight and Charlotte Baldwin and their eight kids from 1838 till 1871.

Dwight Baldwin's job was both to save souls and to heal bodies. He was the only physician/missionary on all of Maui, Lana'i and Moloka'i. He was not eager to practice medicine, he wanted only to work with the spirit, but he was needed to do both. Thus, one room of the house was his medical dispensary.

Open daily 9:30 to 5; small admission fee.

Masters' and Mates' Reading Room
Next to the Baldwin house, it was built for seamen who preferred reading to carousing. Many learned to read and write here with the help of the Baldwins.

Rev. Baldwin wrote in his journal: *"The seamen's library of 400 volumes which has been gathering here is now nearly all floating on different parts of the ocean...The 50 spelling books are nearly all gone, owing to the number on board whale ships who cannot read."*

It now houses the offices of the Lahaina Restoration Foundation...a group that restored many of Lahaina's historic buildings.

Jodo Mission
On the Japanese Buddhist temple grounds, weighing in at 3.5 tons, is the largest Buddha figure outside Japan. It was dedicated in 1968 to commemorate the centennial of the 1868 arrival of the first Japanese immigrants. The Buddha sits outside, ever ready for tourists, but the temples are not open to the public.

BEACHES & PARKS

Launiupoko State Wayside Park

An obvious park—a sign plus picnic tables give it away. Not the prettiest beach, however...dirty gray sand and a rocky ocean bottom. There's more grassy area than sandy beach, so it's good for picnics.

Facilities: toilets, changing rooms, drinking water, showers, paved parking lot, grills and picnic tables.

Puamana Beach Park

A long skinny white beach, a narrow band of grass and a parking lot—not terribly exciting, but decent enough swimming. A sign marks the beach.

Facilities: picnic tables and paved parking.

Lahaina Beach

This narrow beach stretches from Puamana condo property at the south end of Front Street to the boat harbor at the north end. Public access at the harbor and at the left side of Lahaina Shores Hotel. Not bad for swimming, but close to the harbor it can be dirty. There's decent surfing near the harbor.

No facilities.

Pu'unoa Beach

Turn makai at the small sign on Pu'unoa Street. The beach is small, in fact, it's tiny. Bottom's a bit rocky for swimming. Not popular, not crowded.

No facilities.

Wahikuli State Wayside Park

Very large, very popular park and beach. Large grassy areas with numerous covered picnic tables. Good swimming.

Facilities: toilets, showers, drinking water, covered picnic tables, grills, paved parking lots.

Hanakao'o Beach Park

Similar to its neighbor, Wahikuli Park. This is a nice sandy beach with a large grassy area. Popular with residents and tourists both. It has everything, including its own beachside graveyard.

No need to die, however, there is a lifeguard to save you from tombstone territory.

Facilities: toilets, showers, drinking water, covered picnic tables, grills, paved parking lots.

HOTELS

Maui Islander

This looks like an apartment complex, and it once was. It was converted to a hotel with 372 rooms in 1982. These include 148 standard-sized hotel rooms, 90 studios with small kitchens, and 134 two-bedroom suites with kitchens. All are air conditioned, are bright and cheery and are worth the reasonable price.

The location is residential, in the middle of Lahaina, two blocks from Front Street shopping and three blocks from the ocean. No beach close, but the hotel has a swimming pool (and a tennis court).

Mid-range.

660 Wainee Street, Lahaina, HI 96761 • 667-9766 • (800) 367-5226.

Lahainaluna Hotel

This could best be described as seedy—rickety wooden staircase leading up to a cigarette-burned hallway where 18 small, dingy rooms await...like a stage set for a Tennesse Williams' play. There's even a noisy bar below.

The place has plenty of character, and it's been around a long time, but it really needs a white washing. The price, however, can't be beat. It's okay if you just want a bed and a shower.

Very budget.

127 Lahainaluna Road, Lahaina, HI 96761 • 661-0577.

Pioneer Inn

This is a landmark building in Lahaina. It sits right in the center of the action—on the wharf just behind Front Street. Artists who paint old Lahaina scenes often focus on the Inn. Originally built in 1901, its Victorian style is copied by new buildings trying to look old.

The lobby itself is small and funky, and full of sailing ship paraphernalia. A creaky wooden staircase leads from the lobby to the old section of the hotel. Here you find the cheapest rooms—13 small, very basic boxes, some with bath, some without (bath down the hall). Noise can be a problem—these rooms are above the Pioneer's rowdy bar.

The newer wing, built in 1966, has nicer rooms, all with baths, private lanais and air conditioning. These are bigger rooms and have better furniture than the old. They overlook a central courtyard.

Most of the rooms, both old and new, are simply functional, nothing fancy. Still, the Pioneer has a charm and a romance to it that no other Maui hotel has. It's a place of days gone by.

Budget.

658 Wharf Street, Lahaina, HI 96761 • 661-3636.

CONDOS

High Condo: On Beach

Lahaina Shores is the only condo complex that is both right in Lahaina town and is also on a sandy beach. Actually it calls itself a hotel, but its 200 rooms are privately owned and all have full electric kitchens. It is run like a hotel, however, with a lobby registration desk and daily maid service. The rooms are quite large; most are studios, though there are some one bedrooms. The entire seventh floor is seven penthouses. The building's exterior is striking and a bit odd—an antebellum facade of Greek columns and white balustrades. *475 Front St., Lahaina, HI 96761 • 661-3309.*

Expensive Condo: On Beach

Seemingly light years away from the hustle of Lahaina and Ka'anapali is the gracious **Puamana**. This resort has the spirit of a residential village with 60 lowrise buildings spread over 28 acres of grass and trees and flowers. Some of the 230 units (1, 2 & 3-BR) are 20 years old, but they are all comfortable and homey, places where you can put up your feet and feel right. And no one lives above you, no unit is built on top of another. A large, old-fashioned clubhouse is the heart of the village. Ping pong is played in a lacy gazebo behind the clubhouse. Tennis is played in front. Two swings hang under a huge banyan tree that graces the side yard. Two large mango trees shade the front. Palm trees dot the sandy beach that lines Puamana. Everything is peaceful and private. Close to Lahaina, but not of Lahaina. *P.O. Box 515, Lahaina, HI 96761 • 667-2551.*

Stratosphere Condo: On Beach

Not a detail is missed at the **Puunoa Beach Estates**. The solid koa wood front door leads you into professionally-designed, spacious rooms with high cedar ceilings and fancy etched windows. The manager calls the Puunoa "the most prestigious that Maui has to offer," and he could be right. The furnishings and artwork, much of it Asian, are all top quality. Koa is used extensively throughout—kitchen cabinets, mirror frames, all doors, wet bar, even the staircase banister. The huge bathrooms have Roman spa (whirlpool) bathtubs and French bidets. All kitchens have trash compactors, microwave ovens and separate pantries. Every unit has its own garage. With only 10 units (2 & 3-BR), Puunoa is small and private. There are no other condos near it, and it is far from the hub of Lahaina, down a quiet deadend street. *45 Kaipali Pl., Lahaina, HI 96761 • 667-5972 • (800) 642-6284.*

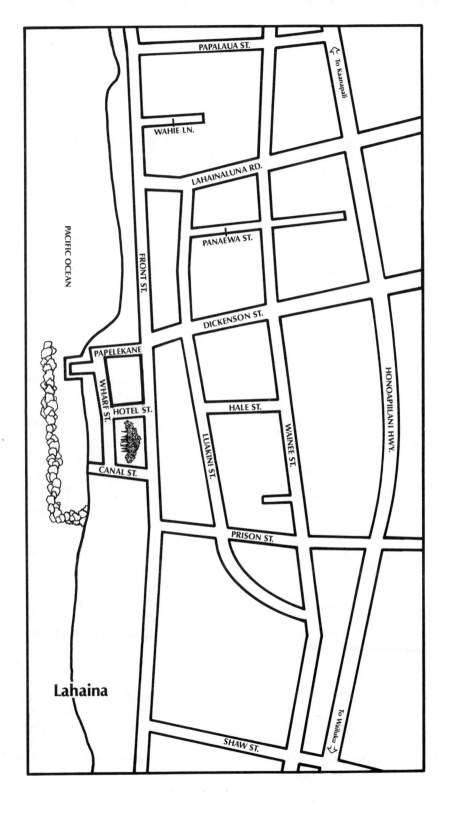

Lahaina

RESTAURANTS

$ Budget

Golden Palace: Looks like you stepped into a Hong Kong restaurant here—same booths and round tables and red decor found all over HKG. Menu has more than 150 Cantonese dishes, most under $5. Take-out service also. Hours: 11-2 p.m. & 5-9 p.m. *Located in Lahaina Shopping Center • 661-3126.*

Hamburger Mary's: Mary's has long been famous for its huge hamburgers and its irreverent customers. In San Francisco it's a hang-out for punks and gays; it's a bit more sedate here, but still popular with gays. Fun place. Restaurant hours: 11 a.m.-10 p.m.; bar hours: 11 a.m. to 2 a.m. *Located at 600 Front in an open-air backyard area • 667-6989.*

Happy Days: A cafe straight out of the Fifties...soda fountain counter, juke box, uniformed waitresses, old style malt glasses. Place is big and bright; food is basic Americano...cheeseburgers, chili, hot dogs, sandwiches, milkshakes, apple pie. Hours: 7 a.m. - 11 p.m. *Located in Lahaina Market Place • 667-6994.*

Longhi's Pizzeria Deli: Can a deli be chic? Longhi's does its best. Choose from 20 sandwiches from cheeseburgers to Peking duck. Or get pasta, salad or terrific pizza. This is also the place for gourmet items— quail eggs, imported peperoncini, grape seed oil...an eclectic choice. Nowhere to sit, this is take-out. Hours: 8 a.m. to 11 p.m. *930 Wainee • 661-8128.*

Naokee's Too: This place has atmosphere because it doesn't try to have it. It's a local joint—a Spam & eggs breakfast, saimin lunch, fried fish or pork dinner type of restaurant...no pretense, just food, honey. Nothing over $5. Ambiance is strictly tile floor and formica table top. The whole building, not just the roof, is made of corrugated tin. A very simple place in a very beautiful spot—right on the ocean. Open windows all around take advantage of the sea air. Hours: 8 a.m. to midnight. *1307 Front • 667-7513.*

Sunrise Cafe: Best little hang-out coffee bar in town. Very casual, intimate, slightly funky place. Pastries, coffee drinks, sandwiches and light entrees...also great spot for breakfast. La Bretagne's owners run the cafe, so it's in good hands. Food is sent from La Bretagne's wonderful kitchen. Hours: 5:30 a.m. to 10:30 p.m. every day. *693-A Front, on a side street, around the corner from Front • 661-3326.*

Thai Chef: Feel the urge for Pad Pramuk (sauteed squid) or Pohpia (spring rolls)? This is the place. Menu is in Thai with English subtitles. More than 50 items, including a page of vegetarian specialties. Only 12 tables, so it's intimate. Hours: 11-3 p.m. except Sun. Dinner nightly 5-10. *In Lahaina Shopping Center • 667-2814.*

Zushi: Simple Japanese cafe...working class feel to it. Small menu, small place—only 4 booths & 3 tables. Noodles and sushi type of lunch; dinner menu slightly larger. Take-out counter open for lunch only. Hours: 10-2 p.m. & 5-9 p.m. *888 Wainee • 667-5142.*

$$ Mid-Range

Alex's Hole in the Wall: Opened in 1974, and has consistently kept its reputation as best Italian restaurant on Maui. Food is fresh, sauces are homemade by Alex. Recipes are a family affair—passed down from the grandparents. Hours: 6-10 p.m. Closed Sunday. *Located off 834 Front down Wahie Lane • 661-3197.*

Chart House: Good, solid reputation for steak and fish, plus they have an excellent salad bar. The building is perched up high—great for views of ocean and sunset. The interior is artistically designed, all wood and lava rock with a beautiful bar and a small outside lanai. Hours: 4:30 to 10 p.m. *1450 Front • 661-0937.*

Chris's Smokehouse BBQ: Only authentic BBQ place on Maui. Charcoal broiled fish, smoked chicken and ribs, ribs, ribs. Everything's cooked over kiawe (mesquite) wood. The owner graduated from the Culinary Institute of America, so he knows how to cook. The BBQ sauce draws raves. Hours: 11:30-9:30 p.m.; Sundays 5-9:30 p.m. *Located in Lahaina Square Shopping Mall • 667-2111.*

Kimo's: A very popular place right on the ocean. Great for sunsets. Good honest fish and meat kind of food. Not fancy, but fresh and substantial. Hours: 11:30-2:30 p.m. & 5-10:30 p.m. Bar open till 1:30. *845 Front • 661-4811.*

Kobe Steak House: The chefs put on a show right at your table. You sit with 6-8 people and watch the food prepared teppanyaki-hibachi style...cutting, flaming, sizzling all done on a grill in mid table. Sushi bar also for those who like their food raw. Beautiful restaurant, Japanese country inn style. Hours: 5:30-10 p.m. Sushi bar 6-1 a.m. *136 Dickenson • 667-5555.*

Longhi's: The IN spot in town. Been "in" a long time, not just a fad. A great restaurant with a chic ambiance. Can sometimes be a "scene," but that's part of the fun. Food changes daily and is always fresh. No written menu, the waiter/waitress verbally runs through the selections. Italian is stressed. This is one of the best and most successful restaurants in Hawai'i. But no reservations accepted, so take your chances. Dancing to a live band Fri. & Sat. after 10:30 p.m. Hours: 7:30 a.m.-10 p.m. *888 Front • 667-2288.*

Marco's: Has the flavor of an intimate European bistro, sophisticated, yet casual. An unusual place for Front Street. The interior is sleek, white and chic. Cuisine is northern Italian, and it is excellent. Famous for their gelatto ice cream. Hours: lunch M-F 12-2:30; dinner 5:30-10 nightly. *Located in back of Mariner's Alley at 844 Front • 661-8877.*

Oceanhouse Restaurant & Seafood Cafe: An airy, brass & wood, crispy clean type of interior. Chic place right on the ocean. Actually two restaurants under same management. Downstairs is the Oceanhouse—fine dining that verges on expensive; some of the food is Cajun-Creole cooking. Seafood Cafe is upstairs—less expensive; has a seafood bar, plus many pizza and pasta dishes. Seafood Cafe hours: 11:30 a.m. to 10 p.m. Oceanhouse hours: 6-10 nightly. *831 Front • 661-3359 • 661-3472.*

Sang Thai: Thai cuisine—great, fresh food. Many vegetarian dishes. You can order it mild, medium or spicy hot. No MSG used. Impeccable service. Serene feel to the place. Hours: 11a.m.-10 p.m. *Located at The Wharf, 658 Front • 667-9581.*

$$$ *Expensive*

Gerard's: This is a small, simple place with just 19 tables. It is not fancy or elegant looking. It is sweet and unpretentious...brick floor, local art on the walls, casual atmosphere. "People come for the food," a waiter says, and he's right. Gerard's is a French restaurant extraordinaire. The food and service have impeccable reputations. Gerard Reversade is a Frenchman who cares about his tiny establishment. Hours: 11:30 to 2:30 M-F; 6-10 nightly. *Corner of Lahaina Market Place and Lahainaluna Road • 661-8939.*

La Bretagne: Darling little place with a country French interior. Used to be the home of a past Maui sheriff, and it still has a homey feel. The front yard is a jungle of plants and flowers. You can eat inside or outside on the screened-in lanai. Food is exquisite, and so is the service.

Place is friendly, not stuffy.   Hours: 6-10 p.m. *562 C. Front down an unmarked side street between Shaw & Prison Streets* • *661-8966.*

SHOPPING

Lahaina seems to be nothing but one small shop after another, yet the stores are generally not very innovative. Front Street, especially, seems to fester with ticky-tacky souvenir joints. Lots of cheap stuff, not enough original ideas.

505 Front Street
The gray wooden buildings here are reminiscent of a New England seacoast town...whaling days supposedly. Two of the shops feature made-in-Hawai'i souvenirs. **The Art Affair** has handcrafted arts and crafts (mostly crafts) from Hawai'i, with an emphasis on Maui artisans. This tiny store is filled with knickknacks, ceramics, cards, jewelry, shawls, wooden pieces.

The Old Lahaina Lu'au Gallery and Shop has slightly more expensive, more specialized items...of both modern and ancient Hawaiian design. Only shop on island where you can get ancient (kahiko) crafts—small musical instruments, gourd helmets (makini) and feather leis. Ni'ihau shell jewelry is also sold here. It's usually expensive since fewer than a dozen Ni'ihau women still string the shells. The shop is headquaters for the Old Lahaina Lu'au...buy tickets here.

The Wharf, 658 Front
These four floors of 55 shops and 6 restaurants has a lot that you don't need and a bit that you do. Most shops are open 9 to 9:30.

Maui Mad Hatter, the best and only hat shop on the island, is a circus of headgear—hundreds of straw hats of all kinds. Once your head is outfitted, time to pamper your feet. Have custom leather sandals made at **Island Sandals**. Choose from three sturdy styles. Takes half a day from fitting to wearing.

Island Coins and Stamps is the only such store in Maui County. They sell worldwide stamps and coins, but specialize in Hawaiian. Hawai'i issued 82 different stamps between 1850 and 1899 when it was a republic and a monarchy. In 1900 the U.S. Postal Service took over. Hawai'i also had its own coins, including a half-dollar sized 1¢ copper coin.

The classy **Chase Collection** has hand-made, one-of-a-kind jewelry and bronze sculptures...all displayed in beautiful wooden cases. **Nature's Emporium** is a small shop devoted to animals...whale and dolphin paraphernalia, Greenpeace T-shirts, animal books, etc.

Outfit the tykes, aged 6 months to size 14, at **Little Polynesians**, a store full of Hawaiian wear. A mu'u-mu'u in size 1? Can hardly live without it.

Want a poster of Hawai'i? Try **Posters Maui** on the top floor.

The only bookstore in Lahaina is **The Whaler's Book Shoppe and Coffee Shop.** Good selection of Hawaiian titles, and for those who like dessert and coffee with their books, this shop serves both. There's a larger selection of desserts on the first floor at the **Old Lahaina Towne Bakery.** Coffee too—they have an expresso machine.

Front Street...Main Drag

It's a cute street, but a disappointment for shoppers...unless you want T-shirts and inexpensive souvenirs. The street goes on for several blocks, though, so there are bound to be a few winners.

The cheeriest place on the street has got to be **High as a Kite** (703 Front), a colorful shop overflowing with kites. **Sea & Shell** (713 Front)

is a classy little place full of jewelry, shells, corals and other tropical souvenirs.

The prettiest sidewalk and entrance on Front Street belongs to **The Gallery Ltd.** (716 Front). You feel like you've stepped into a Hong Kong antique store here. Netsukes, snuff bottles, carved ivory, cloisonne, jade, jewelry...it's down Hong Kong's Nathan Road you go.

Local company **Island Tan** mixes up their own batches of moisturizers and tanning lotions right here at 760 Front Street. Their skin care products have an aloe base, no mineral oil allowed, so it's greaseless. They claim that people who never tan will tan with their potions.

The run-down little shacks at 819 Front used to be an old poi factory. Now it's a crazy mish-mash of three tiny stores, a lei stand, jewelry stands, and wild animal flotation rafts...all together under a canopy of trees. One of the stores, **Pacific Visions,** sells deco objects and handpainted white clothes...all very hip. Fun little area...definitely perks up the street.

Front Street etching by David Warren

Get your portrait done in 20 minutes right on Front Street. Painter **Marcia Young** does charcoal portraits for the unbelievable price of $12.50. She's quick and she's good—she's done it more than 30 years. Her easel is set up nightly in Mariner's Alley.

The Dolphin Gallery (834 Front) sells high quality doo-dads from bronze and glass figurines to exquisite glass perfume bottles to expensive jewelry to...the list is ever changing.

A rambling and ramshackle affair, the **South Seas Trading Post** (851 Front) looks just like it should. It has the funky flavor of a real trading post. Treasures from all over the Pacific—New Guinea to Fiji. Nothing expensive, most items are moderate to cheap.

Dan's Green House (133 Prison Street) is a block from Front Street. Here amidst screeching tropical birds you can buy inexpensive, souvenir type bonsai trees—all of them schefflera, a common house plant...hard to kill. It's a good introduction to the Japanese bonsai art. Most of Dan's trees are 5 years old when sold.

Ivory and scrimshaw lovers should visit **Lahaina Scrimshaw Factory** (854 & 718 Front). It's a store full of scrimshaw—pictures etched on bone, teeth or tusks. Most are modern pieces etched recently, though there are a few antiques.

Amazing tale about **Crazy Shirts**—the T-shirt store (865 Front) that sells heavy cotton shirts with popular tourist designs. Seems the owner started out in the Sixties selling from a bamboo shack in Waikiki. His first shirt he sold straight off his back (for $5). He now has a chain of stores and a big business going. He can be credited for much of the painted and sloganed T-shirt craze. His first shirts said "Draft beer, not students" and "Fly the friendly skies of Cambodia." Now they say "Maui Beach Club" and "Maui Wine."

Lahaina Printsellers are on Front Street, but way down quite a ways from the shopping district. They're located in the historic Seamen's Hospital, worth a visit for the building alone. The Printsellers are exactly that—a store that sells prints, all of them old engravings. Owner Charlene Walker says, "I emphasize that these are antiques, not reproductions. I have a real hard time making people believe that. They're so overwhelmed—they can't believe we have such an incredible collection." Walker and her husband Alan specialize in maps, though they also have a big selection of botanical drawings. The maps are generally from the 19th Century and earlier. Charlene says, "I don't think there's a place we don't have a map of—we have all the states, most American city plans, all the foreign countries." It's an unusual store, definitely one of a kind. Hours are 9-5 daily.

The Cannery

This was once an old corrugated metal building, big as a warehouse. It was built in 1919 as a pineapple cannery, and it functioned as such until 1963 when the cannery shut its doors. By 1987 the cannery was open again, but with a total makeover. The old building was torn down (the structure was not sound), and a similar "cannery" replaced it. This one has 50 spaces for shops and restaurants. Most are open 9:30 to 9:30. The best of the lot include:

Reyn's, a store with classic aloha fashions, some women's dresses, but mostly men's shirts...all made with the Hawaiian fabric that looks printed inside-out. **Blue Ginger Designs** has women's clothing, plus some kid's clothes. All are made with a distinctive cotton batik design that resembles gingham, but isn't.

For old-fashioned-girl type dresses, try **Mama & Me**. It also has little girl clothes. Small, cute store. For more kids' clothes, go around the corner to **Superwhale**. **Alexia** is the women's clothing chain that specializes in raw silk clothing made in Greece. The clothes are generally simple and elegant.

Hobie Sports is worth visiting just to see the collection of old surfboards that lines the walls. The oldest is a battered redwood board made in 1922. The shop sells new boards and casual clothing.

Lahaina Scrimshaw and **Dolphin Gallery** are two island businesses seen in several other locations on West Maui. Both have unique and beautifully-displayed objets d'art.

Maui Folk...

Luckey Lahaina

Jim Luckey aptly describes Lahaina's Front Street as "a sort of Wild West Virginia City false front modified Polynesian hodgepodge." And he loves it. He has dedicated his life to a few city blocks in this tiny historical town.

Jim is the executive director of the Lahaina Restoration Foundation, an organization that restores and preserves Lahaina's historic buildings and sites. Set up in 1962, the Foundation's first project was the missionary Baldwin House. Other finished projects include the Brig carthaginian, the Seamen's Hospital, Hale Pa'i and Wo Hing Temple.

Jim came to the job in 1972 fresh from the Mainland with nothing but enthusiasm as his resume. He was from Oregon, in the lumber business, when he and his wife decided to take their first Hawaiian vacation.

"I had reached a turning point in my business, and in the process of that change, we came to Maui. In that two-week vacation we absolutely fell in love, in a very deep way, with Maui, and with Lahaina in particular.

"We went back and sold our home. Burned our bridges. We moved here with no work. We did not come here to retire; we came for a second career. There was not much going on in 1972. It was difficult for a middle-aged haole to find work then. Fortunately, the work with the Foundation opened up that year." Luckey was indeed that.

"I had a gut reaction to this place. I had an emotional trauma when I went back to the Mainland. Then I was flooded with aloha on my return when the plane landed."

Jim believes that "Lahaina is one of God's very special places on earth.

"I don't want to sound too maudlin," he says about his emotional attachment to the town. "We had, as any visitor has, some serious adjustments to make—economic, social, political, ethnic. There is a culture shock because Hawai`i in general and Lahaina in particular is not just any place in the world."

As he describes it: "It was suddenly learning how to appreciate the wisdom of someone else's culture; to understand the truths in someone else's religion; to enjoy the taste of someone else's food; to hear with joy the sound of someone else's music; and to appreciate the color of someone else's skin.

"We were able to make those adjustments because of a strength, a feeling of support, from many directions. This is the strength and power of Lahaina.

"The word that describes it is aloha, and that is still the gift we have to offer our visitors, particularly the people who embrace us, who put themselves out even just an inch."

Jim considers his work "a gift," and says, "I have never lost my enthusiasm for it over the years.

"The idea of preserving Lahaina and bringing it back to life was a good sound idea nurtured by dozens of talented people. We're just concerned with Lahaina; we don't branch out and argue about airports and hotels. We have a very small world and grand vistas."

What's his reply to critics who say Lahaina is too cutesie or too big? "I see the town through rose-colored glasses. I see it as a brighter, cleaner, safer, more vital place to live than it was in the early Eighties. It is a live, constantly changing flux. It is maturing."

But there are certain parts of town that will remain constant...it's Jim's job to keep them historically intact. "Through it all," he says, "these oases of history, the real heartbeat, will never change—the temple, the Baldwin House, the Pioneer Inn—they are guaranteed in perpetuity. They cannot be sold. They cannot be developed, by law. And that is an advantage that very few communities have."

Jim does acknowledge that Lahaina's popularity and growth causes problems for its residents. The cost of housing is "criminal," he says. "But they do pay it. For every person who has to leave because they can no longer survive, there are ten people standing in line. I don't know how long that can go on, but it's been going on as long as I've been here.

"The plan for Lahaina's restoration was to create jobs for the local people because there were no jobs at the time. There are now hundreds of excellent job opportunities in Lahaina."

Of his own job, Jim never thinks of leaving it. "Every morning is a new challenge. I have a hospital, a print shop, a tree, a whale boat, a cemetery, an old church, a prison—what more could a man want? I've got all the toys I can use."

Ka'anapali

1950s: Ka'anapali was three miles of great beach, but it was surrounded by scrub land. Pioneer Mill Company (owners of the land) couldn't raise sugar on it. It was useless, unprofitable. But an idea was brewing...

AMFAC, Pioneer Mills' parent company, dreamed a scheme—build a huge, classy resort, first such idea with a master plan (condos, hotels, golf courses). No one had ever built such a resort in Hawai'i. It was a gamble. It cost them millions. Hindsight proves they won big.

Ka'anapali is a great resort. Sunshine, sand and luxury. It is not elite, there are crowds of tourists. Some of it is expensive, much is moderate, nothing is budget.

HISTORY

It is believed villages existed here since the 1100s. It is definitely known that one great (or horrible) battle was fought up and down Ka'anapali's shores during the early 1700s.

In this notorious fight, two half-brothers fought to the death over who would succeed their deceased father (Maui chief Kekaulike). One son had 600 warriors from O'ahu join him; the other son had 8000 warriors from Hawai'i. Easy guess which side won. The battle raged for four days and is called Koko-o-na-moku, meaning "blood of the Islands."

A sweeter history...

The Ka'anapali area was plantation land from the mid 1800s until the mid 1900s. Pioneer Mill was established in the 1860s to process the sugar cane.

Henry Baldwin, son of the famous missionary, started growing pineapple on his Honolua Ranch, and in 1919 he opened a cannery in Lahaina.

Villages once again sprouted in Ka'anapali, but the faces of the inhabitants were quite different from the century before. These were the immigrants who worked the fields, and their villages were strictly company towns.

SIGHTS

Black Rock/ Pu'u Keka'a

This large black lava "rock" is actually a cinder cone, and is the western-most point on Maui. To the Hawaiians, it was a very sacred place. This was a "leaping place of the soul," one of the sacred places where souls of the dead would go to leap into their ancestral spirit land. There was a heiau and burial ground on top of Black Rock, but neither is there today. The Sheraton Hotel built over the area.

The great Maui king and warrior Kahekili, who lived in the mid 1700s, was known for his skill and courage in cliff leaping. Few men would dare the spirit world to leap alongside the dead at Pu'u Keka'a. Kahekili did, and in doing so, rallied his men behind him in battle. Seeing his bravery at Pu'u Keka'a, they were encouraged to carry on with their many battles.

Kahekili's great leap is re-enacted nightly at sundown by a diver from the Sheraton Hotel. People sit at the hotel bar, near the ancient burial grounds, and watch the performance. Luckily, there are no more bones to turn in their graves. When the hotel was building itself into the side of Pu'u Keka'a in the 1960s, many of the ancient burial sites were dug up. The bones were buried elsewhere, but for quite a time the hotel was thought to be haunted.

Whalers Village Museum

This is a fascinating display of whale and whaling artifacts, plus terrific old-time photos. The museum takes you through the whole whaling process—from the chase, to the harpooning, to cutting up the whale and storing it aboard ship. There are descriptions and photos of the whaling "men" (often boys). Their tales of hardships and grim conditions are riveting.

The museum was built by the James Campbell Estate which owns the shopping center. The original James Campbell was a whaler who sailed from New England in the 1840s. He later became an entrepreneur, and founded Maui's Pioneer Sugar Mill.

Every half hour, from 10 a.m. till 4:30 p.m., the museum shows whale videos.

Located on the third floor of Whalers Village. Hours: 9:30 to 9:30, closed from 1 to 1:30 for lunch.

Other sites?
"...sugar cane and pineapple plantations, and more recently, the resort developments along this coast, have destroyed virtually all the archaeological sites in the area."
"Survey & Salvage—Honoapiilani Highway"
—Archaeological Research Center of Hawai'i

BEACHES & PARKS

Ka'anapali Beach

Need anything be said? This is obviously an incredible beach...but hardly pristine. The place is jumping with hotels and condos. Always crowded. Never a dull moment...speedboats, jetskis, windsurfers, parasails, small planes...it's the happenest beach on the island (unless, of course, you seek peace and quiet).

Public access is way down by the airport road on the far side of the Sheraton, but the dirt path is hard to find. An easier public path is by the Hyatt's parking lot. Frankly, you can ignore both these legal routes and just cruise casually through the hotels.

Facilities: wherever there's a hotel, there'll be toilets and showers.

HOTELS

Sheraton Maui

In 1963 when it opened, the Sheraton had Ka'anapali all to itself. Perhaps because it was first, it has the primo location—on a sandy beach that winds into dramatic Black Rock, supposedly built by Pele, the fire goddess.

In '63, the opening of a luxury hotel was a grand event in Maui. United Airlines flew in a special DC-8 full of hotel guests. Kids got off school and people jammed the airport to see what is commonplace now—tourists and airplanes.

As tourism grew, the Sheraton kept adding structures, so there's not a consistent feel to the whole. There are 26 "cottages," two towers, four motel-like buildings on the ocean, an upper lobby, a lower lobby...it's a big place, 510 rooms on 23 acres. It still has the best location, but its property and its rooms are no longer the best on the beach.

Tip: don't get a cottage near the lu'au grounds unless you like lu'au music in your bedroom seven nights a week.

Mid-range.
Ka'anapali Beach, Lahaina, HI 96761 • 661-0031 • (800) 325-3535 • (800) 268-9393 (eastern Canada) • (416) 869-1414 (Toronto) • (800)268-9330 (western Canada).

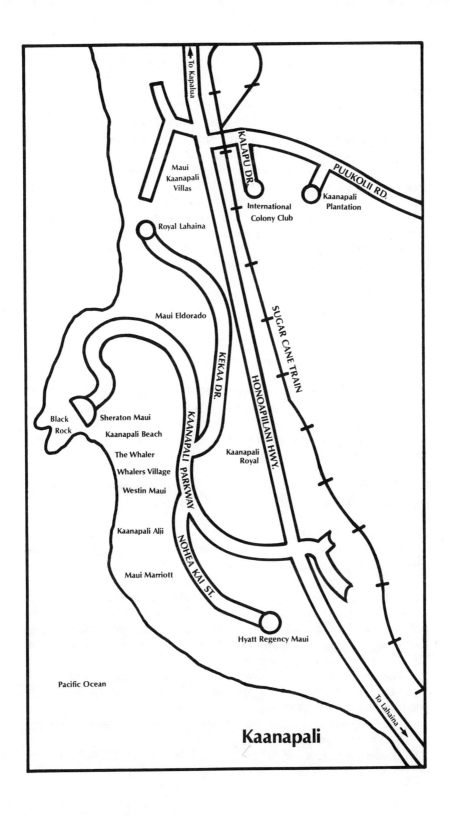

To Kapalua

KALAPU DR.

PUUKOLII RD.

Maui
Kaanapali
Villas

International
Colony Club

Kaanapali
Plantation

Royal Lahaina

Maui Eldorado

SUGAR CANE TRAIN

KEKAA DR.

HONOAPIILANI HWY.

KAANAPALI PARKWAY

Black
Rock

Sheraton Maui

Kaanapali Beach

The Whaler

Whalers Village

Westin Maui

Kaanapali Alii

Kaanapali
Royal

NOHEA KAI ST.

Maui Marriott

Hyatt Regency Maui

Pacific Ocean

To Lahaina

Kaanapali

Hyatt Regency Maui

This hotel is pure ritz and glitz and pizzazz. Sometimes considered a three-ring circus...but just know you'll never be bored. Lots of action, lots of people, lots of food, lots of lots. Nothing, absolutely nothing, has been forgotten. Want a pink flamingo? You've got it.

It was built in 1980 to be a fantasy, and it is. Exotic birds (your pink flamingos for one) have the run of the 18.5 acres. Two miles of waterfalls and streams run through tropical and Oriental gardens. Art worth $2 million decorates the interiors. The half-acre pool with its 130-foot water slide is the best on the island.

It took $80 million to build it. It takes 1200 employees to run it. The 815 guest rooms make it the biggest hotel on Maui.

Expensive.

200 Nohea Kai Drive, Lahaina, HI 96761 • 67-7474 • (800) 228-9005.

Maui Marriott

Not as fancy, and not as expensive, as its neighbor the Hyatt, the Marriott holds its own as a nice, comfortable hotel. Its rooms are as big as the Hyatt rooms, but the interiors are not as sophisticated.

The lobby is all open air with fountains and greenery galore. Much of the lobby area seems to be shops—22 of them. You feel you're in a bazaar, not a hotel.

The 720 rooms are divided between two nine-story buildings. Ninety percent have ocean views.

Expensive.

100 Nohea Kai Drive, Lahaina, HI 96761 • 667-1200 • (800) 228-9290 (U.S.) • (800) 228-2180 (HI).

Royal Lahaina Resort

The lobby here always seems so busy busy, yet once inside the grounds (26 acres), the place is peaceful and quiet. Could be due to the 22 wooden "cottages" spread out on the property. Few new hotels can now afford low-rise cottages, but the Royal Lahaina was built in 1962 when Ka'anapali was not so expensive for developers. Cottages definitely add a graceful touch. Most of the 514 rooms, however, are located in a 12-story tower building. Not as charming, but the rooms are actually nicer than the cottage rooms.

The hotel has 10 tennis courts plus a stadium court (seats 4,000 people). There are three swimming pools and a whirlpool...not to mention the perfect blue ocean.

The AAA people consistently give the place a Four Diamond rating.

Mid-range to expensive.

2780 Kekaa Drive, Lahaina, HI 96761 • 661-3611 • (800) 227-4700

Ka'anapali Beach Hotel

This is Ka'anapali's second oldest hotel and its buildings do show their age. It's comfortable and it's located on a perfect beach; it just doesn't have the pizzazz some of the others do. It also doesn't have the high prices.

There are 431 rooms in four buildings, three to seven stories high. The buildings form a U-shape around the 10.5 acreage. Pool and lawn area are in the middle.

Employees here may be able to answer questions better than most. The hotel has mandatory quarterly classes to teach employees about Hawaiian culture and values.

Mid-range.

P.O. Box 8520, Honolulu, HI 96830 • 661-0011 • (800) 227-4700.

CONDOS

High Condo: Off Beach

Quiet and secluded and relatively unknown, the **International Colony Club** hardly seems as if it could be part of the Ka'anapali scene. Built in 1964, it was the original condo in West Maui. Too bad the rest did not follow suit in design. This place was built with grace and with care for esthetics. Forty-four lovely, homey wooden cottages are spread over a gently sloping hillside. Flowers ring every cottage. Dozens of variations of flowers and trees create paradise throughout the ten-acre property. The two pools are heated since many of the guests and residents are elderly. The Colony Club never advertises; word of mouth and decent prices keep the cottages full. The one bedrooms are high range, but the two bedrooms are moderately priced. *2750 Kalapu Dr., Lahaina, HI 96761 • 661-4070.*

Expensive Condos: Off Beach

The **Maui Eldorado** does not sit on the beach; instead, it overlooks a lovely golf course. The lack of beach is overridden by three big pools. Plus, a short walk leads you to Ka'anapali's shoreline where the Eldorado has a beach cabana for its guests. This condo was built in 1970, so it has a slightly older feel than some of the other Ka'anapali hotels and condos. The Eldorado has a gracious charm. Ten lowrise buildings dot ten acres of a beautifully manicured hillside. Lots of trees and flowers. The 204 apartments (studios, 1& 2-BRs) have no ritz and glitz, but they're spacious and comfortable. A lovely place. *2661 Kekaa Dr., Lahaina, HI 96761 • 661-0021 • (800) 421-0767.*

Built in 1980, the **Ka'anapali Royal** has snazzy modern units, 105 of them spread out in 15 buildings. All are large, 2,000 square-foot, 2-

BR units. But, if you only need one bedroom, you can occasionally get a cheaper price, especially during the summer low season. Golfers can step right out their doors into the adjoining golf course. Tennis players have two courts on the grounds. A whirlpool and sauna are also on property. *Reservations c/o Hawaiiana Resorts, 1100 Ward Ave., Suite 1100, Honolulu, HI 96814. • 667-7200 • (800) 367-7040.*

Stratosphere Condo: On Beach

Everything at the **Ka'anapali Ali'i** is so well done you almost forget you're in a huge complex of four 11-story buildings. The 264 apartments (1 & 2-BR) are all large and exquisitely furnished. A chaise lounge in a bedroom window alcove, a sunken living room, a steel safe in a closet, Chanel toiletry in the bath, a bidet and a whirlpool tub, oak cabinets in the kitchen, a separate dining area—nothing is lacking in these spacious living quarters. The Ali'i is run like a hotel with daily maid service and a 24-hour front desk. The concierge keeps guests busy with a daily activities list of ocean sports and tennis. *50 Nohea Kai Dr., Lahaina, HI 96761 • 667-1400 • (800) 367-6090.*

RESTAURANTS

$ Budget

Chico's Cantina: This is a hip Mexican restaurant with good, plentiful food. The interior is very eclectic...a blue marlin on the wall next to a '56 red Chevy front. For those who don't know a fajita from a chimichanga or a quesadilla, there are explanations on the back of the menu. Hours: 11:30 to 2:30 and 5-10:30. *Located in Whalers Village • 667-2777.*

Chopsticks: They call theirs a "grazing menu"—the idea is to order several appetizer-size dishes and graze your way through several countries. The menu lists food from Hong Kong, Thailand, Mainland China, Micronesia and Japan...so all the munching is done in the Pacific. Hours: 5:30 to 10 nightly. *Located in the Royal Lahaina Resort • 661-3611.*

$$ Mid-Range

Leilani's: This is a big place located on a lovely spot on the beach. They have 60 koa-wood tables, and they do hundreds of meals every night. The menu is steak, chicken, seafood...American fare. Plus, there's a 4-item kids' menu. The interior is beautifully designed...all wood with windows open to the ocean. Hours: 5 to 10:30 nightly; bar open 4 to 1:30. *Located in Whalers Village • 661-4495.*

Lokelani: This is the Marriott Hotel's fine dining restaurant, and it's a very pretty place. Fish is the specialty (5 different fresh fish offered nightly), but meat and chicken are also available. It's an elegant, but casual place...all open air with a view of a courtyard. Hours: 6-10 nightly. Located in the Marriott • 667-1200.

Moby Dick's: This is an imaginative seafood restaurant (with a few items for meat eaters). It has a simple, elegant interior, nothing fancy or fussy. Hours: 5:30 to 10:30 nightly. Located right on the golf course at the Royal Lahaina Resort • 661-3611.

$$$ Expensive

Nikko: Reputed to be one of the best Japanese restaurants on Maui, Nikko's is a steak house, food served teppanyaki style. People sit around a grill where all food is prepared by an entertaining chef who wields a knife like a samurai. Hours: 6-10 nightly. Located in the Marriott Hotel • 667-1200.

The Peacock: The gracious entrance leads over a trickling stream, past a koi pond surrounded by tropical vegetation. The interior is lovely and low-key with windows opening to the golf course. Worth going just to sit in the rattan fan peacock chairs. Dinners are American fare— chicken, fish, meat. Hours: 11:30 to 2; 6-10 daily. 2550 Kekaa Drive • 667-6847.

Swan Court: The Hyatt couldn't have picked a lovelier spot for its best restaurant—the Swan Court sits on the edge of a pond full of swans with a Japanese garden bordering the pond. Everything is elegant and gorgeous...perfect place for a special date. Their award-winning, imaginative menu includes Continental, Polynesian, Oriental and American cuisine. Hours: (breakfast) 6:30 to 11:30; (dinner) 6 to 10:30. Located at Hyatt Hotel • 667-7474.

SHOPPING

Whaler's Village
If you're going to own a shop in Maui, this is the place to have it. Of course you'd never get a space because no retailer ever leaves. Business is too good. There's a captive audience in the Ka'anapali resorts.

This is a classy mall. Most of the shops are unique, many are expensive. **Silks Ka'anapali** is a good example—gorgeous, original women's clothing in silk and cotton, much of it handpainted by local artists.

Another woman's store is **Foreign Intrigue, Ltd.**—elegant, fancy, very different clothing for the woman who knows how to dress with panache. Not faddish, but not boringly classic.

Super Whale Children's Boutique is, as to be expected, cutesie. Stuffed toys, funny hats, Hawaiian clothes in itty bitty sizes. Next door is **Crazy Shirts**, the always popular T-shirt chain store. Crazy Shirts cottons and designs are quality.

Liberty House has a branch store here. Not their big department store variety; this smaller version features casual clothes suitable for Maui...naturally enough.

Eyecatcher Accessories takes care of your eyes—sunglasses of all types, chic to cheap. **Island Tan** covers your skin—a local skin care company that uses aloe vera as a base for its lotions. They claim you *will* tan with their ingredients (presumably with the sun's help).

Waldenbooks is the biggest bookstore on West Maui, and it is not all that big. (Book lovers will note that Maui has a dearth of bookstores.) Waldenbooks always has a good selection of Hawai'i and Maui books.

Sea & Shell is a wonderful little shop full of seashell related gifts. Very clever items, all well crafted. **Scrimshaw Factory** is an elegant store devoted, of course, to scrimshaw. But, you can also buy a $15,000 rare Narwhal tusk that looks like a unicorn horn. If you have more mundane tastes, pick up a pair of elephant tusks. **Dolphin Gallery** has a changing array of bronze sculptures, glassware, posters, jewelry, ceramics, etc.—all fancy stuff.

Lahaina Printsqellers is a unique shop...almost a museum. Here you can buy original lithographs of maps, botanical artwork or Hawaiian prints, all antique engravings. This is a smaller version of their larger store in the Seamen's Hospital on Front Street in Lahaina. Serious art collectors should stop by Front Street.

Do notice the sperm whale skeleton on display in front of Whaler's Village. Along with these huge bones are exhibits of other whale species. Check these out, then go up to the whale museum on the third floor...it is excellent.

Honokowai

Honokowai is the Kihei of West Maui...one condo after another. Most of them not particularly attractive. There's little to say about this strip—nice beaches, too many condos, very little to see. No hotels (just condos), no restaurants, no shopping. No historical sites...anything ancient has been condo-ed over.

One plus: it is possible to get reasonable room rates here, and that's a rarity in West Maui.

BEACHES & PARKS

Honokowai Beach Park

Right across from the Honokowai Superette. It's not a pretty beach or grassy area. Not good for swimming due to large shelves of rocks. The rocks create a nice pool for kids, though.

Facilities: showers, picnic tables, paved parking.

CONDOS

Budget Condo: Off Beach

The only budget condo on all of West Maui is the **Honokowai Palms**. On the outside it looks like big city welfare housing—three orange concrete block buildings. But the interiors of the 1 & 2-BR units are clean and well equipped. Pat and Monty Nelson, the cheery managers, were hired to upgrade the place, and they have done so with pride. "I wouldn't rent the units out if they weren't sharp," says Pat. "We've done a lot of work on them. Now the place is homey, friendly and relaxed. The guests leave here just thrilled." Pat encourages the friendliness by serving coffee every morning at the pool. Bananas from the 100-some trees on property are also gratis. *3666 Lower Honoapiilani Highway, Lahaina, HI 96761 • 669-6130.*

Moderate Condos: On Beach

The **Maui Sands** has a dramatic ocean-front setting. There is a small sand beach, but most of its shoreline is lava rock and coral. Seven low-rise buildings housing 76 units face towards the ocean, though the oceanfront units have the best view. The back units enjoy a lovely yard area that has both tropical and Japanese touches. Oceanfront units are more expensive (in the high range). One-bedroom garden units are budget and two bedrooms are moderate. *3559 Lower Honoapiilani Highway, Lahaina, HI 96761 • 669-4811 • (800) 367-5037.*

The **Kuleana Maui** does not look like much from the road...from there you get a view of the parking lot. But once inside, the view changes. The four and a half acres are beautifully landscaped with lots of flowers. The original two wooden buildings were built in 1968. Two years later five concrete block buildings were added. If possible, stay in the wooden buildings—the rooms are much larger and cheerier. One, two and three bedroom units are all avaiblable there. The concrete buildings have only one bedroom units and they're rather small. The management is very proud of the pool—81,000 gallons large. *3959 Lower Honoapiilani Highway, Lahaina, HI 96761 • 669-8080 • (800) 367-5176.*

Flowers, flowers, flowers—the lawn of the **Mahina Surf** is full of hibiscus, lilies, gardenias, et al. Three wooden buildings with 56 units (1 & 2-BR) are U-shaped around the lawn, all facing the ocean. No sandy beach, just lava rocks, but Ka'anapali beach is close by. The condos are modern and pleasant. Second floor units are especially spacious due to their high wooden ceiling. *4057 Lower Honoapiilani Highway, Lahaina, HI 96761 • 669-6068 • (800) 367-6086.*

A layered roof of brown shingles dominates the 3-story **Kulakane**. All 42 units (1 & 2-BR) are ocean front and all are very modern. There is no beach, waves slap against a retaining wall. A small lawn area between the building and the ocean is decorated with two picturesque Japanese rock gardens, a delightful touch. In front of the condo stands a large rubber tree that looks much older than its 15 years. *3741 Lower Honoapiilani Rd., P.O. Box 5236, Lahaina, HI 96761 • 669-6119 • (800) 367-6088.*

High Condos: On Beach

Noelani means "heavenly mist," but there's not much rain here in the sunshine belt. This complex of three low-rise buildings is the last condo in Honokowai. A great little fishing cove separates it from the monolithic condos of Kahana. Sixteen of Noelani's 50 units are large studios. The kitchens are in a nook off the main room and the bathroom is a separate area with a little dressing room. The 1, 2 & 3 bedrooms are also large and comfortable. All sit on the edge of the ocean and have great views of sunsets, whales and waves. *4095 Lower Honoapiilani Highway, Lahaina, HI 96761 • 669-8374 • (800) 367-6030.*

A favorite place in the **Polynesian Shores** is a wooden patio set at the edge of the rocks overlooking the ocean. Great place for barbeques and picnics, even greater for reading and thinking. Three sets of wooden steps lead down to the ocean. No sandy beach, but very lovely lava rock coastline. The three wooden buildings house 52 modern units with 1, 2 & 3 bedrooms. Second floor apartments have lofts, so they're more spacious than the lower floor units. *3975 Lower Honoapiilani Highway, Lahaina, HI 96761 • 669-6065.*

Expensive Condo: On Beach

The **Papakea** is a large complex, but the 364 units are spread out amongst 11 low-rise buildings on six acres. Stands of bamboo line the walkways between buildings, adding graceful privacy. Two large lily pod lagoons are stocked with expensive koi fish. Two swimming pools, two whirlpools, two saunas, three tennis courts, two 18-hole putting greens, plus numerous classes (swimmercize, snorkeling, pineapple cutting) make this an active place. Studios, 1 & 2 bedrooms. *3543 Lower Honoapiilani Highway, Lahaina, HI 96761 • 669-4848.*

Stratosphere Condo: On Beach

Kaanapali Shores is a very busy place. It has the largest number of units (462) of any condo complex on Maui. Yet somehow it does not overwhelm. It's run efficiently like a hotel with a 24-hour front desk and daily maid service. The concierge has daily activities planned that can keep you busy during your entire stay—aerobics, 15-minute free massages, scuba lessons, poolside parties, Polynesian revue. The tennis pro keeps his three courts busy with weekly free tennis clinics. During the summer he runs a tennis camp for kids. Also during the summer, the complex has a "camp" to keep guests' children busy. Daily "camp" activities include lessons in swimming, surfing, juggling, hula, lei making, plus nature walks and boating trips. Studios, 1 & 2 bedrooms. *100 Kaanapali Shores Pl., Lahaina, HI 96761 • 667-2211 • (800) 367-5124.*

Kahana

Kahana begins with an army of huge concrete condos that jut upwards and spread out down the beach. These end abruptly and fade into a section of private homes, many here for years. The homes give you an idea of what the area was like before tourism took a firm hold.

BEACHES & PARKS

Kahana Beach
Public access is on the S-curve in the road between Honokowai and Kahana. It's a small beach right next to the road, so cars are as prevalent as waves. No facilities.

Keoneuli Beach
Pretty white cove almost entirely taken over by condos. No public access. No facilities unless you stay at the condos.

CONDOS

Moderate Condo: On Beach (and Off)

The **Pohailani Maui Resort** has something for everyone...even a pickleball court, whatever that is. For those who like the beach, there are two buildings of 29 studios smack on a sandy beach. The studios are large with full-size kitchens and baths. The exteriors of the two buildings are very plain, possibly ugly. So, for those who prefer cheerier, quainter accommodations, just cross the street and there you have a village of 43 wooden duplexes spread over 7.5 acres of landscaped greenery. Charming to beat the band. The duplexes are not fancy, they are simple, homey two-bedroom units. Price is moderate and they are worth every penny. This is the most unusual complex in Kahana. *4435 Lower Honapiilani Highway, Lahaina, HI 96761 • 669-5464.*

Expensive Condos: On Beach

A woman who owns 9 of the 16 units in the **Kahana Outrigger** raves about the place. "It's very private," she says. "There's never anyone on our beach. We never have hordes of people coming and going." The four wooden buildings are like well-designed houses, all modern and spacious. Interiors were done by a Maui decorator, so colors and furniture match beautifully. Even the bedspreads match the living room sofa. The large kitchens have microwaves, ice makers, blenders, everything you need. Each bathroom has two sinks and a large tub/shower. All 16 units have three bedrooms. *4521 Lower Honoapiilani Highway, Lahaina, HI 96761 • 669-5544.*

Right next door in a similar setting is the **Kahana Village.** These seven buildings also look like beautiful wooden homes. There are 42 units (2 & 3-BR), so it is a bigger complex than the Outrigger, but the two do look much alike. The rooms here are all large and airy, and are beautifully decorated. The grounds are large and manicured, and feature a perfect little fish pond plus the only round condo pool on Maui. *4531 Lower Honoapiilani Highway, Lahaina, HI 96761 • 669-5111 • (800) 824-3065.*

Want your own beach set in your own private little cove in Kahana? Stay at the **Kahana Sunset.** This place has a magical setting. The cove is secluded and quiet. The six wooden condos are the only buildings in sight. All of them slope down a gentle incline facing the ocean. A lovely garden area and a 60-foot heated pool are the center of the grounds. But the focal point is the magnificent beach. Sixteen of the 79 units are one bedroom; the rest are two bedroom. The two bedrooms are townhouse style with both bedrooms upstairs. They cost more, but the two bedroom ocean front units are worth it. Sit out on one of your two lanais and it's just you and the ocean. *P.O. Box 10219, Lahaina, HI 96761 • 669-8011.*

Stratosphere Condo: On Beach

The **Sands of Kahana** looks and acts like a big hotel. Clerks at the 24-hour registration desk check you in, a bellman takes your bags, a maid makes your beds daily. There's no need for room service, however, because you have your own kitchen, and a big, beautiful one at that. The apartments (1, 2 & 3-BR) are large and modern, and are decorated well. There's nothing low-key here—the four buildings are imposing highrises. There's much beach activity going on. Plus, there are three tennis courts, an 8-hole putting green, a weight room and a whirlpool. A busy place. *4299 Lower Honoapiilani Highway, Lahaina, HI 96761 • 669-0400 • (800) 367-5124.*

RESTAURANTS

$$ Mid-Range

Erik's Seafood Grotto: A display of fish on ice is right inside the door...make no mistake, this is a seafood restaurant that's proud of its very fresh fish. Right behind the fish is a tank of lobsters. The restaurant has a beautiful interior with all kinds of fish and boat paraphernalia on the walls. As would be expected, the menu is mostly seafood, but there are four items "from the feedlot," as they say. Hours: 5-10:30 nightly. *In the Kahana Villa Condos • 669-4806.*

SHOPPING

Farmer's Market
Local politician and County Council member Wayne Nishiki brings his traveling produce show to Kahana twice a week (Mon. & Thur.). He sets up in the parking lot at the Eatery Restaurant on Lower Honoapiilani Highway. It's an open-air market with excellent fruits and vegetables at fair prices. Much of the food is locally grown. Nishiki is a local character...he got the most votes for council in the last election, and only spent $37 doing so!

12:30 to 4:30 Monday; 9 to 12 Thursday.

Napili

Napili is a classy address to have, though it's not as fancy as its neighbor Kapalua. It's mostly a bedroom community of condos and hotels situated in beautiful, sandy coves.

BEACHES & PARKS

Honokeana Bay
Means "the cave bay." It looks great, but it's hard to get to. No decent access unless you stay in one of the numerous condos.

Good swimming and snorkeling.

No facilities unless you stay at the condos.

Napili Bay
Beautiful cove, beautiful beach. Great for swimming and snorkeling. Sometimes the surf is good, but there's also a strong rip current too.

Public access from Napili Place and Hue Drive.

No facilities unless you stay at the condos.

CONDOS

High Condo: On Beach

A good snorkeling bay is just a few feet from your doorstep at the **Honokeana Cove.** The beach is rocky, but a stairway leads over the rocks into the water. You share the coral formations with only a few of your neighbors. Set right at the edge of the cove, this condo's four wooden buildings are small and private. They form a U-shape around a small yard and pool. It's a quiet area dominated by graceful palms and the sound of waves. Condos have 1, 2 or 3 BRs. *5255 Lower Honoapiilani Highway, Lahaina, HI 96761 • 669-6441.*

Expensive Condo: On Beach

Napili Point is also on the same sweet cove (with the same great snokeling) as the Honokeana Cove Condos, but it is three times as big as its neighbor (115 units with 1 or 2 BRs). This is a cleverly-designed complex. Twenty-seven of its units are "underground," though they actually face the ocean and have the best views. These are not really underground, they're built into the side of a cliff....hard to explain, just know it's an innovative design. All cliff units are one bedroom. The two bedrooms are up higher on the cliff. *5295 Lower Honoapiilani Highway, Lahaina, HI 96761 • 669-5611 • 669-9222.*

HOTELS

Coconut Inn
Not exactly a B & B (though breakfast comes with the room), not exactly a condo (though each of the 41 studios & 1 BRs has a kitchen), and not just a mundane hotel....this place likes to think of itself as a country inn.

Whatever, it's a great little hotel...up an obscure road far from the beach. It was once a seedy apartment building. Then a Californian who knew nothing about hotels bought it, put $1.5 million into it and opened in 1984.

Owner George Gilman thought it was tough to find reasonable rates on this end of the island, so he kept his place moderately priced. It's a homey joint despite the fact that it's obviously two modern apartment buildings. The lobby is like a comfy living room and the grounds and pool are lovely.

Mid-range.
P.O. Box 10517, Napili, HI 96761 • 669-5712 • (800) 367-8006.

Mauian Hotel
They call themselves a hotel, but they're much like a condominium. All 44 rooms are individually-owned studios. All are furnished the same...nothing fancy, mostly functional. All have small kitchens with full-sized fridge and stove. Baths have showers, no tubs. There's no air conditioning, no phone, no TV. The large lawn area is flat and grassy with few exotic plants.

Basically it's a simple place—three 2-story wooden buildings right on a sandy beach.

Mid-range.
5441 Honoapiilani Rd., Lahaina, HI 96761 • 669-6205 • (800) 367-5034.

Napili Kai Beach Club

This is a quiet, low-key place. It's very nice, though not fancy; still, it has an exclusive "club" air about it. It was built in 1962 by Jack Millar, a retired Wing Commander of the Royal Canadian Air Force. Jack is now deceased, but wife Margaret and daughter Dorothy still run the hotel as a family affair. About 70% of their guests are return visitors, so even they feel the family atmosphere. One couple has visited twice a year since the '62 opening.

The 137 rooms are mostly studios and 1 bedrooms (three are 2 BRs). Rooms are spacious and all have tiny kitchenettes.

The large grounds have four pools, a whirlpool, two tennis courts and two 18-hole putting greens (one adult, one kiddie).

The "club" has its own school—a group of youngsters funded by the hotel to study Hawaiiana. They perform every Friday night in the hotel's Sea House Restaurant.

Mid-range.

5900 Honoapiilani Road, Lahaina, HI 96761 • 669-6025 • (800) 367-5030.

RESTAURANT

$ Budget

Orient Express: It has budget to mid-range prices, but a fancy reputation. The chef is from Thailand, so the food is mostly Thai with a touch of Chinese. Service and food are both wonderful. Hours: 5:30 to 10 p.m. *Located in Napili Shores Condo • 669-8077.*

Kapalua

This is pineapple country...thousands of acres of the Brazilian fruit. The land is owned by the Maui Land & Pineapple Company, one of Maui's most powerful corporations.

Kapalua is classy and exclusive. The hotel and condo villages have a monied, elegant air. You expect to see Hollywood moguls and CEOs, and you do.

HISTORY

H.P. Baldwin owned 23,000 acres along the coast near Kapalua. Initially it was ranch land, raising both cattle and hogs.

Then in the early 1900s the first commercial pineapple plants were planted and a whole new industry started up. A cannery was built. Hawaiians and immigrants began moving into Kapalua plantation villages to fill the jobs.

Simple villages for the workers were situated where luxury condo villages stand today. The Honolua General Store, built in the 1940s as a plantation store, is a last reminder of the plantation days.

The present resort was the dream of Maui scion (and missionary descendant) Colin Cameron, president of Maui Land & Pine. It was built in the mid 1970s, and was part of the family business until 1985 when hard times forced Cameron to sell to investors...who are keeping up the standards.

BEACHES & PARKS

Kapalua Beach

As classy as the hotel...very pretty little beach. Great swimming area, considered very safe. Access is the road between Napali Kai Beach Club and the Kapalua Hotel.

Facilities: toilets, showers, paved parking.

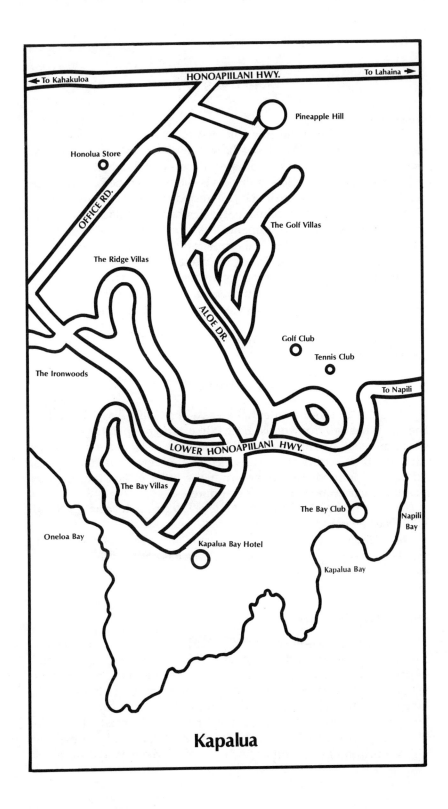

Kapalua

HOTELS

Kapalua Bay Hotel

This is considered the only true first-class, luxury resort on West Maui. The TV show "Lifestyles of the Rich and Famous" rated it the best resort in the U.S. Still, it's no ornate palace—Kapalua has a low-key, understated elegance. Everything feels classy beige here, nothing is splashy. The 194 rooms are lovely, but they don't knock your socks off.

Kapalua's draw is its seclusion. It's perched above its own bay with no other hotels around. The Kapalua Villas are near, but they're all part of the resort—750 acres of it. This acreage is surrounded by thousands more acres of pineapple fields...hence the seclusion.

Two gorgeous golf courses, ten tennis courts, various celebrity-drawing tournaments, a yearly classical music festival and a wine symposium add to the exclusive, wealthy air. Prestige is the name here. Expensive.

One Bay Drive, Kapalua, HI 97761 • 669-5656 • 800) 367-8000 (continental United States).

CONDOS

Kapalua has four residential areas—The Golf Villas, The Ridge, The Bay Villas and Ironwoods. Each is like its own separate village, yet all are quite similar in appearance. There are 528 condos in the four villas and the Kapalua Hotel runs the rental program for 160 of them. All 160 are individually owned, but the hotel insists that owners maintain their units to first class standards.

To rent through the hotel, write: *One Bay Drive, Lahaina, HI 96761 • (808) 669-5656 • (800) 367-8000.*

Jack Nowell's Ridge Realty also rents out several of the condos, usually at cheaper prices than the hotel. He has a 5-day minimum. *888 Wainee St., Unit 207, Lahaina, HI 96761 • 667-2851 • (800) 367-8047 ex. 133.*

Stratosphere Condos: Off Beach

The **Ironwoods** is the most expensive of the villas (and, in fact, it is the most expensive condo on Maui). This is where movie stars and moguls come to stay. The Ironwoods has touches that the other three villa areas don't have—a main security gate, garages for each unit, living room fireplaces, solid koa front doors, marble foyers, sunken living rooms, huge separate his and her baths off the master bedroom. The square footage is 2,200 to 3,000 feet, the largest units of the four villas. Furnishings depend on each owner. Some have typical island rattan furniture, nice but not fancy; others are so luxurious that everything is hand-dyed silk, specially woven fabric and stained glass windows. The setting is spectacular—on a rocky cliff right at the ocean's edge. A short path leads down to a small sandy beach.

The other three villas, Golf, Ridge and Bay, are somewhat inter-changeable. All are equally luxurious and all have beautifully-land-scaped grounds. Price of each unit depends on the view, cheapest being mountain view, next is golf fairway view, next is ocean view and most expensive is ocean front. These three villas have both 1 & 2-BR condos; Ironwoods has 2 & 3-BR units.

The **Golf Villas** are all priced "fairway view" since these villas overlook the Kapalua Golf Course. The surprise is that from the lanai most units have a view also of the ocean. The Golf Villas are the only condos with air conditioning.

The **Ridge Villas** have slightly larger interiors than the Golf and the Bay Villas. They have ocean, fairway and mountain views. None are oceanfront since the Ridge sits up high on a hill.

The **Bay Villas** were the first condos built in Kapalua (1977). They are closest in distance to the hotel—just a short walk. They are also close to the ocean, set at the edge of Oneloa Bay with a sandy beach just a blink away.

RESTAURANTS

Kapalua has a class act—all its restaurants are good, two are excellent.

$ Budget

The Market Cafe: Great place for breakfast, terrific for desserts, perfect for a cappuccino. For lunch and dinner there's a little bit of every-thing—salads, sandwiches, burgers, fish, chicken. It's a sweet little place, both a sit-down restaurant and a deli (a fancy, expensive one). Hours: 8 to 9 daily. *Located in the shopping area next to the hotel • 669-4888.*

$$$ Expensive

The Bay Club: There's almost a casual atmosphere here—the koa wood interior is open air right above the ocean. There's nothing casual about the food or prices, though. Food is wonderful; prices are steep. This is one of the Kapalua Hotel's restaurants, and it reflects that excellence. Hours: 11:30 to 2 (lunch); 6-9:30 (dinner). *Located on the hotel grounds • 669-5656.*

Plantation Veranda: This has been a Holiday award-winning restaurant since 1980. It has fancy continental food in lovely, country-style surroundings. Nothing stuffy...it's a bright, cheery place with a courtyard outside the many windows. Dinner music is either a classical guitarist or a harpist. Hours: 6:30 to 10 p.m. *Located in the Kapalua Hotel • 669-5656.*

SHOPPING

Kapalua Shops

This is a small retail area connected to the hotel, and like the hotel, it is exclusive. Many of the shops cater to those with fat wallets.

Brioni is the most expensive, elegant women's apparel store on the island. Instead of predictable designer brands, Brioni has originals of fluid, artistic styles. It's wearable art.

Thick Thai silk and slinky Hong Kong silk...all made up into beautiful outfits at **Mandalay Imports**, a tiny shop of women's clothing.

It's always party time at **Michele's**—sequins, lace, feathers, beads...fancy, expensive clothing for women.

Auntie Nani Children's Boutique is sweet and original. Not just clothes, also quilts, toys, wall hangings.

Distant Drums is the clever name of this gallery of primitive artifacts. Tribal art, handicrafts and jewelry from all parts of Asia, New Guinea and the South Pacific.

Kahakuloa

Kahakuloa is a single Hawaiian hamlet on the north coast of West Maui. However, locally, it also is a way of referring to that whole wild side of West Maui—the side seldom driven, the side with the bad road, the unpopulated side...the Kahakuloa side.

Kahakuloa road leads into old Hawai'i—a land of sheer cliffs and crashing ocean on one side, and green, mysterious valleys on the other.

The tiny village, seemingly lost in time, stands at the mouth of giant Kahakuloa Valley. It is postcard perfect.

The Road

From mile marker 32 near Honolua Bay to downtown Wailuku, the trip is 27 miles. Travel time along that distance is an hour and a half. Or rather, it used to be. In April, 1987, stormy weather damaged the road to such an extent that it is now impassable. The road used to be impossible enough—it was narrow and dangerous, and unpaved for two very rutted miles. Until it is rebuilt (and on Maui, don't hold your breath), it is not possible to go from Kapalua to Wailuku on this side.

HISTORY

In the early days there were fishing villages located in the bays and valleys along this end of Maui. Certainly the village of Kahakuloa is a rebuilt hamlet from times past...one of the oldest and most secluded in Maui.

Ka haku loa means "faraway master"—thus named because it was the property of a chief (haku) who lived isolated, far off in this village.

Archaeologist Winslow Walker visited the village in 1931 when three grass houses were still in use. Walker said there was a place of refuge near the chief's house, no longer used in modern times, but in earlier times kapu breakers could find refuge from punishment there.

Walker also found many burial caves in Kahakuloa Canyon. Not all were ancient burials, though. He found bottles, nails and a pipe with the bones.

SIGHTS

Kahakuloa Head
A volcanic dome that juts up from the valley floor near the village. It is visible for miles along the road. It looks quite like Half Dome in California's Yosemite Park.

Nakalele Point & Blowhole
A small white lighthouse on a cliff above the sea marks the area. Past the grassy field down towards the ocean is a volcanic moonscape region locally known as Hobbitland. Here lava spattered over the ground, creating strange and wonderful shapes. A local artist put a Hobbitland rock on a pedestal in his living room, and friends believe it to be a sculture molded by man.

Past the spatter cone area is a powerful blow hole that sends spray 50 feet in the air. Large surf is typical here. It crashes into the hole and jets upwards.

The Nakalele area is a bit difficult to find without a guide.

BEACHES

D.T. Fleming Beach Park
Obviously a popular park—there are always lots of cars. It's a very pretty, sandy cove. Can be dangerous; strong currents have caused several drownings.

Named after a Scotsman who managed the Honolua Ranch for the Baldwin family. Fleming was the first to grow pineapple as a commercial crop.

Facilities: toilets, showers, picnic tables, grills, paved parking.

Honolua Bay
Famed as one of the best snorkeling spots on the island...amazing coral formations, lots of fish. Also famed for its waves—surfers say it's one of the world's best spots.

Hard to find since it's not marked. Snorkelers and swimmers should go a quarter mile past the Honolua-Mokule'ia Bay Conservation sign. Park just off the road and walk down a Jeep trail to the beach. Surfers go a bit farther up the road.

Activities

Humpbacks

Maui's favorite and most frequent tourists are the ever popular humpback whales. Loyally they return year after year to Hawai'i's temperate waters to give birth, and it is thought, probably to mate.

They swim 3,000 to 4,000 miles from their summer home in the Arctic seas near Alaska. It's a whale of a reunion they hold here...it is estimated that nearly 60% of the North Pacific's humpback population winters in Hawai'i.

All Hawaiian islands get a share of the whales, but Maui County (Maui, Moloka'i, Lana'i, Kaho'olawe) is definitely the most popular.

When?

The first ones arrive in November, the last ones leave in June, but peak season is January through April.

Why Maui?

No one knows why the humpbacks return yearly to Hawaiian waters, but the theory is survival of the species. Calves are born blubberless, poor little one and two ton darlings, so they could never exist in Alaskan waters.

They waste little time putting on fat. They consume 130 gallons of mother's milk a day and gain as much as 200 pounds daily. They have a long way to go to reach mama's weight of 40 to 50 tons.

A birth has never been witnessed by scientists, neither has nursing, and neither has mating. Birth they know happens in Maui (because the calves suddenly appear), but Maui mating is still a theory. They are private animals who can go to great depths to keep their bedroom habits to themselves.

They definitely don't come to Maui for the food. They don't eat the entire time they're here. Sometimes four to six months they go without a morsel. Luckily, they're surrounded by a foot or so of blubber which they live off during their fasts.

Flukes and Guesses

Humpbacks have been studied live in their ocean habitat only since the mid Seventies. Not all questions are answered; much is still speculation. Scientists, armed with cameras, sit in little rubber boats on the mammoth ocean and hope to see a few familiar flukes.

Some, like whale researcher Debbie Glockner-Ferrari, jump in with the whales and try to figure out the boys from the girls. And she finally did—which was a big breakthrough in 1980. Debbie discovered and photographed a golf ball-sized lobe near the genital slit of female humpbacks. Males also have the slit, but they have no lobe. Until Ferrari's discovery, no one knew this basic biology.

Known Facts

—Humpbacks are the fifth largest whale.
—Whales are mammals, not fish; they breathe air and are warm blooded.
—Adults come up to breathe every 10 to 15 minutes.
—Calves come up every 3 to 5 minutes.
—They breathe through a blowhole on top of the head.
—A "blow" is expelled at 300 miles an hour.
—Their lungs are as big as a compact car.
—Females are slightly larger than males. They average 45 feet long, while males average 43 feet.
—They weigh about a ton per foot.
—The largest humpback thus far recorded was an 88-foot female.
—Their tongues weigh one to two tons.
—Their eyeballs are only the size of an orange.
—They see well both below and above water, but only for short distances.
—They have no vocal cords, yet they "sing," sometimes for hours.
—They have complex brains.
—They eat plankton, krill and small fish...a ton at a time.
—They get water from their food; they do not drink sea water.
—Their "sleep" is limited to 15-minute naps underwater.
—Their flippers (pectoral fins) are like arms with bones similar to human hands and arms. They use them to steer. A mother also cuddles her calf with a fin, wrapping it around the calf to hold it close.
—No one knows how long they live, possibly 30-40 years.
—Unlike fish, which swim by a side-to-side movement of their tails, whales propel themselves with an up and down movement of their powerful tails.
—Their tails are all muscle, no bone.
—A typical pod is only two whales; they don't travel in big groups.

—A male "escort" often accompanies a mother and calf, but he's mostly interested in lust...it's thought he wants to be the first in line when mother comes into estrus.

IDs Please

Each humpback has its own set of "fingerprints"—unique markings that allow scientists to identify and recognize the same animal over the years.

The underside of every tail fluke has distinct markings and coloring. Scientists photograph the flukes when they flip in the air during dives. These "fluke prints" do not change as they age (except for battle scars).

They also have distinct markings on their flippers, plus "lip grooves"—markings along each side of the head.

A Whale of a Song

Humpbacks sing very complicated songs, considered the longest, most complex songs in nature. For some reason they sing in the winter (in Maui), not in the summer. And, most likely, only the males sing. Could be a mating game.

A typical song is 6 to 18 minutes long, but an animal can carry on with several songs for hours. The Pacific Whale Foundation once recorded a crooning fellow for 14 hours nonstop.

What does it sound like?—a cow mooing, a door creaking, a guinea pig squeaking, a roaring, a chirping, a grunting, a moaning...a very versatile little aria.

Gentle Giants?

They have never been known to hurt a human, but they are not gentle with each other. Males draw blood and throw around tons of weight when battling for females.

Whale expert Debbie Glockner-Ferrari once saw numerous males stage a ferocious battle off Ka'anapali and was horrified to see tourists swimming out to join the "play." Forty tons of rage does not gingerly hurtle past gawking humans. Luck won that day and no one was hurt.

Another time Debbie was swimming with a calf when its mother awoke and swam up to investigate. Debbie held her breath as mom swept her powerful tail inches from Debbie's head. Nary a hair undone.

Humpbacks can be curious about us. One fun-loving guy lay under a large whale-watching boat for two hours occasionally lifting it and often "blowing" on the hundred tourists on board.

A Whale's Tale, Sad, but True...

We nearly killed them off until they were put on the endangered species list in 1966. Where once there were thousands of these creatures, there are now only about 1,000 to 1,500 left...a mere drop in the enormous ocean where they are kings.

They are now protected by law. Boats are restricted 100 yards from them, aircraft 1000 feet. From Makena to Olowalu, believed to be calving areas, boats must keep 300 yards away.

Greg Kaufman, president of the Pacific Whale Foundation, says PWF "created the whale watching industry." They started taking boatloads of tourists out in 1979 and every smart boat captain followed suit.

During whale season, almost every charter boat has whale watching trips. PWF has its own boat with a research scientist on board to answer questions and give a narrative. The boat goes out several times daily during whale season. Call 879-8811 for times and costs.

Boating

There are so many good boats and salty sea captains on Maui that it's hard to choose one. These listed below have been in business at least two years...so they've had some success.

Unless you book a private charter and go where you want, most of the boats have similar trips. Whale watching is a biggie November through May; after that the whales go back to Alaska.

Snorkeling trips usually go to Molokini, Lana'i, Olowalu, Honolua Bay or along West Maui's coast. Molokini is definitely the favorite. Because of that, it's often very crowded. Snorkeling gear is usually provided on snorkel cruises, you needn't bring your own.

On sunset cruises you generally just cruise around for a couple hours watching the sunset and drinking. Some boats cater a full dinner, and some have hula entertainment.

The larger boats have the space for a mini floor show, which usually means a live band and a hula dancer. You might even get to don a grass skirt and coconut bra yourself.

Sailboats generally have motors too. Some advertise a "sailing cruise," yet motor most of the trip. So, if you prefer sailing, better say so when you make your reservation.

GLASSBOTTOM BOATS

Coral See
Lahaina Harbor, Slip #1
P.O. Box 218, Lahaina, HI 96767 • 661-8600
65' glass bottom motor boat; 143 passengers
Trips: *Whale Watch*—2.5 hr.; no food, cash bar. *Molokini Snorkel*—5-6 hr.; breakfast, lunch, open bar, snorkel gear.

Lin Wah II
Lahaina Harbor, Slip #3
P.O. Box 1376, Lahaina, HI 96761 • 661-3392 • (800) 843-8113

65' glassbottom Chinese junk with motor & sail; can carry 137 passengers
Trips: *Cruise West Maui Coral Reefs*—1.25 hr.; diver enters water and feeds fish;
cash bar.

RAFTS

Blue Water Rafting
Kihei Boat Ramp
P.O. Box 10172, Lahaina, HI 96761 • *879-7238*
20' rubber Bombard; 6 passengers
Trips: *Molokini Snorkel*— 3.5 hr.; lunch, beer & sodas, gear. *Whale Watch*—2 hr.;
pupus, beer & soda. *Private charters.*

Capt' N Kirk's
Mala Wharf
P.O. Box 98, Lahaina, HI 96761 • *661-5333* • *667-9740*
22' rubber Bombard; 6 passengers
Trips: *Whale Watch*—2 hr.; soft drinks. *Snorkel Trips* (West Maui or Lana'i)—
half day, lunch, snorkel gear.

Captain Zodiac
Mala Wharf
P.O. Box 1776, Lahaina, HI 96767 • *667-5862* • *667-5351*
23' Zodiac; 15 to 17 passengers
Trips: *Whale Watch & Snorkel to Lanai*—2.5 or 3.5 hrs.; snacks, juice, gear.

Painting by David Ridgway

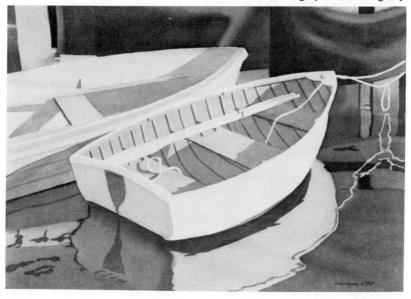

SAILBOATS

Aikani
Ma'alaea Harbor, Slip #82
P.O. Box 1221, Wailuku, HI 96793 • 879-2307
46' world's first racing catamaran. Unofficial entry in 1957 Transpac Race (first to finish). Tries to sail as much as possible. 35 passengers
Trips: *Molokini Snorkel*—breakfast, lunch, beer, wine, soda, gear. *Private charter.*

Alihilani
Kihei Cove Park
P.O. Box 1052, Kihei, HI 96753 • 242-4076
43' catamaran cutter; 6 passengers
Trips: *Molokini Snorkel*—breakfast, lunch, beer, wine, soda, snorkel gear, free underwater camera. *Whale Watch*—2-3 hr.; snacks, beer, wine, sodas. *Sunset*—3.5 hr.; snacks, beer, wine, soda. *Private charters.*

Apollo
moored at Kealia Beach
101 N. Kihei Rd., Kihei Rd., HI 96753 • 874-0643
40' trimaran; 6 passengers
Trips: *Olowalu Snorkel*—lunch, beer & soda, gear. *Sunset Sail*—pupus & champagne.

Cinderella
Moored in front of Kealia Beach Plaza, Kihei
101 N. Kihei Rd., Kihei, HI 96753 • 879-0634
50' Columbia sloop; 6 passengers
Trips: *Olowalu Turtles*—full day; breakfast, lunch (steak or seafood), snorkeling gear. *Private charters.*

Capt. Nemo's
moored off Lahaina
150 Dickenson St., Lahaina, HI 96761 • 661-5555 • (800) 367-8088
58' racing catamaran; built in 1967, owned by actor James Arness (Matt Dillon of Gunsmoke); won every race it ever entered. Named Sea Smoke. 32 passengers
Trips: *Snorkel & Scuba to Lana'i*—1/2 day; breakfast, lunch, beer, wine, champagne, gear. *Sunset Whale Watch*—2 hr.; snacks and beverages.

Foxy Lady
Ma'alaea Harbor, Slip #49
107 Waipuilani, Kihei, HI 96753 • 879-4673
27' Cal sloop; 6 passengers
Trips: *Molokini Snorkel*—bring along own lunch & beverage; snorkel gear & sailing lessons provided. *Private charters.*

Genesis
Lahaina Harbor
P.O. Box 10697, Lahaina, HI 96761 • 667-5667
48' Irwin cutter rigged ketch with 2 double staterooms (each with head & shower); 18 passengers
Trips: *Whale Watch*—2.5 hr.; juice. *Lana'i*—1/2 day; lunch, sodas, snorkel gear. *Dinner Sail*—2.5 hr., catered by La Bretagne, guitar player, champagne, beer & wine. *Private charters.*

Kiele V
Hyatt Regency Boat - moored in front of hotel • 667-7474 ext. 3104
55' catamaran; 49 passengers
Trips: *Snorkel*—4 hr.; breakfast, lunch, open bar. *Cocktail*—1.5 hr., open bar, pupus. *Private charters.*

Lavengro
Ma'alaea Harbor, Slip #80
P.O. Box 1221, Wailuku, HI 967693 • 879-8188
60' Topsail pilot schooner. Built in 1926 in Biloxi, Miss. as a shrimper. 27 passengers
Trips: *Molokini Snorkel*—breakfast, lunch, beer, wine, soda. *Whale Watch*—3.5 hr.; snacks, beer, wine & soda. *Sunset Sail*—2 hr.; dinner catered by Longhi's, guitar player.

Leialoha
Cove Park in Kihei
P.O. Box 530, Kihei, HI 96753 • 242-7026
42' Coronada; 6 passengers
Trips: *Molokini Snorkel*—breakfast, lunch, open bar, snorkeling gear. *Whale Watch*—beer, wine, soda.

Maika'i Makani II
Mahana Maia
Ma'alaea Harbor, Slip #76 & #47
P.O. Box 0, Wailuku, HI 96793 • 667-9739 • after 5 p.m. 879-8585
49' & 58' catamarans; 49 passengers
Trips: *Molokini Snorkel*—breakfast, lunch, free underwater cameras, gear, hula show. *Whale Watch*—2.5 hr.; snacks, beer, wine, sodas.

The Phantom
Lahaina Harbor, Slip #72
P.O. Box 1742, Lahaina, HI 96767 • 661-5888
36' Lancer, mono hull, has fresh water shower. Capt. Rolly is an Aussie with many years in Maui's waters. 6 passengers
Trips: *Snorkel & Sail*—half day; pupus, beverages, snorkel gear, whale watch. *Sunset Sail*—2 hr.; beverages, pupus. *All Day* (either to Honolua Bay, Lana'i or Olowalu)—lunch, beverages, snorkel gear. *Private charters.*

Sail Hawai'i
Kihei Cove Park
P.O. Box 573, Kihei, HI 96753 • *879-2201*
37' & 40' Endeavour, single hull; 6 pax
20' Zodiac raft; 10 passengers
Trips: *Molokini Snorkel*—breakfast, lunch, beer & soda, gear (on Zodiac: no frills, just gear & soda). *Private charters.*

Scotch Mist I & II
Lahaina Harbor, Slip #11
P.O. Box 845, Lahaina, HI 96767 • *661-0386*
36' Cal & 50' Santa Cruz, both mono hull; 6 to 19 passengers
Trips: *Olowalu Snorkel*—3 hr., pupus, beer, wine, soda, gear. *Champagne Sunset Sail*—2 hr., pupus, champagne, beer, wine, soda. *Full-Day Sail*—place varies; lunch, beer, wine, soda, snorkel gear.

Sea Sails on Ka'anapali Beach
Pick-up on beach in front of hotels
661-0927 • *661-8957*
50' Beachabel catamarans (2); 43-49 passengers
Trips: *Whale Watch*—2.5 hr., juices. *Snorkel/Sail*—location depends on weather, 3.5 hr.; lunch, juice, beer, mai tais, snorkel gear. *Champagne Sunset Sail*—1.5 hr.; sail by the Sheraton's high diver; champagne, beer, mai tais.

Seabird Cruises
Lahaina Harbor, Slip #4
P.O. Box 1553, Lahaina, HI 96767 • *661-3643*
60' Viejo & 65' catarmans (2); 75-110 passengers
Trips: *Lana'i*—full day, breakfast, BBQ lunch on beach, open bar, snorkel gear, van tour of island. *Moloka'i*—full day, breakfast, van tour of historic sites, BBQ lunch, open bar, snorkel gear. *Dinner Sunset*—2 hr.; dinner, open bar, hula show, live band.

Suntan Special
Moored in front of Kihei Kealia Beach Plaza
145 N. Kihei Rd., Kihei, HI 97753 • *874-0332*
50' Santa Cruz, racing yacht; tries to sail, not motor, depending on the winds; 16 passengers
Trips: *Molokini Snorkel*—5-6 hr.; breakfast, lunch, beer, wine, soda, veggie tray, snorkel gear. *Whale Watch or Afternoon Sail*—2 hr.; beverages & pupus. *Sunset Sail*—2 hr.; heavy snacks, beer, wine, champagne, sodas. *Private charters.*

Trilogy Excursions with the Coon Family
Lahaina Harbor or Ma'alaea Harbor (Slip #7)
P.O. Box 1121, Lahaina, HI 96767 • *661-4743* • *(800) 874-2666*
3 boats: 54' diesel-powered catamaran, 52' diesel-powered trimaran, 40' diesel-powered trimaran, 40' Hawaiian catamaran; 20 to 40 passengers

Trips: *Lana'i*—full day, breakfast, lunch, sodas, van island tour, snorkel gear. *Molokini Snorkel*—half day, breakfast, lunch, sodas, snorkel gear. *Private charters.*

Wailea Kai
Ma'alaea Harbor, Slip #58
3750 Wailea Ala Nui, Kihei, HI 96753 • 879-4485
65' catamaran; 95 passengers
Trips: *Molokini Snorkel*—breakfast, lunch, beer, wine, mai tais, gear, rent fishing lines for trolling. *Sunset Sail*—2 hr.; dinner, open bar, live band, hula dancer. *Whale Watch*—2 hr.

Windjammer Maui
From Lahaina Harbor Slip #1
P.O. Box 218, Lahaina, HI 96761 • 667-6834 • (800) 843-8113
65' 3-masted sailing schooner; 117 passengers
Trips: *Sunset*—2 hr.; open bar, meal, Polynesian show
Lana'i (all day) M-F—breakfast, BBQ lunch on beach, ground tour of Lanai City, snorkeling, open bar on trip home.
Sunset Dinner Sail—nightly for 2 hours; open bar & dinner.

LARGE POWER BOATS

Leilani
Lahaina Harbor, Slip #3
P.O. Box 218, Lahaina, HI 96767 • 661-8600 • 800- 843-8113
49' Uniflite motor boat; 49 passengers
Trips: *Molokini Snorkel*—breakfast, lunch, open bar, gear.
Moloka'i—June through November, all day trips.

Luckey Strike
Lahaina Harbor, Slip #50
P.O. Box 1502, Lahaina, HI 96761 • 242-9277
45', custom built diesel cruiser; 22 passengers
Trips: *Whale Watch*—2 hours.

Maka Kai
Ma'alaea Harbor, Slip #62
3750 Wailea Ala Nui, Kihei, HI, 96753 • 879-4485
65' power catamaran; 125 passengers
Trips: *Lana'i*—full day; breakfast, lunch at Hotel Lana'i, bus land tour, snorkel gear. *Whale Watch*—2 hr.; cash bar.

Prince Kuhio
Ma'alaea Harbor
831 Eha Street, Wailuku, HI 96793 • 242-8777
92' double-deck; largest boat in Maui waters; 150 passengers

Trips: *Molokini Snorkel*—breakfast, lunch, open bar, gear.
Whale Watch. Private charters.

SMALL POWER BOATS

Adventure I
Ma'alaea Harbor, Slip 78
RR1 Box 337 #210, Wailuku, HI 96793 • *242-7683*
35' Radon motor boat. Designed for Hawaiian waters, for speed and comfort.
25 passengers
Trips: *Molokini Snorkel*—breakfast, lunch, open bar, snorkel gear including
lightweight wetsuits and prescription lenses.

Maui Impulse
Kihei Boat Ramp
P.O. Box 119, Kihei, HI 96753 • *874-0034*
30' Wellcraft ocean cruiser; 6 passengers
Trips: *Molokini Snorkel*—lunch, beer, wine, sodas, snorkel gear.
Other trips—scuba diving, waterskiing, sport fishing, *private charters.*

Fishing

Charter fishing boats come completely equipped (rods, reels, bait, tackle, ice, etc.). All you need do is pack a lunch, bring a beverage and get on board. You don't even need a fishing license. Most boats have fighting chairs, and some have fancy equipment that help find the fish.

Clients generally may keep fish they catch, but each boat has its own regulations. Most tourists only want a filet or two from the fish; they can't really eat 150 pounds of mahi during their stay. Some boats will filet, freeze and ship the fish, if you want to send the meat home. Tourists cannot sell their fish to local restaurants; one needs a commercial fishing license to do so.

Usually the captain keeps the fish and sells the meat. One captain calls this money his slush fund—when the boat's down for repair or lack of business, the fish money keeps the crew going.

You can get a copy of Hawai'i fishing laws and rules from the State Department of Land and Natural Resources, Divisions of Aquatic Resources, Kalanimoku Building, Room 330, 1151 Punchbowl St., Honolulu 96813.

It's open season on most salt water fish all year round, with restrictions on size if the fish are speared, caught with certain small-eye nets or traps, or sold commerically. Shell fish (spiny lobster, 'opihi, clam) must meet size limits even for home consumption. There is a closed season on spiny and slipper lobster, Kona crab, 'ama'ama (mullet) and clam. The Hawaiian monk seal and various sea turtles are endangered species.

TV fishing shows

Look for local fishing shows on television. "Mike Sakamoto's Fishing Tales" airs on channels 3 and 9 at 6:30 p.m. Hari Kojima's "Let's Go Fishing" shows on channels 2 and 7 at 5 p.m. Sunday.

FISHING BOATS

Carol Ann
Ma'alaea Harbor, Slip #109
111 Kahului Beach Rd., D223, Kahului 96732 • *877-2181*
33' Bertram, 2 fighting chairs; 6 passengers

Finest Kind, Inc.
Lahaina Harbor, Slip #7 & Ma'alaea Harbor, Slips 13 & 61
P.O. Box 10481, Lahaina, HI 96761 • *661-0338* • *661-5559*
4 boats: 37' twin diesel Merritt, 31' Bertram, 43' Delta, 35' Bertram; tournament equipped, IGFA; 6 passengers

Kahu O Ke Kai
Ma'alaea Harbor, Slip #71
1431 Kahoma St.., Lahaina, HI 96761 • *661-4112* • *661-5749*
38' Luhrs Sport Fisher; 6 passengers

Kanoa
Lahaina Harbor, Slip #52
P.O. Box 1502, Lahaina, HI 96761 • *242-9277*
31' Uniflite Sport Fisher with twin diesel engines; 2 fighting chairs; 6 passengers. Request no oily suntan lotion.

Lahaina Charter Boats
Lahaina Harbor, Slip #8
P.O. Box 12, Lahaina, HI 96767 • *667-6672*
3 boats: 42' Trawler; 36' Sportsfisher; 26' Bertram; fighting chairs; 5-7 passengers.

Luckey Strike
Lahaina Harbor, Slip #50
P.O. Box 1502, Luhaina, HI 96761 • *242-9277*
45' custom-built diesel cruiser, has color fish finder, 2 fighting chairs; 6 to 8 passengers.

Rascal Sportfishing
Ma'alaea Harbor, Slip #69
479 Pauu Place, Lahaina HI 96761 • *661-0692*
31' Bertram, twin diesel, fighting chair, fish sounder; 6 passengers

Diving

Mike Severns Scuba Diving
P.O. Box 627, Kihei, HI 96753 • 879-6596

Mike Severns is an adventurer and explorer like none other on
Maui. He discovered and mapped the first underwater archaeological
site in the Hawaiian Islands. He found the longest underwater cave
system (900 feet) off Maui. He discovered several critters (a worm, an
eel, a lobster, etc.) that had not yet been collected and categorized in
Hawai'i. He's considered an expert on Hawaiian tree snails...which has
nothing to do with diving, but Severns is a scientist and a naturalist. He
mostly takes "comfortable, experienced divers" out, but he will take
beginners because he enjoys their questions. He doesn't teach SCUBA
and he doesn't have a shop. Most of his diving is off the beaten path, but,
he says it's not risky. He will go to Molokini, but prefers the remote
areas. Severns has his own 22' power boat, and he provides all scuba
equipment needed.

Chuck Thorne
P.O. Box 1461, Kahului, HI 96732 • 572-6759

Chuck Thorne wrote the book on diving; in fact, he wrote two—*The
Divers' Guide to Maui* and *The Divers' Guide to Hawai'i*. This man is a
serious diver who takes out advanced divers, no more than two or three
at a time. He doesn't mess around; he flatly states: "I'm not interested
in babysitting. I want the kind of guys who have been diving for years
and have their own equipment. It's not safe to take them in caves with
rental gear. Your equipment has to be an extension of yourself." He
scoffs at diving Molokini. "You could send your grandmother there,"
he says. Instead, he four-wheel drives to the south side of East Maui, to
Kaupo, Kipahulu and Hana, and does shore dives. "Nobody else goes
there. I have all kinds of secret places," he says. "I do a lot of caves. I
know about 80 caves just on the south side of Maui alone. I love to show
a person some really hot stuff. Every time I go out I'm like a kid on

Christmas Eve. I take 'em to unpicked-over reefs, but I never do anything dangerous. I watch the currents. I know the tricks for rough water." Thorne does not advertise. He does not have a shop. Most of his clients come by word of mouth.

Hana Bay Divers
P.O. Box 481, Hana, HI 96713 • 248-7289

The Hana area is "virtually unexplored dive territory," say Diana and Michael Brandon, owners of Hana Bay Divers. "It's not like the other side of the island where people get herded out. Hana is set apart," says Diana. "You can dive and not be crowded." The Brandons offer PADI certification courses, beginning, advanced and several specialty. They also do a lot of snorkeling trips. They usually dive Hana Bay, but also explore Ke'anae and Nahiku coastlines. All their dives are shore dives. "Hana's a small area, so we can individualize our tours," Diana says. "We feel people out and see what they want to do." One problem with Hana diving, though, is the weather. "We are very dependent on the weather here," Diana says. "There are blocks of time when we can't go out because the water is too rough."

Blue Chip Charters
P.O. Box 5159, Lahaina, HI 96761 • 661-3226 • 667-7474 ext. 3267

Blue Chip has a brand new 38' motor boat specially designed for diving. It has a full galley, a head and a fresh water shower. The boat can carry 18 passengers, but they prefer just 12. The boat goes to Molokini twice a week and to Lana'i four days a week. The excursion includes a lunch and a 2-tank dive (if certified). For an extra charge, they'll take photos or a video of your dive. They also have four beach dives a day...much cheaper than going on the boat. These go off reefs by the Hyatt or by Black Rock. With 2-day notice, you may request other areas. They have a 4-day PADI certification course which is more expensive than other dive shops, but they offer nine dives with it—four during the training, then five days of diving afterwards. Other training includes advanced and specialty courses (photography, night, deep, hunting & collecting).

Dive Maui
Lahaina Market Place, Lahainaluna Rd., Lahaina, HI 96761
667-2080 • 661-4363

This outfit is the only Maui shop that can give full certification programs (from basic SCUBA through instructor) in all three training programs—PADI, NAUI & SSCI. All three have similar training, all are good internationally and are valid forever. Certification takes four days, six hours a day. Dive Maui also has three 26' power boats, that take a maximum of six passengers, both certified and beginners. Their dives are along Maui's coastline, plus Lana'i and Moloka'i. Their shop in Lahaina Market Place sells and rents equipment.

Dive Shop
1975 S. Kihei Rd., Kihei, HI 96753 • 879-5172

They can do everything for you—rent or sell equipment, train you or take you diving. They have a 4 or 5-day PADI certification program (includes 4 dives), plus about 40-some advanced and specialty PADI courses. They own two boats, a 25' power boat and a 40' sailing trimaran, both limited to 6 passengers. They mix snorkelers, beginners and certified divers together on a trip. Being an East Maui operation, they dive Molokini and the Kihei-La Perouse coastline.

Extended Horizons
P.O. Box 10785, Lahaina, HI 96761 • 667-0611

Owner Eric Stein generally does custom trips for his customers...what they want is what they get. His 25' power boat seats a maximum of six, and unless it's a charter group, he does not mix beginners and advanced divers. Beginners he prefers to teach on the beach, but will teach out of the boat if asked. Stein has no shop and does not sell equipment; it's diving he does. He supplies all equipment for dives and classes (PADI training). He dives off Lana'i and off remote areas of Maui (like Hobbitland); he will not dive Molokini because he thinks it's overcrowded.

Hawaiian Watercolors
P.O. Box 616, Kihei, HI 96753 • 879-3584

Owner Ed Robinson is a well-known underwater photographer, hence the name Hawaiian Watercolors. His company takes certified divers out in two 21' power boats (6 passengers per boat). He can provide scuba instruction, but he's not a scuba school. His boats go along the Kihei/Wailea coastline out past La Perouse, plus Molokini, Lana'i, occasionally Kahakuloa and Molokini.

Lahaina Divers
710 Front Street, Lahaina, HI 96761 • 667-7496 • (800) 367-8047 ex. 102

In business since 1978, Lahaina Divers is a PADI Five Star instruction center...which means they can train beginner to instructor level. They own two dive motor boats, custom built especially for divers with boarding platforms and gear storage space. Beginners learn in a 5-day course. Certified divers can take advanced instruction, or just go out on a 2 or 3-tank dive (usually to Molokini, Lana'i or Moloka'i). Night dives are also available.

Maui Adventures
P.O. Box 1267, Lahaina, HI 96761 • 661-3400

Maui Adventures has a 40' power catamaran docked at Slip #5 in Lahaina's Harbor. Both scuba and snorkeling is done off the same boat (passenger limit 15). If a husband wants to scuba and the wife doesn't (or vice versa), the wife can snorkel and watch her husband below. Since 1976, the boat has been going to the same spot near Lahaina, so the fish are now trained. They also have a turtle dive near Puamana for experienced divers. They do offer a 4-day PADI course when asked, but it's not their main business.

Maui Dive Shop
Azeka's in Kihei • 879-3388; Rainbow Mall in Kihei • 879-4188
Lahaina Cannery • 661-5388; Kahului • 871-2111; Kihei Town Center (Seasport Shop) • 879-1919; P.O. Box 1018, Kihei, HI 96753

This is Maui's biggest retailer for scuba/snorkel equipment, both sales and rentals. They also give diving instructions—half-day programs for those who just want a diving experience or the full 5-day PADI course. They do not own a dive boat; instead, they book divers with Ocean Activities' boats.

Maui School of Diving, Inc.
P.O. Box 330684, Kahului, HI 967333 • 871-7681

Owner Wayne Peterson is a one-man operation. He does, he says, "Everything related to diving." He certifies in 4-day PADI or NAUI courses. If you have your pool and paperwork done on the Mainland (and have your form), he'll give you the four open-water check-out dives. He prefers to dive along West Maui's coast, but also goes to Lana'i and Molokini. He also does night dives in West Maui. His trips are limited to six.

Ocean Activities Center
3750 Wailea Ala Nui, D-2, Kihei, HI 96753 • 879-4485

OAC is a big activities outfit—they can book you for anything. They have several stores and many activities desks in hotels. For SCUBA, they have their own 37' motor boat in Ma'alaea Harbor. Seven days a week they take certified divers on 2-tank dives all over Maui County. They do not have an instruction program, but they do offer introductory dives for beginners. They do not mix scuba and snorkel on the same boat. Snorkelers they take to Lana'i or Molokini.

Outer Reef Charters
P.O. Box 343, Kihei, HI 96753 • 879-4296

This is a small, personal operation run by Jim Kimball. He takes his 24' power boat from Kihei to Molokini—a quick 15-minute ride. He'll go anywhere else if chartered to do so. He takes certified divers, beginners and snorkelers together, but has a maximum load of six. For an extra charge, he'll take your photo under water, or he'll give you the camera and let you shoot your own film.

SCUBA Schools of Maui
1000 Limahana Pl., Lahaina, HI 96761 • 661-8036 • 667-7500

One of the oldest SCUBA outfits on Maui, SCUBA Schools offers four-day, four hours a day, PADI certification training. They also have 3-day advanced training. They do 1 & 2-tank dives off their two motor boats. On full-day trips you can both dive and fish from the boat. The boats carry a max of six divers. Molokini, Lana'i and Moloka'i are their favorite dive areas, but they also do night dives off Black Rock in Ka'anapali.

Steve's Diving Adventures
1993 S. Kihei Rd., Bay 22, Kihei, 96753 • 879-0055

This is a full service scuba store—they sell, rent and service equipment, plus they give PADI instruction (from beginner to instructor). Their courses include 4-day certification, 2-day refresher course, 3-day advanced course (mostly diving), dive master and instructor. Their 23' motor boat takes divers mainly to Molokini, but sometimes they dive along the coast from Kihei to La Perouse. They do not dive West Maui or Lana'i.

Tropical Hydro
711 Mill St., Lahaina, HI 96761 • 871-2686

Molokini is Tropical Hydro's main destination because Molokini is what they say visitors want to see. Their 28' power catamaran takes six divers, both intro and certified. Certified divers go down 85 feet on the first dive, then 35 feet on the second. Beginners get instructions during the first dive, then dive with the others on the 35-ft. dive. The company does not sell or rent equipment, but it does offer a 4-day PADI course.

Valley Isle Divers
36 Keala Pl., Kihei, HI 96753 • 879-3483

Valley Isle is a full-service dive store (sells and rents equipment, services it, trains divers and does dive trips). They're particularly proud of their $30,000 air compressor; they claim it's tested as the purest air on Maui. Though the store's small, they employ a large number of trainers—5 full-time SCUBA instructors, 2 master instructor trainers, plus several dive masters. Their courses are extensive...intro dives, 3-5 day PADI certification, 3-day advanced (includes 5 dives). They also certify in specialty areas—photography, deep diving, cavern diving, night diving, underwater hunter (shells or game). Their 20' power boat generally goes to Molokini, but they also frequent more than 100 dive spots along the Kihei-La Perouse coastline.

SNORKEL

Snorkel Maui
P.O. Box 1107, Makawao, HI 96768 • 244-7572

This is a one-woman show, and she knows what she's talking about. In fact, she wrote the book. *Hawaiian Reefs and Tide Pools* is the book; the author and snorkel guide is Ann Fielding. Being a marine biologist, Fielding briefs her snorkelers on what they're about to see, then takes them where the reefs are best. Olowalu, despite its snorkel reputation, is often murky, so Fielding prefers Honolua Bay, Ahihi-Kinau Bay or Ulua Beach. Her trips are four hours in the morning. She'll take 2 to 8 passengers, including children. You can hire her to do specialized tours, and she can also do SCUBA.

WHERE TO SCUBA & SNORKEL (LEGALLY)

WEST MAUI

Kahakuloa Bay	scuba: A
Mokolea Point	scuba: A
Honanana Bay	scuba: M to A
Nakalele Point	scuba: A
Honokohau Bay	snorkel or scuba: M
Honolua Bay	snorkel & scuba: B to M
Mokuleia Bay	snorkel or scuba: B to M
Kapalua Bay	snorkel or scuba: B
Black Rock	snorkel or scuba: B
Olowalu	snorkel: B
Pali	scuba: M
Scenic Lookout	scuba: M
Manu'ohule	scuba: B to M
McGregor Point	scuba: M

EAST MAUI

Kama'ole Park 2 & 3	snorkel: B
Ulua Beach	snorkel or scuba: B
Mokapu Beach	snorkel or scuba: B
Wailea Beach	snorkel or scuba: B to M
Polo Beach	snorkel or scuba: B to M
Haloa Point	scuba: B to M
Five Graves	scuba: M to A
Molokini	snorkel or scuba: B to A
Oneuli Beach	scuba: M
Makena Beach	snorkel or scuba: M
'Ahihi Bay	snorkel or scuba: B to M
La Perouse Bay	snorkel or scuba: B to M
Kanaloa	scuba: M to A
Kahawaihapapa Point	scuba: A
Nu'u Bay	snorkel or scuba: M to A
Haleki'i	scuba: M to A
'Ohe'o Gulch	scuba: A
Hana Bay	snorkel or scuba: B to A
Waianapanapa	scuba: M to A
Kawe'e Point	scuba: M to A
Pauwela Point	scuba: M to A
Maliko Bay	snorkel or scuba: M to A

CODE: B = Beginner; M = Intermediate; A = Advanced

This list and map are taken, with permission, from Chuck Thorne's book, *The Divers' Guide to Maui*.. The book has detailed maps and descriptions of each site listed above. Books can be purchased in most dive shops, or can be ordered by writing Thorne at P.O. Box 1461, Kahului, HI 96732.

Surfing

Ua pi'i mai ka nalu!
Surf's up!

Never forget the plain, humble surfboard. It existed way before athletes began rigging sails on its back and "windsurfing" into the waves. Used to be that every man, woman and child in old Hawai`i had a board. They were prized possessions. Villages would empty when the waves were in.

"The thatch houses of whole villages stood empty. Daily tasks such as farming, fishing and tapa making were left undone while an entire community—men, women and children—enjoyed themselves in the rising surf and rushing white water."
—Missionary William Ellis (1831)

Hawai'i is in the path of the Pacific's major swells. These perfect waves combined with the temperate water make the islands a surfer's playland. Many of Maui's favorite windsurfing spots are also great for board surfing—surfers and sailors just learn to stay out of each others' waves.

HISTORY

The sport of surfing is hundreds of years old. No one knows which islanders rode the first boards, however. Early white explorers saw surfers in Tahiti, Tonga, Samoa and most major island groups. Boards were also seen off the coasts of Africa.

It is speculated that only the Hawaiians used boards long enough to stand on. Short boards typical in other islands could only support a prone body. Hawaiian surfing chants, one of the few historical references to surfing, indicate that Hawaiians knelt, stood and sat on their boards.

The ali'i did it best, and thus surfing is called the sport of kings. Frankly, the ali'i had more leisure time than commoners. They also had the great surf spots (like Waikiki) to themselves. Such areas were "kapu" to commoners. Gliding in on a king's or queen's wave could be your last ride.

The ali'i were expected to be strong and athletic. Kamehameha I and his wife Ka'ahumanu were both expert surfers. They, and many other chiefs, had personal surf chants that expounded their skills.

Making the old wooden boards

Ali'i boards were usually made from heavy koa wood, sometimes weighing as much as 150 pounds. Commoners had lighter boards made from wili wili trees.

As with everything in Hawaiian life, there was a religious overtone to the game. Nothing was done without considering the gods.

When a tree was cut down to make a board, a red fish was left by its roots as an offering of thanks. There was a sacred ritual to carving the board—it was chipped with a stone axe, then smoothed with coral, then stained with either ti root or pounded kukui bark juice or banana bud juice, then finally it was oiled with kukui nut oil.

There was no special surf god, but there may have been surf heiau where people could pray for good waves.

The Makahiki...Hawaiian Olympics

The Hawaiians had their own Olympics, dedicated to the god Lono. Called the Makahiki, this was a three-month celebration (in the fall and winter) of tournaments, feasts, dances and games. Surfing contests were paramount. Everything shut down but fun...war was outlawed, work was ignored..it was three months of play and thanksgiving to the gods.

"No important contest was engaged in without approaching the gods with prayers and offerings to win their favor. Some god presided over every sport. When a man felt he was in harmonious relations with the mysterious forces about him he was quite likely to accomplish superhuman feats of strength and skill."
—Dr. Kenneth Emory of the Bishop Museum

Then came the missionaries. Put on your clothes, stop screwing around, get to work...words to live by, if your name is Hiram Bingham. Surfing, particularly surfing naked, was truly a no-no with Bingham and his crew of zealots. Hawaiian waves had nobody to play with for quite a while.

Surfing Revival

King David Kalakaua (the "Merry Monarch") came to his senses during his reign (1874-1891) and started surfing again at Waikiki.

In the early 1900s haoles began picking up the sport. In 1908 a bunch of haole boys founded the Hawaiian Outriggger Canoe Club on Waikiki. They sponsored contests and promoted the sport. They thought it might lure tourists to Hawai'i.

A rival club formed with mostly local boys. Hui Nalu, Club of the Waves, was started by the great Duke Kahanamoku and his buddies.

Duke

Duke was legendary stuff. He was the first to introduce a 10-foot board. He was the first to ride tandem with a woman on his shoulders. He won three Olympic gold medals and two silvers for his swimming; the only man who could beat his swimming record was Tarzan himself—Johnny Weissmuller, one of Duke's pals during his Hollywood movie days.

Duke made surfing international. He took it to Southern California in 1912 and to Australia in 1915. He taught scores of people, including Douglas Fairbanks, Jr., and the Duke of Windsor, former king of England.

"I soared and glided, drifted and sideslipped, with the blending of flying and sailing which only experienced surfers know and fully appreciate."
—Duke Kahanamoku

From Duke's days the sport took off. No longer the sport of kings, even the tousled-haired Beach Boys could sing its glories. Their songs could never be compared with Hawaiian surfing chants. This is strictly Southern California culture:

Let's go surfing now,
Everybody's learning how,
Come on a safari with me.
Come on, baby, surfing safari...

BEST SURF SPOTS

According to Brad Dugan, "Maui has two of the best waves any-where in the world." Dugan should know, he's surfed here for years, and now judges surfing contests. When not surfing, he runs his surf shop, Lightning Bolt, in Kahului.

Dugan says, "Honolua Bay and Ma'alaea are world class waves. When they're firing, I don't think there's any place better in the world." Ma`alaea is his favorite "because it's so fast and so hollow—it's like nowhere else on earth."

He cautions that waves are not always consistent in the two areas because Maui is blocked by several other islands (Lana'i, Kaho'olawe, etc.) , and that makes it difficult for swells to get in.

According to Dugan and his crew of surfers, Maui's best surf spots include the following:

Mala Wharf: long left handers (waves break to the left); good for long boards; best in summer.

Lahaina Harbor: breaks to the right, fairly consistent waves; best in summer, not good in winter.

Lahaina Breakwall: breaks left; good in sumer.

Olowalu: less crowded than Lahaina; soft peaks; summer and winter, but better in summer.

Thousand Peaks: (between Olowalu and beginning of Pali) not crowded; good in summer for body boards and long boards.

Ma'alaea: one of best and most famous waves on south shore; one of fastests waves in world; rarely breaks because it needs a really big swell; it's fickle.

Kihei to Wailea Coast: small shore breaks; good for body surfing; not much of a swell.

La Perouse: experts' spot; big surf breaks right in front of lava flows so access in and out of water is tricky; best in summer.

Hana Bay: good surf; summer swells bring fast tubes; winter swells produce small, choppy surf.

Hana to Ke'anae: rugged coastline; a few spots known to locals that break with the right swells, but isn't worth the drive unless you know the area. Locals are secretive about "their" spots.

Ho'okipa: most consistent spot on Maui to find surf, in summer and even in winter; have two-foot tradewind swells year-round.

Ho'okipa to Kahului: reefs are a quarter mile out, so long paddles; only good on Kona wind days in winter.

Baldwin Beach: sometimes good for beginners.

Kahului Harbor: breaks inside the harbor on a north swell; winter break.

Paukukalo: breaks left off point; winter spot during Kona winds.

Windmill: waves are hard-breaking, hollow left; need Kona w i n d s or no winds; winter spot; seldom crowded.

Honolua Bay: premier winter spot for quality waves; better waves than Ho'okipa, but not as consistent; needs large west or northwest swell; expert spot.

"S" Turn: (between Honokowai and Kahana there's an "S" turn in the road) gentle rolling waves; good for beginners.

Windsurfing

Is the wind up?
Is the wind blowing?
How's the wind?

They come seeking the wind, these young troops with sunburned eyeballs. Wind, water, waves...the ingredients of the sport. But mostly it's the wind. They can boardsail with no surf, but they've got to have the wind.

They come from around the world—Germany, Sweden, Japan, Australia. Maui's wind and water are that important. Pa'ia is their Mecca. Ho'okipa the beach of their dreams...the greatest place on earth to catch the wind in their sails.

Why Maui?

It's strictly the weather. Maui's wind and water combine for perfect sailing...not every day, of course, but enough to be legendary in the world of surfing.

The tradewinds, so-called because they powered the clipper ships of the 19th century traders, blow across Maui most of the year. The trades come from a high pressure area northeast of Hawai'i, blowing more in the summer than in winter. But winter brings other winds, including the fierce Kona winds, and these are stronger than the trades.

Wind and storms create swells on the ocean. They travel thousands of miles until they meet up with land and become another force altogether. Surf.

The perfect beach

Ho'okipa is it. No other spot comes close. Since 1981 they've held international competitions here. Hawai'i's north shore swells create primo wave-jumping conditions. The waves are consistently 10 to 15, sometimes 25 feet high, and the tradewinds blow at a steady pace.

The area was "discovered" in 1979 by Mike Waltze, who at that age (19) had not yet won his many championships. There were few windsurfers living on Maui then, and those few surfed Lahaina's waters. One day Waltze drove to the other side to see the famous Hana Road. What he saw were the virgin waves of Ho'okipa. What he wondered was why no one was windsurfing them. Wonder no more. Waltze is now called "Mr. Ho'okipa."

Ho'okipa is on the windward side of Maui. As the winds come through, they're blocked by Haleakala and sent down the coast to whip through the plains of central Maui.

Ho'okipa just happens to be in the perfect spot to catch these winds at a right angle to its beach. It lies near the most northerly point of East Maui, and thus receives the winds with no interference from other islands or other parts of Maui.

Pa'ia town

Only two miles from Ho'okipa, Pa'ia has naturally been dubbed the Aspen of windsurfing. However, Aspen was never this funky. Pa'ia started out in the late 1800s as a sugar cane workers' town and grew to have a population of 8000—the biggest town then on the island. By the 1950s it was a ghost town, having lost its inhabitants to the newly-built Kahului. The hippies discovered its sleepy spirit in the Sixties and Seventies, and the town still has much of their laid-back attitude. Now the windsurfers claim it as theirs.

Equipment

With so many pros living on island, Maui has the best boards and sails and paraphernalia in the world. Better equipment is always being built, often tested by the pros themselves. These small shops and factories are names known the world over...Sailboards Maui, Hunt Hawai'i, Hi-Tech, Simmer Style, Second Wind, Ezzy Sails, Da Kine Hawai'i.

There are those who claim Maui waters need equipment unique to Maui. They suggest leaving personal equipment home and renting while on island. Numerous small shops and factories rent equipment— check the Yellow Pages under windsurfing and make a few calls.

SURFING SPOTS

Ho'okipa: Only experts sail here. Anyone else may be resented and may get in trouble. The coastline is mostly rock and reef with waves breaking in shallow water. Big waves and strong currents can smash even the pros on Ho'okipa's numerous rocks.

There are four breaks to sail at Ho'okipa, each one with different conditions. The Pavilions is near the cliff to the right (as you're looking out towards the ocean). It's surfer territory and is rarely sailed. The other three–Middles, H'Poko and Lanes—are all good for sailors, but sometimes dangerous for equipment. Rocks and coral can eat you up.

Kanaha: Great beach, everyone's favorite—beginner to expert. Lots of grass lawn and sandy beach to rig and break down. Toilets, showers, picnic tables, paved parking and oodles of other windsurfers to meet...terribly civilized place. When Ho'okipa is howling with impossible winter swells, just go down the road to Kanaha. It's a long, narrow area, so there's plenty of room for all levels of sailors.

Spreckelsville: This is the windiest spot on the north shore. When other areas are windless, Spreckelsville might still be puffing. During normal tradewind times, sailing is great here; during winter Kona winds it is not so great. Generally these waters are for intermediates and experts; shallow reefs make it rough on beginners. There's another reef a mile from shore that has awesome waves, but only experts should seek it out.

Waiehu: Not a great spot to sail, so it's seldom crowded. Only intermediates and experts should try it because it can be tricky—beginners can bust up equipment if they're unaware of the often low, shallow tides with waves breaking in shallow water. North winds during winter can send in excellent sailing waves.

Bit hard to find—take Kahului Beach Road out of Kahului, turn right onto Waiehu Beach Road and follow the signs to the Waiehu Golf Course. The beach park is just beyond the golf course. It's a very local place. No tourists.

Ma'alaea: This is a windy area. It's on the isthmus of central Maui. The wind is blocked by Maui's two big mountain/volcanos, so it whips through the isthmus instead. Average wind speed in Ma'alaea is 24 knots. The waves created are some of the fastest in the world, great for speed sailing, tough on beginners. This is expert sailing. During the winter Kona winds, Ma'alaea may be the only spot on island worth sailing.

Kihei: Kihei is all beach—about 6 miles of it from Ma'alaea to the end of Kihei's strip. In the summer months the area is calm, the water flat. In winter Kona winds and south swells make the going a bit more exciting.

Experts like to sail from Kihei across the bay to Ma'alaea. Favorite beaches are Mai Poina 'Ole La'u (Memorial Park—also known as Ohukai) and Waipuilani Beach. Best spots for beginners to learn are at the far southern and northern ends of Kihei.

Lahaina: Beginners to experts can find what they want off Lahaina's Front Street, but locals don't favor the area...too many tourists, too busy-busy, plus the harbor is always crowded.

The four areas usually surfed are: 1. in front of Lahaina Shores Condo—great for beginners from April to November, but very windy, expert sailing during the winter months; 2. breakwater (by the harbor)—waves can get high here, but watch for shallow reef; 3. Lahaina Harbor—sailable, but lots of boat traffic, plus oily water and shallow coral reef; 4. in front of Chart House restaurant—never any waves, but the windiest spot in Lahaina; beach is very rocky.

West Maui: Strong tradewinds cruise the shore from Kapalua to Ka'anapali during much of the year. They blow offshore a bit, so you may have to paddle or float out to meet them. It's a long shoreline with areas suitable for beginners to experts. If you're confident enough, you can sail the whole strip in a half hour—from D.T. Fleming Park past the Ka'anapali hotels.

One of the easiest areas from which to launch is Kapalua Bay. Hanakao'o Park and Wahikuli Park are also good for beginners. Experts can try to sail across the channel to Lana'i.

RULES

Windsurfers have certain unspoken, generally understood laws. Nothing's carved in stone, but Miss Manners would approve. Sailboard rules are similar to boating regulations where the smaller or less powerful craft always has the right of way.

1. Swimmers have the right of way.
2. Surfers have the right of way.
3. Windsurfer going out has right of way over sailor coming in.
4. S/he who catches the wave first has right of way.
5. Upwind sailor has right-of-way over downwind sailor.

Contests

Competition is getting stiffer by the year. Just how high can a human jump off a wave? How many loops can a body make with sail and board attached? New tricks make the old tricks look easy. The pros and the upstarts all live here, so Maui is the place to watch the show. Some of the best world competitions are held in Maui's waters.

April: Marui-O'Neill Invitational • wavesailing-jumping
            —Ho'okipa
            Windsurfing Maui Contest • freestyle
            —Alakapa-Lahaina

May: World Race & Wave Sailing
            —Ho'okipa to Kanaha
            Kanaha Team Slalom (May through August) • slalom
            —Kanaha Park
            Maui Super Sessions • sinker freestyle
            —Spreckelsville
            Ho'okipa Race • downwind racing
            —Ho'okipa to Kanaha

August: Hawaiian Pro-Am • slalom races
            —Maui to Moloka'i long distance; Molokini roundtrip

October: Maui Grand Prix • wavesailing, jumping & surf slalom
            —Ho'okipa
            Aloha Classic • wave sailing
            —Ho'okipa

Certain data is taken, with permission, from the *Windsurfing Guide to the Islands*. This is a detailed, indepth source of information on windsurfing. The guide can be ordered by sending $9.50 to P.O. Box 52, Paia, Maui, HI 96779.

Hiking

The ancient Hawaiians were great hikers. They had to be. They were a stone-age people who had no concept of the wheel. Feet were it.

They had miles of trails all over the island. Their major road, probably built in the 1500s, linked all parts of the island. It is believed that the great Maui king Pi'ilani and his son Kiha-a-Pi'ilani built the road. Some of this King's Highway (or Pi'ilani Highway) still exists, particularly in the La Perouse and Kaupo areas.

For those looking for it—it is generally a very wide path, paved with lava stones, often with high curbs of lava on both sides. A hike along it is a hike back in time. Best place to find it is in the La Perouse area. Just walk the road from La Perouse out to the lighthouse and beyond. You'll be on the King's Highway.

On most of the island the ancient trails are now overgrown or obscured. Many of today's trails are not much easier for someone trying to go it alone. Most trailheads are not marked, and are thus difficult to find. Only three areas have posted trailheads—Haleakala Crater, Polipoli Forest and 'Ohe'o Gulch. Luckily, these are some of the best hikes on island.

HALEAKALA

Haleakala is an eerie moonscape, full of desert colors. For the hiker, it has the same awe-inspiring feeling of majesty and solitude that one finds in the Grand Canyon. There are several trails, but all feed into these three major trails:

Halemau'u Trail: This rocky trail was built in 1937 by the National Park Service. Halemau'u means "grass house," named after a thatched roof shelter that used to be near the trailhead. The trailhead is near 8,000 feet elevation, and is a mile from the rim (the walk to the rim is along a gentle grassy slope). From the rim it's a switchback trail 1.9 miles down to the crater floor at 6,640 feet. Trail is rocky. Scenery is rough a'a lava with some greenery, plus views of Ko'olau Gap.

Sliding Sands: As the name indicates, this is a sandy, cinder trail, easy going down, tough going up. It starts near the summit at 9,780 feet, and descends 4 miles to the crater floor. Scenery is desert-like, colorful and dotted with cinder cones.

Kaupo Gap: Usually traveled to exit crater. Begins near Paliku Cabin at 6,400 feet and descends down the gap through private ranchland, eventually to Highway 31 by Kaupo Village. The trip can easily take 8 hours. It is all down hill, but not to be taken lightly—people occasionally pop off toenails and ruin their knees.

Hosmer Grove: This is a forested area reached .7 miles after entering the park, just before Park Headquarters. Named after the first territorial forester, Ralph Hosmer, who planted temperate-zone trees at this altitude in the early 1900s. The nature trail here is an hour walk through both native and exotic trees and shrubs. A brochure available at the trailhead maps and describes the trail well.

Haleakala Hiking Mileage
2.9 - Halemau'u trailhead to crater floor
3.9 - Halemau'u trailhead to Holua Cabin
2.5 - Sliding Sands trailhead to first cinder cone (Kalua o Ka Oo)
7.4 - Sliding Sands trailhead to Holua Cabin
5.8 - Sliding Sands trailhead to Kapalaoa Cabin
9.8 - Sliding Sands trailhead to Paliku Cabin
3.7 - Kapalaoa Cabin to Paliku Cabin
9.0 - Paliku Cabin down Kaupo Gap to Highway 31

'OHE'O GULCH

'Ohe'o is also part of Haleakala National Park, but it is far different than the crater. It is lush and green, with pools and waterfalls and running streams. Kipahulu Valley, above the pools, gets more than 250 inches of rainfall a year. The pool area is often called "Seven Sacred Pools"—an incorrect appellation given it years ago to promote tourism. There are closer to 20 pools along the first mile of 'Ohe'o Stream from the ocean up. There are two wonderful hikes up from the main pools.

Makahiku Falls: This is a half mile from the parking lot to a railing overlooking the falls. The hike follows a cattle trail through a pasture.

More adventurous types can go down to the stream and sit on rocks right at the head of the falls.

Caution: Look before you leap. Do not jump from high places into pools unless you know the pool is deep enough. Hitting bottom or rocks is a good way to break your neck.

Waimoku Falls: From Makahiku Falls overlook, continue on for another 1.5 miles. Highlight of the trip is a long walk through a dark and silent bamboo forest. Carry on up the stream until you deadend at the base of Waimoku Falls...good area to swim and cavort. Seldom any people there.

POLIPOLI FOREST

In olden days this was a naturally-forested area of native trees and shrubs. It took less than a century for newly-introduced critters to destroy this vegetation. Cows and goats were introduced to the island in the early 1800s and were allowed to roam free. Their numbers multiplied, and by the early 1900s they had eaten the area bare.

In the 1920s the government began reforesting. In the 1930s the Civilian Conservation Corps joined forces and planted many of the redwoods, pine, ash, sugi, cedar and Monterey cypress. The planting continued until the 1940s.

Polipoli is a park within Kula and Kahikinui Forest Reserves. The trails lead through massive groves of redwoods, then cedar, then ash, then...each grove with its own personality. Like Hansel and Gretel, you walk deeper and deeper into the magic. Mist rolls through. Birds call out. Silence prevails.

To reach Polipoli, go out Highway 377 past Haleakala Road to Waipoli Road. Go straight up Waipoli Road until you reach the park. Do not go when it's wet; 6.5 miles are unpaved, and this dirt road becomes slippery mud. Major trails in the park are:

Redwood Trail: Starts at the picnic/camping area at 6,200 feet elevation and winds through groves of massive redwoods and other conifers. Ends near the ranger's cabin at 5,300 feet. The cabin is nearly surrounded by hydrangeas. Plum trees, which bear fruit in June, are below the cabin. Easy one-hour hike.

Haleakala Ridge Trail: This goes along the southwest ridge of Haleakala for 1.6 miles. Much of the trail is not forested, so there are great views galore. The trail leads through cinders, tall grass, native brush and some forests. Near the end is a small cave within a cinder cone; used for shelter; not bad for sleeping. Easy hike.

Upper Waiakoa Trail: Begins at 6,400 feet elevation and goes 7 miles up Haleakala to 7,800 feet. Begins in the trees, but becomes increasingly rougher until the land is nearly barren. Great vista views at the top. Not an easy hike.

Skyline Trail: Trailhead is near Science City just outside Haleakala Park near the crater area. Begins at 9,750 feet and descends down the mountain for 6.5 miles till it meets Haleakala Ridge Trail. Terrain is barren and rough, and plants are scarce near the top. Gets greener as you descend. Great views.

Kahua Road: Starts in a grassy area called Ballpark Junction at 7,100 feet. Called that because the CCC used to play softball there in the 1930s. This is a dirt road that goes 3.5 miles through rough lava to the Kahua cinder cone. Country is rugged, vegatation sparse. Motorcycles and 4-wheel drives are allowed on the road, so hunters use it.

OTHER HIKING AREAS

There are some areas of Maui that are not hard to hike, even though their trailheads are not marked. 'Iao Valley has one trail that is particularly spectacular. Go up the steps to the viewing shelter, climb the railing on the left and ascend an obvious dirt trail high above the stream. It's a 2-mile trip up to a tableland plateau way behind 'Iao Needle, seemingly near the center of the West Maui Mountains. From this perch you see the massive expanse of the West Maui crater while being surrounded on three sides by mighty cliffs...the kind of place that makes you an instant philosopher.

Waianapanapa State Park has several trails along one of the most beautiful coasts on Maui...crashing sea into jagged black lava rock. One trail follows the coast from the park 3 miles to Hana Bay. In the opposite direction the trail goes past several burial sites into rugged, eerie land.

On the road to Hana, stop at the first bridge past mile marker 2 (Ho'olawa Bridge). Go through the gate up the jeep trail to **Twin Falls**. This is an easy family hike; good place for picnicing and swimming in the pools. First pool has twin waterfalls (small), but the second, a quarter mile up stream, has a larger pool and taller falls. This is private land, so be considerate.

Maui Folk...

Listen to the Earth

"Nothing is overlooked on Schmitts's hikes."

—*Chicago Tribune*

"A well-read, erudite man, Schmitt seems to have a thoughtful answer to every question."

—*Los Angeles Times*

"Equal parts mystic, hippie and Renaissance man...our charismatic guide..."

—*Texas Homes Magazine*

Ken Schmitt draws raves. And rightly so. He's good. He offers a service unique on Maui...hiking trips into the Hawai'i of tropical dreams, where nature reigns, lush and elegant.

His company, Hike Maui, is the only such service on the is-

land. Those who hike with him are fascinated by this quiet, reflective man of gentle spirit.

An art dealer from the East Coast, who had done little wilderness trekking before, went on four of Ken's hikes. "I spent a month on Maui," he said, "and the time I spent with Ken was the most memorable, not just for the beautiful places he took me, but because of the person he is."

Ken knows his territory well. He has been on island since 1978, with four of those years spent living outside, hiking Maui and contemplating life.

He was drawn to Maui, he says, by "an inner prompting which I could only understand several years later. I had to leave a life filled with concerns of business and finance, and be forced to part with everything I then considered valuable. Finally, my deepest questons began to find answers."

He took his search for wisdom into Maui's jungles, learning all he could from books and nature. When he finally came out of the wilds, he decided he wanted to share his knowledge of the island. A hiking company seemed the best way to go.

"Most of Maui," he says, "is wilderness. I like to introduce people to the spirit of the earth— to show them the wonder and beauty of it all."

"We have learned to live in an artificial environment, alienated from nature and her ways. We seldom walk on the bare earth or listen to the birds and the wind and the running water. We need to sit under more trees and waterfalls. When we quiet our minds and our emotions, we learn to identify with the earth."

An unpretentious, modest man, Schmitt is not one to toot his own horn. His friends, and clients, however, are not so restrained. As one friend says, "Ken is much more than a hiking guide. I watch people fall silent when he talks. They ask him questions as if he has the answers to the universe."

"I just speak what comes through me," Schmitt says with a shrug. "It feels to me as if I am a teacher. Actually, ever since I was a child, I knew that was my role."

Right now his classroom is nature and his teaching vehicle is Hike Maui.

In his 50-some hikes he details the history, geology, botany, plant and animal life of the area. He learned classical languages in college, and can give the Latin genus and species of most plants along the path. If clients are interested, he'll add his own particular interests—spiritual and esoteric studies, including the lore of ancient Hawai'i.

Schmitt tailors his hikes to what his clients want, and he goes at the pace of the slowest hiker. He can do both tough and gentle hikes.

Most visitors don't want to push their limits, he says. They just want to trek a few miles off the beaten path and see a secret waterfall. That's fine with Ken.

His easiest hike is a half-day coastal trip, a series of half-mile walks at three points along a rugged seacoast. A side trip into a cow pasture unveils a huge stone structure, like a mandala or an Indian medicine wheel. Nobody knows its origin or *raison d'etre*. It is an unmarked, uncategorized treasure, way off the tourist track.

The toughest hike is an all-day West Maui Mountains trip—16 miles, up 4,500 feet, then back down again. It journeys through three distinct botanical zones—arid desert area, grassy meadow and boggy rain forest. "It requires you to keep breathing heavily all the way up," he warns, "and it takes its toll on your knees on the way down."

The 'O'heo Gulch waterfall hike is very popular, mostly due to the appeal of the Hana coast. Schmitt takes his hikers on a four-hour walk past 400-foot waterfalls and through a dark bamboo forest. Unguided tourists can find some of the many waterfalls at 'O'heo, but few can locate them all. Schmitt can. And that is reason enough to follow his lead. *Address: PO Box 10506, Lahaina, HI 96761. Phone: (808)-879-5270.*

Horseback Riding

Adventures on Horseback
P.O. Box 1771, Makawao, HI 96768 • 242-7445 (24 hr) • 572-6211
Frank Levinson has 8 to 10 registered quarter horses, Arabians and Appaloosas..."the kind you'd like to take home with you," he says. "They're well trained, and I train people how to ride along the way." Levinson does only one ride a day—a five-hour trip through private property along the north shore of Haleakala. "This is not a nose-to-butt trail ride of just ambling along," he says. "This is a unique adventure into most peoples' Hawaiian fantasy—lush, secluded, tropical, pristine country...no development. We go to rain forests where there are private waterfalls. We swim and party; everybody is served gourmet picnic lunches at the falls." He takes only six people per day.

Hotel Hana Maui Stable
Hotel Hana Maui, P.O. Box 8, Hana, HI 96713 • 248-8211
The hotel has 10 horses available for one and two-hour rides. Priority is given to their hotel guests, but nonguests are welcome when the rides aren't full. Every day but Sunday they have hour-long rides that go up into the pastureland, then down to the sea coast. Mondays and Thursdays they have a breakfast-cookout ride that follows the pasture-coast route, but then ends at a cookout on the beach. On Tuesday nights there's a dinner cookout ride, and on Friday nights you can ride to their dinner lu'au.

Ka'anapali Kau Lio
P.O. Box 10656, Lahaina, HI 96761 • 667-7896
Lio means horse, Kau means back, so ranch owner Jim Bruce put them together to get "horseback." He has 20 horses on his ranch, six miles above Ka'anapali Resort. The ranch is inaccessible—five miles up a dirt sugar cane road—so Bruce picks clients up at their hotels or at the Puukolii Sugar Train Station. He offers 2 & 3-hr. rides (but they're 3 &

5-hr. trips including the travel and saddling time). He rides up in the West Maui Mountains to a forest reserve that has many native plants. The 3-hr. ride goes up an old rain gauge trail above Napili.

Makena Stables
7299-A S. Makena Rd., Kihei, HI 96753 • 879-0244
This is a two-person operation—Helaine and Pat Borge. They ride twice a day, 2.5 hours per ride, half-way up the 'Ulupalakua Ranch. Deer, cattle and wild turkeys are often seen along the trail. The Borges have 13 horses, but they take out only 6 people at a time. Thus, the horses can be rotated and kept fresh.

Pony Express Tours
P.O. Box 535, Kula, HI 96790 • 667-2202
They focus on riding in Haleakala Crater. "Probably the only ride in the world that goes into a dormant volcano," speculates owner Doug Smith. They have a 4-hour ride from rim to crater floor, 7.6 miles roundtrip descending 2,500 feet. Their 7-hour trip goes down Sliding Sands trail to Kapalaoa Cabin. This is a "heavy-duty trip," says Smith. "Anybody can do it, but it's better if you feel comfortable on a horse." They offer shorter trips, 1 & 2 hours of ranch riding, on Haleakala Ranch.

Rainbow Ranch
P.O. Box 10066, Lahaina, HI 96761 • 669-4991 • 669-4702
Located in Napili, just minutes from the hotels, this is a breeding and trail horse ranch. Only about 20 of the 60 horses are used for trail rides. Whenever one of the 20 loses its enthusiasm, it's switched with another and given a long rest. "A trail stable is only as good as its horses," says ranch president Kimo Harlacher. "We take pride in keeping our stock healthy and alert." They do beach rides along the north coast or they ride into the West Maui Mountains...they have 10 different rides from which to choose. Rides are 1 to 3 hours, with a limit of 6 riders.

Thompson's Riding Stables
RR 2, Box 203, Kula, HI 96790 • 878-1910
This is one of Maui's oldest cattle ranches, started in 1902 by Charlie Thompson. His son Jerry now runs the show and has been offering ranch trail rides since the 1960s. The ranch is on the slopes of Haleakala, 3,700 feet up. They have about 15 horses, but prefer to send out only 10 people at a time. The ranch rides are 1.5, 2 or 3 hours long. They also offer Haleakala Crater rides, half-day, full or overnight.

Biking

There is only one place in the world where it is possible to bicycle 10,000 feet down in just 38 miles. Haleakala. Three bike companies make good money doing just that.

Cruiser Bob's was the first. The original cruiser himself, Bob Kiger, got the idea on his 36th birthday when he treated himself to a fun ride down the mountain. From that 1982 birthday ride blossomed the whole shebang. Now thousands of people ride down every year. Cruiser Bob's company and his two competitors will take 8-year olds to 80-year olds...anyone who can peddle.

Kiger claims, "This is the steepest paved road in the world. No other road rises 10,000 feet vertically in 38 miles." Because of this, the bikes are fitted with special drum brakes.

This ain't no Ironman Ride

It sounds like it might be a strenuous adventure for the truly fit. It is not. It is actually a very tame ride. No one is allowed to blast banzai down the mountain. For an athlete, there's no challenge. The pace is slow, and you stop often to let cars past. You barely need to peddle. The road is all downhill, except for a third of a mile stretch of small hills.

The trip takes you through a variety of climates and botanical zones...from the cold, desert-like crater, through green cattle country, through eucalyptus groves to the beach at Pa'ia. It's an all-day affair, though only three to four hours are spent on the bike. All three companies have hotel pick-up service, and all three feed you well. Windbreakers, rain pants, gloves and helmets are provided.

The trip is safe and easy, and it's a spectacular ride with glorious views. Anybody can do it, and anybody has.

Cruiser Bob's
505 Front St., Lahaina, HI 96761 • 667-7717 or (800) 654-7717

Maui Downhill
333 Dairy Rd. Suite 201 D, Kahului, HI 96733 • 871-2155

Maui Mountain Cruisers
P.O. Box 1356, Makawao, HI 96768 • 572-0195

For the independent biker...
Those who like to bike it alone should know it can be suicidal. Maui's roads are no longer big enough for the traffic the island now generates. On some streets, notably Kihei Road and the road to Hana, there is no room for cycles. Bikers still ride, but it is nerve wracking.

Safe rides include the upper Kihei road (Pi'ilani Highway), the Honoapi'ilani Highway from Wailuku through Lahaina and all the way to Kapalua, all Upcounty/ Kula roads and the Haleakala Highway.

Mountain bike riders can ride around to Hana the back way by 'Uluplakua and Kaupo. Another great ride is the back way to Lahaina via Kahakuloa. For a wild, bumpy ride, go down the back side of Haleakala by Polipoli Forest...it's downhill most of the way.

Call the Cycle and Sport Shop (877-5848) for information on the Maui Bicycle Club. They know about races, and they have day trips that serious bikers are welcome to join.

Renting bikes
If you don't bring your own, these are the places to check out:

AA Go Go Bikes Hawai'i: single or three-speed bikes by the day or week. *30 B Halowai Drvie, Ka'anapali; 661-3063.*

Scooter's Bike Rental: single-speed mountain bikes by the hour, day or week. *1223 Front Street, Lahaina; 661-8898.*

Fun Rentals: single, five, ten-speed bikes by hour, day or week. Has some 18-speed bikes which are rented only by the week. *193 Lahainaluna Road, Lahaina; 661-3053.*

Abrams Bike Shop: high-quality Italian bikes, mostly 12 speeds, valued up to $2,500. Rented by day, by appointment only. *642C Luakini, 667-2033.*

Hunting

Want to stalk wild pig in a jungle, armed with knife or bow and arrow...pack of trusty dogs sniffing a trail ahead of you?

Most days somewhere on Maui visitors with a hunting yen are doing just that. Of course, not all hunting trips are Rambo-style excursions. Hunters also track goats and wild birds (pheasant, quail, partridge, francolin, doves). Mouflon and axis deer are hunted on Lana'i.

You need a hunting license, and must abide by game laws set by the state. These are described in pamphlets available from the Department of Land and Natural Resources, Division of Forestry and Wildlife, 54 South High Street, P.O. Box 1015, Wailuku, HI 96793.

Visitors may bring their own rifles, but must register them within 48 hours of arrival. In lieu of your own, hunting guides can rent rifles.

Pig & Goats

Pigs and goats are hunted year-round in certain state forest areas of both East and West Maui, particularly in the Ko'olau and Hana forest reserves along the north coast of East Maui. Also good is the Kahikinui Game Management area on the south slopes of East Maui, but it's open only February through June.

Hunting is possible every day on private lands, but hunting there without permission is poaching.

For pigs and goats, a variety of rifles, muskets spears, knives and bows and arrows are allowed. Different rules apply when dogs are along; these are listed in the state hunting pamphlets.

Birds

Bird hunting rules are strict. Each species has a specific season with certain hunting days, and there's a daily limit. Birds are hunted in the Kula Forest Reserve and the Kahikinui Game Management area, both on the south slope of Haleakala below the crater.

Bird hunters must use only shotguns with BB or smaller shot or bows and arrows.

What's a mouflon?

Dictionary definition: a wild sheep of the mountains of Sardinia and Corsica with large curling horns in the male. Rather than go to Sardinia or Corsica, take your rifle to Lana'i. Here you can hunt mouflon or axis deer, but each has separate days for hunting...can't hunt both on the same day.

Mouflon are hunted only on Sundays in August. Axis deer are hunted only on nine consecutive Sundays, ending with the last Sunday in April.

Both can be bagged with either rifles or bows and arrows. However, rifle hunters must participate in a public drawing in order to hunt either animal.

HUNTING GUIDES

Hunting Adventures of Maui
645 B Kaupakalua Road, Haiku, HI 96708 • 572-8214

Guide Bobby Caires went full-time with his guide business in 1984. He specializes in trophy hunts for goat on private land—'Ulupalakua, Haleakala or Kaupo Ranches. Because he has permission to hunt on private land, he can take people out any day of the week. Caires is fully insured. He provides a full day's hunt with a hot lunch. He picks up hunters at the airport or meets them in Pukalani. If needed, he can sell a hunting license, rent a rifle and ammo, and lend boots or camouflage gear.

He prefers small hunts, no more than three people. He guarantees a trophy on goat hunts, but promises only 65-70% success on pig hunts. He hunts pig without dogs, because, he says, there's more challenge in stalking the animal and less likelihood of baby pigs getting killed.

A taxidermist, Caires can prepare the head for transport home and the meat for meals, if the customer so desires.

No Ka Oi Outfitters
P.O. Box 556, Wailuku, HI 96793 • 572-6046

Provides one to three-day hunts, with helicopter transport to and from hunting grounds. Sighting and shooting opportunities guaranteed. All equipment and meals supplied; hunting license and taxidermy service available.

Bus Tours

If you don't rent a car, you may want to take bus tours, and there are many companies willing to accommodate. The ride is often only as good as the driver. Drivers give narrations during the tours, and hopefully they know the facts.

Don't forget to tip

When the drivers are good and caring, as they often are, a tip is in order. Their salaries are not exactly top scale.

Akamai Tours
532 Keolani Pl, Kahului, HI 96732 • 871-9551
14-passenger Ford vans
Tours: Haleakala, Hana, West Maui circle island

Aloha Nui LoaTours
P.O. Box 1592, Kihei, HI 96753 • 879-7044 (24 hours)
two 15-passenger Dodge vans
Tours: Hana, Haleakala

Ekahi Tours
205 Pukalani St., Pukalani, HI 96788 • 572-9775
14-passenger Dodge vans
Tours: Hana, Haleakala, Ke'anae, Upcountry

Grayline Maui
273 Dairy Rd., Kahului, HI 96732 • 877-5507
57-passenger buses & 11-passenger vans
Tours: Haleakala, Hana, Upcountry, 'Iao Valley & Lahaina, all-day Maui tour from airport (Haleakala, 'Iao & Lahaina)

Tropical Excursions
P.O. Box 597, Pai'a, HI 96779 • 579-8422
15-passenger Dodge van (but only they carry 10); VIP van with 7 velour captain's chairs
Vans stop at Tropical Garden Cafe (owned by the excursion company) in Pai'a for breakfast or lunch (included in tour price).
Tours: Hana, Haleakala

No Ka Oi Scenic Tours
P.O. Box 1827, Kahului, HI 96732 • 871-9008
15-passenger Ford vans
Tours: Hana, Haleakala, Upcountry

Roberts
P.O. Box 1563, Kahului, HI 96732 • 871-6226
49 & 57-passenger buses; 10, 21, 25, 28-passenger mini buses; 14-passenger vans; limos
Tours: 'Iao/Lahaina; 'Iao/Haleakala; Hana Haleakala/'Iao/Lahaina; Kula/'Iao/Lahaina/Haleakala

Transhawaiian
845 Palapala Dr., Kahului, HI 96732 • 877-7308
47, 53, 57-passenger buses; 15, 17, 22-passenger mini buses; 10 &14-passenger vans
Tours: Hana; Haleakala; 'Iao; Haleakala/'Iao/Lahaina; 'Iao/Lahaina

Tennis

Tennis on Maui ranges from the sublime to the municipal. Key points to consider, besides costs, are weather and time of day. Hot areas close to the beach resorts are often scorching at midday. Early and late hours are better, but the courts are more crowded.

Many hotels and condos have their own courts, but for guests only. There are 36 courts in Ka'anapali, for example, but only a few are open to outsiders.

The following list includes the major resort courts open to the public, plus the county courts—not fancy, but free.

RESORT COURTS

Wailea Tennis Club

World Tennis magazine rates Wailea Five-Star. This is top of the line—14 courts, including three grass courts, Wimbledon style, the only public grass courts in Hawai'i.

Four courts of their courts are lighted for night play. They have a tennis stadium which has several tournaments each year.

There's priority for play, plus slightly lower fees, for guests of the Wailea hotels and condos. Grass court fees are per court hour. Hard court fees are by the day. Players may keep playing if no one is waiting after the first hour, and may return later to play again.

Lessons by one of five pros are at hourly rates or are part of a Wimbledon West Tennis Academy package. Lessons include instant replay video and ball machines. Hours: 7 a.m. to 8 p.m. Phone: 879-1958.

Makena Tennis Club

This is the newest of Maui's tennis clubs, opening in August, 1986, as part of the Makena Resort (which includes the Maui Prince Hotel). Six hard courts, unlighted. There are no pros and no lessons. Playing priority and lower fees are given to Maui Prince guests. Hours: 7 a.m. to 6 p.m. Phone: 879-8777.

Royal Lahaina Tennis Ranch

This is Ka'anapali's major tennis center. Its 4,000-seat stadium hosts several tournaments each year. Six of the 11 courts are lighted at night. Reservations needed for early morning or late afternoon hours. Pay by the hour. Courts are open 7 a.m. to 7 p.m.

The "ranch" is directed by Peter Burwash International. Lessons include demonstration and instruction clinics, advanced workout with the pro and round-robin social tournaments. Phone: 661-3611.

Maui Marriott Hotel

Three of the Marriott's five courts are lit at night. You can play by the hour or get an all-day pass. It's smart to book reservations during the peak tourist seasons (winter and summer). Lessons are available. The Marriott sponsors no tournaments. Hours: 7 a.m. to 8 p.m. Phone: 667-1200.

Sheraton-Maui Hotel

The Sheraton's three courts are all lit for night play. There's a pro on staff, so lessons are available. Pay for courts by the hour; reservations are a good idea because it's a big hotel and has many guests. Hours: 8 a.m. to 9 p.m. Phone: 661-0031.

Napili Kai Beach Club

Their two courts are not lit, so night playing is not possible. Priority for both courts goes to guests, but the public is welcome when guests aren't playing. Pay by the hour. Lessons available. Open during daylight hours. Phone: 669-6271.

The Tennis Garden, Kapalua

The magazines seem to love it—Tennis magazine calls Kapalua "one of the top 50 U.S. Tennis Resorts," Tennis Industry magazine rates it the 1986 "Court of the Year," World Tennis magazine gave it a "5-Star Tennis Resort" rating.

Ten courts are set within a landscaped garden where a number of tournaments are held each year. Four courts are lighted for nighttime play. Court time is at a daily rate, lower for Kapalua guests and property owners. Private and group lessons are available, and there are seven tennis camps for adults each summer...3 to 5 days of instruction, plus video analysis and unlimited additional court time. Hours: 7:30 a.m. to 8 p.m. Phone 669-5677.

COUNTY COURTS

These are all free and first-come, first-served. Play is one hour for doubles, 45 minutes for singles. If no one is waiting, play on. The busiest courts are in Lahaina, Kihei and Wailuku.

Central Maui
Kahului Community Park: *Onehee Ave. & Uhu St.*
—2 lighted courts, restroom
Kahului Salvation Army: *Kamehameha Ave. & Kaulawahine St.*
—2 courts, not lit
War Memorial Center: *Ka'humanu Ave. & Kanaloa Ave.*
— 4 lighted courts, restrooms, locker rooms
Wells Park / Wailuku Community Center: *Wells & Market St.*
—6 lighted courts, restrooms

Kihei
Kalama Park: *S. Kihei Rd. & Kealia Pl.*
—4 lighted courts, restrooms
State park area: *behind Maui Sunset and Luana Kai Condos*
—6 courts (not lit) on a large grassy field by the ocean ;

Upcountry
Eddie Tam Memorial Center: *Makawao Ave. & Mahola St.*
—2 lighted courts, restrooms
Haliimaile Park: *Haliimaile Rd. & Makomako St.*
—1 lighted court, restrooms
Pukalani Park: *Pukalani St. across from shopping center*
—1 lighted court

Hana
Hana Park: 1 lighted courts, restrooms

Lahaina
Lahaina Civic Center: *across from Wahikuli Park*
—5 lighted courts
Malu Ulu O Lele Park: *Front & Shaw St.*
—4 light courts, restrooms

COLLEGE COURTS

Maui Community College at Ka'ahumanu & Wakea Avenues has four courts...open during daylight hours (no lighting). Anyone can use them for free when tennis classes are not being held. First come, first served basis.

TOURNAMENTS

April: Kapalua Doubles Championship—men, women, mixed.

May: Kapalua Tennis Jr. Vet/Sr. Championships—men and women (over 35) in singles, doubles and mixed.
            Hal "Aku" Lewis Memorial Tennis Tournament

September: Kapalua Open Tennis Tournament—top players from around the state compete for one of largest tennis purses in Hawai'i.

December: Kapalua/ Betsy Nagelsen Tennis Invitational—Nagelsen, Kapalua's touring professional, plays host to other women tennis pros. Pro-doubles competition and a pro-am tournament.

Golf

Maui's golf courses are gorgeous, especially in the resort areas. They are also expensive. Ka'anapali, Wailea, Makena, Kapalua can cost up to $80 for 18 holes. Anyone can play in the resort courses, you needn't be a hotel guest.

There are two public courses, both priced more reasonably than the resort courses. Due to their locations, they generally have cooler weather than courses near the hotels.

"Mad dogs and Englishmen go out in the noon-day sun"...or so the ditty goes. Golfers do too, though all courses open by 6 or 7 a.m., so midday sun can be avoided.

RESORT COURSES

Royal Ka'anapali Golf Course

Ka'anapali has two 18-hole courses. The North Course, designed by Robert Trent Jones, Sr., is the longer and more challenging of the two. The South Course, originally designed as an "executive" course for high-handicap players, was redesigned by Arthur Jack Snyder as a regulation championship course.

Both courses are run by Director of Golf Ray DeMello, born and reared in Lahaina, who started with Ka'anapali in 1963, the year the North Course's second nine opened. DeMello began as a driving range attendant and worked his way to the top.

Pro shop, restaurant, rentals. Carts mandatory. Tee times up to two days in advance for resort guests; outsiders one day in advance. First tee-off is 7 a.m.

Sunseeker Golf Schools (P.O. Box 10930, Lahaina, HI 96761; 667-7111) provides lessons at Ka'anapali. Variety of instruction—from a lesson to a three-day package. Every day but Sunday.

Reserve in advance. Phone: 661-3691.

Kapalua Golf Courses

Kapalua's two courses, both designed by Arnold Palmer, offer quite different views to distract the golfer. The Bay Course, site of the nationally-televised Isuzu Kapalua International tournament, lies on the coast, with one hole requiring a shot across an ocean bay. The Village Course rises above the resort on the slopes of the West Maui Mountains.

Pro shop, restaurant, rentals. Carts mandatory. Bay course has a driving range; both have putting greens. Proper golf attire requested (no cut-offs or tank tops). Lessons and videos available for individuals, clinics for seven or more. Guests given preference for tee times and lower green fees. All rates cut during "twilight"—after 2:30 p.m. First tee-off is 6:30 a.m.

Phone: 669-8044

Makena Golf Course

Maui's newest course, designed by Robert Trent Jones, Jr., is set on the sunny coast of Makena, with views of the ocean and Haleakala. Pro shop, restaurant, rentals. Carts mandatory. Driving range and putting greens available. No restrictions on tee time reservations. First tee-off at 7 a.m. No lessons or major tournaments.

Phone: 879-3344.

Wailea Golf Courses

Both the Blue Course and the Orange Course at Wailea have been ranked by national organizations as among the nation's best courses. Designed by Arthur Jack Snyder, the courses have views of the ocean and Kaho'olawe.

The Orange Course is considered a tougher course; it has more trees, is at a higher elevation and has narrower fairways. It also has uniquely Hawaiian hazards—lava-rock formations and stone walls left from ancient villages. Some village sites are still intact in the scrub kiawe forests that border the golf course.

Pro shop, restaurant, rentals. Carts mandatory. Two putting greens for each course plus a single driving range. Lessons available from pros; driving range has video equipment. Tee times up to three days in advance for members (Wailea property owners can be members), two days for resort guests, and otherwise one day. Resort guests given lower green fees. First tee-off at 6:36 a.m. Tournaments include the Asahi Beer/Kay Ohashi in January or February and the Hal "Aku" Lewis Memorial Celebrity Tournament in May.

Phone: 879-2966.

PUBLIC COURSES

There are two public courses, both priced more reasonably than the resort courses. They generally have cooler weather than courses near the hotels.

Waiehu Municipal Golf Course
Set on the northeast coast of West Maui, past Wailuku, with ocean views on one side and the mountains on the other. Pro shop, restaurant, rentals. Carts available, but not mandatory. Lessons for beginning to advanced players by one of four teaching pros. Call up to two days in advance for tee times. Rates lower on weekdays. First tee-off at 6 a.m. Phone: 244-5433.

Pukalani Country Club
This course is in the midst of a suburban community on the western slope of Haleakala. Views of the West Maui Mountains, the entire central plain and the ocean on each side. Pro shop, restaurant, rentals. Carts mandatory. Lighted driving range and putting green are open week nights until about 9 p.m. Lessons from teaching pro Cliff Council (572-8062), ranging from an hour of instruction to a three-hour playing lesson. Video of lessons on request. Call up to three days in advance for tee times. First tee-off is 6:30 a.m. Course is the site of the pro-am for the Maui Open and of the Hawai'i Women's State Golf tournament in May. Phone: 572-1314.

TOURNAMENTS

Jan./ Feb.: Asahi Beer/Kay Ohashi Tournament at Wailea

May: State Women's Tournament at Waiehu or Pukalani
Hal "Aku" Lewis Memorial Celebrity Tournament at Wailea.

June: Maui Open Golf Tournament—played at several courses. For information write: Charlie Aruda, at the Maui Beach Hotel, 1770 Ka'ahumanu Ave., Kahului HI 96732.

November: Isuzu Kapalua International at Kapalua. Grand masters compete for $600,000. Admission free to watch four rounds.

Fitness

All gyms offer daily, weekly and other short-term rates for visitors. For those who prefer yoga instead of aerobics or gyms, watch the bulletin boards at the health food stores—classes are often posted.

CENTRAL MAUI

Nautilus World Fitness Center

Nautilus machines and free weights, whirlpool, sauna. Three or four aerobics classes each weekday, one on Saturday. Open M,T,W from 7 a.m. to 9 p.m.; Th,F from 7 a.m. to 8 p.m.; Sat. 8 a.m. to 7 p.m.; Sun. 9 a.m. to 2 p.m.

1325 Lower Main, Wailuku • 244-3244 .

Valley Isle Fitness

Paramount machines and free weights, circuit training, saunas, juice bar, massage therapist, pro shop, nutritional and fitness counseling. The most aerobics classes of any gym on island—41 a week. Open M-F 6 a.m. to 9 p.m.; Sat. 7 a.m. to 7 p.m.; Sun. 9 a.m. to 2 p.m.

Wailuku Industrial Park (850 Kolu A-3) • 242-6851.

Maui Racquetball Club & Spa

Dyna-Cam machines (a division of Nautilus), free weights, whirlpool, sauna, steam room. The island's only racquetball court. Separate charge for court use in addition to membership fee; may reserve court up to two days in advance.

Daily stretch class at 8:30 a.m.; aerobics class at 5:30 p.m. Exercise videos available for those who would rather follow a video than a class. Membership rates some of the lowest on island. Open daily except Sunday, 7 a.m. to 10 p.m.

25 Kahului Beach Road • 242-4974.

Maui Family YMCA

The Y is now building a facility which will include a gym, but for now its low-impact aerobics classes are held in a rented facility. First visit is free. Classes M,W,F at 9 a.m., 5 p.m.. and 6 p.m.

Address is a bit complicated, so call for directions. *242-9007.*

Keiki Gym

Kids from 4 months to 8 years get to play here. These are not structured classes; they're free play on equipment designed to be safe but challenging—slides, swings, ramps, pillows for jumping. The idea is to develop coordination, motor skills and self confidence while having fun. Parents must stay with kids under three years. Payment is by the class or monthly. Classes at 9 a.m. M, T, Th; 10 a.m. M, T, W, Th.

572-0733 (call for address).

KIHEI/WAILEA

World Gym

This is a muscle gym, run by people who ripple. They have universal weight machines and free weights, plus a computerized "Life Cycle" (stationary bike that gives information like how many calories the rider is burning.) Of course there is no lack of mirrors. Open M-F 7 a.m to 9 p.m.; Sat. 7 a.m. to 5 p.m.; Sun. 9 a.m. to 5 p.m.

1325 S. Kihei Road • 874-0101.

Maui Workout

Held in the World Gym facilities, but not part of the gym. Aerobics program is owned and run separately. Co-ed aerobics classes only; low-impact and regular; 25 classes a week. First class on weekdays at 7:30 a.m., last one at 8:15 p.m. On Sat. & Sun. only one class a day.

1325 S. Kihei Road • 879-8907.

The Waves at Wailea

This is an intensive fitness program created by local fitness educator Gloria Keeling. The six-day program (held at the Maui Inter-Continental Hotel) includes daily aerobics, yoga, seminars on wellness topics, massages, personal fitness evaluation, plus typical Maui sports like snorkeling and hiking. Package price includes accommodations and gourmet meals at the hotel.

P.O. Box 758, Paia, HI 96779 • (US) 800-367-8047 ext. 217 • (Can.) 800-423-8733 ext. 217 • (local) 575-2178

Strong, Stretched & Centered at the IC

Stephenie Karony, Gloria Keeling's sister, teaches an aerobics course at the Inter-Continental Hotel each morning at 8 a.m. Free for guests, but open to the public for a small fee. The class is held outside on grass by the ocean. Bring your own mat and towel.

Hotel Inter-Continental • 575-2178

WEST MAUI

Lahaina Health Club

This is a gym with a wide variety of weight machines of several makes, plus free weights, and a massage therapist. Aerobics classes daily at 9 a.m. and 5:30 p.m.

Across from Maui Ka'anapali Villas • 667-6684.

Lahaina Civic Center

Exercise classes led by West Maui Workout teachers organized by Laura Cody, who has been teaching on Maui and O'ahu for years. Aerobic classes 9-10:30 a.m. M-Sat.; 5:30-7 p.m. T,Th. Low-impact aerobics M,W 5:30-6:30 p.m. Showers are available; bring own mat and towel.

Mauka of highway by post office • 661-4685.

Kahana Gym

They have 1,000 square feet full of free weights and free weight apparatus. There's always someone available to help. Rates are by day or by month. Open 7 a.m. to 8 p.m. M-Sat.; 9-2 Sunday.

4310 Lower Honoapiilani Highway, Apt. 119 • 669-7622.

HANA

Workout at Helene Hall

Typical of friendly, community-minded Hana, this is a free workout organized by a local woman, Sina Fournier. She does it "for the fun of it," she says. She lost 40 pounds when she first started aerobics, and now says "I don't dare stop." Sina plays her exercise tapes M-F at 5:30 a.m. and about 3:40 p.m. at Helene Hall in Hana Bay. The classes are 45 minutes to an hour. Just show up.

ISLAND-WIDE PROGRAMS

Strong, Stretched & Centered

Gloria Keeling has nearly 20 years experience in various types of body work. She has taught numerous exercise programs, and now she teaches others how to teach. Her six-week instructors' course has yoga, weight training, jazz dance, exercise physiology, diet and nutrition, cardiopulmonary resuscitation, dance, Tai Chi Chu'an, fitness testing, and more. She also teaches instructors to market their courses.

Fee for the program includes housing, meals, transportation, excursions and massage therapy. There are four Maui sessions each year, plus two in Montana, conducted by Keeling's associate Nancy Myrick. *P.O. Box 981, Pa'ia, HI 96779 • 575-2178.*

Strong, Stretched & Center Exercise Classes

Anybody can take these classes, they're not as hard as one might think. Gloria Keeling and her instructors teach Keeling's exercise method of aerobics/yoga/stretching in Pa'ia, Kula and Lahaina. Call Keeling for times and locations. *575-2178.*

HOTELS WITH CLASSES OR GYMS

Ka'anapali Beach.....Pool aerobics M,T,Th,F at noon. Public welcome. No charge.

Hyatt Regency..........Health spa with weights, sauna, massage therapy, whirlpool. Aerobics class daily at 9:30 a.m. Water aerobics in pool every afternoon at 2:15. Limited to guests; no charge for classes and gym.

Marriott.....................Weight room. Aerobics class 9 a.m. daily except Sunday; $3 for nonguests, guests no charge. Water aerobics in pool T,Th, Sat at 1 p.m. No charge; nonguests welcome.

Stouffer's...................Aerobics class 8 a.m. M-F. Guests only. No charge.

Inter-Continental.....Aerobics daily at 8 a.m. No charge to guests. Nonguests $4.

Kapalua.....................Aerobics M-Sat. 8 a.m. $6 a class for guests or nonguests.

JOGGING/ RUNNING

Runners can join in monthly "all comers" sessions at the War Memorial Stadium (Ka`ahumanu & Kanaloa Avenues) in Wailuku. Runners vie at standard race distances (from 1,500 meters to a mile or 10-K) on what Jerry Horton, running columnist for *The Maui News*, calls "one of the finest tracks in the world." The track is made of rekortan, a yielding, textured substance also used on the 1984 Los Angeles Olympic track. These meets are usually held the second Wednesday of each month at 6:30 p.m. Call the Valley Isle Road Runners codaphone, 242-6042, to make sure the meet is being held.

Public courses

There are two parcourses on Maui for those who like to break up a run with some calisthenics. One is located at the Kahului Community Center at Onehee and Wakea Avenues, and the other is in Wailuku at the War Memorial Complex.

The resort areas, particularly Wailea and Ka'anapali, have long strips of beach and lawn great for joggers. Stouffer Wailea Beach Resort gives out a jogging map (at the guest activities desk in the lobby) that details four courses from Kihei to Makena.

Long strips of uninterrupted sand are also found from Ma'alaea to Kihei and from Kanaha to Spreckelsville.

Races

Competitive runners should call the codaphone for weekly reports on races (locations, times, etc.). There are three major runs held every year—the Maui Marathon, The Run to the Sun and the Hana Relays.

The Maui Marathon, held in March, travels the standard 26 miles. Participants run from Kahului to Ka'anapali along the Honoapi'ilani Highway.

The Run to the Sun, in August, takes runners 36.2 miles up the dormant volcano, Haleakala. Most runners who try this one feel like winners if they just finish the run—it goes from sea level to 10,023 feet...relentlessly up all the way. The leaders of the pack do it in less than five hours.

The Hana Relays, in September, include teams of 500-some runners. They take turns running parts of the road between Kahului and Hana, a twisting 54-mile course.

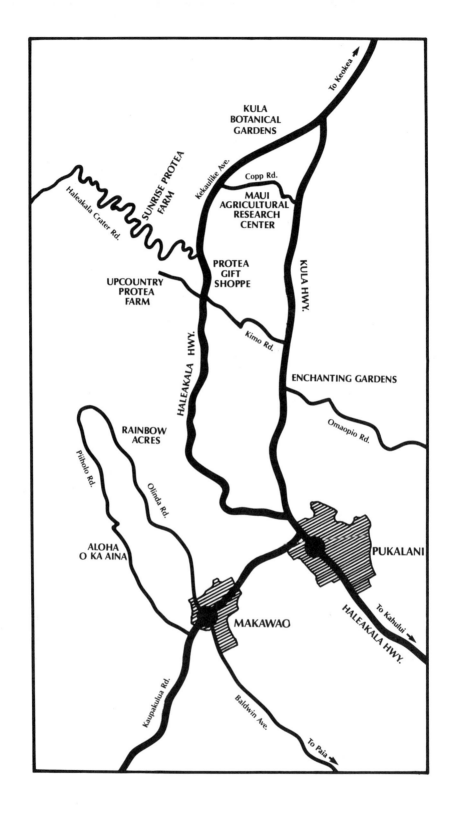

KULA
BOTANICAL
GARDENS

To Keokea

Haleakala Crater Rd.

SUNRISE PROTEA
FARM

Kekaulike Ave.

Copp Rd.

MAUI
AGRICULTURAL
RESEARCH
CENTER

PROTEA
GIFT
SHOPPE

UPCOUNTRY
PROTEA
FARM

KULA HWY.

Kimo Rd.

HALEAKALA HWY.

ENCHANTING GARDENS

Omaopio Rd.

RAINBOW
ACRES

Piiholo Rd.

Olinda Rd.

ALOHA
O KA AINA

PUKALANI

MAKAWAO

To Kahului

HALEAKALA HWY.

Kaupakulua Rd.

Baldwin Ave.

To Paia

Garden Tours

Flower lovers should head Upcountry. That's where most of Maui's commercial flower farms are. That's also where the unique and famous protea flowers grow...nearly one million of them annually (and their popularity is on the rise).

Kula carnation growers produce almost all the carnations needed in Hawai'i for lei making—32 million flowers a year. Fields of carnations grow next to fields of onions and fields of wild prickly pear cactus. The diversity is great Upcountry. The district of Kula is like one big garden. It has rich soil and a sunny, but cool climate.

KULA LOOP TOUR

The following loop tour goes through Kula's gracious countryside. It winds around on the side of Haleakala at 3,000 to 4,000-foot elevation. There are scores of farms here, but most cannot be visited. Those that can always have a sign welcoming visitors.

Enchanting Gardens
The first one along Kula Highway is a garden, not a farm. Enchanting Gardens looks like a mass of colors from the road. Once inside, the smell alone is worth the walk through the six acres of flowers. Narue and Makota Nitahara opened the garden in April, 1986, and it's thriving well for such a short time. They don't sell any flowers here; this garden is strictly for looking. They seem to have one of everything—not just flowers, but also fruit trees, taro, pineapple, an orchid section and an herb garden. The garden is open from 9 a.m. to 5 p.m. daily. Admission charge.

Maui Agricultural Research Center
A side jog off the highway goes to the University of Hawai'i's research center (up Copp Road, then left to the end of Mauna Place). There's nothing commercial about this place; it's a working farm where

the university does research on vegetables and flowers.

In 1965, the first proteas grown in Hawai'i were planted here. Within a few years, scientists were testing proteas as a commercial possibility. They obviously did their research well.

Walking through the various gardens is strenuous exercise up a steep hill. The less ambitious can skip the higher plots and just see the proteas growing close to the office.

Maps are handed out at the office for a self-guided tour. Hours are 7:30 to 3:30 (closed at lunch hour); open Monday through Friday. Pesticides are sprayed on Mondays, but the farm is still open.

Kula Botanical Gardens

Warren and Helen McCord started with bare land and a dream in the late Sixties. By 1971, their Kula Botanical Gardens was ready to open. By now it is grown up and lush. The three acres are beautifully landscaped with a koi pond and two streams trickling through.

This is not a flower garden (though there are many); there are plants and trees of all kinds here. The predominant color is green. It is designed so that something is in bloom during every season.

There's a small section called the "tabu garden" that contains poisonous and toxic plants. There's also an aviary with several exotic birds.

Located on Kekaulike Road; open daily 9 to 4 daily. Admission charge.

Sunrise Protea Farm

A short way up Haleakala Highway towards the crater is Sunrise Country Market, a little grocery/deli that also sells protea. A few protea grow next to the market, but a whole field of them are just one and a half miles up the road at their Sunrise Protea Farm. They sell the flowers either fresh or dried. They're certified for shipment to the Mainland. Hours: 7:30 to 5 on week days; 8:30 to 4:30 on weekends.

Protea Gift Shoppe

The Hawai'i Protea Cooperative has a retail outlet, the Protea Gift Shoppe, next to the Kula Lodge. Fifteen local growers sell their flowers to the Co-op, which supplies almost half the local protea market in Hawai'i. Fresh flower bouquets start at about $30 here; they do not sell individual flowers. Hours: 8 to 4 daily.

Upcountry Protea Farm

At the very end of Upper Kimo Road is a lovely little farm called Upcountry Protea Farm. They grow about 35 species of protea, plus bird of paradise, orchids and ginger. Visitors are welcome to browse anywhere on the two and a half acres, including the greenhouse and nursery where baby proteas are sprouting.

Owners David and Lisa Morrison enthusiastically answer questions about protea. Neither of them knew about plants before they bought the farm, but they've learned by doing. They give customers written instructions on how to grow the flowers and how to dry them properly. They sell individual stems and bouquets, and they're certified to ship out of Hawai'i.

Lisa reports that the best selections are on Tuesdays and Fridays because they pick the flowers Mondays and Thursdays. Hours: 8 to 4:30 daily.

MAKAWAO LOOP TOUR

Want more countryside, but different types of gardens? Head towards Makawao and take a right up Olinda Road at Makawao's main intersection. Olinda curves into Pi'iholo Road and loops back down to Makawao. The loop is a gorgeous drive, much like northern California. Eucalyptus line the narrow road and pine trees grow in the fields.

There are only two gardens along the loop, and neither are really geared for visitors. They're in business to sell plants, not show them, but browsers are welcome. The drive is the attraction, more than the gardens.

Rainbow Acres

Rainbow Acres is a succulent and cactus farm open to visitors only Fridays and Saturdays, 10 to 4. The rainy hills of Olinda are not prime land for cactus growing, but owner Chuck Weidner likes living in Olinda, and succulents are his hobby. Anyway, the business started as a hobby. Now Weidner has more than a thousand varieties, and his is the largest succulent nursery in Hawai'i.

Aloha o Ka 'Aina

Downhill on Pi'iholo Road is Aloha o Ka 'Aina Farm (means Love of the Land).   This nursery specializes in ferns and has a large greenhouse full of them. They also sell potted trees and plants. Hours: 10 to 4 Tuesday through Saturday.

Helicopters

There's nothing like a helicopter's birds-eye view of canyons and waterfalls. Then again, there's also nothing like the noise a helicopter generates. That's the dichotomy in the helicoper business.

Visitors often love the whirlybirds. For an average $100 fare, they can fly into remote areas they'd normally never see. Instead of hiking for hours into 'Iao Valley, they can fly over the whole of the West Maui Mountains.

Residents, however, are not charmed. People who live in the remote areas do so because they want peace and quiet. Helicopters are an intrusion in their lives. Some complain that a helicopter takes off every 15 minutes on the island.

Haleakala's silence disturbed

Those who hike through Halekala's crater are amazed by the silent eeriness of the place...until the eggbeaters whirl past. Sound is amplified by the bowl-like crater.

It is an unresolved problem. To their credit, the helicopter companies have a Helicopter Environmental Liason Office (HELO) that anyone may call with complaints. Their hotline is 244-7511.

LOVE thy neighbor

Residents have their own hotline which they would prefer visitors call. Their organization is LOVE (Love Our Vital Environment), and its number is 248-7756.

Hana resident Paul I. Fagan, III, of LOVE, says the helicopter industry is "growing in leaps and bounds, and new laws have to be written." Fagan says LOVE is trying to "collect information and recommend solutions to protect our quality of life."

HELICOPTER COMPANIES

ALEXAIR Helicopters
P.O. Box 330626, Kahului, HI 96733 • *871-0792* • *(800) 722-0201*
Take-off from Kahului Heliport
2 Hughes 500 Jet Copters; 4 passengers
Trips: 35 min. West Maui Mts. • 1 hr. Haleakala/ Hana • 1 hr. 20 min. whole island tour.

Hawai'i Helicopters
P.O. Box 330010, Kahului, HI 96732 • *877-3900*
Take-off from Kahului Heliport
2 French AStar 350B, 6 passengers
Trips: 1.5 hr. Haleakala to Hana • 35 min. tour of West Maui Mt. • 2 hr. whole island.

Kenai Helicopters Hawai'i
P.O. Box 685, Pu'unene, HI 96784 • *71-6463* • *(800) 367-2603*
Take-off from Kahului Heliport & Ka'anapali Heliport
Bell Jet Rangers; 4 & 6 passengers
Trips: 35. min West Maui Mts. • 1 hr. Haleakala/ Hana; 1 hr. 20 min. West Maui/ Hana/ Haleakala • 1 hr. West Maui Mt./ Moloka'i.

Maui Helicopters
P.O. Box 1002, Kihei, HI 96753 • *879-1601*
Take-off from Kahului Heliport & Wailea Helipad
3 Hughes 500 Jet Copter; 4 passengers
Trips: 55 min. East Maui/ Hana/ Haleakala/ La Perouse • 45 min. West Maui Mt. • 1 hr. 45 min. whole island tour • 1 hr. 45 min. West Maui/ Moloka'i.

Papillion
P.O. Box 1690, Lahaina, HI 96767 • *669-4884*
Take-off from Ka'anapali Hills Heliport & Kahului Heliport
7 French AStar Jet Copters; 6 passengers
Trips: 30 min. West Maui Mt. • 1 hr. whole island tour Haleakala/ Hana/ West Maui Mt. • 1 hr. West Maui Mt./ Moloka'i.

Richard's Helicopter Tours
Airport Road, Kahului, HI 96732 • *871-2882* • *871-5993 (8 a.m. to 4 p.m. Mon. to Sat.)*
Take-off from Kahului Heliport

1 Hughes 300; 2 passengers plus pilot
Trips: 1 hr. coastline to Keanae/ Upcountry/ West Maui Mt.

South Sea Helicopters
536 Keolani Pl., Kahului, HI 96732 • 871-8844
Take-out from Kahului Heliport, and has 2 exclusive landing spots in Hana
Bell Jet Ranger B3; 4 passengers
Trips: 30 min. West Maui Mt. • 1 hr. Hana/ Haleakala; 1.5 hr. island tour

Sunshine Helicopters, Inc.
P.O. Box 1286, Lahaina, HI 96767 • 871-0722
Take-off from Kahului Heliport
2 Bell Jet Rangers; 4 passengers
Trips: 20 or 30 min. West Maui Mt. • 1 hr. Haleakala/ Hana • 1.5 hr. island tour; 1 hr. 45 min. West Maui/ Moloka'i

Nightlife

Jazz, rock, Hawaiian, contemporary, classical...whatever your tune, it's playing on Maui. Just check Friday's "Night Beat" column by Jon Woodhouse in *The Maui News*. Jon's a fun-loving, knowledgeable guy who keeps tabs on who's playing where.

Most hotels have several musical happenings every day. Sunset time there's usually a Hawaiian group or a contemporary pianist playing the sun's finale in every large hotel.

LONG-LIVED MUSICAL REGULARS

JAZZ

—Blackie's Bar, Lahaina. 5 to 8 p.m. M, W, F, Sun. 667-7979.
—Idini's, Kihei. 2:30 to 5 p.m. Sunday. 879-1356.
—Julian Kay Trio, big band and jazz sounds in the Garden Lounge at Kapalua Bay Hotel. 8 to 12 p.m. Mon. through Sat. 669-5656.

CONTEMPORARY & HAWAIIAN

—Waiehu Sons, well-known Hawaiian trio in the Sunset Terrace at Stouffer Wailea Beach Resort. 5:50 to 8:30 p.m. Monday through Friday. 879-4900.
—Hapa, a guitar-playing duo, at El Crab Catcher Restaurant, Whaler's Village, Ka'anapali. 9:30 p.m. to 12:30 a.m. Th, F, Sat. 661-4423.
—Willie Kahaialii, member of a large and well-known musical Lahaina family, Whaler's Pub, Lahaina. 6 to 8 p.m. M, W, Sun. 9:30 p.m. to 661-3303.

CLASSICAL

—Vance Koenig, classical guitar at Gerard's Restaurant in Lahaina. Nightly from 7 to 10 p.m. 661-8939.
—Holly Angel, harpist, plays everything from Bach to Led Zepplin, so be prepared for her eclectic selection, at the Plantation Veranda

Restaurant at Kapalua Bay Hotel. Nightly except Tuesday, 7 to 10:30 p.m. 669-5656.

—Joel Robeson, classical piano, at the Bay Club Restaurant at Kapalua Bay Hotel. Sundays from 6:30 to 9:30 p.m. 669-5656.

—Classical string trio in the Maui Prince Hotel's courtyard. Nightly from 7 to 9:30 p.m. 874-1111.

DANCING

For traditional dancing, the kind where you touch your partner, try the Pavilion Courtyard at the Hyatt Regency. Tropical Breeze plays nightly, 7:30 to 10:30, for dancing under the stars.

On Sundays, "Swing is Back" at the Maui Inter-Continental Hotel's Inu Inu Lounge, 5 to 7 p.m.

Square dancing

There are two groups of square dancers on Maui. The Maui Mixers meet every Thursday at 7:30 p.m. at the Kahului Community Center (Wakea and Onehee Avenues). Contact number: 244-0440. The Up-country Squares meet Wednesday nights at 7:30 in the Pukalani School cafeteria (2945 Iolani). Friday nights at 8 p.m. they have a workshop for advanced dancers at the Makawao library (close to the intersection of Baldwin and Makawao Avenues). Contact number is 572-1721.

Rock & Roll...

Rock is found most frequently in disco land. Some bands, like Hauula at Lost Horizon Disco (at Stouffer Wailea Beach Resort), stick to their territory. Other groups like Jimmy Mac and the Cool Cats may be found in different rooms every week.

DANCING CLUBS

LAHAINA

Moose McGillycuddy's
844 Front Street, Lahaina • 667-7758

A beer and T-shirt joint. Fun-seeking crowd in their 20s and 30s out to cruise. Often called a meat market. Rock and roll to records seven nights a week, 9 p.m. to 1 a.m.

Longhi's
888 Front Street, Lahaina • 667-2288

Only place on West Maui with a live band. They frequently have well-known performers play a gig. Good dance floor. Draws the upscale, hip local crowd. Relaxed atmosphere...people go to dance and see their friends. Open for dancing only Fridays and Saturdays, 10:30 p.m. to 1:30 a.m.

KA'ANAPALI

Banana Moon
Marriott Hotel • 667-1200

Clever name, fancy place. Two stamp-sized dance floors plus backgammon tables. Crowd is youngish, New Wave. People and place have an L.A. slickness. Wear your hippest clothes. Open nightly, 8 p.m. to 2 a.m.

Spats
Hyatt Regency Hotel • 667-7474

Older, more professional crowd than at Banana Moon...more conservative. Good sized dance floor. DJ spins records. Dress code: no flip-flop shoes, tank tops or shorts, but jeans and sneakers are okay. Mondays and Thursdays at 11:30 p.m. the Passion Dancers, a professional local dance troupe, performs for a half hour. They are great. Open weekdays 10-2; Fri. & Sat. 10-4.

KAHULUI

Maui Beach
Red Dragon Room • 877-0051

Young, young, young, very local. Flashing, colored lights above a large dance floor keeps the crowd hopping to disco records. The room is a large Chinese restaurant by day, so Chinese lanterns are in evidence. Open W, F, Sat. 10-2. Cover charge.

Maui Palms
East-West Dining Room • 877-0071

The same crowd 30 years later. Dancing to a live band—a local trio that's been there ages. Slower, more conservative music to dance to. Open Fridays and Saturdays, 9 p.m. till closing.

Pizza Factory
Maui Mall Shopping Center • 877-3761

Here you can eat pizza, drink beer and dance the night away. The dance floor's small and so is the place. It's very casual and usually attracts locals. Can be crowded if there's a good band. Live bands only on Saturday nights; Mondays through Fridays it's disco records. Open for dancing 10 p.m. to 1 a.m.

WAILEA

Lost Horizon
Stouffer's Hotel • 879-4900

Live music every night; been the same local band for the past few years...a good, lively group. Draws a mixed crowd—young/ old, singles/ couples, tourists/ residents. Not a cruise scene. Tues.-Thur. 9 p.m. to 1 a.m.; Fri. & Sat. 9 p.m. to 2 a.m. Closed Sun. & Mon.

Inu Inu Room
Inter-Continental Hotel • 879-1922

Large room with a small dance floor; there's also an outside lanai room with seating. Attracts a hip dancing crowd. Band is live, and is usually very upbeat and charged. Bit of a cruise scene, but not heavy-handed. Lounge opens at 5:30 p.m.; dancing starts at 9 p.m.; bar closes at 2 a.m.

KIHEI

Sailmaker's
Azeka Shopping Center • 879-4446

Has an uneven reputation. The bar used to be rowdy, then it changed hands and changed style. Now it attracts both locals and tourists. Can be dead, can be lively. Nothing special, just a small dance floor and bar. Open 10 p.m. to 1 or 2 a.m. for dancing (food served before 10). Dancing to DJ music Wednesdays and Thursdays; live Hawaiian music Fridays; live band Saturdays.

MAKAWAO

Partners
1188 Makawao Ave. • 572-6611

This is an unpretentious, dance-your-heart-out and don't worry about the new steps from L.A. kinda joint. It's big and roomy with a large hardwood dance floor. Makawao is cowboy country, so it attracts a local crowd of good ole boys—those friendly types with "Bill" or "Joe" tooled into their belt leather. Wednesdays and Thursdays dance to disco records; Thursdays draw a New Age crowd. Fridays and Saturdays there's a live band and a cover charge. Dancing from 8:30 to 1 a.m.

Lu'au Shows

The Hawaiian people are great eaters. The lu'au is testimony to that. Any celebration is a good excuse for a lu'au—a wedding, a birthday party, a fund-raiser.

A tourist lu'au is not like a Hawaiian lu'au. Real Hawaiians do not have fire-eating Samoans or Maori war chiefs perform at their parties. Nor do they have six nubile nymphs do a Polynesian revue. Real Hawaiians are not nubile nymphs.

But this is as close as most can get. And what the heck...the dancers are always terrific, the food is generally decent, the music is Hawaiian, the energy is good and the sunset view is tropical. There's fun to be had. Roll the dice and pick a show. Some of the best are featured.

Old Lahaina Lu'au
Behind Whaler's Marketplace, 505 Front Street, Lahaina
667-1998

One of the most Hawaiian and most natural of the lu'au. Hawaiian songs and hula are stressed. A Maui family caters and serves the very Hawaiian food.

The setting is perfect—just steps from the ocean. Grass and palm trees and setting sun.

The opening number is dramatic and lovely. Six Tahitian dancers carrying torches walk along the beach, up through the audience, then onto the stage where they do a Tahitian dance. A lone maiden left on the beach dances a sensual, sad hula, waving goodbye to the Tahitians who left their island to find Hawai'i. After this, all the dances and songs are Hawaiian. No Samoan fire dancers, no Maori warriors wagging their tongues, no Tongan drums. The eight dancers show the evolution of the hula— from the ancient hulas danced to chants to the modern hapa haole hulas danced to English songs.

Every Tuesday, Thursday and Saturday at 5:30 p.m.

Bishop Museum Photo

Lu'au at Stouffer Resort
Stouffer Wailea Beach Resort • 879-4900

This is a fast paced, professional show with no corn. Emcee Rodney Guerrero gives facts, not jokes between numbers. He doubles as a falsetto singer—the only show that demonstrates this typical Hawaiian mode of singing.

Three women dancers start the show with two fast Tahitian numbers, then there's no more shimmying hips...all the rest is hula. Maui's history is told through dancing—sailors, missionaries and modern "swing."

The ever popular Samoan fire dancer comes out of nowhere in the midst of all this hula. It doesn't fit with the flow, but the dancer is very good. And the crowd always likes fire tossed around, so no complaints.

Tuesday nights at 6.

Hotel Hana Maui Lu'au
Hotel Hana Maui, Hana • 248-8211

The most informal and Hawaiian of all the lu'aus. The family spirit of the hotel pervades. It's relaxed, spontaneous and intimate. The maid who makes your bed by day may dance the hula for you by night.

Nothing is organized or choreographed. No one comes out wearing grass skirts and coconut bras.

A musical trio plays through dinner, then they casually suggest a hula dancer would be nice...and bingo, the old woman who just served dinner pops on stage and dances beautifully in her mu'u-mu'u. Next song, another of the hotel staff dances. Guests can hula if they feel like it. The whole evening is infused with a laid back and loving spirit. What else in Hana?

The setting is Hamoa Beach. You can ride there from the hotel by horseback, by hay wagon or by bus. State your preference when you make the reservation.

Fridays at 6:30 p.m.

Other Lu'au Shows

Sheraton's Aloha Lu'au
Sheraton Hotel, Ka'anapali • 661-0031
Nightly at 5 p.m.

Royal Lahaina Lu'au
Royal Lahaina Resort, Ka'anapali • 661-3611
Nightly at 5:30.

Inter-Continental Hotel Lu'au
Maui Inter-Continental Wailea • 879-1922
Every Thursday at 5:30 p.m.

Maui Lu
Maui Lu Hotel, 575 S. Kihei Rd., Kihei • 879-5881
Every Saturday at 5 p.m.

Jesse's Polynesian Revue
Behind the Island Fish House at 1945 S. Kihei Road • 879-7227
Every Wednesday, Friday, Saturday at 5 p.m.

DINNER SHOWS

Hyatt's Drums of the Pacific
Hyatt Regency Maui, Ka'anapali • 667-7474

Trust the Hyatt to have an extravaganza. Maui's fantasy hotel keeps its image with this Polynesian revue. The dinner is good, the service great and the show very well done. It's exciting show biz, and it's fun.

They don't have just one Samoan fire dancer, for instance, they have three. These three don't just twirl batons, they toss them, roll on the them and eat them.

A three-piece band sets the pace for the dancers while three additional drummers bang out a primitive beat on various types of wooden/skin drums.

Tihati Productions of Honolulu has produced the show for the hotel since 1980. Emcee Francis Kamahele, who has a beautiful singing voice, has hosted the show since the beginning.

Monday through Saturday at 5:30; just show, no dinner at 7:15.

Tropical Plantation Bar-B-Que & Country Party
Tropical Plantation, Highway 30, Waikapu • 244-7643

There's no Hee-Haw nonsense here...this is a high spirited, entertaining show. A country show could easily be corn; instead, emcee and singer Buddy Fo sets a fun, professional tone. He sings throughout the evening, and at the very end throws in a mean conga drum number for a surprise.

Two dancing beauties add their expertise. They both look like they dance because they love it, not because it's a job.

The food is good and plentiful. Plus, free mai tais, wine and beer.

Go a little early, if you want to square dance. The Maui Mixers, a local square dance club, demonstrates do-ce-doing and will teach anyone who wants to learn.

Monday and Wednesday at 5:30 p.m.

Other Dinner Shows

Here Is Hawai'i
Ka'anapali Beach Hotel • 661-0011
Nightly at 6 except Mondays.

Maui, Moonlight and Magic
Sheraton Hotel's Discover Room • 661-0031
Nightly at 8:30, except Tuesdays when the show starts at 8 p.m.

Art

Art is redundant on Maui. The island is art itself. Yet art and artists abound here. There's something going on in Maui on a creative-consciousness level that fires up the artistic scene.

Of the 18 galleries detailed here, 15 of them are owned by Mauians. This keeps the art business homegrown...local business people and local artists making Maui an art center in the Pacific.

ART GALLERIES

Center Gallery
Hyatt Regency Hotel, Ka'anapali • 661-1200
Marriott Hotel, Ka'anapali • 661-1220
758 Front Street, Lahaina • 661-1250

Center has a different focus than all the other galleries. It's more upscale and expensive, concentrating on international, rather than local art. It's known to be the most financially successful of all Hawaiian galleries, and, with the other six Center Galleries on O'ahu, it's one of the largest art galleries in the world.

This is not a gallery that nurtures local talent. You forget you're even in Maui when you step through Center's doors. Marc Chagall, Joan Miro, Salvador Dali, Norman Rockwell, Leroy Neiman—these are their big sellers. But their biggest money-maker is TV comic Red Skelton and his clown faces. This is "investment art." Definitely not art for art's sake here. Prices range from $50 to several million.

Coast Gallery
Inter-Continental Hotel, Wailea • 879-2301

Coast is the only gallery in the world where you can buy writer Henry Miller's childlike paintings. That's because Miller lived in Big Sur, CA, and the original Coast Gallery opened there in the late Sixties.

This is their second gallery.

All art objects find a home here—painting, jewelry, wood, pottery, glass...all exquisite. More than 40 artists and artisans exhibit, most from either Hawai'i or California.

The gallery's director, Patrick Robinson, is a man who obviously knows and loves art. A chat with him is worth a visit to Coast.

Gallery Makai
1770 S. Kihei Road, Kihei • 879-9177

Owner Dick Delaney changed toys—from gun to paint brush—when he opened this gallery in '83. Once an L.A. cop, he and wife Lindy are now forces in the local art scene. The gallery keeps him so busy that he's hung up his paint brush along with his gun.

Gallery Makai shows about 35 artists regularly, all of them residents of Hawai'i, most from Maui.

Gallery 1993
1993 E. Main, Wailuku • 242-8063

Art, posters, framing—this place covers three bases. The art includes paintings, pottery, photography, ceramics, and all is local.

Interior designer Paul Alexander has an office right behind the gallery, and though both are separate, they work together. This is Maui's only art/design center.

Grycner Gallery
758 Front, Lahaina • 667-9112

You step into New Mexico here. The familiar forms of R.C. Gorman's Navajo women take over this gallery. That's because Gorman, the famous Navajo painter, is friends with the owners. They've been doing business for years in the Grycner Gallery in Taos. Maui is their second home.

Other New Mexico artists are also featured, but Gorman is the drawing card.

Lahaina Galleries
17 Lahainaluna Road, Lahaina; 661-0839
728 Front Street, Lahaina • 667-2152
Whalers Village, Ka'anapali • 661-5571
Kapalua Hotel, Kapalua • 669-0202

Before owning all these galleries, Jim Killett had never been in business and had never bought a painting. In 1976 Killett was a phys ed teacher for the military looking for a new life.

He opened his first Maui gallery that year and sold in a year what he currently sells in a month. From his meager start, he now has a big business.

"Very few galleries in America do the volume we do," he says. "We have no low ticket items. I draw the line at $500. Our art falls between $500 and $30,000. I don't have any starving artists. They're very successful because they're very good."

Of the 40-some artists he shows, only a dozen or so are Hawai'i residents, yet they make up 90% of his sales.

Painting by Eddie Flotte

Maui Crafts Guild
43 Hana Highway, Paia • *579-9697*

In 1982 Maui craftworkers banded together to sell their work. What started out as just a Christmas show is now a full-time, excellent gallery...the only crafts gallery on the island. Great place to get made-in-Maui souvenirs. Handmade baskets, pottery, weaving, jewelry, wooden bowls, handpainted silk clothing...the island's best crafts are here.

The 30-some artists who belong to the co-op run the whole show. They create, they sell, they dust the shelves. Prices are great because there's no gallery mark-up.

It's a very Maui place. The gallery is in a two-story, funky wooden house on the Hana Highway. Back yard is the beach. Buy here and you'll know you've got an island treasure.

Montgomery Gallery
136 Dickenson, Lahaina • *667-9704*

There's a big city, New York-L.A. feel to this gallery. Owner Ed Waznis hangs artists with Mainland reputations, though none are so famous they'll break your wallet. Typical prices are $1000 to $1500.

He sells no island artists because, "I haven't found any art I respond to here." The one exception is Captain Kenny Neizman, a local legendary character who hangs out in a Lahaina park. Largely ignored and sometimes scorned by the art community, Neizman paints child-like drawings reminiscent of primitive folk art. Waznis considers him the "last of the authentic island artists."

Captain Kenny also sells his own art. His portable "gallery" is a shopping cart full of paintings done on cardboard. Prices are cut-rate, often depending on how pretty you are or how hungry he is.

Old Jail Gallery
649 Wharf, Lahaina • *661-0111*

This is a great little gallery located in Lahaina's historic courthouse (near the banyan tree). Four holding cells are still intact, thus the "Old Jail" name; but they hold art now, not prisoners. Off the beaten track of Front Street, the gallery does not get the traffic it deserves.

It's run by a co-op of artists who price their own work conservatively because they don't have to pay a gallery's overhead. Thus, there are bargains here. It's all local art, mostly paintings and sculptures.

Buy here and get a tax break. The Lahaina Arts Society, formed in 1965 as a nonprofit group, runs the gallery. They take 25-35% of the price tag, and that percentage is tax deductible. You've "donated" to a nonprofit organization. The Society has over 300 members, but only about 50 at a time show their work.

Village Galleries
The Cannery Shopping Center, Lahaina • *661-3280*
120 Dickenson, Lahaina • *661-4402*

Lynn Shue opened Maui's first gallery in 1970. "We wondered why we did it the first two years," she says. "It was very quiet back then. But we did have a lot of support from the local artists."

Now she returns the favor by selling mostly local art. Shue is an artist herself. "I love art," she says. "It's something very tender and very special that people do from their hearts."

She sells jewelry as low as $10 and paintings as high as $25,000, though most of the art ranges around $1000.

One-Man Shows

There are six artists brave enough to run their own galleries, combining business and creative talents. Some hang other artists on their walls, but most feature themselves.

The Curtis Wilson Cost Gallery
Kula Lodge, Haleakala Highway, Kula • 878-6544

This is a simple, elegant little gallery located downstairs at the Kula Lodge. Only Curtis Cost is shown here, usually no more than 10 paintings at a time. It takes Cost several months to finish one of his detailed, realistic works; he does not pump them out.

Cost paints Maui. He favors the high Kula area because he has lived there 14 years. "I'm in Kula the most," he says simply. "It's a gorgeous area. I like the open pasture land and the serenity of it."

A Cost painting runs from $2,800 to $20,000. Wife Jill runs the gallery; Curtis is seldom there. He does allow interested buyers to see his studio, but by appointment only.

Larry Dotson Gallery
143 Lahainaluna Road, Lahaina; • 661-3838

Artist and gallery owner Larry Dotson came to Maui in 1982, started painting tropical scenes and never left. Landscapes and seascapes in oil are his specialties.

Posters and lithographs from other artists are also sold here, but the focus is Dotson's work.

Gallery at the Wharf
658 Front St., #170, Lahaina • 667-2722

Artist Manor Shadian runs the gallery to showcase his paintings, though he does show several other artists. A few years ago Shadian's paintings looked similar to Gauguin's. Now he's attracted to surrealism.

Shadian came to Maui in 1987 after eight years in O'ahu. He was born in Iran, but raised in Israel, and has been in the U.S. since the Seventies.

Macario Pascual
551 Wainee St, (second floor, Hongwanji Mission) Lahaina • 667-6166

By appointment only...this is Macario Pascual's personal gallery attached to his studio. He calls it a "little showroom for myself." He says only 5 or 6 couples come by each month, but they're not just browsing, they're serious customers.

Pascual came to Maui from the Philippines at age five. His father was a plantation laborer, so the family lived in a large sugar plantation village in what is now Ka'anapali Hillside.

That is what he paints in oil—plantation life of the 1960s and 70s. His first job at 14 was in the fields, and years later he still remembers it on canvas.

Resta Studios
313 West Kuiaha Rd. (Pauwela Cannery Bldg.) • *575-2203*

Piero Resta's studio is perfect for an artist...just what one would expect of Piero—a happy, giving Italian with a love of people, parties and life. The studio is in a cavernous metal cannery building. It has a high ceiling and a loft area, and is filled from top to bottom with colorful, splashy art. It's an eclectic clutter of paintings, sculptures, mosaics and art tools. Piero's a talker and a gracious host. His cappuccino machine is always ready for the next guest.

Piero is a Florentine, from Italy, but has lived since 1964 in the States—first New York, then San Francisco where he was attracted to the beatnik scene. He and wife Gail came to Maui in 1978 for the birth of their daughter Bella. His bright paintings now show both European and Polynesian influences.

Son Luigi is the business manager. He calls it an "informal studio," but says it's best to call before dropping in.

Sands Beachfront Studio
Whalers' Marketplace, Lahaina • *661-5495*

You can watch owner Stephen Sands paint right on the spot. All the paintings sold in the gallery are his oils; he's here seven days a week working on them. The gallery is small with a lanai facing the beach. Prices, Sands says, are "budget"—$150 is his typical tag.

Art Mart
Not an art gallery per se, but an open-air market held every Saturday under Lahaina's famous banyan tree. Artists and artisans from the Lahaina Arts Society show their wares from 10 a.m. to 4 p.m.

ART SOCIETIES

If you want to meet the island's artists, or if you want to take art classes, there are two art societies you can join. Both have a $20 membership, though both will take nonmembers in their classes.

Hui Noeau
2841 Baldwin Ave., Makawao • *572-6560*

The first art society on Maui, the Hui began over 50 years ago as a wealthy ladies' afternoon painting group. Now it's no longer a dilettante bunch; the current artists are dedicated.

Best thing about this group is the house where they hold their classes—it's the old Kaluanui mansion built in 1917 by Harry and Ethel Baldwin (of the famous missionary and sugar family). Fabulous place of days gone by. Paint in one of the bedrooms, throw a pot in the stable, be a resident artist and live in the house for a week (while giving classes).

The house is not a gallery, it's a place to produce art. Art is sold, though, in the frequent shows the Hui exhibits. These generally feature one or two artists' work at a time.

Lahaina Arts Society
649 Wharf St. (old courthouse), Lahaina • *661-0111*

This is a busy group of 300-some artists and art devotees. They hold monthly potlucks to keep in touch with each other. They sponsor free art classes and workshops. They raise scholarship money for Maui high school seniors. They put out a monthly newsletter.

Curious about them? Get more information and see the fruits of their labors in their Old Jail House Gallery.

ART TOURS

Maui Art Tours
P.O. Box 1058, Makawao, HI 96768 • *572-1022 or 878-2706.*

Tourists can now walk right into the homes and studios of Maui's best. Painters, wood sculptors, fabric designers, stained glass workers—they're all available through Maui Art Tours.

The idea is to get patrons and artists together, to make the artists seem less illusive. For the tourists it's fun and educational—a day-long academy of art. At least four artists are visited in their homes or studios. A gourmet lunch is included in the price.

Genesis of the tour began with a book put out by local publisher Barbara Glassman, a spirited, can-do kind of woman. The book, *Maui Art and Creative People*, features Maui's major artists, and only they are on the tour.

Hyatt Art Tour

Unbeknownst to nonguests, the Hyatt Regency's hotel and grounds are a quasi-museum...open to all. More than $2 million worth of Oriental and primitive art is placed around the hotel, most of it right in the open air...very little is behind glass.

All the art was bought in the Orient. It is owned, by the hotel's developer, Chris Hemmeter and his wife Patricia.

Huge cloisonne vases, bronze lions from Thailand, wooden Burmese drums, 19th century Thai Buddha head, a mischievous stone badger from China, New Guinea war shields and spears...none of it is ancient art and few pieces are even a century old. It's not modern, though; most pieces are done in the style of the old masters.

Tours explaining the art are given every morning at 10 except Tuesdays and Sundays. Meet at the concierge's desk. A booklet about the art is available from the concierge.

ANNUAL SHOWS

Art Maui

This is a yearly show held in the spring featuring Maui's best artists. Painters, sculptors and crafts people submit work to a jury of experts who then choose the best of the lot. All the chosen work is exhibited together for two weeks. Watch the paper for the dates (they change each year). Best and only chance to see Maui's top art shown in one place.

Maui Marine Expo

Held every spring for two months in the lobby of the Inter-Continental Hotel. This is a display of marine art...dolphins, whales, sea birds, etc. This being Maui, whales are particularly predominant—in jewelry, paintings, sculpture, pottery and photos. It's a classy exhibit, worth a look.

Island Life

Drawing by Piero Resta

History

The traditions about the Hawaiian Islands handed down from remote antiquity are not entirely definite; there is much obscurity as to the facts...

The reason for this obscurity and vagueness is that the ancients were not possessed of the art of letters...

When traditions are carried in the memory it leads to contradictory versions.

...certain learned men have searched into and studied up the origin of the Hawaiian Islands, but whether their views are correct no one can say, because they are but speculations.

—Hawaiian historian David Malo in *Hawaiian Antiquities*

Thus wrote David Malo in the 1800s. His words still stand—ancient history is still speculative. Theories abound, but there is still much "obscurity and vagueness."

Ancient Hawaiians were a stone-age people. They had no metal tools, they had not invented the wheel, and they had no written language. With no writing system, they could only transmit their history through songs, chants, genealogies, stories and myths—colorful, but not always accurate.

Stone-age or not, they were brilliant, adventuresome navigators. Hundreds of years before Europeans put their toes in the water, Polynesians were scooting around the massive Pacific Ocean in wooden canoes. No other primitive people could travel as they could. They did so by following nature's signposts—the sun, the currents, the stars, the birds, the clouds.

Europeans headed across the Atlantic in the 1400s. By then, the Polynesians had finished all their exploring. They had discovered and settled New Zealand, Tahiti, Hawai'i, Tonga, Samoa...the list goes on.

As Kenneth Emory, dean of Polynesian archaeologists writes, *"The Polynesian people are remarkable in world history. They were the first people, in their double canoes, to discover every island within a vast 10 million square miles of the Pacific Ocean."*

Homeward Bound

Legends speak of the mystical homeland Hawaiki from whence the Polynesian ancestors came and to where the people assumed they would go after death. Hawaiki was the promised land sought by many of the early voyagers. This is perhaps what drove them on over thousands of miles from island to island.

The unknowns about these peoples produce many a theory. They include the following, some more scientific than others. None are proven.

—They were an Austronesian race originating in southern China maybe 7,000 years ago.

—The lower caste people were a Mongoloid/Negroid race from Southeast Asia; the high caste were a Caucasian race, possibly from Europe or India.

—Early Mormon missionaries considered them one of the lost tribes of Israel.

—Certain Polynesian words are like similar words from ancient Mesopotamia, from the kingdom of Baluchistan and/or from ancient India.

The truth as we know it...

Most believe the first group to reach Hawai'i came from the Marquesas Islands, possibly as early as 300 to 500 A.D. Some speculate they were here by the first century. The next wave of migration came from Tahiti in the twelfth or thirteenth century. With them they brought pigs, dogs, fowl, taro, bananas and other plants. They conquered the earlier people, and their ali'i became the ruling class.

Perhaps they believed they were finally home. Once here, the constant voyaging ceased. They lived in isolation for several centuries until...

Captain Cook

The white sails of Cook's two ships heralded a new era for the islands. These were the first white men seen by the Hawaiians. They brought with them iron nails, metal implements, alcohol, guns and venereal disease.

British Captain James Cook was the most remarkable explorer of his day. This was his third trip to the Pacific region. On the first two he missed Hawai'i completely and sailed on to Tahiti. Finding Hawai'i on the third trip was an accident; he was heading to the Americas to find the illusive Northwest Passage.

The Death of Captain Cook

Hawai'i State Archives

On Maui Cook could find no anchorage, but his ships were visited by canoes of curious Mauians. Kahekili, the great and fierce Maui king, came out looking a sight—half his face and body were heavily tattoed. He dressed in his best—a crested feather helmet and a red and yellow feather cape. The cape he left as a gift.

A few days later, off the coast of Hana, several Big Island warriors visited the ships. These included a youthful Kamehameha I. Though not yet a great warrior, Kamehameha's presence was impressive enough for Lt. James King to write of him: "...as savage a looking face as I ever saw...his disposition...was good natured & humorous, although his manner showed somewhat of an overbearing spirit..."

Cook sailed on to the Big Island where he finally found safe anchorage. Here the stage was set perfectly—the visit coincided with a celebration to the god Lono. The ships' white sails were thought to be Lono's tapa banners. The ships themselves were floating islands transporting Lono—none other than Cook himself.

Cook and his men were welcomed as gods. People prostrated themselves before them. Food and sexual favors were offered freely.

For four weeks the two ships stayed anchored in Kealakekua Bay. Eventually, several natives became suspicious. One of Cook's men died...quite unlike a god. Most of the others had voracious sexual appetites...also unlike gods. These "gods" did not observe the kapu system. And they were not very polite—they stocked their ships heavily, depleting the natives' food.

When they finally sailed out of the bay, it was definitely time to go. Unfortunately, they had trouble with a mast and had to return. This time the welcome was not the same.

Within days Cook was killed by the same people who had called him Lono. He had gone ashore seeking a stolen boat. Tempers flared, shots were fired, and Cook was stabbed in the back of the head. He fell face down in the ocean and was stabbed and clubbed to death. Kamehameha was supposedly there.

King of the islands

Mauians first noticed Kamehameha's courage during one of their many battles with Big Island warriors. In this one at Kaupo, a warfare teacher of Kamehameha's was struck down. Though Maui warriors were winning, Kamehameha bravely led his men back and rescued his teacher.

Battles were constant between Maui and the Big Island. Kahekili, who ruled Maui for about 25 years, was a fierce, ruthless leader. By the end of his career, he ruled Maui, Moloka'i, O'ahu and Kaua'i. The Big Island and Kamehameha stood in his way for a complete kingdom.

The aged Kahekili died in 1794 still short of his goal. Kamehameha soon made mincemeat of Kahekili's son, driving his warriors to their deaths over the cliffs at Nu'uanu in O'ahu.

Kamehameha had already won Maui four years earlier in the bloody battle of 'Iao Valley. Now he had only Kaua'i to gain. Diplomacy, not bloodshed won that island, though, and by 1810 Kamehameha was king of a first-time unified Hawai'i.

He is called Kamehameha the Great because he was. Political genius, courageous warrior, cunning leader—the only man to unite a chain of islands in the Pacific. Only he could stop Hawai'i's constant warfare.

He strictly followed the old traditions of kapu and worship, yet used the white man's ways when needed. In 1819 he died and left no trace. His two closest friends took his bones and buried them secretively. They have never been found.

The end of the old

Kamehameha's two most powerful queens helped bring down the kapu system and the ancient religion. Perhps tired of the restrictions placed on women and aware that kapus were routinely broken by the white men, they decided the time was nigh. Favorite queen Ka'ahumanu and highest ranking "sacred" queen Keopuolani were Hawai'i's first feminists.

Liholiho, Kamehameha's son and heir, officially broke the kapu by eating with these women, but he did so only with much persuasion and alcohol. His mother, Keopuolani, and his stepmother, Ka'ahumanu, were the persuaders. The alcohol was his idea.

In truth, there was discontent and discussion for a long time about abolishing the system. Eating with the two queens was a symbolic act that brought the end.

The Hawaiians were now a people with no religion and a wavering social structure. They were an open slate for all that came. Times were confusing. Alcohol muddled them and foreign diseases killed them by the thousands. In the 40 years between Cook's arrival and the death of Kamehameha, nearly half the population was wiped out by illnesses. The Hawaiians had no immunity to the simplest of diseases. Liholiho himself and his half-sister bride died of the measles while visiting London.

The righteous arrive

Two weeks before the kapu system was broken, the first group of missionaries left New England. They were on their way to change Hawai'i for good.

It is easy now to denigrate the missionaries. They were a tragi-comic, dogged bunch of ultra conservative Calvinists. They viewed man as suffering and sin-ridden. The Hawaiians had no concept of sin.

The missionaries wore sweltering, long-sleeved woolen clothing; they did not bathe often or go swimming; they deplored surfing and hula dancing; they were easily shocked by Hawaiian ways.

Rev. Hiram Bingham, leader of the first missionaries, wrote of their feelings after landing here: *"...the appearance of destitution, degradation and barbarism, among the chattering, and almost naked savages...was appalling. Some of our number, with gushing tears, turned away from the spectacle. Can these be human beings!...Can they be Christianized? Can we throw ourselves upon these rude shores, and take up our abode, for life, among such a people for the purpose of training them for heaven?"*

In fairness to them, the missionaries were brave, selfless people, true zealots who had one goal and lived it every moment. They were responsible and dedicated. They learned the language, wrote an alphabet and set about teaching these "lost souls" how to read and write their way to God. They built a printing press, opened schools, and healed with Western medicine.

In the process they also created cultural genocide. The Hawaiians began to have little self worth. Many were ashamed of their roots. It was a schizophrenic time, and their identities floundered.

The tragic princess

A sad example of the split between old traditions and new ideas was Kamehameha's and Keopuolani's daughter Nahi'ena'ena. Her brother, Kauikeaouli, was King Kamehameha III (after Liholiho's death). They had been betrothed since they were children as was the custom with offspring of high ranking chiefs. Their high mana together would produce a child of even higher mana to continue Kamehameha's dynasty.

This was a big no-no to the shocked missionaries. Incest, they called it. While a teenager in Lahaina, Nahi'ena'ena was taken under their wing and taught Christianity. Still, she loved her brother deeply. She secretly met him often, and became pregnant, probably by him. The old ways were not to be, however—the baby died and so did Nahi'ena'ena not long after. Her alternating life of drinking and partying versus Christian piety and guilt ended at age 21.

In his grief, her brother began to mend his previous wild and drunken ways. He moved his capital to Lahaina to be near the mausoleum he had built for his sister and their mother. Later he moved back to Honolulu, and, as he matured, he wrote the first Hawaiian Bill of Rights, the first constitution and the land division called the Great Mahele.

Grog and women

Everything happened at once after Kamehameha died in 1819. The kapu system was broken, the religion was destroyed, the missionaries arrived and then so did the whalers. God, sin and commerce in one fell swoop.

Lahaina was a sweet little town in 1820. The whalers quickly changed that. They weren't interested in whales here, they wanted R & R, better known as grog and women. Hundreds, sometimes thousands, of them roamed Lahaina's Front Street looking for both. By 1825, there were 23 grog shops within Front Street's one-mile strip.

These New England whalers had fished out the Atlantic Ocean, so they came west looking for whales. Sperm whales were rumored to be plentiful in Japanese waters. From New England to Japan was a very long voyage. They came around the Horn, and by the time they reached Hawai'i, they were due for more provisions. The captain's goal was to restock the ship; the whalers just wanted to get off it.

Whaling life was very tough. Many of the "men" were mere boys, and they all signed on to live together for 3 to 5 years. Life on board ship was rough...filth, cockroaches, scurvy, rotten food, whale oil over everything. Wages were minimal; a greenhand could earn as little $30 take-home, a captain as little as $380, for four years at sea.

Saints and Sinners

The whalers met their match in the missionaries. The whalers declared "no god west of the Horn," but the missionaries would have none of that. They disapproved of easy women and alcohol—the sailors' favorite pastimes.

The missionaries had the ali'i on their side. Both queens Ka'ahumanu and Keopuolani were Christian converts, and their conversion swayed many of the chiefs.

When the sailors rioted through town and threatened the lives of the missionaries, the ruling chiefs built a jail and enforced a sundown curfew. Still, Lahaina had a hard time containing them. During the heyday of 1840 to 1860, 50 to 100 ships, each carrying 25 to 30 men, were anchored in the harbor. Town was a bustling place.

All this died, however, by 1871 when whaling abruptly stopped. That year 33 ships were lost in an Arctic disaster. Previously, during the Civil War, numerous ships were reconverted for war puposes. Besides the lack of ships, petroleum oil was discovered in Pennsylvania, and it replaced whale oil in lamps. Whaling became too expensive and dangerous, and it was no longer a profitable business. Lahaina fell back asleep...until it awoke with the sugar plum fairy.

Sugar Cane

As Lahaina went, so went Maui. Sugar filled the economic void and soon became king. Sugar grew wild on the island, but those who tried to tame it into plantations did not do well until the Civil War. Then Southern sugar became unavailable in the North, so the Hawaiian crops turned great profits.

Sugar created a quiet agricultural community, and eventually an exotic, multi-ethnic population. Over the years, there were sugar plantations on almost every part of Maui, from Lahaina to Wailuku and from Pa'ia to Kipahulu.

The children of the missionaries, and in some cases the missionaries themselves, championed sugar. Converting souls was a thing of the past; it was now time to turn a profit.

Two of the most successful missionary sons were the founders of the still powerful Alexander & Baldwin, Inc. Henry Perrine Baldwin (son of Dr. Dwight Baldwin of Lahaina) and Samuel T. Alexander (whose father once headed Lahainaluna School) purchased 12 acres between Pai'a and Makawao.

Alexander worked as manager of the rival Haiku Sugar Company while Baldwin set up their own plantation. In time they acquired controlling interest in the Haiku Company and their holdings included thousands of sugar acres.

Claus Spreckels enters the game

The good-old-boy missionary network was broken when an upstart sugar refiner from San Francisco entered their sugared ranks and did enormously well. Claus Spreckels was never trusted and he never played fair; he was a character used to getting his way.

He came to Maui with the Reciprocity Treaty. For years Hawaiian planters had sought this duty-free treaty for their sugar, but Louisiana sugar planters opposed it. Spreckels had opposed the treaty, but when Congress passed it in 1876, he boarded the same ship that brought the news to Hawai'i. Moving quickly, Spreckels bought up more than half the 1877 crop before prices had time to rise.

This did not tickle his competitors, and many of his future actions gave him a rascal reputation. He became a crony of King David Kalakaua. He lent the king and several of his ministers enough money to keep them indebted to him. When a cabinet balked at giving him water rights on East Maui, Spreckels called his cards and had the king dismiss the cabinet.

Both Alexander & Baldwin (A & B) and Spreckels' Hawaiian Commercial and Sugar Company (HC & S) irrigated Maui's dry central areas with water from rainy East Maui. They did so by an engineering feat—miles of ditches were built to reroute stream water into the fields.

The two companies maintained an uneasy standoff for years until Spreckels fell from prominence. A key figure in the controversies and scandals of Kalakaua's time, he eventually lost favor with the king and returned to California. By 1898 A & B took over its rival HC & S in a deftly-maneuvered stock purchase.

The monarchy doomed

Scandals and overspending by Kalakaua caused much discontent with the government, and the king was forced to bow to a new constitution, one that greatly limited his power. He died four years later in 1891, and his sister, the spirited Lili'uokalani, took charge. She aimed to restore the monarchy; but, in fact, lost it.

Businessmen, particularly sugar growers, decided it was time to annex Hawai'i to the United States. They did not trust Lili'uokalani; they wanted a stable government, one that would be good for business. They plotted against the queen, and they won. She signed a surrender paper under protest, and though President Grover Cleveland agreed with her that her kingdom had been illegally overthrown, he was unable to reverse the revolution. Kamehameha's dynasty, the Hawaiian monarchy, was no more.

This mini revolution of 1893 left Hawai'i with a temporary government, officially a republic. During its five-year duration, a small uprising to restore the monarchy occurred. It was quickly squashed, and Queen Lili'uokalani was confined to 'Iolani Palace as a well-kept prisoner. She then formally abdicated her throne and pledged her allegiance to the republic. By 1898 Hawai'i was annexed as a territory of the U.S..

Sadly, the Hawaiian people were losing more than their kingdom. Plagued by foreign diseases, uprooted from their land, cut off from the rituals which once gave life meaning, their race was dying at an alarming rate. The population when Cook arrived was estimated at 300,000 or more. By 1900 there were only 30,000 Hawaiians.

Immigrants or slaves?

Life on Maui was quiet and productive in the years between the turn of the century and World War II. Immigrants kept the sugar industry rolling. Without them, it could not have worked.

These workers came to Hawai'i, beginning in the 1850s, as cheap labor. With sugar's growth, and the addition of pineapple early in the 1900s, labor was essential. Hawai'i imported 46,000 Chinese between 1876 and 1897, about 17,500 Portuguese between 1878 and 1913, about 61,000 Japanese between 1886 and 1900, nearly 6,000 Puerto Ricans in 1901, and about 8,000 Koreans in 1904 and 1905. Almost 8,000 Spaniards came between 1907 and 1913, and more than 12,000 Filipinos arrived between 1907 and 1931.

Conditions in the early days approximated slave labor, but the immigrant pioneers adapted and thrived. Most came on contract, expecting to return home eventually, rich from their sojourn. Many stayed on, though, and the races eventually mingled, developing a culture that took a little from each.

World War II

Maui's peace was disturbed very little by World War I, but WW II was different. When the Japanese bombed Pearl Harbor, all Hawai'i went into blackout and martial law. No one knew where the next attack might occur, and, in fact, Kahului was shelled.

Japanese who had been living in the islands for years were questioned and regarded with suspicion, but unlike California, Hawai'i built no internment camps. Many Japanese Americans volunteered for service. They fought in Italy and France, establishing a distinguished combat record. They came home more sophisticated with no intention of returning to cane or pineapple. Armed with the GI Bill, they educated themselves and became leaders of their communities.

On Maui, thousands of servicemen from the Mainland practiced jungle warfare so they could defend the Pacific. The island became an armed camp, with bunkers on the beaches and air bases on the central plain. The people grew fond of the strangers...they were the first tourists modern Maui would see.

After the war, Maui's population dwindled. The economy was depressed during the 1950s, and children of the immigrants went elsewhere to find jobs. Cane and pineapples were not their row to hoe.

In the 1960s the hippies came to town...the oddest bunch of immigrants yet. Young, transient dreamers, they built shacks in banana patches and set up communities on beaches. Many roamed the island, genuinely searching for peace and beauty.

Tourism brought Maui back to life...some say the slumbering island awoke to a nightmare of commercialism. Condos popped up out of sandy beaches; hotels sprang forth on manicured lawns; restaurants and shops came and went in a whirlwind. Maui was reborn as a glittering, sophisticated beauty.

What next?

Ancients, missionaries, whalers, immigrants, tourists...each vignette of history shows an island ever ready to change. Every new wave had an act of its own, every character a role to play. The drama moves on into the next decade. Cast and characters stand in the wings. Hold the applause until the curtain rises.

Maui Folk...
Two Strong Queens

Two women, born into a world in which women were far from liberated, nevertheless, were probably the most influential and powerful Hawaiians in a time of great change for the islands.

Keopuolani and Ka'ahu-manu were married to the same man, Kamehameha I, who united the islands into one kingdom. Both women were born on Maui, of the royal line of Kekaulike; both died Christians after becoming early converts to the first missionaries.

Otherwise, they were very different. And yet, despite their differences, and despite their husband-sharing arrangement, the two queens apparently got along quite well, complementing each others' strengths and working as a team to help revolutionize their culture.

Ka'ahumanu, born in a cave in Hana, was married to Kamehameha at an early age. She was never able to bear heirs for the king, but she was his favorite wife. That favor gave her great power, as did her own strong personality and intelligence.

Ka'ahumanu was tall, beautiful and athletic. She was passionate in nature and given to fits of temper.

Fascinated by the ways of the outside world, she met many of the early explorers and traders.

George Vancouver, on his first visit to Hawai'i in 1792, was much impressed with Ka'ahumanu, then about 16. He said she *"did credit to the choice and taste of Kamehameha, being one of the finest women we have yet seen on any of the islands."*

The next year, when Vancouver passed through again, Ka'ahumanu had gone home to mama, reportedly after her husband became angry about her affair with another chief. Vancouver lured Ka'ahumanu aboard his ship, called Kamehameha out of hiding, then disappeared while the lovers made up.

Kamehameha eventually tried to keep other men away from his wife by placing a kapu on her body, but Ka'ahumanu was not to be corraled by any man, even the great conqueror, and it is doubtful whether the kapu was very effective.

When Kamehameha conquered Maui, he named Ka'ahumanu's father, Ke'eaumoku, governor of the island. Ka'ahumanu's strength was further enhanced by the appointment over the years of many of her relatives to positions of power, and she herself joined the council of chiefs after her father's death.

By the time Kamehameha died in 1819, Ka'ahumanu was so powerful that she became Kuhina Nui, or regent, sharing power with the young king, Liholiho. Her first order of business was to get rid of the troublesome kapu system that kept women down.

She had the unlikely assistance of a woman who sat at the pinnacle of that system, the Sacred Queen Keopuolani.

Keopuolani's life story is not unlike that of a fairy tale princess. Born at the Pihana and Halekii heiau which still overlook Wailuku, she was of the highest sacred rank, the only child of a brother-sister liason.

The 19th century historian, Samuel Kamakau, in his book, *Ruling Chiefs of Hawai'i*, described her parents as *"tabu chiefs of divine rank."* Their union produced a child of even higher rank and mana.

Unfortunately, incest does not always produce great physical specimens. Kamakau describes the child as *"homely and puny looking."* Her guardians, a high ranking ali'i couple who helped raise her, apparently considered switching their baby daughter (because of her "excellent physique") for the baby Keopuolani. But fate did not allow it. As Kamakau explains, a dog entered the house where both babies slept and bit off the fingers on one hand of the guardians' daughter.

The dog played his role. The switch could not be made. Keopuolani was meant to be Keopuolani. Kamakau writes: *"The servant might have been the chiefess had not God willed it otherwise."*

Keopuolani was of such high rank that *"neither chief nor commoner dared approach or touch her, and anyone who disobeyed this tabu was burned to death"* (Kamakau).

Thus she lived a sheltered and secluded life. If her shadow fell on someone, the person must die, so she rarely went outside before sunset. However, Kamakau writes that no one was ever put to death for breaking her kapu. She was, he says, *"a good mother, respectful to the chiefs, to her husband, and to all people."*

When Kamehameha and his Big

Island army battered the Maui army in the battle at 'Iao, the child Ke'opuolani was carried through the West Maui Mountains. Then she and her family escaped to Moloka'i.

The victorious Kamehameha followed them, offering protection to the family. Thus Keopuolani became Kamehameha's ward, and eventually his wife, though her rank was so far above his that he supposedly approached her on his knees.

Kamehameha had a political purpose for making Keopuolani his wife—to obtain her mana for his heirs. With the sacred mana inherited from their mother, and the mana acquired by their father's victories, the children would be secure in the monarchy he was creating for them.

Keopuolani did indeed provide the king with heirs. Two sons and one daughter survived her many pregnancies (though Kamakau writes that she *"was not made his constant companion, for he slept with her only from time to time in order to perpetuate the high chiefly blood of the kingdom"*). Their two sons became Kamehameha II and III.

It was the first of the two sons, Liholiho, who had to contend with these two strong women, one his mother and the other his foster

Queen Ka'ahumanu

Hawai'i State Archives

mother, after his father died in 1819.

No sooner were the dead king's bones hidden in their secret burial place than both women had eaten forbidden foods in the presence of men. The dietary restrictions on certain foods (no pork, coconuts or bananas for females, for instance), plus the separation of men and women during meals, were especially irksome to women. They had certainly noticed that foreigners were completely unaffected by breaking kapu. And foreign men often encouraged women to eat with them.

At first Liholiho tried to ignore the challenge by the two queens, but eventually, he capitulated, and ate with the women. This act by the king symbolized the end of the kapu system. Liholiho went all the way with his break, commanding that heiau and idols be destroyed all over the islands. He faced, and with the help of Keopuolani's counsel, defeated a rebellion by those who wanted the kapu system to remain.

If nature abhors a vacuum, then the Christian missionaries were fulfilling some natural law when they sailed from Boston at the time the old religion was being destroyed. By the time they reached the islands, the Hawaiians were an open slate—a religious people with no religion.

However, Ka'ahumanu initially treated them with disdain, mostly ignoring their presence. She was busy with politics, which in her case included marrying the still semi-independent king of Kaua'i, thus ensuring the unity of all the islands, and then also marrying the king's son.

Keopuolani, though she did not embrace the missionaries' teaching at first, did approve their request to stay in Hawai'i. Within a few years,

she observed the value of some of their instruction, began to study herself, and made sure her two younger children learned to read and write.

When Keopuolani moved from Honolulu to Lahaina on the island of her birth, she requested that missionaries be sent with her. Each day, the two who accompanied the queen held services for the royal party at a kou grove near the beach, and soon she ordered mission buildings erected for them.

While she still enjoyed native ways, the queen grew in her affection for the missionaries and their teachings. When she lay dying in Lahaina in 1823, she asked them to baptise her. They did so, naming her Harriet after the wife of one of her favorite missionaries. Thousands gathered for her funeral, which combined the rituals of the old culture with the religion of the newcomers.

Ka'ahumanu, meanwhile, was finding her own way to Christianity. Her attachment to Kaumuali'i, the king of Kaua'i, who was a student of Christianity, had something to do with it, as did the deaths in quick succession of Keopuolani, Kaumuali'i himself, and Liholiho and his queen, who caught measles on a trip to London. When Ka'ahumanu got sick, she was nursed back to health by a prayerful missionary wife.

She then reversed her previous disdainful attitude, began to study, and quickly learned to read. She started going to church and called herself Ka'ahumanu Hou, or the New Ka'ahumanu.

With such a powerful patron, who actually ordered her people to learn to read and write and to study the new religion, the success of the missionaries was assured.

Maui Folk...
A Modern Hawaiian Warrior

Dana Naone Hall is a determined Hawaiian woman, her life devoted to restoring Hawaiian pride and culture. She is a visible and vocal force for Hawaiian rights, often present at hearings that affect Hawai'i's people and environment.

"As a Hawaiian today, I'm dedicated to being as much a part of the decision-making process as I can," Dana says.

Why? Because "much Hawaiian culture has been lost." She thinks the early missionaries were "hellbent on extinguishing what they considered the immoral and licentious aspects of the culture...looking at it from their own warped perspectives."

Photo by Ron Youngblood

She believes those in power today are not much better, being "not only lax, but in league with the developers."

"How do we change that?" she asks. "As a Hawaiian, one often finds oneself on the outside of political influence and power. Those who are in power don't care. So it's our job to make sure that our concerns are brought up constantly.

"In doing so, we become stronger, our identities become sharper. As a Hawaiian, you have to become very strong and sure of yourself to understand that what this dominant society is dictating to you is not something you have to accept and bow under to.

"Even given the knowledge of our great loss, whatever we have today is enough to keep us alive and whole as a people. But because there is so little left, it becomes that much more precious.

"So, whenever one more part of our culture is taken away, one more heiau destroyed, an ancient trail removed, our ancestor's bones dug up from their burial places...then a death knell is sounding for our culture. But by protecting and preserving what we have, we can grow from this foundation again. In the last 15 or 20 years, there's been a deep desire in Hawaiians to know who we are. What we're interested in is regenerating ourselves as a people."

Dana grew up in Kaneohe, O'ahu. Of her first ten years, she says, "It was a very small town feeling. One had the sense at that time of knowing everyone in the place."

But the next ten years, things changed, as the whole windward side of O'ahu became suburbanized. "I watched a very rural, close-knit, intimate place bulldozed into something completely different. The development of Kaneohe mirrors the development of Hawai'i in the past 20 years. It's been so fast paced that it's really shocking."

Dana is currently trying to slow things down—"to let the land breathe again." For the past few years, the focus of her work has been Hui Ala Nui o Makena, an organization formed to fight the closing of the Makena Road in front of the Maui Prince Hotel. The hotel wanted privacy, but the Hui insisted the road was part of the 15th century Pi'ilani Highway, and thus should be open to all. A compromise was struck— the road is closed to vehicular traffic, but open to foot traffic.

"The Hui has gained political substance," Dana says. "We can threaten the powers that be with our own resistance. Our purpose is to use whatever appropriate means there are to make sure that our culture is not obliterated."

The Hui is Dana's way to ensure this survival. "We're talking about our pride, and our dignity," she says. "We come from a rich and vital culture. We stand on equal footing with anyone in this land. In fact, as the bearers of the original culture of this place, we have a primary right to be here, and we're due a kind of respect that we're not getting.

"It's not for other people to tell us anymore who we are. It's for us to figure it out and say to others, `This is who we are, and you can't take advantage of us anymore. You can't relegate us to the side position—to be brought on stage for a few musical numbers and then sent out the back door. This is our home, this is our land.'

"I cannot allow in my lifetime the Hawaiian people to lose their deep and ancient connection to the land and surrounding seas, to become nobody. The time for not knowing who we are is past. We know who we are.

"As long as we have our culture, we'll be able to overcome everything; but once we lose our culture and our land base, there is no ground from which to move out—the firm sense that you belong to this place, that spiritually you are a child of the land. As long as Hawaiians have that sense, and it is not severed, we will continue to exist as a people, and Hawai`i will continue to be Hawai`i, celebrated for the power and beauty of its land and people."

Crops

SUGAR CANE

Sugar cane is one of the most important ingredients in the history and development of Hawai'i's culture and economy. It was cane that brought in the immigrants—cheap labor from Japan, China, Spain, Portugal, the Philippines, Korea. It was the immigrants, thousands of them, who changed the people of Hawai'i into the multiple faces of today.

Cane came to Hawai'i with the original Polynesian settlers, who chewed the stalks for the sweet juices. The first mill on Maui was started in 1828 by two Chinese businessmen. Others began toying with the idea of sugar grown commercially, and by the end of the 1900s, cane was king.

Now, almost a century later, the health of the sugar industry depends largely on support by the U.S. government. Other countries, which subsidize their nation's sugar crops, tend to dump their surpluses on the world market, lowering the price so much that in recent years there have been lay-offs and shutdowns in Hawai'i. The state must have aid in the form of loans or import quotas if its crop is to compete.

Maui's plantations and mills

On Maui, the Wailuku Sugar Mill closed its mill several years ago and the Pioneer Mill in Lahaina has walked a narrow tightrope for years.

Maui's most viable plantation, Hawaiian Commercial & Sugar Co., HC & S, was the only sugar company in the state that reported a substantial profit in 1985. The industry as a whole experienced a loss that year for the fifth year in a row. HC & S is the largest sugar company in the state. Its 37,000-acre plantation supplies cane to mills in Pu'unene and in Pa'ia.

The king loses control

Once, what was good for sugar was considered good for Hawai'i, and if some people didn't agree, they lacked the power to do anything about it. Today, however, Mauians are concerned about the problems of cane smoke, dust from the fields and pesticide use.

Cane smoke is hard on people with respiratory problems. Cane smoke's natural content is carbon dioxide, water vapor, dust particulates and a tiny bit of carbon monoxide. Only two things are likely to add chemical pollutants—an herbicide and plastic irrigation pipes.

The herbicide, Glyphosate, is sprayed on the fields two months before harvest. It is in the Polado brand used to dry the plants before they're burned. Sugar spokesmen say 83% of it dissipates by the time the cane is burned. They insist only a tiny amount of it makes its way into the smoke.

Plastic irrigation pipe found all over the fields burn during cane fires. Again, sugar experts say not to worry. Most of the pipe is polyethelene, which breaks down to carbon dioxide and water vapor. A small amount of polyvinyl chloride is used at the edges of the irrigaton systems, but because it is expensive, the companies either bury it deeply in the soil or carefully salvage the PVC parts before burning. And anyway, say some sugar scientists, PVC just won't burn in the 30 minutes most cane fires last.

Tell that to an environmentalist, however, or to a parent whose child has an asthma attack whenever cane is burned. To many people there is just no way to explain away a thick cloud of smoke on the horizon.

One study, by a University of Hawai'i professsor, suggested the worst problem may be the dirt that cane fires stir up, sending tiny particles into the air and into lungs.

Are we breathing pesticides?

Some people worry about the pesticide residues that may enter the air when the crop is burned. Sugar companies say this is not a big problem. The fields are sprayed with herbicides only at the beginning of a two-year crop cycle, and once the cane grows up it crowds out any weeds, eliminating the need for further spraying. Insects and diseases are controlled largely by a pest management program the state's growers have worked on for years. Research scientists constantly try new cane varieties to find those most resistant to problems, and use natural predators to keep insects under control.

The cane fire conflict is one that likely won't be solved for years, if ever, because sugar mills are set up to squeeze cane which has had most of its leaves removed by burning, and it no longer is economically feasible to do it any other way.

Sugar culture

The sweet white crystals of table sugar begin as a liquid squeezed from the thick stalks of sugar cane.

To produce that cane, workers plant two-foot sections of the stalk, whose nodes produce sprouts that can grow as tall as 30 feet in the two years of a crop cycle. While the cane grows, it is fed liquid fertilizer in the water that flows through drip irrigation lines along its roots. It takes a ton of water to produce a pound of sugar. Most of this irrgation water is brought in from rainy areas of East Maui by a sytem of ditches built in the 1870s.

About seven months before harvest, irrigation intervals are extended from every 14 days to about every 30 days. This fools the plant into thinking it may die, and it begins to store sugar for survival.

About 60 days before harvest, all irrigation stops, so the plant, which is 75% water, begins to dry before burning.

After the fields of cane are burned, bulldozers push the blackened stalks into piles. Giant "cane grabs" pick up the piles, a ton or so at a time, and drop them into specially-designed trucks that haul to the mill.

At the mill, the stalks are washed and then crushed to release the precious juice. The juice is purified by the addition of lime, which also prevents the sucrose from changing to other types of sugar. HC & S maintains a lime kiln at Pa'ia, near Baldwin Beach Park, which burns coral to supply lime for this purpose.

Next, the juice is heated, then filtered to clarify it. It is run through evaporators to remove the water and to crystalize the sugar into clear granules. A whirl in a centrifuge separates the crystals from molasses, and the resulting raw sugar is then shipped to California for processing. The California and Hawai'i Sugar Company refinery in Crockett, California, the largest refinery in the world, is cooperatively owned by Hawai'i's sugar growers. A small plant on O'ahu refines the sugar used in Hawai'i.

Meanwhile, back in the fields, a second crop is sprouting from ratoons, the small pieces left in the field after harvest. Each field will yield three crops before it is time to begin again with a new planting.

PINEAPPLE

The first written record of pineapple being in Hawai'i was in 1813. It was not planted on Maui until 1903 when Dwight Baldwin brought it to his Haiku fileds. Shortly thereafter, he opened Maui's first cannery.

Today, Maui County grows 70% of Hawai'i's pineapples. The fruit was once a rare delicacy, but it is now the state's second largest agricultural product.

Maui Pine, a subsidiary of the Maui Land & Pineapple Company, is one of the state's most successful pine producers. The company plants 8,000 acres on two plantations, one in the area from Haiku to Pukalani, and the other on West Maui at Honolua.

Maui Pine, plus independent Maui farmers, plant the Smooth Cayenne, a variety researchers have improved over many years.

The pineapple is a member of the bromeliad family. Its bluish-green rosette of leaves grows close to the ground, around a central stalk with the fruit developing at its top.

The pineapple's flower is a beauty, a cluster of flowers at the top of the central stalk with pink brackets and bluish-purple petals. Each flower, blooming for one day, will develop into one fruitlet. The whole pineapple is a collection of these fruitlets grown together into a single fruit whose "eyes" are the remains of the flowers. The fuit matures in 14 to 17 months.

Pesticide problems plague pineapple

The pest problem has been an urgent one recently, as one by one the chemicals the pineapple industry used for years have been banned because of their environmental effects. The blows to the industry have been serious ones, forcing closure of some Hawai'i plantations.

Chemicals have appeared in a few Maui wells, mostly in the area between Pa'ia and Haiku. Maui Pine chemists say there was an exceptionally heavy use of dibromochloropropene, DBCP, in some fields in the area many years ago. The company was the last in the United States allowed to use DBCP. It wanted to finish up the last of its supplies because it could find no other effective treatment to get rid of the nematode, a root worm that plagues pineapple. Public opinion won out, however, and DBCP no longer is used.

Growers have had to figure out how to keep up their production without using the convenient and functional chemicals. Maui Pine's efforts to practice good agriculture won it an award in 1985 from the National Association of Conservation for its environmental and conservation efforts. So far, these efforts seem to be working.

Hawaiian Language

Hawaiian is a language which uses a few sounds to create many meanings. For a newcomer, pronouncing the words formed from the mere 18 sounds can be difficult. Syllables are similar. Vowels appear to run together. And then there are those peculiar little backward apostrophes known as glottal stops. Plus, there's the macron—a short line above an occasional vowel.

Learning to say the words is not the end of the confusion. With so few letters (an alphabet of 13), there are many homonyms—words with several meanings.

Just what particular sweet potato did you want?

The Hawaiians named everything around them, from rocks and trees to wind and rain. They lived in such constant, close contact with nature that they were aware of things like changes in the wind from one part of a valley to another. There are 12 named winds in one Moloka'i valley alone.

And while there is no equivalent term in Hawaiian for such English words as sex, weather or scenery, the Puku'i-Elbert English-Hawaiian Dictionary lists 33 entries for cloud and 179 for sweet potato.

Survive & Revive

This subtly complex language was nearly dead until just a few years ago. After annexation, young people were forbidden to speak it; mastering English was considered the key to success and progress.

With the renewal of pride in Hawaiian culture, the language is also being revived. People of all races are learning to speak Hawaiian.

Polynesian family of languages

The language has a long history. It is part of the family of tongues known as "Austronesian," used by sea-going travelers who came into the Pacific about 3,000 years ago. The descendants of these people are now scattered across this ocean, their similar language providing a clear sign of their relationship.

Even the untrained ear can hear that relationship. Aloha in Hawai'i is the same as alofa in Samoa and aroha in Tahiti. Captain Cook was able to communicate with the "Indians" he found in Hawai'i because they spoke almost the same language he'd heard farther south.

Grammar: no gender, few tenses, no plural

Alike as the Polynesian languages are, they are quite unlike English. One word may be a noun, adjective, verb or adverb, depending on its use. The Hawaiian speaker does not use gender, but does indicate whether the subject of a statement is God-given (a parent) or acquired (a spouse). There is a near lack of tenses, and sentences may contain verbs without subjects, or have no verb at all. There is no verb "to be."

Adjectives always follow the nouns. The name "Puanani" is translated literally as "flower pretty." "Aloha nui" is "love great."

Plurals are indicated by the article "na," a plural version of "the." Although "s" is commonly added to Hawaiian words today, there is no "s" sound, and no such plural in correct Hawaiian. Thus, rather than say "leis," one should say "na lei."

There are two versions of the Hawaiian singular "the"—"ka" and "ke." That's one reason so many Hawaiian words start with K. For example, the town Kahului is Ka-hului, which probably translates as "the winning."

PRONUNCIATION

Every letter counts since there aren't very many of them...eight consonants and five vowels, a 13-letter alphabet.

The eight consonants are—p, k, h, l, m, n, w, plus the glottal stop. Most are pronounced much as they are in English, with the exception of W. It is a "v" sound after I and E, and a "w" sound after U and O. When in doubt, stick to a slightly aspirated V—use of too harsh a V tends to sound affected if not said correctly.

' ...what is it?

The unique symbol, the glottal stop ('), is one of the eight consonants. It is something like the sound between the two "ohs" in "oh-oh." When it's indicated, simply make a clear break between the letters it separates.

A,E,I,O,U and don't ask Y

The vowels—a, e, i, o, u—are a bit more complicated than the consonants. The difference is in the macron, a short horizontal line above the vowel to indicate it is longer than other vowels. It is a difference detectable only to the trained ear, however. (This book does not use the macron because we do not have the typesetting capability.)

Most vowels are pronounced as if they were Spanish or Italian. Say A as in lava; E as in they; I as in the Y in city; O as in no; U as the oo in moon.

Some vowels slide together in dipthongs—ei, eu, oi, ou, ai, ae ao, au. They blend together, but they and all other vowels should not be skipped over. In a complicated string of vowels, take the time and pronounce them all.

Each syllable ends with a vowel, and there are always vowels between consonants. Generally, the next to the last syllable is accented.

Humuhumunukunukuapua'a is the longest Hawaiian word. It's a type of fish. It is not a hard word to reel out...pronunciation is simple, 22 letters, 12 sounds.

HAWAIIAN WORDS

'aina—land, earth; meal
akamai—smart, clever, wise
akua—god, goddess, divine spirit
ali'i—chief, chiefess, noble person
aloha—love, affection, compassion; greeting or farewell
'aumakua—ancestor god, spiritual ancestor
auwe—Oh! Alas!
haku—lord, master, overseer, employer
hale—house
hapa haole—part Caucasian
hapai—to carry, lift; pregnant
haole—foreigner, someone without geneology; usually Caucasian
heiau—ancient pre-Christian place of worship, temple
he mea iki—you're welcome; "It's a small thing."
holoholo—to go for a walk, ride or sail; on a trip or excursion
holoku—Hawaiian gown with a train
hou—new, again, more (hana hou means "do it again" or "encore")
hui—club, association, partnership
hula—Hawaiian dance
huli—to turn, or change. Hulihuli chicken is turned frequently as
    it's barbequed over a fire.
hukilau—to fish with a seine net
'ike—to see, know, feel; knowledge, understanding learning
imu—underground oven

ka—the (singular)
kahiki—Tahiti; any foreign country
kahiko—old, ancient; old person; the ancient style of hula
kahuna—priest, sorcerer, expert in any profession
kai—sea
kalua—to bake in the imu
kama'aina—a person born in Hawai'i; literally "child of the land"
kanaka—human being, man, person
kane—male, husband, man
kaona—hidden meaning in Hawaiian poetry
kapa—tapa, a cloth made from bark
kapu—taboo, sacred, forbidden; no trespassing, keep out
ke—the (singular)
keiki—child, offspring
ko'a—fishing shrine
kokua—help, assistant
kona—leeward side of an island; name of a leeward wind
kukui—candlenut tree whose oily nuts were burned for light
kula—plain, field, open country; an area on Haleakala mountain
kuleana—small land holding within the mountain-to-sea district
    called ahupua'a; also a person's area of responsibility or function
kupuna—grandparent, ancestor
lanai—porch, patio
lani—sky, heaven; spiritual; very high chief, royal
lau—leaf, as in lau hala—the leaf of the hala tree
laulau—wrapping; package of ti or banana leaves containing cooked
    meat, fish or taro
lehua—the flower of the 'ohi'a tree
lei—a flower garland, necklace
lele—to fly, jump, leap
limu—seaweed; any plant living under water
lolo—stupid
lua—hole, pit, toilet
lu'au—Hawaiian feast; young taro tops
mahalo—thank you, thanks
makai—toward the sea
malihini—stranger, newcomer, guest
mana—supernatural power
mauka—inland, toward the mountains
mauna—mountain
mele—song or chant; to sing
menehune—legendary race of small people who worked at night
    building fish ponds, roads, temples

moana—ocean
mu'u mu'u—loose Hawaiian gown
na—the (plural)
nani—pretty, beautiful
nui—big, large, great, many
'oe—you
'ohana—family, relatives
'oi—best, superior, as in the island motto: "Maui no ka 'oi."
'ono—delicious
'opala—trash, rubbish, garbage
'opihi—a small limpet that clings to rocks on the shore
'opu—stomach, belly
pali—cliff, steep hill
pau—finished, ended, completed
pa'u—a divided skirt or sarong worn by women horseback riders
pilau—rotten
pilikia—trouble of any kind, great or small
pua—flower
puka—hole, perforation
pune'e—couch; often a single bed used as a couch
tutu—grandparent
wahine—woman
wikiwiki—hurry, hurry up

Pidgin

Wen you stay holoholo dis side, you going hea some plenty da kine talk.

In other words, when you travel in Hawai'i, you're going to hear a lot of pidgin...the local style of speech, a combination of several languages spoken with a unique lilt.

Actually, linguists say this style of speech is not really pidgin, which is defined as a simple, marginal language developed in a bilingual situation.

Instead, the descendants of field workers from many countries developed a creole language—a stew of words from a multi-lingual community.

Whatever it's called, the way locals talk is part of what defines their "localness." Most learn correct English, but talking pidgin is like relaxing in bare feet and old clothes...comfortable and familiar.

Pidgin's peculiar pattern of speech developed from fragments of Hawai'i's past. The sentence order, for example, sometimes echoes that of Hawaiian. "Ono ka palaoa" becomes "Good, da bread." "Auwe ka nani" becomes "Oh da pretty!"

It is liberally sprinkled with Hawaiian words. From "akamai" for "smart" to "wahine" for "woman," bits of Hawaiian survive in this everyday speech.

Kaukau...chowchow

Some words and phrases come from the true Cantonese pidgin used by traders who stopped in Hawai'i in the late 1700s and early 1800s. The very word "pidgin" may be a Cantonese pronunciation of the word "business," so called because the dialect was used in doing business. Other adoptees from Canton include no can (can't do), bumbye (by and by) and kaukau (food, chow). Kaukau sounds Hawaiian, but isn't; it probably comes from the Cantonese pidgin "chowchow" for food.

Mo' bettah drop dat

Even when not speaking pidgin, consonant sounds and dipthongs are often dropped. The final "d" may not be pronounced, as in "grin" for "grind," or "wen" for "went." "H" is not heard in "thing" (ting), or becomes "d" in "that" (dat).

The "r" disappears from many words. "Spark" becomes "spahk," "more" is "moah." This stems in part from the type of English first heard since most of the original haoles were from England or New England.

What you mean, brah?

The wise visitor should never try speaking pidgin in public. It takes exposure to the accent to get it right. But it pays to be familiar with some of the colorful expressions.

Across—across from. "Da new place stay across Azeka's."

An'den—"And then? So what?"

Any kine—anything. "Him, he eat any kine."

'Ass why hahd—That's why it's hard; life is tough. "I call him, but he no stay. 'Ass why hahd."

Beef—fight, as in "You like beef?"

Befoah, befoah-time—earlier, in the past; "Befoah, I never like go, but now I like. Befoah-time, we was staying Wailuku side."

Benjo—Japanese for restroom or toilet.

Bento—Japanese-style box lunch.

Blala—a local guy, usually Hawaiian, usually tough.

Brah—brother, or "bruddah," usually a friendly form of address.

Broke da mout'—delicious food.

Bumbye—by and by, after a while, pretty soon.

Bummahs—expression of disappointment, a "bummer."

But—used at the end of a sentence like though or however. "My bruddah wen tell me fo' leave. I never like go but."

Chee!—local pronunciation of Gee!

Chicken skin—goose bumps.

Chop suey—all mixed up, as in a person whose ancestry includes a mixture of races.

Cockaroach—to steal. "Who wen cockaroach my da kine?"

Cool head main ting—A cool head is the main thing; stay calm.

Crack seed—Chinese treats made from dried and salted plums, one with seeds cracked to add a bitter taste; a favorite of local kids.

Da kine—a constantly-heard expression which can mean whatchamacallit, or the best or any number of things apparent to speaker and listener at the time of use. "She wen ask me to da kine her da kine, but I nevah had time." "Dat sashimi is da kine."

Every time—all the time, always. "He every time promise me, but still yet he nevah do."

For—used in place of "to," which is the single preposition most often left out of pidgin speech. "I no like fo' do dat kine job."

Funny kine—strange, unusual. "He get on one funny kine shirt."

Garans or garans ballbarans—guaranteed. "Garans ballbarans dat space case going fo'get to bring da kine."

Geev'um!—Go for it! Go all out!

Get—have. "I get hard time for learn slack key."

Go—used to form the future tense. "I go play one song."

Go for broke—The motto of the famous WW II 442nd Regimental Combat Team, the Japanese from Hawai'i who fought in Europe. It means "give it your all."

Good fun—really enjoyable. "Da lu'au was good fun."

Grind—to eat. "I stay some hungry. Le's grin'!"

Guys, or dem, or folks—added on to a name to indicate someone and their gang or family. "Alice-guys wen go movie, but Calvin-folks not going go. Us go wit' Auntie-dem."

Hawaiian time—late. "Da show wen sta't Hawaiian time."

Howzit—greeting, like hello or aloha. "Eh, howzit, brah! How you stay?"

Humbug—a hassle or nuisance. "Humbug, dis television—no catch channel 9!"

Junk—bad, lousy. "Dat was one junk idea."

Junks—what haoles would call "junk." "My car get plenty junks inside."

Kaukau—food; to eat. This word probably is from the Cantonese pidgin word "chow-chow," meaning food.

Like—to want. "I like go beach today, but my bruddah no like go."

Local—someone from Hawai'i. Local style is a typcal island way of doing things. Local haole is a Caucasian born and reared in the islands.

Lu'au feet—big feet. "If you no wear shoes, bumbye you get lu'au feet."

Make A—to make a fool (or ass) of oneself. "Hey, brah, lighten up; no make A."

Moke—a really tough local guy. "Look out, or dat moke going bust you head."

Mo'bettah—better. "Mo'bettah we hurry up or we come late."

Nevah—"Never" plus the simple form of the verb is used in place of the standard negative contraction. "I nevah see him yet."

No act—don't act that way; don't show off.

No make li' dat—don't act like that.

No moah, no mo' notting—none; not just out of something, but don't have and never did. "You get one fishing pole?" "No moah. We wen try catch fish today, but no mo'notting."

No need—unnecessary. "You like I help you carry?" "No need, I can handle."

No shame—don't be ashamed or shy. "No shame, Joe, eat plenty!"

One—a, an, or each.

Plenty—lots.

Poi dog—a dog of mixed ancestry.

Shaka—A hand signal with thumb and pinkie extended from a closed fist, used in greeting. The word also is used to express delight or excitement.

Shave ice—ground-up ice with flavored syrup poured over it. A sno-cone.

Shibai—Japanese for nonsense; lies of the variety politicians tell.

Shishi—Japanese for urination. "Mommy, I like go shishi."

Shoyu—soy sauce.

Small-kid time—phrase used in recollections of childhood. "Oh, he was one rascal, small-kid time."

Some-very, as in "some good, some ono."

Spark—to see or catch sight of someone. "I wen spa'k him coming down the street today."

Stay—to be. "I stay some hungry."

Still yet—still, yet or but.

Stink eye—a dirty look. "My maddah giving me stink eye."

Suck wind—to lose out, or go without. "If we no get job pretty soon we going suck wind."

Talk story—to talk, shoot the breeze. "We wen Jojo's house, talk story all night."

That's all right—A local substitute for "no thank you." "You like some sushi?" "'Ass awri', I get plenty fo' eat."

Tita—a tough local girl. "No can use da bat'room at dat school, cause get plenty tita inside, ready fo' beef."

Try—Substitute for the polite "please." "Try pass me da rice."

We go—Let's leave.

Wen—went; added to other verbs to form a past tense. "We wen spa'k him on da way to da movie."

Yeah?—May be scattered through a sentence somewhat as "you know" is in standard English, or added to the end of the sentence to form a question. "I saw Robert, yeah, and den I wen go back to da office." "We go eat shave ice, yeah?"

Zoris—rubber thong sandals, also known as slippers.

Local Eats

"Onolicious" is a local way to describe a favorite dish. This combination of the Hawaiian word "ono" (good) and the English word "delicious" is like island cuisine—a blend of different cultures.

HAWAIIAN FAVORITES

Kalua Pig: Pig cooked whole in an underground oven (called an imu). The imu hole is lined with stones which absorb the heat of the fire in the pit. A few hot stones are placed in the abdominal cavity of the gutted pig. The body is wrapped and laid on crushed banana leaves to protect it from scorching. The leaves also provide moisture for steam. Usually it is an overnight, at least 5-hour, slow cooking process, using both roasting and steaming.

Laulau: Bits of pork or fish, wrapped in green taro leaves (called lu'au), and cooked along with the pig in the imu. Inedible ti leaves, often used by the Hawaiians as disposable cooking containers, cover the laulau and the lu'au. The cooked taro leaves (lu'au) are good, tasting somewhat like spinach.

Poi: Often compared to wallpaper paste, poi is an acquired taste, but it's good for you. Vitamins and minerals in poi include calcium, phosphorus, iron, thiamine, nicacin and riboflavin. Hawaiian babies are fed poi early. It is made from the corm, or underground tuber, of the Polynesian staple called taro or kalo. Poi is best sampled with a bite of kalua pig or lomi salmon.

Lomi salmon: Salted salmon combined with chopped tomatoes and onion. Lomi means to rub or massage. While soaking in water, the salted salmon is rubbed to remove the salt from the meat and the meat from the bones.

Chicken lu'au: Made from chicken, lu'au (taro) leaves and coconut milk. Cooked like a stew.

Haupia: A white, pudding-like dessert made with coconut milk, sugar and cornstarch.

'Ulu: Breadfruit—a staple starch for the early Hawaiians. It grows on a tree, and can be baked, steamed, boiled or fried. Breadfruit chips, available in supermarkets, are similar to potato chips.

'Opihi: Tiny shellfish of the limpet family (same as abalone) which cling to rocks along the shore. They are considered delicacies, eaten raw, and sell for $125 or more a gallon. When you see the waves that collectors have to brave to pry loose a few 'opihi, you understand the price.

JAPANESE FAVORITES

Teriyaki: Beef marinated in soy sauce.

Tempura: Vegetables or seafood dipped in a batter and deep fried.

Sushi: Rice and bits of fish or vegetables rolled in a sheet of seaweed or stuffed into a shell made of fried tofu. Another type of sushi—piece of fish draped over a hunk of white rice. Green wasabi (hot horseradish) is often used as spice.

Sashimi: Raw fish usually dipped in wasabi and soy sauce.

Saimin: Soup made with noodles in a broth flavored with meat or vegetables. Noodles are thin, somen type, not the larger udon noodles. Locals like saimin so much they eat it for breakfast.

PORTUGUESE FAVORITES

Portuguese soup: Made with kidney beans, vegetables and Portuguese sausage (linguesa—a spicy pork sausage also good with eggs for breakfast).

Portuguese sweetbread: Round, fluffy white loaf which used to be baked in backyard wood-fired ovens.

Malasadas: Much like donuts, but without the holes.

KOREAN FAVORITES

Kimchi: The most famous of Korean dishes, this is a hot, spicey, pickled mixture usually made with Chinese cabbage, turnips, radish and other vegetables. In Korea, kimchi is fermented and stored underground in earthen pots during winter months. It is served with every meal, and is rich in vitamins A, C, K, plus potassium and calcium.

Kalbi: Short ribs roasted in a marinade.

Pulgogi: Strips of beef charcoal-roasted over a brazier at the table. Beef is marinated in soy, sesame and spices.

CHINESE FOOD

Cantonese, Hunan, Szechuan...they're all here with their multiple zillions of dishes. None are typically Hawaiian; they're the same as found elsewhere, whether in Asia or the Mainland. Beef broccoli and fried rice are favorites that generally show up in most local delis.

Poi Eaters

HOW TO MAKE POI

Wash, but don't peel, taro corms. Place in a pot with water to cover. Bring to a boil, then turn down to medium and cook till it's soft enough to insert a fork, as you would test a potato. This may take several hours, and it's a good idea to change the water a couple of times.

Cooking well is essential to destroy the tiny, sharp oxalic acid crystals in raw taro, which will irritate mouth and throat.

When the taro is cooked, cool and peel. It's edible at this stage—with butter, in chunks in stew, or sliced and fried.

To make poi, break the cooked corm into pieces, put a few on a shallow pan and break into still smaller pieces with a potato masher.

With wet hands, turn the mashed taro; wet potato masher and continue to alternate mashing and turning; keep hands and masher wet.

When poi is thick and smooth, put it in a bowl and add water a little at a time, mixing by hand until it's the desired thickness. Traditional way to measure thickness is by the number of fingers needed to get a glob from bowl to mouth (one-finger poi is thicker than two-finger poi).

To keep poi sweet, refrigerate it. To develop a tart and tangy flavor, leave it covered on the counter.

Lithograph courtesy of Lahaina Printsellers

Music

In the beginning was the chant. History and legends were told through its poetry; geneology was chanted; culture was "sung" from generation to generation. Thus, the chanter was an important member of the ancient society, the poet preserver of tradition and history.

Chants (mele) were composed by haku mele, song masters. Chanters underwent long training and strict dicipline in the halau, originally temples of worship usually dedicated to Laka, the diety of the hula.

A chant could honor an individual, welcome a newborn, record the genealogy of a chief, or lament the loss of a loved one. One of the most famous chants still in existence is the Kumulipo, whose 2102 lines tell of the earth's creation and the evolution of life.

There was often a kaona, or hidden, symbolic meaning, in the words of a chant. Nature usually provided the symbolism—the fragrance of a fern or flower might refer to a sweetheart; rain or water had many possible meanings, from life and growth, to romance and erotic love, to grief and hardship.

Ancient mele had little melody, but the near-monotone was arranged in complex and changing rhythms, and singers cultivated stylized and distinctive voice qualities. There are at least 60 Hawaiian terms for specific voice styles and qualities used in the chant. Certain voice "ornaments" used by ancient chanters—breaks, glides, vibratos, changes of pitch—are still part of the unique sound of Hawaiian music.

Many chants were lost in the past two centuries, and no one knows exactly how the ancient chanters really sounded. There has been some simplification and westernizing of the current style of chanting.

The missionaries...at it again

While the mele of old times declined, driven underground with the hula by the missionaries, a new Hawaiian music was born.

The missionaries brought hymns in 1820, and Hawaiians were immediately enthusiastic about this new music. Learning to sing the western scale was not easy for ears trained by the mele's subtle tones, so missionary Hiram Bingham set up singing schools.

The well-loved missionary Lorenzo Lyons, or Liana, brought the folk gospel tune to Hawai'i which set the style of Hawaiian music for years to come. Lyons translated about 900 hymns, including "Hawai'i Aloha," which has become an unofficial state song. Today, islanders automatically rise and join hands when this anthem to Hawai'i is sung (to the tune "I Left It All With Jesus").

Hawaiians began composing mele in the new style, meshing the simple hymn tunes with the beautiful poems and complex rhythms of Hawai'i. Royalty was especially adept at music, and four noble siblings have a special place in the history of Hawai'i's music—King Kalakaua, Queen Lili'uokalani, Prince Leleihoku and Princess Likelike. Songs written by these four are still sung today.

Queen Lili'uokalani was one of the most gifted of the royal composers. Her song "Aloha 'Oe" is perhaps the world's best known Hawaiian song. Her brother, King David Kalakaua, was responsible for a revival of Hawaiian music and dance after decades of Calvinist efforts to stamp out the "lewd" native arts.

The Prussians are coming...

A Prussian bandmaster, of all people, was the next big influence on Hawaiian music. Heinrich (Henry) Berger arrived in 1872 to lead the Royal Hawaiian Band, and stayed the rest of his life. His composition, "Hawai'i Pono'i" (with words by King Kalakaua) is the official state song.

Berger was taken by what he called, the "hauntingly beautiful music of the Hawaiians." He arranged as many songs as he could, plus he pioneered printing them...thus preserving what might otherwise have been lost.

Later, composer Charles E. King preserved and popularized Hawaiian music in two now-classic collections. The original 1920 "blue book" and its companion "green book" of his *Book of Hawaiian Melodies* are still used today. King, a part-Hawaiian raised among the ali'i, was a student of Queen Lili'uokalani. He knew both contemporary songs and the ancient mele.

Hapa Haole

This type of song became popular in the late 19th century. Hapa means half; but, in fact, the songs are written mostly in English with a smattering of Hawaiian or pidgin words (though some are all English). Hapa haole songs usually have a Hawaiian theme and the singer may use Hawaiian vocal styles.

"Tiny Bubbles," "Little Grass Shack" and "Lovely Hula Hands" are tourist favorites of the hapa haole genre. Since many current composers do not speak Hawaiian, hapa haole is the fastest-growing category of Hawaiian music. Recent hapa haole hits are "Honolulu City Lights," "Paniolo Country" and "Ku'u Home o Kahalu'u."

The Hawaiian renaissance of the past two decades has brought Hawaiian culture back, and with it the music that once faced a swan song. Current groups like The Sons of Hawai'i and the Brothers Cazimero produce the ancient music with a new life and a lively sound, appealing to young people while remaining faithful to Hawai'i's roots.

THE INGREDIENTS

The rhythms of the ancient hula were created by implements found in nature. Some are still in use today.

The **pahu** is a drum, usually made from the trunk of a coconut tree, turned upside down so the narrow end of the trunk's natural taper is at bottom. The wide top is covered with a sharkskin tied onto the drum with sennit, a cord made from coconut fiber.

A small drum, the **puniu**, is made with coconut shell covered with shark or fish skin. The puniu is tied to the knee and played in a rhythmic pattern along with the pahu.

The **ipu heke** is made by gluing together two hollowed-out gourds to make a figure-eight shape. The chanter slaps the ipu heke to set the beat, while a dancer may beat a single gourd (ipu).

'Ili'ili are small, smooth, flat rocks clicked together somewhat like Spanish castanets.

The **pu'ili** is a piece of bamboo, split lengthwise into many narrow widths with a small space between each strip. A dancer strikes the pu'ili against the body or against another pu'ili to make a rattling or rustling sound.

The **'uli 'uli** is a small gourd topped with a circlet of feathers, usually in bright colors. The gourd is filled with seeds which rattle when shaken.

The **'ohe hanu ihu**, or nose flute, actually is played by blowing through the nose into a hole drilled in a length of bamboo. Pitch is changed by the fingers covering other holes. It is often used as accompaniment to love songs.

Man-made instruments

Two instruments are closely associated with modern Hawaiian music—the **'ukulele** and the steel guitar.

The **'ukulele** came to Hawai'i as the braguinha, a small four-stringed guitar first played in 1879 by a Portuguese immigrant over-joyed to be on land after four months at sea. Portuguese instrument-makers were an immediate success in Honolulu as Hawaiian musicians eagerly learned to play.

The Hawaiian name 'ukulele means "jumping flea," and there are several stories why. One of the most likely is that the player's rapidly moving fingers reminded Hawaiians of a jumping flea. Also, the 'ukulele is tuned to the notes G-C-E-A, which players remember by singing "My dog has fleas."

The 'ukulele's popularity was partly due to the enthusiastic support of King David Kalakaua. It was his favorite instrument. It joined the guitar and the double bass as an automatic part of any Hawaiian band, and gradually developed from taking the rhythm parts to solo status.

In the early 1900s, the 'ukulele became a fad on the Mainland, after its introduction by traveling Hawaiian bands in the late 19th century. Tin Pan Alley got into the act with pseudo-Hawaiian songs like "Yacka Hula Hickey Dula" and "I Can Hear the 'Ukuleles Calling Me."

Simple to tune and to play, small enough to carry easily, the 'ukulele continued to be popular on the Mainland until the 1920s. It has never lost its popularity in Hawai'i.

The **steel guitar**, with its wailing tones, has had lasting impact on Mainland music with its adoption by country-western groups. It was introduced to the Mainland in the early 1900s by the same Hawaiian bands that brought the 'ukulele.

Birthplace of the steel guitar was Hawai'i, but there's dispute about the inventor. Most likely candidate is Joe Kekuku, an O'ahu youngster who experimented in 1885 with various hard objects. He tried a comb, a glass and a knife until he settled on a steel bar he made in school shop.

The guitar is laid across the lap. Instead of picking or strumming with the fingers, a steel bar is slid along the strings. The bar may be oscillated to produce a vibrato or tremolo.

Western music players electrified the instrument in the mid 1930s. Pedals were added a few years later, increasing the chord possibilities.

Slack key and falsetto

Two techniques are associated with the unique sound of Hawaiian music—slack key and falsetto.

Slack key is a style of guitar playing long practiced in Hawai'i. The six steel strings are loosened, or slackened, in their tuning. Many different tunings exist; often developed by players who kept the tuning within the 'ohana (family) where it was handed down by the generations. In slack key, the strings are predominantly plucked, rather than strummed, for both melody and bass.

No one knows just when the guitar came to Hawai'i, but by the days of Kalakaua, the instrument was a favorite, and now it's a basic component of modern bands. The modern master of slack key was Gabby Pahinui, an O'ahu musician who died in 1980. His records are still available.

Falsetto is a common vocal technique developed from unknown sources over the past two centuries. It is thought that some chanting techniques may be akin to falsetto; it may have been the trademark sound of some ancient chanters...no one knows for sure. Later European influences and the yodeling of paniolos (cowboys) may also have had an influence.

The falsetto singer uses breaks in his voice when he moves in and out of falsetto, and he often adds yodeling. Though falsetto is possible for female singers, the technique really is a physical feat of male singers, particularly tenors. They deliberately use only a portion of their vocal cords.

There are many beloved falsetto singers, including two brothers who live quiet lives on Maui, Rick and Sol Hoopii. Occasionally, they perform at a local event, trilling along with their distinctive yodeling.

HAWAIIAN AIRWAVES

One of the best places to hear a variety of Hawaiian music is on the radio. Most local stations play Hawaiian songs off and on during the day, and some have regularly-scheduled shows.

For length of listening, KPOA, 93.5 FM, is tops. The only Hawaiian music FM station in the state, KPOA play 19 hours of Hawaiian music every day (switching to jazz between 8 p.m. and 1 a.m.). Listeners in West Maui and Kihei can hear this station on the radio, and folks elsewhere can catch it as the audio on cable television's channel 3.

Sundays from 11 a.m. to 4 p.m. on KMVI, 55 AM, Ki'ope Raymond plays Hawaiian music, then gives interesting comments on the songs in both Hawaiian and English...a rare opportunity to hear the Hawaiian language.

Other shows which feature Hawaiian music:
—KMVI, 55 AM, Jesse Nakooka, 7 to 11 a.m. Sundays; and Paul Douglas, "the local boy with the haole name," 3 to 7 p.m. weekdays.
—KHEI, 11 AM, and KVIB, 94 FM, Saturday noon to 1 p.m.
—KAOI, 95 FM, Hawaiian sunset show, Saturday & Sunday, 5 to 7 p.m.

Hula

Hula is one of the world's most recognized forms of ethnic dance. The hula maiden, swaying under the palm trees near the shore, has become a symbol of all that is tropical and romantic.

However, the image of the "little brown gal" with the "lovely hula hands" is a product of Western influence. To the ancients, hula was an important art...there was nothing sexy or cute about it.

The ancient hula, now called kahiko, was a ritual of religion and communication with diety. The dancers were dedicated, sometimes from birth, to the correct performance of this demanding art.

The hula of popular image, called 'auwana, is also demanding and graceful, but it has no religious meaning and its beauty is sometimes cheapened by the modern tourist culture.

Ancient hula

The halau hula (hula school) was the center of a dancer's life in old Hawai'i. A halau was run by a kumu hula, a master of both the dance and the chants.

The dancers were called 'olapa, named for a tree whose leaves shimmer and shake in the wind as if they were dancing. Some dancers had rigorous, but nonreligious training. Others were hula kapu, dancing in halau dedicated to a god, and worshipping through their dance. These dancers could be consecrated to the hula before birth. If a kumu hula dreamed that a child was kapu, the baby would be hanai (given in adoption) to the hula master, then reared under strict guidance, immersed in the hula from birth.

By age eight or so, these children had absorbed most of what their teachers knew, and their kapu would come to an end in a ceremony called uniki. Then they were returned to the outside world.

The dance misunderstood

Early visitors apparently never understood that the hula was part of the Hawaiian spiritual life. Sailors and traders saw what they wanted to see—semi-nude women with swaying hips. There is an erotic aspect to some hula, and it was eagerly encouraged by the crude newcomers.

The missionaries had a different viewpoint. They were shocked at what they saw as "lascivious." They had come to convert, not to dance. In their opinion, the hula had to go.

And so it was driven underground, nearly killing the art. Hula

Drawing by Ben Kikuyama

survived partly because some royalty, despite their Christian conversion, continued to support the dance sporadically. Certain families also quietly passed their knowledge to succeeding generations.

Hula reclaimed

There was a revival of the art under King Kamehameha IV and Queen Emma. They had a court troupe of dancers and chanters, but missionary influence was evident in the covered-up costumes of the dancers.

It was King David Kalakaua who sparked life back into the old culture. Kalakaua is remembered as the Merrie Monarch for his love of song and dance (as well as his great capacity for wine). The annual dance festival held in Hilo is named for him.

Kalakaua's coronation in 1883 and his birthday celebration in 1886 were landmarks in hula history. The king called in his kingdom's best performers. At his coronation, more than 260 chants and dances were performed. Dozens of dancers performed inside and outside the elaborate 'Iolani Palace Kalakaua had built.

Modern hula

Kalakaua was fascinated with things foreign, so a new hula began to emerge...one that included steps of contemporary dances. Guitars and ukeles now accompanied the drum beat of the pahu and ipu. From this hula ku'i, or "joined hula," came the modern style, 'auwana.

After Kalakaua died, and his sister Lili'uokalani lost her throne, hula began a long decline into the TwentiethCentury. The new name, 'auwana, was like a prophesy—the word means to wander, drift, go from place to place, to stray morally or mentally. Hula did wander, traveling around the world with the Hawaiian bands popular in the early 1900s. Hula strayed also from the state of mind that was Hawai'i, the very basis of existence of the old dance.

Hula became "haolefied." Hawaiian musicians began to compose in English, and people who'd never been to Hawai'i wrote songs and danced on Mainland stages. The old mystery of Hawai'i was cheapened by a hootchy-kootch image. Then Hollywood caught on and made it glamorous. Meanwhile, back home in the islands, Hawaiian culture was being suppressed. Children were punished for speaking Hawaiian in school, and culture, history and dance were never officially taught.

Still, the kumu hulas carried on in their quiet, traditional way. So, when the revival of Hawaiian pride began in the late 1960s, the dancers were ready. Once more the chant was heard, and the flashing movements of kahiko were again seen in public.

Maui Folk...
Kumu Hula: Hula Master

Hokulani Holt-Padilla cannot remember a time when she did not hula. "There was no beginning," she says. "It just always has been.

"I came from a hula family. My tutu was a kumu hula. Of her seven daughters, three are. And I am the next generation."

Hoku, as she's called, is a warm, smiling woman, one who embodies the Hawaiian word aloha. She works at the Maui Historical Society in Wailuku because her roots are important to her. But that's just her 8 to 5 job. Her passion is the hula.

"To me," she says, "hula is everything. Beyond my family and my church, it is my life."

Traditional kumu hulas spent most of their lives studying the hula. Along with the dance, they were also taught Hawaiian culture and lore. Hoku tries to give her students the same, though modern dancers seldom live solely for the dance.

Hands, feet, culture, et al.

"I teach them not only hand, body and feet movements, but also culture, language, history, values, philosophy, botany. Hula encompasses all of it.

"Everything that my people felt was important is located in the chants and the dances. Since hula is the visual representation of these words, it lets you see those things that the Hawaiians felt were important.

"They had no written language prior to 1820, so all that information was by spoken word and most of it was in the form of chants.

"I teach cleanliness—more than just physical, also spiritual and mental. Basically, the overall philosophy of the hula is perfection in whatever you accomplish...sticking to it until you master it."

Hoku teaches both kahiko (ancient) and 'auwana (modern) hula, but prefers kahiko because, she feels, "It is the classic of Hawaiian dance. Kahiko is a measure of a good hula dancer, more so than 'auwana. For me, it is the basic element of the people, of the culture. In it you can feel the connection to the elements much stronger. For the Hawaiian, nature was alive, it was not inanimate, it was animate. To be in touch with the elements was to be in touch with the life of the land and the sea...all of it."

Hoku began her halau in 1976. In ancient times a halau was a "school of learning where you spent all your time under strict kapu until your time of learning was over...24 hours a day. It has changed today to a place to go and learn the hula."

Pa'u O Hi'iaka is the name of Hoku's halau, named after Hi'iaka, sister of fire goddess Pele. Hi'iaka is the patroness of the hula, and, according to legends, the first goddess to perform the dance.

Descendant of Pele

"My family is from the Pele family," she explains. "In Hawaiian culture, geneology is very important. In the Hawaiian way of thinking, the gods and goddesses were real, flesh and blood, and they became deified. They are seen as real people, but deified. They had progenitors and ancestors themselves. The family name indicates what gods and goddesses you're associated with."

Hoku grew up on Maui in the home of her grandmother. All 50 of the first cousins were taught the hula, but Hokulani is the only one who stayed with it, the only kumu hula.

She has a good knowledge of Hawaiian culture and history, but does not speak the language.

"I understand a great deal, and I speak some, but I'm not fluent," she says. "My tutu spoke English to me because she did not want me to suffer when I went to school. Tutu was horsewhipped in school when she spoke Hawaiian."

Those bad old days are turning around nowadays as people are genuinely interested in the past. Hoku's classes are always racially mixed—as many haoles and Orientals as Hawaiians.

All races can hula

Race does not make a good hula dancer, aptitude and attitude does. When Hoku watches dancers, she watches not just the mechanics of the dance.

"I also see whether they understand what they're doing, beyond the hand and feet movements," she says. "The inner understanding of the hula shows through the face and the eyes. The eyes indicate the spark of understanding...the feeling where the dance transcends itself."

And what does she think of tourist lu'au hula dances? "I'm saddened by the need to compromise what visitors want or expect to see with what hula really is. The more we give in to others' expectations (who have no understanding at all), the more we will lose what makes the hula

unique.

"My halau has performed at hotels for conventions, but I tell them right at the beginning that we don't do Polynesian. We do only Hawaiian—no Tahitian, Maori or Tongan. And we do not show a lot of skin.

No coconut shell bras, please

"I don't see the necessity for putting coconut shells and clam shells on. The hula is so much more than that.

"I don't feel it's necessary to show skin to portray what the words are saying. I do not use it as a thrill-seeking tool. I use it if it fits the particular hula I'm doing."

Obviously, Hoku loves to dance herself. "I dance around my kitchen. I take classes myself. You never stop learning, not only the dance, but also the culture and history. There's always something new you can learn. That's what makes hula such a creative art. You can have the same chant, but with ten different kuma hulas it can be choreographed ten different ways."

Aloha

On Living Aloha

Old Hawai'i, calm and soft, still exists under the glitter and clatter of the new. It is in the beauty of the land and sea and sky...in the velvet feel of the air...in the songs that emanate from nature...in the warmth of the people.

How few visitors are aware, as they swim and golf and play, of old Hawai'i, still here in modern garb, with its feet firmly planted in earth and sea, yearning to preserve a way of life unique on the planet.

Visitors sensitive to this land and its peoples find themselves accepted and adopted, as has been the custom in Hawai'i for those who can live in harmony with what is here.

Island communication is often nonverbal. The vision is aloha, a word that means many things—hello, goodbye, compassion, love. This gentle, loving philosophy is what makes Hawai'i unique.

The source of its power is the meaning described by Maui's legendary Inez Ashdown, who learned it from the queen who became her mentor when Inez arrived in Hawai'i in 1907. Queen Lili'uokalani was Hawai'i's last monarch, a woman of great spiritual strength and wisdom.

As Inez says: "Aloha, my queen taught me, means 'I see God in you, in all he created, and God is in me. We are his children, to take care of his earth, not to desecrate the land or the sea.'"

Other Lands

Once part of a joined Maui when the sea level was lower, these are now separate lands, one an islet, the other an island. Both are uninhabited, both are quite barren.

Molokini is a tuff cone...a bit of earth splattered up, shaped like a horseshoe. The bay within the horseshoe is a great marine area for snorkelers and divers. It is sometimes too popular and too crowded with boats. The fish are quite tame, fed daily a questionable diet of bread and chips.

Kaho'olawe is a single volcanic dome, possibly one of the older islands in Hawai'i. It is 45 square miles with a high elevation of only 1,472 feet.

Once the soil on top was deep, but now it is blown off. Overgrazing by cattle and goats, combined with high winds and bombing have left the island barren and dry.

Meanings of Place Names

| Molokini | "many ties" |
| Kaho'olawe | "the carrying away (by currents)" |

Molokini

Hawaiian legends say Molokini is part of a beautiful woman turned to stone by a jealous Pele. Both women loved the same man. The volcano goddess ended the dispute, as she often does, with her fiery temper, cutting the woman in two and turning her to rock. The head of Pele's rival is supposedly Pu'u Ola'i, the cinder cone by Makena Beach.

Scientists say the island is a tuff cone, the remains of explosive volcanic eruptions. As molten lava met sea water in the depths of the Alalakeiki Channel, steam formed and blew the magma apart into ash. Because the explosions took place at the surface, rather than deep inside the earth, the ash formed a broad cone instead of a steep-sided cinder cone. Some of this ash solidified into a substance called tuff, forming the islet. Part of the tuff eroded away, leaving the horseshoe-shaped island to shelter many coral reefs.

Molokini's cone stands 156 feet above sea level. It is the tiniest in Hawaiian's chain of islands. It is barren, inhabited only by a lighthouse to guide navigators.

Molokini's rich fish population is protected by law. The islet is a Marine Life Conservation District. Though divers may look, they may not catch or remove fish.

Tour boats crowd the crescent harbor daily, sometimes dropping anchors onto the precious reefs and breaking off chunks that took hundreds of years to form.

The island was once used for military target practice. Bombs left embedded in the ocean floor also caused damage when the Navy exploded them in place to ensure that no diver touched off an accidental blast. The ordnance experts have improved their techniques in recent years. They now remove bombs without damage to the reefs.

Never try to swim or paddle to Molokini—currents in the channel are dangerous.

Kahoʻolawe

The island of Kahoʻolawe has been a prison for convicts, a grazing grounds for thousands of sheep and goats, the nemesis of a dedicated rancher and the target of Navy bombs.

It was originally believed to have been a temporary fishing station. No records were kept of life on the island. The first records are of its use as a prison, beginning in 1830 when the Hawaiian monarchy exiled convicts there. The convicts led a wretched life, sometimes near starvation. Luckily, the "prison" did not exist for long.

From prison to ranchland

After the last convicts left in the mid 19th century, various efforts were made to turn the island into grazing land. One after another, the efforts failed, but sheep and goats were left behind. Their grazing seriously advanced the erosion already depleting the island's thin top soil.

The first to have near success was Angus MacPhee, a rancher from Wyoming who managed several Maui ranches in the early 1900s. MacPhee leased the island from the territorial government in 1918 for $200 a year, with the stipulation that he rid the island of sheep and goats within four years.

MacPhee and his cowboys managed to kill more than 12,000 of the critters within two years, while building water tanks and fences and planting grass and windbreak trees. The government was sufficiently impressed with his work to extend the lease, though a few of the elusive sheep and goats still lurked in out-of-the-way places.

Legendary curse

While the reclamation of Kahoʻolawe proceded at a slow but steady pace, MacPhee was plagued with the bad luck that seemed to dwell there. A freak wave killed a young Hawaiian cowboy. A poorly constructed 50,000-gallon water tank collapsed under a pouring rain storm. MacPhee was near bankruptcy, but Harry Baldwin of Maui became his partner, and Baldwin pumped more capital into the venture.

It began to seem the endless years of work and the nearly $200,000 invested were to pay off—grass flourished, feeding cattle and horses.

Then came Dec. 7, 1941. The military commandeered the island, and the partners were lucky to get their thoroughbreds back to Maui. Kaho'olawe was now a target.

Targeted territory

Even when the war ended, though MacPhee and his daughter, Inez MacPhee Ashdown, tried for years to regain their rightful lease, the military hung on, claiming undetonated shells made the island too dangergous for further use. In 1953, President Eisenhower issued an executive order officially taking Kaho'olawe for Naval operations.

In the late 1960s, with Vietnam providing the military with a reason to practice bombing more than ever, Mauians grew weary of the bombing from across the channel. Then-mayor Elmer Cravalho began to campaign for the restoration of Kaho'olawe, which he regarded as part of his county.

The state got permission to plant on part of the island. The Navy restricted its target practice to one-third of the island to let the reforestation efforts take hold. The state also began killing off the sheep and goat herds that had grown from the stragglers MacPhee's cowboys never caught.

Sacred 'aina

The debate continued for years, but the action that really changed the fate of Kaho'olawe came from native Hawaiians who saw the bombing as desecration of the sacred 'aina (land). In 1976, they formed the Protect Kaho'olawe 'Ohana, and began unauthorized trips to the island. Feelings ran high during these early radical days of the 'Ohana. Several members were jailed for their trespassing protests. The group filed a civil suit, claiming the bombing violated environmental and historic preservation laws.

The most tragic event of these times happened on one of the illegal access trips. Singer George Helm of Moloka'i and park ranger Kimo Mitchell of Ke'anae, Maui, paddled surfboards to the island, spent some time there, but never returned. They disappeared at sea while paddling back on their boards.

Despite the tragedy, the 'Ohana persisted. Eventually their civil suit resulted in a court-ordered Consent Decree naming the 'Ohana as stewards of Kaho'olawe. The Navy was ordered to allow the group regular access to the island.

Ancient sites

Meanwhile, an archaeological survey found 544 archaeological sites, including the second largest adz quarry in the state and more than 400 petroglyphs. Heiau, fishing shrines, burial sites and village ruins were found. Evidence from the ruins indicates that the early people were fishermen, not farmers.

The earliest sites were dated about 1,000 A.D., with growth until around 1,600. The notion of Kaho'olawe as a temporary fishing camp was gone; the island was an archaeological treasure trove. It was listed in 1981 on the National Register of Historic Places.

Now the Hawaiians and their supporters had proof of the significance of this desolate island in the story of Hawai'i's past. They began to make regular visits, bringing sprouted coconuts, sweet potatos, taro and other native plants to the island.

Still the bombing went on. When the U.S. offered to share its target island with other Pacific nations in 1982 exercises, 'Ohana members once more occupied the island illegally in protest. "Uncle" Harry Mitchell, whose son Kimo had been lost at sea, made his own statement in a solo occupation of the island, then paddled back to Maui on a surfboard. Uncle Harry was 62. Greenpeace became involved in the protest, with two members hiding on Kaho'olawe while bombs fell.

Bombing continues

Today, the bombing goes on, but so do the regular access trips. The Navy limits its bombing to 26 targets, all located in the center third of the island, with the eastern and western thirds unbombed. The Navy also has planted thousands of trees, built dams to stop erosion, and cleared thousands of acres of unexploded ordnance.

'Ohana members and friends spend long weekends on Kaho'olawe, finishing a thatched building in the style of their ancestors, planting native gardens, and clearing trails to the archaeological sites. Each year, they celebrate the Makahiki season in the fall with ceremonies harking back to their spiritual past. Their dream is an island free of bombs, useful once again to the people.

Maui Folk...
"Pride to the Land"

She was just a little haole girl who moved to Hawai'i from a Wyoming ranch, but she grew up to be a bridge between the people who remembered the old ways and the young ones who would need to learn them.

Inez MacPhee Ashdown was seven years old when she moved to Hawai'i in 1907. Her father, Angus MacPhee, had won the world's championship roping contest at the Cheyenne Frontier Days, and with it a trip to the islands. MacPhee found his home here, and became manager of 'Ulupalakua Ranch. His daughter, given into the care of a Hawaiian cowboy, loved riding the hills of Maui with this kahu, or guardian, who told her tales of old Hawai'i.

Queen Lili'uokalani

During her first year in Hawai'i, Inez also met Queen Lili'uokalani, who provided inspiration for her life by telling the child to "help my people to remember their heritage of aloha."

Inez spent her growing-up years traveling back and forth between Maui and the Mainland, as her parents divorced and her mother moved away. During her late teens she lived in Makawao with the family of Louis von Tempsky, whose daughter Armine wrote the classic *Born in Paradise.*

In 1916, MacPhee won the lease on Kaho'olawe, which he'd wanted for years despite warnings of a curse on the island...that no good could come to anyone associated with it.

Legendary curse

Inez remembers Kaho'olawe since her first trip to Maui. "Since the night Mama and I arrived from the S.S. Mauna Kea and met Papa at the Makena Wharf," she says, "Kaho'olawe has been a part of my life. That midnight, the island loomed up on the black, alive sea. The ship's captain had told Mama and me that it is the island of death with a curse on it, and it is separated from the rest of the Maui kingdom by the Sea of 'Alala-keiki, Weeping Child."

Taming Kaho'olawe took

"four years of death and hell," Inez says, as the island lay "like a monstrous inert carcass putrifying and blistered by the sun," covered with the bloated bodies of goats and sheep slaughtered by MacPhee, his cowboys and even his young daughter Inez. As part of his lease agreement, MacPhee had four years to rid the island of sheep and goats, animals that were destroying the soil and vegetation. Within two years 12,000 animals were dead.

The work paid off. "We had always laughed and claimed that the first seeds and seedling of grasses and trees grew because the earth was wet with our sweat and the sweat of our horses," Inez says. "Kaho'olawe thrived. The feed was belly high where cows and fattening steers and new calves grazed with the cowponies and workhouses."

The military takes over

In 1939, when war seemed imminent, MacPhee and his partner Harry Baldwin voluntarily leased the southern tip of the island to the military for bombing practice. The day after Pearl Harbor, the military took over the entire island, and the work of more than 20 years was lost.

By this time, Inez had married Charles Ashdown and settled into the life of a young matron and mother at Honolua Ranch, in West Maui, where her husband worked as a timekeeper. She befriended elderly Hawaiians in Lahaina, and began to learn the history of that area.

She also began to write for magazines and newspapers. When she wrote about a Maui performance by the famous dancer 'Iolani Luahine, she was given the name "'Aina Kaulana" by the Maui Hawaiian Women's Club. It means she brings "pride to the land."

Archaeological pioneer

Inez was a pioneer in the preservation of historic sites such as the Baldwin House in Lahaina. She acted as guide and assistant to visiting scholars like archaeologist Kenneth Emory.

At age 68, Inez was hired by the county, and spent the next 10 years collecting information on historical and archaeological sites. She published some of this information in *Ke Alaloa o Maui*, one of several books she has written about Maui and Kaho'olawe.

Named Maui County's Historian Emeritus in 1982, Inez slowed down only slightly with old age. She has served as grand marshall for all three of Maui's major parades, and rode on horseback in the Makawao 4th of July parade at age 86.

In her eighth decade, almost completely blind, Inez appears each week as mistress of ceremonies for a hula show at the Kapalua Shopping Mall, where she shares her favorite stories of old Hawai'i...a world that no longer exists.

Drawing by Pamela Hayes

Artists

Cynthia Conrad (page 151)

Cynthia makes time for her watercolors when not working full-time as the art director for the local advertising agency, Faught & Myashiro. Cynthia came to Maui in 1970 from Berkeley, California, where she received a BA in painting. She has been in numerous Hawai'i and Maui shows since the early Seventies.

Her work can be purchased from the Coast Gallery or directly from her (phone 572-6548).

Curtis Wilson Cost (page 96)

Curtis is one of Maui's foremost realist painters, a man whose work represents where he lives—Upcountry. He has lived in the Kula area since the early 1970s, finding continual inspiration there for his detailed paintings. He likes the seclusion and the rural living of Kula. "We're peaceful here," he says. "You can't help but be. The area is so beautiful and has the subject material I like." Curtis had no formal training for his precise art; instead, he learned from his father, artist James Peter Cost, who owns a gallery in Carmel, California.

His wife Jill sells Curtis' work at their own gallery, downstairs in the Kula Lodge.

Eddie Flotte (pages 86, 87, 90, 293)

Eddie grew up in a tough factory town near Philadelphia—a place, he says, "rich with old fashioned buildings and old fashioned ethics." He came to Maui in 1985 and immediately fell in love with Pa'ia...a town he thinks has the same kind of character and characters as his own hometown. "Every building was a picture waiting to happen," he says. He has painted much of the town and its people, and is now known as Pa'ia's painter.

He sells his own work from his studio/home. Phone Eddie at 579-9641 for an appointment.

Pamela Hayes (pages 92, 350)

Pam took only four hours each to sketch the two Makawao street scenes for *Magic Maui*. She lives in Makawao, so she has a feel for the buildings. Her preferred medium, however, is watercolor. Her paintings are bright and friendly—vividly colorful pictures of flowers, cats, frogs, nature. All these have inspired her since moving to Maui in 1978. Before then, she studied and lived in Los Angeles, Florence, Italy, and London, England.

Pam's paintings are found at both Village Galleries and Gallery Makai.

Ben Kikuyama (pages 165, 338)

Ben is a rarity among Maui artists—he was actually born on the island. He never left, in fact, until he went off to college on an art scholarship. But college couldn't hold him for more than a year; an injury from a car accident, plus a homesickness for island life has kept him here. Ben draws with painstaking, realistic detail in black and white.

He sells his work through Coast and Village Galleries, and can be reached at home for commisioned art (572-9349).

Richard Nelson (cover artist)

Dick is well known in Hawai'i as both an art teacher and an artist. For 22 years he chaired the art department at the prestigious Punahou High School in Honolulu. He has been in Maui since 1978, pursuing his own painting career. He paints with watercolors, using a three-color technique he discovered while working with printers. He creates all his paintings, including *Magic Maui's* cover, with only the three primary colors...from these he gets the entire rainbow of hues. It's a simple, but radical approach that he nows teaches in various workshops in Hawai'i and on the Mainland.

Dick's work can be found in Coast, Village and Makai Galleries.

Piero Resta (page 219, 354)

Self-described as an "eclectic person," Piero has the exuberance and zest for life of a true Italian. After formal art training in Florence, he left his native Italy to travel the world. He joined the "beat" scene in New York and San Francisco in the Sixties and Seventies. He settled in Maui in 1978. Coming to the island, he says, "allowed my art to unfold." Here, he adds, "art is my life, my meditation."

Piero's son Luigi sells his dad's art in Piero's studio in the Pauwela Cannery in Haiku. Phone 575-2203 for an appointment.

David Ridgway (page 225)

David moved to Maui from Maine in 1985 to see if he could make a go of a painting career. He quickly made a name for himself with his watercolors. He organized a show of several Maui watercolorists in 1987. The same year his painting of a dinghy (shown on page 225) was selected as the poster art for Art Maui '88. He is a self-taught watercolorist, but credits the cover artist, Dick Nelson, for helping him develop his sense of color. David now uses Nelson's tri-color technique.

He is represented by Gallery Makai, Village Galleries, Coast Gallery and the Lahaina Arts Society.

David Warren (188, 189)

David Warren's move from Minnesota to Hawai'i completely changed the direction of his artwork. "The gracious dignity of the people, and the incomparable beauty of the islands," he says, are now the main influences for his art, both painting and printmaking. Most of David's work has a Hawaiian theme.

His art is shown in the Coast Gallery, the Village Galleries, through the Lahaina Arts Society and at the Maui Crafts Guild. He also sells from his studio in his Haiku home (phone 572-1864).

Painting by Piero Resta

Bibliography

Abernathy, Jane Fulton and Suelyn Ching Tune. *Made in Hawai'i*. Honolulu: University Press of Hawai'i, 1983.

Ariyoshi, Rita. *Maui On My Mind*. Honolulu: Mutual Publishing, 1985.

Ashdown, Inez MacPhee. *Kaho'olawe*. Honolulu: Topgallant Publishing Co. Ltd., 1979.

_____. *Ke Alaloa O Maui*. Wailuku: Kama'aina Historians, 1971.

Beckwith, Martha. *Hawaiian Mythology*. Honolulu: University Press of Hawai'i, 1970.

_____. *The Kumulipo, A Hawaiian Creation Chant*. Honolulu: The University Press of Hawai'i, 1972. (First edition, Chicago, 1951.)

Bird, Isabella L. *Six Months in the Sandwich Islands*. Rutland, Vt.: Charles E. Tuttle Company, Inc., 1974. (First edition, London, 1890.)

Buck, Peter H. *Vikings of the Pacific*. Chicago: The University of Chicago Press, 1938.

Carlquist, Sherwin. *Hawaii A Natural History*. Kaua'i: Pacific Tropical Botanical Garden, 1980.

Carr, Elizabeth Ball. *Da Kine Talk*. Honolulu: University Press of Hawai'i, 1972.

Clark, John R.K. *The Beaches of Maui County*. Honolulu: University Press of Hawai'i, 1980.

Daws, Gavan. *Shoal of Time*. Honolulu: University Press of Hawai'i, 1968.

Day, A. Grove. *History Makers of Hawai'i*. Honolulu: Mutual Publishing, 1984.

Elbert, Samuel H. and Noelani Mahoe. *Na Mele O Hawai'i Nei, 101 Hawaiian Songs*. Honolulu: University Press of Hawai'i, 1970.

Emerson, Nathaniel B. *Pele and Hi'iaka: A Myth from Hawai'i*. Rutland, Vt.: Charles E. Tuttle Co., 1978.

Fornander, Abraham. *An Account of the Polynesian Race: Its Origin and Migrations*. Rutland, Vt.: Charles E. Tuttle Co. , 1969.

Gray, Francine du Plessix. *Hawai'i: The Sugar-Coated Fortress*. New York: Random House, 1972.

Gutmanis, June. *Kahuna La'au Lapa'au*. Honolulu: Island Heritage, 1976.

Handy, Edward Smith Craighill. *Native Planters in Old Hawai'i; their life, lore and environment*. Honolulu: Bishop Museum Press, 1972.

_____ and Mary Kawena Pukui. *The Polynesian Family System in Ka'u, Hawai'i*. Rutland, Vt.: Charles E. Tuttle Co., 1972.

Hopkins, Jerry. *The Hula*. Hong Kong: Apa Productions, 1982.

Kamakau, Samuel Manaiakalani. *Ka Po'e Kahiko: The People of Old*. Translated by M.K. Pukui. Honolulu: Bishop Museum Press, 1964.

_____. *Ruling Chiefs of Hawai'i*. Honolulu: The Kamehameha Schools, 1961.

Kuykendall, Ralph S. *The Hawaiian Kingdom*. Honolulu: The University Press of Hawai'i, 1938.

_____ and A. Grove Day. *Hawai'i: A History. From Polynesian Kingdom to American State*. Englewood Cliffs, N.J.: Prentice-Hall, Inc., 1948.

Kyselka, Will. *Maui, How It Came to Be*. Honolulu: University Press of Hawai'i, 1980.

Lili'uokalani. *Hawai'i's Story by Hawai'i's Queen*. Rutland, Vt.: Charles E.Tuttle Co., 1964 (first edition, Boston, 1898)

Lueras, Leonard and Ron Youngblood. *On the Hana Coast*. Honolulu: Emphasis International, Ltd., 1983.

Luomala, Katharine. *Maui-of-a-Thousand-Tricks: His Oceanic and Euro pean Biographers*. Honolulu: Bishop Museum, 1949.

Lyons, Barbara. *Maui, Mischievous Hero*. Hilo: Petroglyph Press, Ltd., 1961.

Macdonald, Gordon A. and Agatin T. Abbott. *Volcanoes in the Sea. The Geology of Hawai'i*. Honolulu: University Press of Hawai'i, 1970.

Malo, David. *Hawaiian Antiquities*. Honolulu: Bishop Museum Press, 1951.

Martini, Frederic. *Exploring Tropical Isles and Seas*. Englewood Cliffs, N.J.: Prentice-Hall, Inc., 1984.

McBride, Leslie R. *Petroglyphs of Hawai'i*. Hilo: Petroglyph Press, 1969.

_____. *The Kahuna*, Versatile Mystics of Old Hawai'i. Hilo: Petro-glyph Press, 1972.

McDonald, Marie A. *Ka Lei: The Leis of Hawai'i*. Honolulu: Topgallant Publishing Co., 1978.

Mitchell, Donald Dean. *Resource Units in Hawaiian Culture*. Honolulu: The Kamehameha Schools, 1982.

Neal, Marie C. *In Gardens of Hawai'i*. Honolulu: Bishop Museum Press, 1965.

La Perouse, Admiral Jean-Francois Galaup, Compte de. *Voyages and Adventures of La Perouse*. Translated by Julius S. Gassner. Honolulu: University Press of Hawai1i, 1969.

Pogue, the Rev. John F. *Mo'olele of Ancient Hawai'i*. Translated by Charles W. Kenn. Honolulu: Topgallant Publishing Co., Ltd., 1978.

Pukui, Mary Kawena and Samuel H. Elbert. *Hawaiian Dictionary*. Honolulu: University Press of Hawai'i, 1971.

_____. E. W. Haertig and Catherine A. Lee. *Nana i ke kumu (look to the source)*. Honolulu: Hui Hanai, 1972.

_____. Samuel H. Elbert and Esther T. Mookini. *Place Names of Hawai'i*. Honolulu: University Press of Hawai'i, 1974.

Puzon, Julie and Eileen Tamura. *Family, Religion, and Society: Readings*. Honolulu: Hawai'i Multicultural Awareness Project, 1980.

Schoofs, Robert SS. CC. *Pioneers of the Faith,* History of the Catholic Mission in Hawai'i. Honolulu: Louis Boeynaems, SS. CC., 1978.

Simonson, Douglas. *Pidgin to Da Max*. Honolulu: Peppovision, 1981.

Speakman, Cummins E. Jr. *Mowee, An Informal History of the Hawaiian Island*. San Rafael, Calif.: Pueo Press, 1978.

Stone, Margaret. *Supernatural Hawai'i*. Honolulu: Tongg Publishing Co., Ltd., 1979.

Titcomb, Margaret and M.K. Pukui. *Native Use of Fish in Hawai'i*. New Plymouth, N.Z.: The Polynesian Society.

University of Hawai'i at Manoa. *Atlas of Hawai'i*. Honolulu: University Press of Hawai'i, 1973.

von Tempski, Armine. *Born in Paradise*. Woodbridge, Conn.: Ox Bow Press, 1985. (First edition, New York, 1940.)

Walls, Madge Tennent. *Eating Out on Maui*. Kailua: Press Pacifica, 1986.

Wright, Allan B. Jr., *Surfing Hawai'i.* Redondo Beach, Calif.: Mountain and Sea, 1971.

Index

ORDER FORM

Aka Press
P.O. Box 1372-B
Wailuku, Maui HI 96793

Telephone (808) 242-4173

Price of *Magic Maui:* $9.95
Shipping, each book: $1.00

Hawai'i residents add 4% sales tax ($.40 per book).

Please send me _____ copies of *Magic Maui, The Best of the Island.*

I enclose a check or money order for _____.

NAME: _____

ADDRESS: _____

_____ZIP CODE_____

- I can't wait 3 to 4 weeks for Book Rate Mail. Here is $2.50 per book for Air Mail.